Let The Children Come

A Story Of Faith Gone Courageous

To Know Him
And make Him known!
Marc Morrow
Psalm 117:1

25 24 23 22 21 20 1 2 3 4 5 6 7 8

LET THE CHILDREN COME

Library of Congress Cataloging-in-Publication Data:
ISBN: 978-1-949758-97-9 Perfect Bound

Across the globe, God is implanting a desire within the hearts of a generation of young people to do something great for Him. Let The Children Come vividly captures the essence of adventure, testing, and supernatural glory that await those who leave everything to follow Jesus. This is a thrilling page-turner from beginning to end!

— Lance Shumake,
Director of iGo Global (igoglobal.org)

God's heart is moved when the young pursue Him and His ways with passionate love and obedience. D.C. Lee's debut novel is a thrilling journey of faith from small-town USA, deep into the jungles of South America. Prepare to be swept away by this moving story.

— M. Wen,
Cross-cultural missionary and trainer with Youth With A Mission (ywam.org)

Let The Children Come is an incredibly good novel that packs a punch. While fictional, it still presents deep spiritual truths that lead to deeper thought. This book is not "preachy" as much Christian fiction tends to be, rather it is a powerful story that presents honest challenges to us all. A great read for teenagers, college students, and adults alike!

— Matt Murrah,
Vice President for Financial Affairs at Dallas Baptist University

This book is dedicated to my mom, for all the books she read to us at night, for cultivating in me a love of stories, and for teaching me about and modeling the love of Christ.

"In the last days I will send My Spirit on all men. Then your sons and daughters will speak God's Word. Your old men will dream dreams. Your young men will see special dreams. Yes, on My servants, both men and women, I will pour out My Spirit in those days. I will show powerful works in the heavens and on the earth…"
Joel 2:28-30 (NLV)

1 THE PRAYER

The darkness was thick, blanketing the mountains. Underneath, like a body tossing and turning in its sleep, the trees rustled and swayed in the wind. A storm was approaching. Moving between the trees, a group of shadows ran deep into the jungle. Stopping suddenly, one of four figures spoke quickly in Spanish then disappeared into the brush. Only one of the remaining three understood him. The tallest of the shadows translated to the others.

"Manuel says we have to wait here."

"He better hurry, Taylor. You know we're not supposed to leave, especially at night and especially alone." A tone of nervousness and fear was evident in the second and younger voice. The third and smallest figure said nothing.

"Don't worry, Mike. Brad turned off the security cameras, and Ricardo was sleeping on the job, as usual. We'll be back before anyone knows we're gone. Just like always."

"I don't even want any of this stuff!" Mike was having serious second thoughts...again.

Taylor didn't want any drama from his younger friend. He spoke as reassuringly as possible. "It's okay Mike. As soon as we get back, you'll be glad we came. Anything to escape this hell hole, remember?"

"But why couldn't we meet Manuel in town like we always do?"

"I don't know. Maybe he found a new dealer. Everyone wants a piece of our parents' money. We can trust Manuel."

As Taylor said the name, the fourth figure, a dark-haired, dark-skinned teenager, returned, spoke quickly in Spanish, and led them deeper into the darkness. There was one more thing Mike had to get off his chest.

"I can't believe you brought Robert! What were you thinking?"

"I didn't have a choice. It's no big deal. He can handle it. Right, little brother?" Taylor looked at his little brother who stood still and silent while nodding his head. Robert felt a little scared, but he would keep his mouth shut. He was getting to hang out with the big boys, something that rarely happened, and he wasn't going to screw it up.

Eventually, the four boys came out into a clearing where a large fire was crackling and burning brightly. Strong winds howled through the open area causing the flames to dance about. Three other figures were sitting on large logs around the fire. As the boys approached, they immediately noticed the faces of the three sitting were colored white, but that wasn't all – their eyes, noses, and lips had all been traced in black and appeared as large holes. The three American boys all had the same thought: they were staring at skulls. The glow of the fire reflected up onto the painted faces, enhancing their devilish appearance. Mike stood deathly still. He could barely find his voice.

"Taylor, what is going on?

"Relax, Mike and I'll tell..." Before Taylor could finish, Mike spoke again, louder.

"Let's get out of here Taylor!" His voice trembled.

Suddenly two familiar voices filled the night air. "It's okay Mike."

"Yeah, chill out and come over here."

Mike couldn't believe what he was seeing and hearing. Brad and Tommy were there beside the fire, with their faces painted, and grinning as if nothing out of the ordinary were going on. Mike, still frozen in unbelief, watched as Taylor walked over to the fire and gave high fives to his friends.

"Isn't this awesome, Taylor?" Brad, a stocky, red-haired, freckle-faced boy, with an almost psychotic gleam in his eyes, asked.

"Yeah dude, how do we look?" Tommy, a tall lanky boy with bushy, curly brown hair, chimed in.

"Like idiots!" Taylor yelled laughing. "How long have you been here?"

"Maybe 20 minutes or so with gramps here. This dude is chill." Brad motioned with his head toward an older native sitting on a log across from them staring blankly into the fire.

"He doesn't say much," Tommy added, with his customary huge grin.

"By the way," Taylor said, extending his hand towards Brad, "nice job with the security feed again."

Brad shook it firmly. "Thanks. It's getting too easy. The cameras stay on, but they're not recording. And Ricardo can't stay awake to save his own life, let alone ours!"

"I'm just glad he was on duty tonight. Now, give me some paint!"

"Yeah!" Brad and Tommy yelled out in unison.

"Gramps will show you how to put it on."

As Taylor sat, the old native looked over, smiled, and motioned for Taylor to scoot closer. Meanwhile, Tommy faced the others.

"Come on Mike."

"You guys are freaks!" Mike quickly yelled back.

"Just relax!" Brad shouted.

"No way!" Mike's voice cracked and they all knew that meant he was about to start crying, something no one wanted to deal with.

"Just leave him alone guys," Taylor said, just loud enough for Tommy and Brad to hear.

"Do you want to try some Robert?" Tommy asked, walking towards the little boy. Robert shook his head "no" and remained standing at the edge of the clearing.

"Tommy, don't be stupid!" Taylor yelled. "Leave Robert alone."

"I meant try some paint," Tommy mumbled, regretting having opened his mouth at all. He walked dejectedly back over to the fire.

Taylor glanced at Brad and shook his head. Then he looked over at his little brother standing just under the shadows of the circling trees. "Just let him stand there and he'll be okay." Taylor hated dragging his little brother along but didn't have a choice. Robert had woken up just as he was sneaking out their bedroom window. If he had left without him, there was no telling what Robert might do. Maybe he would go back to sleep, maybe not. Taylor wasn't about to risk it. Besides, his little brother was a pretty tough and brave kid. He could handle it.

* * *

Manuel came over and handed each of the three boys a small bag filled with dry marijuana leaves. They quickly shoved them into their pockets. Next, he held out three perfectly rolled joints, which disappeared in an instant. Lighting the marijuana, the three sat back against the logs and relaxed, inhaling and exhaling on the joints in their hands. Mike's voice was heard but ignored,

"I'm leaving! I'm going back guys! I'm..."

"Okay, just shut up and go!" Brad yelled.

"You shut up!" Mike screamed, then looked at Taylor. "I'm going."

"Then go!" Tommy joined in.

Mike paused at the edge of the clearing then slowly turned and looked back one last time. Taylor continued to ignore him. He finally turned and disappeared into the woods. No one was surprised. Mike had only smoked with them a few times before. He always went along and even pretended to be excited about joining them, then he'd freak out, change his mind, and head for home.

"Girl," Brad mumbled.

"Yeah, what a dork!" Tommy remarked, looking at Taylor.

"If he doesn't want to do it then he doesn't have to, it's his choice," Taylor replied calmly. Although he agreed Mike was always too scared to do anything, he was still their friend.

Tommy decided to keep his mouth shut.

* * *

As they finished their joints, the older native lifted up a long wooden pipe from the ground behind him and slowly lit it. He smoked it for a moment then began to pass it around as Taylor finished painting his face.

"Awesome!" Brad whispered looking closely at him.

"Perfect," Tommy interjected, "if only the girls could see us now!" At this, they all began to laugh.

Taylor took the pipe that was handed to him and lifted it to his lips. A scared, soft voice stopped him.

"Taylor, what are you doing?"

"Not him too!" Brad moaned.

Taylor didn't have time for it.

"Robby, just shut up okay!" he yelled back. The drugs were beginning to have their effect. An enormous rush of power and angst pumped through Taylor's veins. He was tired of Robert and his whining. Either he was with them or he could leave, and this Taylor yelled with a rage that Robert had never heard in his brother before.

Robert knew it was only the drugs talking through his brother, but that was what scared him most. He slowly backed out of the clearing and into the woods. Then finding a thick bushy area he crouched down and watched. He had made an unspoken promise to his mom to watch over his brother, and he meant to keep that promise.

Brad asked what was in the pipe before he put it to his lips. The native answered and they all recognized his word without translation from Taylor.

"Is peyote dangerous, Taylor?" Tommy asked.

"This stuff's been around forever!" Brad interrupted. "Don't you chicken out too!"

"I don't know," Taylor answered. "Just try it!"

That seemed to be enough for Tommy who inhaled deeply on the pipe, then coughed as smoked shot out from his lips and nostrils. The other two rolled over in hysterical laughter. Soon Tommy was laughing too and all three began to sway back and forth in their seats on the logs. Brad eventually rolled over onto the ground as Taylor and Tommy stood up and began to dance around the fire. Even Manuel and the older native began to participate in the festivities, as the drugs seemed to bring all of them to a common ground despite their cultural and language differences. Soon they were all on their feet dancing around the circle.

Suddenly, from out of the woods another native emerged – so subtly it was almost as if he had just appeared out of thin air. He was a young man, tall, slim, and muscular, with long black hair that glistened in the moonlight. His skin, only slightly lighter than his hair, shined also. He sat down next to the fire cross-legged, placed his hands on his knees, lifted his face to the sky, and closed his eyes. He seemed unaware or uncaring of all the ridiculous action going on around him.

Robert watched him intensely. Even when Brad got too close to the fire and fell in, sending sparks into the air, burning his hand, and then laughing at the absence of pain – Robert never took his eyes off the man, and the native's eyes never opened. He was painted like the others, but with more colors, and he had feathers attached all over his body. From where Robert sat, he couldn't tell how the feathers were held in place. It was creepy. When Robert looked once again at the man's face, their eyes met. Startled, Robert quickly ducked behind the brush, his heart racing. Something about the man was terribly wrong. In the one-second their eyes had met, Robert recognized an evil presence looking back at him. Slowly, he peered around the brush in time to see the man disappear back into the trees. Had he been seen? Was the man coming over to get him? Robert was terrified. He was about to back up more when the native reappeared and walked up to the edge of the firelight. The wind picked up and began to howl. Something moved in his hand. He raised the object above his head and began to chant out loud. At first, Robert couldn't tell what the man was holding, but then he heard a clucking sound and saw the object squirming, and realized it was a chicken. The hairs on the back of Robert's neck stood up as the blood drained from his face. All he could hear was the pounding of his own heart inside his chest.

All of the others slowly gathered around the fire and sat once again in a circle. The man with the bird continued to speak out in a violent, yet pleading voice. His eyes closed again. Taylor and Brad closed their eyes as did Tommy, though he continually peeked at the other two to make sure he was doing whatever it was they were doing, correctly. A minute later the man walked over to a stump and pinned the chicken down upon it as it protested and squirmed under his hand. Next, he drew a large machete from his side, raised it high above his head, and slammed it down upon the bird's neck. Immediately the body of the bird began to flop around on the ground as blood poured from its open neck.

Robert turned his head and fought back the urge to vomit, but in seconds his attention was once again riveted on the unbelievable scene before him. No matter how fearful he felt, he had to stay, he had to watch Taylor.

The man picked up the headless body and held it over a bowl so that the blood spilled into it. Once the bowl was full, he stood up straight and tall. The fire seemed to grow in height as if also standing up. Something dark and gigantic rose up above them all, expanding onto the trees, surrounding them, swallowing them. Robert had the strange sensation that the man's shadow itself was alive. The man began to chant and the fire hissed, popped, and crackled, joining in with its own incantations. After a moment the man grew silent, raised the bowl to his lips, and took a long, slow drink. Robert watched his Adam's apple bob up and down with each gulp. The dark man passed the bowl to the older native, wiped his mouth with the back of his hand, and began chanting out loud again. This time the others joined him, though it was obvious none of them knew what he was saying. The American boys were chanting and giggling as the bowl drew nearer.

Robert was certain his brother and the others wouldn't drink the disgusting blood. His hopes were shattered as Taylor took a hold of the bowl, lifted it to his lips, and drank, some of the blood overrunning his mouth and dripping down his chin and throat. Tommy went next. He paused for a second, but realizing he had come too far to back out, took a quick gulp and passed it on to Brad who didn't hesitate, but drank quickly, made a bitter face, then smiled as he handed the bowl back to the dark native.

The sight of his brother and friends with their faces painted, eyes closed, and mouths dripping with blood, was too much for Robert to handle. This couldn't be happening! This was a nightmare, he thought as he slowly stood up and began to inch forward. He wanted to run into the circle and scream at the dark man to leave his brother alone, but he couldn't. Then the voice of the young native sent Robert stumbling backward again.

The native began yelling passionately as if talking to a presence only he could see. It was a gut-wrenching cry that caused all the others to come out of their reverie and standstill. The man took the almost empty bowl and threw it into the fire producing an explosion of bright yellow flames. He began to laugh hideously and his eyes rolled back into his head, leaving small white slits in their place. His laughter grew louder and louder, then suddenly he outstretched his arms and curled his fingers in Brad's direction. The stocky boy immediately flew off his feet onto his back and began to flop around on the ground like a fish yanked out of water. Taylor opened his eyes and quickly threw himself onto Brad to try and hold him still but it didn't help, a strength that was not Brad's own moved him. The sight of this sent Tommy into a state of hysterics, screaming and crying all at once. Taylor yelled for him to shut up, but it just made him worse. Taylor looked up and saw Manuel running away into the brush. He looked around to ask the natives for help, just in time to see the younger one approaching from behind with his machete raised above his head. Taylor screamed as the machete began its descent. The older native suddenly appeared, tackling the younger one at his midsection and knocking him to the ground while yelling something Taylor didn't understand.

* * *

At the sight of Brad's convulsions, Robert took a few steps backward, fell over a log, then climbed back to his feet and ran as hard and fast as he could into the woods. Soon his legs began to tire and ache, but he wouldn't let them slow their pace – a pace matching the frantic beat of his heart. Sweat poured down his face and body. He didn't know where he was going. Still hearing the screams of Tommy in the distance, he ran deeper and deeper into the woods and the darkness closed in around him, trapping him even more in fear. He ran and ran, changed directions, and ran some more. Soon the sweat joined with tears and streamed down his cheeks and neck. His legs felt like rubber, and there was no end to the darkness surrounding him. He couldn't stop running, but he couldn't go on. Tripping over a large root, he lost his balance and fell onto his hands and knees. He crawled a few feet under a fallen tree, pulled his knees up to his chest in a ball, and cried. He had left his brother behind. He had done nothing to help. A dread that the worst had happened flooded over his body and he began to shake violently, but no matter how courageous his thoughts were to return to the horrible scene, he couldn't move. He wished his dad were there. With quivering lips, he spoke out loud to the darkness above him, "God please save my brother and friends..."

* * *

Somewhere up above, his prayer was heard.

2 THE CALL

John Parker didn't see Mr. Hall glaring at him, shaking his head from side to side. At the moment he was too caught up in the rhythm and the sound. With his arms flying about, he beat on the drums before him as if on the plains of Africa, but this was no tribal celebration by the village fire, only Monday morning chapel.

Every week, no matter how hard John tried to obey the worship leader's command to play soft and simple, he couldn't help but get caught up and swept away in the music and eventually let loose – putting all his emotion and strength into the rhythm of the songs. In the end there was really nothing Mr. Hall could do about it. Not only was John one of the best drummers at the school, but the only one who would play at chapel and put up with the conductor's strict leadership. So regardless of how Mr. Hall felt, he needed the gifted young drummer. It was a miracle that Coach McKenrick let him participate with the group. No other basketball player had ever been allowed such a distraction. John had practically begged before his coach finally agreed and even then it was only on the condition that his star player was exempt from all the worship team practices. It was with much reluctance that Mr. Hall agreed to Coach McKenrick's terms. No other worship team member had ever been allowed such a privilege. Truth be told, everyone – especially Mr. Hall – knew John Parker didn't need any practice, but he would never admit it.

On the last stanza of "Lord I Lift Your Name on High", John finally opened his eyes and saw Mr. Hall's stern gaze. He smiled back sheepishly, then gently and softly ended the song. The praise team went back to their seats to the hollering and clapping of the students. Some of the basketball players yelled "Pooky", John's unwanted nickname – a lazy alteration of his family name - that had evolved over the years on the basketball court. He looked up and winked at his friends who were now laughing. They had told him to play extra loud that day. He hoped they were satisfied. Honestly, he never did it on purpose, his spirit just couldn't hold back the excitement and joy it felt when performing to praise God. John felt honored just to be on the stage. Though he sometimes struggled with the pride that accompanies performing before large crowds, it was always a bigger problem on the basketball court. Basketball was after all, entertainment. Worship was personal and leading others in the worship and praise of God Almighty, a holy responsibility. When he played the drums he would often close his eyes, the crowds would disappear, and he would be alone before his Savior.

Sitting down on the second row, John quickly glanced around to make sure no one was looking, then opened his backpack beneath him and removed a small book. As the Dean of Student Affairs introduced the speaker for the service, John was already lost in the pages of *Jane Eyre*, cramming for his test in British Literature class immediately after chapel. He knew if anyone saw him reading he would never hear the end of it since he was always nagging his friends for their lack of attention or attendance, but this was an emergency. *Yeah, I've heard that one*, he admitted, feeling guilty, but desperation held on, he had to finish that novel. *It's all up to his first words,* John thought, looking up at the short stocky man who headed towards the podium with only a half-hearted applause to encourage him. From where he sat, John could see him better than most. The speaker had an uncombed looking head of bushy white hair, matched by bushy white eyebrows and a bushy white mustache that almost covered his whole mouth. Small wire rim glasses sat on a plump, bulbous red nose. He wore a pair of dark wrinkled slacks and a short-sleeve, khaki shirt covered in a print that reminded John of the tropics. It looked as if the man had just thrown on something out of his suitcase only minutes before. His face and thick arms were weathered and bronze. John guessed the man had spent much of his life out in the sun. He was sure of it when he caught a glimpse of the worn down looking sandals on the speaker's feet. A ripple of soft chuckling moved through the crowd. John felt pity for the guy, but really what did he expect dressing like that? John looked down at his book, not wanting to be a witness to what was coming…

* * *

"Fellow faculty and students, first of all let me thank you for allowing me to come here today."

Another chuckle rose up from the student body. The speaker's voice was high-pitched and nasally, not at all what John or anyone else had expected from his somewhat burly appearance.

"This guy's going to get eaten alive," John whispered to himself, not even looking up.

"Go and make disciples of all nations..."

Same old Bible verse intro, John thought. He imagined himself in a director's chair yelling, "Cut! Cut! Let's try that again!". *Oh well. I'll hear all the critiques at lunch.* That was the last he heard...

"You say you are a Christian. Tell me what does that mean to you? What is that worth to you? Your future is secure, so now what are you going to do with the present? Young man, what are you going to do with the present?"

It got unusually quiet in the auditorium, the silence pressed down upon John and interrupted his reading. He felt an uneasiness stirring within. Lifting his eyes, John's gaze locked with the speaker's. The man behind the podium was looking directly at John with his index finger aimed towards him. Turning to the left and right only introduced John to more stares. Panic stricken, the blood drained from John's face and his body turned to Jell-O. *What is everyone looking at?! What did the guy say?! Did he ask me something?!* These thoughts and others were screaming in John's head. What seemed like an eternity passed and John was about to ask the speaker if he would please repeat himself, when the man continued on.

"What are you going to do with the present young lady?" This time the speaker pointed to a small freshman on the fifth row who smiled and turned red though not nearly as embarrassed, knowing the man didn't really expect an answer.

"And what are you going to do Mr. Professor, with the present? And you Mrs. Dean?" He now had everyone's attention in the whole auditorium. "Or you Mrs. Custodian?"

If the President of the school had been there he would have asked him as well. John knew this and was captivated by the confrontation in his tone. The high pitch was now deeper, stronger. If anyone assumed he was speaking to be impressive or convincing, they were wrong and John could see it in the seriousness on his face. His heart was being poured out. Something in his eyes stirred John's soul, something John had rarely seen before and he wondered where it came from. The man spoke and answered John's thought.

"I'm looking out upon an audience who claims to know the ever abundant grace, never diminishing love, and unfailing eternal security of God Almighty. The Maker of the entire universe, the Creator of all life, the Establisher of nations and kings, and Judge of all heaven and earth, who sent His very Son to die so that we may know Him, as we claim to do. My question is, if His Son who sought us...wait, let's stop and just think about that statement for a moment. You want to be blown away? Ponder what Christ did, that he sought you out, leaving the bliss of heaven for the torture of earth, the perfection of spirit for the limitations and sufferings of the flesh. He sought YOU and then he bought you with the price of his own life...If this Jesus now lives inside of you and has taken up Lordship over you, how is it you fail to live as he lived? Now, I'm sure you have speakers come in here who say, 'it's all going to be alright, you're trying and that's all that matters, God will bless you and give you the things you ask for, just be patient.' I want to warn you young folks. Listen closely to what I'm about to say. There are many out there today who claim to preach the gospel and all they really preach is selfishness."

Some bodies – many belonging to the faculty and staff – shuffled in their seats. Otherwise, there was complete silence. No one seemed to even breathe.

"Concern for yourself will always destroy compassion for others. Stop worrying about what you're going to eat or wear just as Jesus said. Stop worrying about what movies you should or shouldn't see, what music is appropriate, who likes you and who doesn't, and instead worry about the millions of souls that are headed straight for damnation and are arriving there even as I speak. Now I know you are thinking, 'Dr. Russell, come on. Be realistic about all of this, I can't possibly change the world!' And you know what? You are right, *you* can't. But *you* have been crucified with Christ remember? And it is no longer you who live, but Christ lives in you, and the life which you now live in the flesh you live by faith in the Son of God who delivered Himself up for you. Who is this Christ? He's the Maker of the universe, remember? The Creator of all life, the Establisher of nations, Judge of all heaven and earth…Let me tell you folks, He can change the world." He paused, closing his eyes, then continued. "Believe me," he almost whispered the words, "Jesus Christ can change the world." There was not a person in that auditorium who doubted him, nor doubted that he had seen God do just that in his own life.

Perhaps he's seeing it all again now, John thought, wishing he could peer into the speaker's mind.

Seconds passed in complete silence, then opening his eyes he slowly continued, "And he desires to do so through you. Do you understand? The power of Christ is in you! God brought me here today as a messenger for the dying. How can I emphasize enough the shortness of this life? Each of us only has so much breath inside and sooner or later it runs out for us all. How we spend that breath is all that's going to matter in the end. When Paul encountered Christ on the Road to Damascus he was changed and from that day forward his every breath until his very last was spent preaching about his Savior. I don't understand why we speak so highly of Paul, with no real desire to be like him. He was incredible, people tell me, but extreme. Do you realize that extreme is the only way a Christian can be? God said so Himself, 'Choose ye this day whom ye will serve. You are either for me or against me. Either hot or cold! But because you are lukewarm I will spew you out of My mouth!' Simply put, either love and serve God with all you've got or hate and deny him with all you've got. He says 'Make me your lover or your enemy, but don't dare just consider me an acquaintance!' And so my problem is this, if the encounter Paul had with Christ changed him so much, why do our encounters with Him fail to do so? Has Christ changed? Is He no longer as powerful and amazing as He was when He appeared to Paul? Is He less convincing now? Less appealing? I know Christ has not changed for He is 'the same yesterday, today and forever'. I am therefore afraid that there are many out there who believe they are "Christian" who have never really met Jesus and therefore, though they hope to be different, they simply cannot because they have not been changed. Go to your rooms today and meet with Jesus. Talk with Him, but mostly listen. Read His Word and ask Christ to show you your heart, to open it bare before your eyes and see if it truly belongs to Him. If your salvation is sure then I cannot convince you to strive for things eternal, to look heavenward in all your endeavors. I cannot make you see the lost around you. You must seek to be changed by these truths yourself. God will not force you either. He will not have robots in His service. The choice is yours. Apathy has crept into our hearts like cancer! Pray night and day for the eyes of Jesus to be upon you. I have been all over the world and have seen eyes so full of hurt and empty of hope that it breaks your heart in two. Stop all that you have planned for your future. All the dreams you have made, your spouse, family, job, house, cars – all the thoughts that help make your future comfortable and secure and go lay them before your Father in Heaven and ask Him what He wants you to do. He might just respond, "Go and make disciples of all nations…'"

* * *

The bell rang as he closed the chapel service in prayer. It seemed that for the first few seconds after "Amen" no one moved, faculty and staff included. Soon doors were opened and gusts of icy December air blew into the auditorium stirring everyone out of their thoughts and to their feet. The warmth of the gym was quickly forgotten as students dropped off their chapel cards, crowded through the three double door exits, and walked sleet covered paths to their classes.

3 THE HERITAGE

Tennessee Christian University lay nestled in the Smoky Mountains just outside the town of Lewisville. A beautiful university built in the early nineteen hundreds, with dark red brick buildings trimmed in white, with no lack of ornate pillars and columns supporting them. Bushes and flower gardens lined every path and tall rows of Poplar trees stood regally along the few campus roads. The school, steeped in tradition and patriotism, had established itself as an institution founded upon the Word of God and while other similar universities found themselves weakened over the years by the ever increasing infiltration of liberalism into their faculty and curriculum, TCU had remained true to its founding fathers' vision as a school centered in Christ. A small school, with a student body of around four thousand, allowed the town of Lewisville to claim a population of fifteen thousand for itself during the Fall and Spring semesters.

Lewisville was the type of town where most residents knew each other by name, with the name Parker perhaps known most of all. Rumor had it some in the community tried to change the town's name to Parkerstown in the early 1900s, but failed after the family members themselves argued so strongly against it.

The Parkers were fifth generation Tennesseans. In 1860, at the age of twenty-four, Simms Parker said goodbye to his father and mother in Ireland and journeyed across the Atlantic on board a freighter headed to America. He was going to go and make a name for himself in the new and untamed land bubbling with opportunity. At six foot six inches and 240 pounds, he was strong and hardworking, the kind of man who quickly found himself in high demand. Then a Civil War broke out and instead of the peaceful and abundant life he had dreamed of, Simms Parker was suddenly surrounded by the nightmare of battle. Though some said it wasn't his fight, he considered that the future of the country was his own future as well. With his personal convictions leading him, he joined the Union Army.

There were few soldiers who proved themselves as bold and courageous as Simms Parker. His skills at combat helped him climb the ranks to First Lieutenant in the five years that he served. After the war, at the age of thirty, he, along with other soldiers and their families, moved to the beautiful green valleys of Tennessee and established the town of Lewisville in 1867, naming it in honor of a comrade and friend who had died in the war. Soon Simms was married and just as in everything else he had done, he became a leader of the town. He established and ran the first bank, helped build the first church and school. He raised a family of six children, the eldest of which grew up to be the town's first mayor.

Mayor Parker's youngest son Richard, as tall and strong as both his father and grandfather, after fighting in W.W.II, avoided public office, but took over as president of the bank. He continued the Parker tradition of improving the town by providing low interest loans to build city parks and recreation facilities. Richard's two sons – both star athletes in high school, one in football and the other basketball – upon graduation, went to fight in the Vietnam War. Billy, the oldest and a pilot, was shot down and killed. Todd, the younger brother, returned home from the Marines much grown up and affected by the war and the loss of his brother. He was the first of the Parkers to attend Tennessee Christian University and continued his ball playing there. With skills and competitiveness not seen in many, he rose to stardom in the town as well as in the entire state as a point guard for the Lumberjack basketball team. He lead the program in it's mere third year to a Conference Championship title followed up by another the next year. Later he would say that he always played in memory of his brother whom he knew was looking down, watching him from heaven.

Married and soon to be a father, Todd turned down requests after graduation to play professional ball and instead joined his father at the bank. Though the Parkers had always been a family of faith and members of the church, it was Todd who after playing on a missionary basketball team that traveled to Mexico, surrendered his life totally and completely to the Lord. Along with his responsibilities at the bank, he was also a deacon and on the board of trustees at the church, taught Sunday School, and even preached every now and then. It was into this family that John and his younger sister Megan had been so fortunate to be born.

4 THE REPUTATION

At six foot five inches and 220 pounds, John continued in the stature of the Parker men before him. His hair was dark like his complexion and thick, but cut short with a buzz on the sides, short side burns, and short bangs that stood up in the front. His face was square and set with a jaw that seemed chiseled from stone. His lips, nose, and ears were small and seemed almost out of proportion to the one trait that his mother claimed were the jewels of the Parker men – admitting they had more than once put her under his father's spell – large dark, penetrating eyes. His head sat atop broad shoulders and a large neck that extended from a body cut and defined by years of hard work and exercise. From mowing yards and laying sod to shoveling snow and cutting timber, John had always worked and grew to love the smell of sweat on his shirt and the feel of dirt on his hands – hands that were unusually large and strong, able to perform with a basketball in ways others only dreamed about.

Though John's family was considered wealthy, they had never abused that status, nor allowed it to abuse them. John's father had worked hard all his life, just like those before him and though a successful career had been handed down, he didn't treat it as such but as a blessing that required diligent attention. Mr. Parker had seen what money and greed could do. He had watched his friends sell their lives and souls to it after college. He had seen the lines drawn in a community between people because of monetary status, even in the church, and he had watched the children of those friends grow up to appreciate only what they could get for nothing. This he would not let happen to his own.

Mr. and Mrs. Parker expected John to work for the money he needed to support his adolescent social life. They wanted him to appreciate earning something he sweated for, but most of all they hoped he would see the danger in letting money control him. Mr. Parker also did his part to teach his son humility by making the teenager drive an old pickup truck from the time he got his license all the way through graduation while many of his peers got brand new fully loaded sports cars or completely accessorized utility vehicles. John struggled with it at first, causing a few verbal battles between he and his father. At the time John had thought it a rather dumb way for him to learn a lesson. Really he just dreaded the thought of taking any girl out in the thing. However, it wasn't long until he realized not only how unimportant the whole issue was, but also how much fun he could have with "ol' Bess" as he came to call her. His was the only vehicle that could go to all the backwood hang outs and come out looking no worse than it did going in. For that reason, it didn't take long before everyone who could fit in "ol' Bess" did so, leaving their own jewels out of harm's way. Bess enjoyed all the attention.

John had, of course, already come to recognize his friends' obsession with possessing things, the best and most expensive. He'd also witnessed the contempt that the wealthy and popular could have on those who didn't pretend to have it all together. John had even been a part of it for a while, choosing to play "the game" early on. The game of trying so hard to fit in and be accepted, that you forget who you really are.

John loved to have fun and hang out so it was no surprise that he tried the fast and furious party scene his first year of high school. As a member of the newly admitted class of '92, it didn't take him long to find himself surrounded by guys and girls, classmates and upperclassmen, who were always looking for that next attraction and thrill. John gladly answered their call to center stage. His ego found popularity to be a drug he couldn't get enough of. Weekend after weekend his friends seemed to push him one step further that the weekend before. He quickly built a reputation as someone who always took things to the edge and sometimes past. If someone drank a six-pack, he would chug two. If one of his friends made-out with a random girl, John made out with two or three. He was the first to take risks and the last to back down. Eventually, he was challenged by some upperclassmen at a party, and a bloody brawl ensued. That night, John discovered fighting to be the best rush of all, and from then on things really began to get out of hand. With a small gang of tough guy followers behind him, John's reputation began to leave the campus and make its way all over town.

That was the year of eternal Sundays when Pastor Larry Myers' sermons seemed to drag on forever and were directed solely at John alone, which the pastor's constant heavy gaze in his direction confirmed. John began to hate going to any church or youth group activity because the youth there only reminded him of how he was supposed to be acting, and he imagined they despised him. He didn't have anything in common with any of them, and only a few of the girls were worth flirting with anyway. Week after week he avoided getting caught alone by his youth pastor, Rick Chambers, until finally Rick decided to pay him and his parents a visit at their home. John snuck out the back door as the adults waited for him in the living room. When he returned home hours later, his embarrassed and infuriated parents informed him that he was grounded "until further notice". They also reminded him they were leaving the next afternoon to go and visit an out of town friend who was in the hospital and that he would be responsible for picking up his little sister from school and taking care of her for one night until they returned. "Can you handle that, or do we need to call a babysitter?" His father asked with a hint of condescension, or so John thought.

"I can handle it." He responded, with a heart full of defiance.

The next morning, before he left for school, John was promised a lengthy face to face talk with his father upon their return. In a matter of hours, John's world would come crashing down completely.

5 THE LONG WALK

By the time the afternoon school bell rang, everyone who was anyone at Lewisville High School knew John's parents were out of town and the Parker home was *the* party place to be that night. John never paused to consider the ramifications of what he was doing. He picked up Megan from school and drove her to the Harris' house. The Harris' were longtime friends of his parents and some of the nicest people in town. John had a plan and knew they wouldn't say no. He lied to Mrs. Harris about an important school project that required spending the night at a classmate's house. Mrs. Harris knew his parents were out of town and had no reason to doubt John's explanation. Of course, Megan could spend the night with their daughter, who was also her best friend. John promised to come back soon with his sister's pajamas and toothbrush and drove home with a big smile on his face. Everything was falling into place. By 10:00 pm, John's street was flooded with cars and thumping music and his house was packed wall to wall with rowdy teenagers wreaking havoc. At 11:00 pm the police showed up. A dozen inebriated adolescents were rounded up and taken into custody. John was caught with his shirt off in his parents' bed with Trisha Hastings, a junior, and the daughter of Officer Hastings, who just so happened to be the first on the scene. Thankfully for John, another officer interrupted their make-out session and brought it to a sudden end. John was already in the back seat of a patrol car by the time Officer Hastings found out what his daughter had been up to and with whom. The livid officer had to be restrained when he spotted John and started heading in the teenager's direction. Quite the scene unfolded as a group of officers held Hastings back and tried to calm him down while his daughter cried in the background. John had no idea what was going on. Later, at the police station, the police chief himself called Mr. and Mrs. Parker and didn't argue when they asked him to keep John locked up overnight until they could get back. John was too drunk to remember where he had taken his younger sister to spend the night. It wasn't until early the next morning, with a hangover pounding in his skull, that he remembered dropping her off at the Harris' house…and forgetting to return with her pajamas and toothbrush. His life was over.

Mr. Parker picked John up the next morning. As John climbed into the front seat he already had a lump in his throat, a knot in his stomach, and a cramp in his chest. His father didn't say a word as they drove out of town and up into the mountains. After half an hour, on a dusty forest road, Mr. Parker stopped the car, left it running, got out and began to walk back in the direction of their town. John sat blinking, wondering what in the world was going on. His father's slowly walking figure eventually disappeared over the horizon. John felt nauseous. He slid over into the driver seat and by the time he pulled up alongside his father, tears were beginning to spill from his eyes.

"Dad, what are you doing?"

Mr. Parker looked down at his son with glistening eyes and the look of pain in his expression pierced John's heart. His father didn't say anything, but looked straight ahead and kept walking.

"Dad! Why are you walking? Get in!"

No reply, only the low grinding sound of tires slowly rolling over loose gravel.

"Dad please!"

His father continued to look straight ahead, but spoke quietly.

"John, I can't for the life of me understand how a son of mine – a son who from the day he was born has been loved and cared for, taught and trained, encouraged and prayed for – how this special and precious son of mine could have done what you did to your mom, your sister, and I unless I had somewhere, somehow failed you as a father. You disrespected us, allowed our home to be trashed, and worst of all abandoned your sister…"

John noticed his father's hands were balled up into tight fists.

"Son, it's best if you leave me alone now. I'm going to walk until I either figure out where I went wrong or I get home…" and with that his father immediately veered off the road and headed into the woods. John stopped the car and got out.

"I'll see you at home," Mr. Parker said emphatically over his shoulder.

"Dad wait! Come back!"

Mr. Parker strolled over a ridge and out of sight once again.

"Dad I'm sorry!" John yelled at the tops of his lungs. His body slumped down onto the ground and he cried his eyes out. He had never felt so useless in all his life.

John drove home slowly and all he could see was the look of disappointment on his father's face. He kept looking off in the distance hoping to catch a glimpse of his dad, but he was never there. John also did something else while he drove, something he hadn't done in a long time. He prayed to a God that he had grown up hearing about in church and in his house. A God he had at times been sure was really out there then other times doubted completely. He had even gone forward at one summer camp and prayed to ask this mysterious God in his heart, but he knew then and remembered now how much pressure he had felt to do so. The fact that Susie Jones went forward first and that he had been desperate to get her attention only served to undermine the whole experience even more after it was over.

God, I don't know what I'm doing! I don't know who I am!

His father's question reverberated in his skull…"How could you do this to us?"

John felt one last rush of self-preservation rise up within him. *I'm not my Dad! I'm nothing like him! He's always had it all together. Everyone looks up to him just like they do grandpa and everyone still talks about how great Uncle Todd was. Why did I have to be born into this perfect family?!* Immediately John was ashamed of his thoughts. He felt like the most selfish, ungrateful person earth. From somewhere, deep within or far away he wasn't sure, a voice spoke to him. *You want to do things your own way don't you? You forget that there are others who are affected by the way you live.* John suddenly understood how much it must have embarrassed his parents to be called by the chief of police in the middle of the night. He realized the whole town would be talking about him and that they would ultimately judge his parents for his actions. Why didn't he see this before? *It's time you take responsibility for who you are and live up to the name you've been given.*

John parked the car in the driveway and sat in the front seat waiting for his father to come home. He definitely didn't want to face his mom and sister. Two long, gut wrenching hours passed before John saw his dad round the corner at the end of the street. John bolted out of the car and sprinted to his father. He threw his arms around his dad and buried his face in his father's chest. He sobbed uncontrollably for a whole minute until his father's hand lifted his chin up.

"I'm sorry dad! Please forgive me. I will never, ever do anything again to shame you and mom and Megan. Never."

"Son," Mr. Parker said with a smile on his face, "I think it's time I shared some stories with you about when I was your age…"

An hour earlier, just as John was coming to terms with the responsibility of belonging to a family and living up to others' expectations, his father was beginning to understand his own responsibility to be real and honest with his son. As Todd Parker walked down the mountainside, he vividly remembered what it had been like at times to live up to his father's expectations and the struggles and rebelliousness that he had gone through for a few years as a teenager. He realized he had never shared any of those experiences with John and now he was desperate to connect with his son and help him through this stage of his life…

"Let's go for another drive son…"

* * *

This time they traveled up another mountain and deep into another forest. They came to a stop when the front of their car almost touched the blue sparkling water of one of their favorite fishing lakes. They went for a long slow walk and then sat on the bank and skipped rocks together. That morning John found an understanding friend in his father and Mr. Parker found more of himself in his son than he ever expected. They connected and both of them knew it was a moment they would never forget.

Later, the son and father returned home and enjoyed a sweet reunion with two anxious and relieved females. John shed more tears as he hugged and kissed his mom and sister, asking for their forgiveness and promising them his devotion and obedience. Megan wasn't sure what all the fuss was about, but she was glad to have her old brother back – she hadn't been liking the one that had been around for awhile. When she shared these thoughts, John laughed and wiped away his tears.

"I am back Megan and you'll never get rid of me."

That afternoon and evening the Parker family worked together to clean up their house and then they went out for a night on the town to celebrate the miracle of a family's love. They even kind of enjoyed all the curious stares they received.

6 THE PARTNER

There were only a few weeks of school left before summer and John was grounded for the entire time. Of course with teens, the more trouble you get into the more famous and respected you become and John's party definitely lifted him to "godlike" status among his peers. Their praises and adoration however felt like a weight on his heart and soul. He began to sense that there was something out there more important than anything he'd imagined so far. He wasn't sure what or who it was, but his heart was now capable of honestly searching.

* * *

That summer, to keep his son busy and out of trouble, Mr. Parker enrolled John in basketball camp. John began to practice all hours of the day and his skills improved so quickly and dramatically that the high school varsity basketball coach was informed he needed to come and take a look. It hadn't slipped anyone's attention that John had also grown five inches taller since the beginning of his freshman year. The varsity coach knew potential when he saw it and started John on a serious work out and training routine. He also partnered John with an upperclassman named Scott Mitchell. The two had talked a few times previously, but Scott had never gone out drinking or partying with the other players and John had always thought him a little strange. Now he learned Scott's odd behavior resulted from a personal walk he had with Jesus Christ. Scott was an incredible ball player, but it was something else that caused John's admiration of him to grow everyday. It was the way that Scott carried himself. The way he talked and joked using words that were always positive and uplifting. The way he handled tough situations calmly and prayed continuously, talking to God as if He was his closest confidant. Most of all, the way he noticed others – others that most people didn't take the time to notice – and made them feel special. John was watching and listening and learning that something is truly different about a person whose faith is everything to them. One day after a hard practice, as the two friends sat catching their breath on the bench, Scott asked John the question he needed to be asked.

"John, what's keeping you from giving your life to God? You know He's the one who gave it to you and He requires that you give it back?" Just like he always did, Scott cut through all the crap and got right to the point.

John wiped the sweat off his forehead. "Dude, besides my parents and youth pastor, you're the first person I've known whose walk with God seems genuine..."

"So how many people do you have to meet? Anyway, as far as your soul is concerned it doesn't matter if I'm walking with God or not or your parents or youth pastor or anyone else. In fact, if there wasn't another single person on this earth living for God it wouldn't change the truth of Who God is, what He's done for you, what He requires of you, and what He wants to do in your life. That's between you and Him alone. Bro, I'm glad you can see something different in my life because that means I'm doing something right, but most days I fall so short of how I want to live for God and especially the time I need to spend with Him.

"Scott, come on man. You're the nicest guy I've ever met.

"Listen John. Niceness doesn't cut it. It's an issue of righteousness. You don't know the thoughts that run through my mind or the evil intentions of my heart, but God does. This is why the Christian life is a struggle and a fight. A fight against your very self. It's hard and at times seems impossible, but it's the only thing and I mean the ONLY thing that will ever really and truly satisfy you and that's because it's what we were created for."

"If it's what we were created for then why is it so hard?"

"Because we weren't created to live in this messed up world and sooner than later we'll be right back where God intended, hanging out with Him forever in paradise, but to get there you have to do one thing..."

John had heard all about becoming a Christian at church and youth group meetings and camps, but he suddenly felt as if he was about to hear for real for the first time in his life. He leaned in towards Scott, not wanting to miss a word.

An hour later, John and Scott hugged each other and headed their separate ways. John was a new creation. He announced his decision to his family as soon as he got home. They were overjoyed and his mom was moved to tears. Their ultimate prayer for their son and one they had been lifting up to God from before John's birth, had been answered. Their child was a child of God.

* * *

Over the course of the next school year, the Lord assured John again and again that if he would seek after Him and His ways, he would be filled with purpose and love for others like never before. John discovered a relationship with his Creator that was real and life changing. He desperately needed this assurance as he faced one difficult situation after another, usually involving those he'd once considered his friends and the way they treated him now that he was no longer running with them. Sometimes he still went out to a party, but he didn't drink or get high, he didn't use the same colorful language or laugh at the same jokes, and he usually didn't stay long. His old friends no longer enjoyed his presence and his offer to serve as their designated driver only added to their frustration. Now that John could see how pointless and destructive their lifestyle was, he desperately wanted them to see it as well. His words fell on deaf ears and one night a few of his old buddies, drunk and looking for a fight, decided to turn on him. He took a hard punch to his jaw and fell down onto one knee then stood up slowly, wiped the blood from his busted lip, and walked away from the party and those friends for the last time as they laughed and cursed him for his weakness and hypocrisy. John began doing things with others, Christians and non-Christians, who knew of better ways to spend their time. However, he never forgot his old friends and prayed for their souls and often woke up in a sweat, haunted by their faces.

There were still struggles for John. He found his flesh still craving things he had surrendered to the Lord, especially with girlfriends who seemed all too eager to know him physically and were far from satisfied with just holding hands. He finally decided to cease dating altogether until he met someone who shared his spiritual desires and convictions, a decision that kept him single the rest of his high school career. His vulgar and rude speech didn't disappear as magically as he had hoped, but with each new day his convictions grew stronger and his old ways weakened and diminished. It was an even harder battle with his complaining spirit and sometimes-unpredictable anger, but John slowly and surely found his Lord's promise of setting him free from his old self, to be true. In time he hardly recognized his old sins when they showed up and he never considered letting them hang around. As his faith grew stronger, John found himself longing for more and more of the Spirit filled life. He studied the Scriptures for hours, both alone and with Scott and anyone else willing to join him. He prayed daily for God to lead him and reveal Himself anyway He wanted. The more John discovered, the more he was convinced that trusting his life to Christ was indeed exactly what he had been created for.

Scott was also there by his side every step of the way and John had never known a friend more committed and true. The two spiritual brothers played basketball as an offering to their God and together they led their high school team to an undefeated season and district championship. No one, especially their teammates, was immune from the contagious way the two preached and proclaimed the goodness and mercy of their Savior. Early in the season the team began praying together before and after games. Philippians 4:13, "I can do all things through Christ who strengthens me!" became their motto for the season and posters and banners were held up and displayed all over the gym at every game. Three other players gave their hearts to Jesus that year because of the influence and testimony of Scott and John's lives.

Scott graduated that year and headed off to an Ivy League school on a full scholarship. John was left to carry the torch, but not alone. Many in the school were now walking boldly for Christ, but John was definitely the one they all looked to for leadership and inspiration. God took the outgoing and friendly nature of his servant and used him to touch people. John's heart went out to everyone and serving them in whatever ways he could, filled him with joy and contentment. Over the next two years he became one of the most recognizable figures on campus and though most of his popularity was due to unusual basketball talent, it was his friendliness and willingness to serve that many would remember him for…not to mention his drums.

John had opted out of the piano lessons most of his elementary friends were taking and hating and instead somehow convinced his parents to buy him a drum set. His father had been first and easiest to sway, as visions of stardom lingered in his mind from years of fiddling on a keyboard and perfecting his own unique version of vocal harmony. His son could be the ticket! Eventually mother came around, but only after her boys promised to rearrange the garage into a practice area, more to keep out her husband's singing than John's drums. John took lessons from a neighborhood teenager and then joined the middle school band. From there he never looked back and 10 years and three garage bands later – the last of which headlined at the Senior Prom to the delight of everyone except John's date – John offered his drum skills to the chapel praise team at TCU in hopes of leading others in worship and adoration of the God Who had captured his heart for so long.

7 THE LOSS

John's freshman year at Tennessee Christian had been the busiest of his existence as he attempted to juggle a handful of new ministry and worship opportunities along with basketball and an exciting new social life. The words "over committed" didn't even begin to describe his situation. What was amazing was that he actually somehow made it through two semesters before finally crashing and burning. Well, almost. During finals week John received an unexpected phone call from Scott's mom. Mr. and Mrs. Mitchell had moved out East after Scott left for college and though the two friends had stayed in touch, John hadn't seen or spoken to Scott's parents in years. John could barely understand her choked up words, but the message that Scott had been killed in a car crash got through his quickly numbing skull. He cried with Scott's mom over the phone and after hanging up, fell onto the floor and cried some more.

Like lightning, memory after memory of the life and times he had shared with his brother and friend flashed before his eyes.

Why God?! Why?! How could You possibly need him more than us?! John suddenly found himself face to face with characteristics of God that he had never come across before - His unknowable and unsearchable ways. John didn't know where his next step would carry him, and it was frightening. Only the Word of God rescued him from complete despair, and he took refuge in His Lord's promises, pouring over them from morning 'til night.

* * *

Two days later John flew to New Jersey and joined Mr. and Mrs. Mitchell, along with the rest of their family, at a memorial service held in the gymnasium at Scott's university. Some of his and Scott's high school classmates were also there, including two of their teammates Scott had led to the Lord. Not surprisingly, an unending stream of students, athletes, coaches, and professors all took turns going to the microphone and sharing some fond memory of Scott's life and the impact he had made on them. John couldn't help but notice the variety of the people who shared – attractive and outgoing, unsightly and disfigured, respectable and dignified, weird and eccentric. One girl, who looked as if she didn't have a friend in the world, stepped up shyly to the microphone.

"I don't know any of you really…and none of you really know me. I've spent most of my life feeling like I don't fit in anywhere…and without a friend…until Scott came bouncing into my life…" She smiled as she said Scott's name, but her lips quivered. Many, especially John, were already wiping tears from their eyes.

"Scott talked to me every time he saw me…every time and he always had something funny and kind to say to me. He also asked me how I was doing and then would stop and wait for me to answer. He would encourage me to tell him how I was honestly doing. He would eat with me in the cafeteria and walk me to class. He would talk to me about God and encourage me to read the Bible that he gave me…and…" Now she began to sob. "He told me that he prayed for me all the time. He's the only person who's ever told me that. I've missed hearing that since he's been gone."

There was not a single dry eye in the entire gymnasium.

"I hated God for years. I hated him for the way my father abused me and my mother neglected me. The way no one saw me. The way I felt stuck and alone in this depressing world. Scott changed all that. I went to a church last night that Scott had begged me to go with him to…and I gave my life to Christ." The girl's eyes and face suddenly lit up with a glow. She looked up at the ceiling.

"I don't know why God took Scott away from us, but what's more important to me is thanking and praising God for sharing Scott with me for just a little while."

John's eyes were closed and his fists raised in the air. His spirit could hear the angels rejoicing in heaven over this lost soul come home, and he imagined Scott celebrating there with them. The most painful questions of his heart were being answered. He had planned on sharing something at the memorial, but there were so many others lined up at the microphone that he decided all the good things he and Scott had shared would stay between them. With each new testimony however, the solemn assembly turned more into a celebration. Soon people were clapping, shouting "Amen" and praises to God, and eventually standing to their feet and giving God applause for the life of His servant. It ended with a concert of a local band that Scott had hung out with and discipled. It was a worship concert, and never before had John felt his whole being so in tune with the movement and fullness of God's presence. Later that evening, John and Scott's family and closest friends reminisced long into the night, sharing their own fondest memories of the young man. The also prayed and praised God for all they had witnessed and heard that day in his honor and to the glory of his King.

* * *

John's sophomore year began quite differently from his previous one. He skipped out on the "ministry fair" during the first week of school and refused to obligate himself to one single commitment. By this time he had come to realize that his mission field was the basketball team itself and he needed to focus all his effort and attention on those teammates who were lost. He also stopped worrying about playing the "I've got it all together" part and instead began to really let people get to know him. He felt free to truly be himself for the first time since becoming a Christian. Since the initial shock and anger at Scott's passing, and as a result of his friend's incredible memorial weekend, John's walk with his Savior began to reach a new level of honesty and intimacy. This empowered him to walk by faith – not by sight, thought, or even emotion – like never before. John sensed Scott's delight.

John missed a few chapel services that first semester to the surprise of his buddies. The offer to play drums with the worship band eventually saved him from the threat of making that a habit. John had never been your stereotypical all braun and no brains jock because his parents always pushed academics over athletics. During his freshman year of college, however, he quickly found himself too busy to study and get the grades he wanted. After that first year, he determined to no longer take his college education for granted because he knew one day his basketball journey would come to an end. More and more often he could be found in the library or computer lab reading and researching for a paper or just out of curiosity. He loved attending lectures by distinguished professors with reputations of academic excellence along with the weekly discussions held by the campus' various clubs. That second year John learned and experienced more off the basketball court than on, and even though he led the conference in scoring and earned MVP status for the season, it was his 4.0 grade point average that both he and his parents were most proud of.

Now in his third year, John thoroughly enjoyed a mental challenge as much as a physical one and he loved to come across viewpoints and ideas that disagreed with him because he knew such dialogues informed and sharpened him.

John was a star athlete, but more than that he was a Christian who considered the ability to understand people, whatever their ideas, a noble pursuit. He had been given a life of countless blessings. God's grace had found him and freed him from his slavery to sin. He strived to love his Lord with all his heart, mind, soul, and strength and to love others as himself. There was so much he was sure of…and yet at times the journey seemed a complete mystery.

* * *

Like now.

8 THE WRESTLING

He sat still with his eyes closed long after everyone else had left. The maintenance men began removing the stage, podium, carpet, and chairs, turning the makeshift sanctuary back into the old gymnasium that it was, but John didn't hear them. He was waiting, being still, listening to his heart. The presence of the Holy Spirit was pulsating through his entire body.

Lord what do you want me to do? I neglect the lost around me in so many ways…

Suddenly John felt a hand on his shoulder. He looked up, his eyes squinting as they adjusted back to the light around him. Sam, one of the custodians whom John had formed a friendship with over the years, grinned down at him. His large cap shadowed most of his face, so all one could see was a large smile protruding from beneath his bill. He took his hat off and ran his fingers, cracked and grimy, through his thick curly hair.

"Hey, John you okay?" Sam asked, concern in his voice as he looked into John's red moist eyes.

"Yeah, Sam I'm fine, just having a talk with the Lord."

"Oh that's good," Sam replied, nodding his head, then went on, "Good game on Saturday captain! Another double, double!"

"Thanks."

"You gonna make All-American again?"

"That's a good question, Sam." He had been asked that so many times over the last few months, he tried to avoid the entire subject now. "We'll have to wait and see."

Sam always brought his kids to their games and was what one would consider a loyal fan of their team. John appreciated his and everyone else's support and encouragement, but at times, the game and especially the team's success, seemed to be all anyone cared about. It had gotten to the point where John often struggled to enjoy the game of basketball because of what it had made him on campus and in the entire town for that matter.

At first he had loved being a celebrity – being known, looked up to and admired by all, especially the girls. One day however, as he walked across the campus, five different people he had never seen before in his life came up to him and congratulated him on the game he had played the night before, scoring 25 points and being named the MVP. They didn't want to know anything about John Parker the person. John Parker the athlete was all they cared about. Was that all he was? The adoration he had sought at first, now left him feeling empty. It was also a constant struggle to stay humble amidst the praise and as his flesh continued to seek recognition, his spirit seemed to be more and more removed.

Sam was still talking, now about last season's National Championship game. John remembered the professor who'd hinted that if they won, he would get an A for the semester. A blessing most would think, but only a curse to his soul. He was tired of it all.

The curtains began opening up across the gym floor. John stared down onto the court that had meant so much to him, had filled his life with excitement and praise, success and glory, friendships and memories that would last forever. The curtains continued to move, exposing two goals on each end of the floor. No doubt the Lord had given him a talent to play ball and had allowed him to mature in his faith through the experience. It had also provided him with a full scholarship to attend TCU and for this John would always give God the glory knowing it was His provision. John had used the gift, but now it seemed the gift was using him. The thought came into his mind abruptly from out of nowhere: m*aybe it's time to stop playing.*

He laughed out loud at the absurdity of the idea and quickly dismissed it. He looked down at his watch – it was 25 minutes after 11am. He was late for his test! Grabbing his backpack, he ran out of the aisle and up the steps.

"Don't worry John, we'll git 'er all ready for practice today!" Sam hollered as he swept the gym floor, grinning from ear to ear.

John waved, yelled "See ya Sam!" and was out the doors.

* * *

That afternoon at practice, John was leading the team through their warm-ups when out of nowhere, just as he was balancing on his left foot and stretching his right quadricep, the thought returned. *It's time to quit.*

He lost his balance and fell over, slamming his hands onto the floor, barely avoiding his face. Everyone started laughing. Coach Mckenrick's voice filled the gymnasium.

"Move it! Let's go!"

John was back on his feet and the stretches continued.

The reason John was not only a starter, but also the captain of the team was that he practiced like he played. He knew only one speed, one level of intensity. It was all or nothing all the time. But on this day he was out of sync and out of sorts. Distracted by an insane thought that buzzed around his head and through his mind like an annoying insect that you couldn't kill and wouldn't leave you alone. He mis-timed passes, mis-judged shots, forgot set plays and routes and basically did everything he wasn't supposed to do. After two long and frustrating hours, Coach McKenrick blew his whistle and the team circled up in the middle of the court.

"Sorry guys," was all John could think to say as he placed his hand out in front and they all stacked theirs onto his.

"All or nothing on three. 1, 2, 3!"

"All or nothing!"

Before jogging off the court to the showers, Coach McKenrick made sure to let them know he was not at all pleased with their practice…or their captain.

"We play like we practice boys! And we practice like our leaders practice! Today was unacceptable! We're toast against Belmont if we don't get our heads out of our ashes!"

Some of the team members stopped and looked back.

"I said ashes so calm down! Tomorrow we get it together!"

Every player entered the locker room and exploded in laughter.

"Get your ash in the shower!" Someone yelled from inside a bathroom stall. A few were lying on the floor, unable to stop laughing or breathe.

* * *

John took a long, hot shower and left the gym long after everyone else. He skipped dinner. He tried to work on his term paper for his Philosophy of Education class, but couldn't get his thoughts together. He ended up playing NBA All-Star Challenge on his Sega console for an hour then finally drove into town for a late meal by himself. When he finally got back to his dorm room and fell into his bed, one thought had complete control of his mind…*it's time to quit.*

His roommate and best friend since middle school, Bill, lay in his loft across the room talking into the night about, Susan, his girlfriend. At least that's what John assumed, since she was all Bill had talked about every night for the last two semesters, but John wasn't listening.

Lord if you want to just say out loud for me to quit then go ahead or give me some dream tonight because I don't know what to think. Nothing but silence in his head, heart and soul. *God you know what you want me to do in this situation, but I don't. You also know how stupid and crazy my ideas and feelings can be so please make it evident to me what to do. I will obey what you say. If I'm to play again, I will. If not, I won't.*

He stayed up long after Bill had fallen asleep, thinking about and questioning his future, imagining what would happen with the different decisions he could make. Finally, he fell asleep, his heart feeling torn.

9 THE PROPOSAL

John wasn't sure how long the phone had been ringing when he finally opened his eyes and reached for the receiver.

"Hello?"

"This is your morning wake-up call buddy!"

"Hey Richard." Richard Baxter was the Director of Student Ministries at the University. "What's up?"

"Can you come by my office for a few minutes?"

"Sure, give me ten."

John hung up the phone, stumbled out of his bed and into the shower.

* * *

Twenty minutes later, he walked into the Student Ministries Office. Bonnie, Richard's secretary, sat behind her desk smiling at him as he approached.

"John, you can wait in his office if you want. He'll be back in a minute."

"A minute? Are you sure that's possible?" John asked, smiling down at Bonnie, who quickly giggled. Her offer of coffee to visitors had come to be known as a "bottomless mug" since it took a few refills before her boss appeared. All the magazines on the table looked well worn. Richard Baxter was just too easily diverted. A simple thing like walking across the campus could take him hours.

"Thanks Bonnie," John said, walking into Richard's office and sitting down in his regular spot in front of Richard's big mahogany desk. John couldn't help but reminisce on all the times he had sat in that very chair and shared the things going on in his life with Richard. In the two and a half years that he had been a student at TCU, Richard had become one of his mentors and closest friends. A man of God like no other John knew, Richard would tell you what was on his mind and he would confront your sin, but in such a caring way that you were thankful for his concern. He loved the students and desired more than anything to see them walk with the Lord and live holy lives. But best of all, he was a funny man. His sense of humor was relaxing and made him a true delight to be with. It was hard not to love the guy.

John heard him come into the lobby and tell Bonnie to hold all calls until he was through. He walked into his office, closed the door behind him, and sat down at his desk.

"Good morning sir," Richard said grinning from ear to ear, "You look a little worn out, did you get enough sleep?"

"Almost. I was this close," John said, pinching his fingers together.

"What happened?"

"I'm not sure, but I have this ringing in my ears."

"Must be those drums you beat on." They were both all smiles.

Richard looked at his wife's picture on the wall and John knew what was next. He'd been in Richard's office so many times, the guy's procedure was like clockwork.

"So word has it, you've got yourself a new best friend."

John only smiled.

Richard continued, "So were you going to share this with me or what? After all we've been through. After all the help and advice I've shared, this is how you repay me?"

Richard never failed to play matchmaker at every meeting, something he wasn't very qualified to do since his wife Sharon had practically been forced to propose to herself due to her fiancée's inept romantic skills. It was a story everyone knew and an event most had witnessed...

* * *

At 29 years old, Richard had been TCU's most available bachelor. The single staffers lined up across the campus to get to know him better, but he was busy, focused solely on his work and the students. After three years of employment and not a single date, everyone thought he would never tie the not. Then *she* walked onto campus – a 28-year-old California native who had worked professionally five years and was now returning for her Masters studies. Richard was hooked immediately, but from so long out of the game, he'd lost the ability to reel her in. It was the students, faculty, and staff – from the groundskeepers up to the President himself – who tried their hardest to help Richard and give him advice. He was doomed from the beginning. Nervous and uncomfortable every time he was near her, he couldn't be himself. His humor fell apart. His style, charisma, and charm went out the window. It was fun to watch at first, but as he failed again and again to win her over, it turned depressing. He finally gave up. Things fizzled out.

It's still unclear at what point Sharon Fulton had a change of heart. It was also unclear what truly caused it, but really no one cared. The day Richard and Sharon walked across the campus hand in hand, all other activity stopped. No one could believe their eyes. A few students even clapped. They fell in love, and the campus was thrilled. Later Sharon would tell all the students at Focus, the campus' weekly student led Bible study and prayer time, how Richard had actually won her over with his natural sense of humor, which ironically didn't show up until after he'd given up on her and let her go. But all of this is a preface to the one event that TCU would never forget, and would keep Richard forever stuck in "how not to keep a girl" history.

It was at a Lumberjacks basketball game that Richard left Sharon, his girlfriend of then eight months, sitting in the bleachers while he went to buy some snacks. At half-time instead of the normal dancers, Richard appeared on the court, took the microphone in his hand, asked Sharon to join him on the floor, got down on one knee, and then went blank. He forgot everything. He forgot the English language. The local media were there with cameras and lights as all eyes watched and every ear listened, waiting for words that were somewhere in the Bermuda Triangle. Later, on the evening news, as the camera zoomed in, everyone would clearly see the strain on Richard's face, the perspiration, the dark red shading, the overwhelming panic and then embarrassment as Sharon, calm, cool and collected, took the microphone and told her frightened lover to repeat after her. As if talking to a child she spoke slowly,

"Sharon Wilkerson...will you...marry me?"

Richard paused, then mumbled, "Yes I will," into the microphone she had lowered to his lips. And that was it. They never got another chance because of the riotous laughter that erupted.

At the roaring sound, Richard was brought back to reality, blinking his eyes, as if coming out of a dense fog to suddenly see clearly again. He realized what had just happened and smiled sheepishly at the crowd. He waved, wiped the sweat from his face, and then took Sharon in his arms and kissed her. He swears that you can see on the news footage where he whispered to Sharon after kissing her, asking her to marry him, but Sharon doesn't remember, allowing everyone to continue haunting him with the fact that she never really agreed to marry him and did so only out of pity.

* * *

"We both know how much you could use my help." Richard was straining to keep a straight face. The sentence alone was enough to cause John, still tender from the previous laugh, to start up again.

"What's so funny?"

John's side hurt as he spoke, "You know I wouldn't make a move without consulting you first."

"Good, you'll always be one step ahead of the rest."

"But don't be surprised now, if when it gets closer to the time to, you know, pop the big question, that I...go to your wife for help."

"I'll understand," Richard said grinning, "So you're saying that may be a possibility, huh?"

The smile on John's face said *nice try*, but he didn't take the bait. "I will say this, Rachel is special."

"Rachel. Rachel Nix? Am I right?"

John nodded his head. It didn't surprise him that Richard knew her. He knew all the students, new and old. That was his job and his gift. He could remember more names than anyone.

"Yep, that one has a spark about her," Richard said.

John smiled. *A spark. That's a good way to put it,* he thought.

"Well, just take it slow, have fun, and you know the secret to success…"

"Be friends."

"Wow, you do listen to me."

"Sometimes you do say something worthwhile."

Richard smiled then paused again and looked down at his desk which, John knew, meant it was time to get serious.

"Well, on a more serious note. Let me just begin by saying that this whole thing might be absurd to you and impossible, but I'm going to throw it out to ya anyway, and if you feel immediately there's no way, I'll understand, but just hear me out okay?"

"Okay," John answered back.

"I got a call this morning from an old college friend of mine. Her name was Maggie Garrett, now its Maggie Stevens. To tell you the truth, it was quite a surprise. I hadn't heard from her in over eleven years. She was an energetic and wonderful godly girl, and we spent a lot of time working together at a mission near our university. To make a long story short, after graduation she married her long time boyfriend Paul Stevens, also a classmate of mine, though we were never close friends. It seemed they were headed for the mission field when Paul, whose degree was in business, was offered a position working for an oil company, a position it seems he could not afford to pass up. He became very successful, making a reputation for himself as well as a fortune. Dealing mainly in offshore drilling, his work took him all over the world and not wanting to be away from his family, he took them with him. He started a new venture with four other businessmen about four years ago in Venezuela. They moved their families there, forcing them to practically start over. From what Maggie told me, it's been hard, especially for the children. All five families have kids between the ages of six and sixteen. Maggie and some of the other mothers have decided they want a young adult male to come live with them for at least a semester and be like a youth leader for the kids. Two of the couples there are Christian and, though they tried to start a church, it turned out to be more like a Bible study, then fizzled out completely. Apparently even the non-Christian parents, who are mostly from the Bible-Belt here in the States and are familiar enough with Christianity, think that religion of any form might do their kids some good."

John lowered his head, staring at the floor. This, Richard knew, meant the young man was thinking hard.

"Obviously money is not a problem, at least in the physical sense. In fact, Maggie says its because they've made so much money that they've stayed so long and it doesn't look like they'll be leaving any time soon. Basically they want a young man who is sold out for the Lord to come and live with them and spend time with their kids just as any youth pastor does at church here in the States. They'll provide an apartment, a condominium actually. You'll have all your expenses paid, as well as receive a salary of $2000 a month. There are nine children in all, five boys and four girls. They would want you to start at the beginning of January, right after Christmas and New Years. They'll pay for you to fly to Venezuela and then fly back in six months. So you'd be missing the entire spring semester…the rest of the season. To be honest John, I never had you in mind for this job simply because we both know you can't take it. But during the chapel service yesterday, I was looking over the crowd, praying and asking God who He wanted me to consider and out of the blue your name popped into my head and right after it did, the speaker called you out! You remember that? I saw him looking at you and I saw you staring at him like a deer caught in headlights!"

John had felt his pulse quickening as Richard spoke and now as the memory of that moment replayed in his mind, he started laughing again.

"You saw that?! Was it obvious he was looking at me?"

"Dude, his eyes were on you like a laser?"

"Right? That's what I thought too!"

"So listen. I didn't have you in mind, but once your name came to me, I realized you're probably the only one who could handle this assignment. Maybe that's what God knows too, but anyway, we both know you can't take it."

"Richard," John interrupted, lifting his face. Richard could see the glistening of tears forming in his eyes. "We need to pray."

"Okay John, what's up?" There was a hint of concern in Richard's voice as he had no idea why John would be crying.

"What's up is," John said, a huge smile spreading across his face, "God just might be answering my prayers and I don't want to screw this up." As John finished speaking, he began to chuckle, which relieved Richard, but still left him confused.

John went on to describe the events of the previous day, his experience in chapel, the wrestling that took place inside him all day long, and his prayer before going to sleep.

"I never expected an answer this fast, but like I said, I want to be sure. You know someone once told me that Satan is also interested in blessing your life...only his motives are to make you comfortable and content with how things are, keeping you from relying on God and ultimately making you feel distant from the Lord and apathetic about the gospel. Ever since I heard that, I've realized the importance of having discernment in making decisions. I just don't want to take this job because I'm wimping out on the team and the struggles I have with playing ball."

Richard knew those struggles well as they had discussed and prayed over them many times before.

"John that sounds more like an accusation others would make than one that you believe yourself. I can't tell you what to do, but I will say this, what you've been debating over is not something you thought of yourself. God has placed this situation before you and He's done it for a reason. If you decide to keep playing ball, I believe you'll play with a new passion that will allow you to overcome Satan's attacks and find more and more of your strength in God. If you choose to quit the team and take this job, I believe you'll not only find Satan's attacks continuing, but God's power in your life increasing as you, once again, learn to find more and more of your strength in Him. Remember, whatever you do, do it for the glory of the Lord. He gives you the opportunity to choose."

"You're right Richard," John said smiling, "you didn't tell me what to do at all. I thought I'd get little more direction than that." John's smile quickly disappeared at the seriousness of Richard's tone.

"John, if you quit the team, you're going to upset and confuse a lot of people, especially your teammates. You're going to be misunderstood, attacked, and ultimately despised by some. All this to go and live in a foreign country, leaving your friends and family, surrounded by strangers, and worst of all, stuck with a bunch of spoiled rotten kids who have most likely never been disciplined in their lives. Compared to this, quitting the team will be easy. I say all this to make the point that if you go to Venezuela, Satan has little chance of making you comfortable and apathetic about the gospel, rather you'll find it to be your only means of survival. God says that if you trust and delight in Him, He will give you the desires of your heart. John, that's all the direction you need. Just follow in faith. But right now let's do what you said earlier, let's pray. You have all week to think about this and you need to think. We both know this would change your life and your future."

* * *

After praying with Richard, John went back to his room and sat on his small sofa. He sat and stared at the wall. That verse kept running through his mind, "Delight yourself in the Lord and He will give you the desires of your heart." *What are my desires?* He had a blank stare for nearly five minutes then out of nowhere came laughter. Life never ceased to amaze him. *Where in the world did all of this come from?!* John imagined Scott up in heaven asking God to shake things up in friend's life down below...and offering some ideas of his own. *I wish you were here bro.* Scott's unforgettable last words echoed again in John's head. "Don't go and screw anything up okay!"

I'm trying not to brother.

John began to reach for the phone but stopped. He wanted to call

Rachel, but suddenly felt that this had nothing to do with her. The selfishness of that thought disturbed him. *Must I do this alone?*

The response he heard within was unmistakable. *What are YOUR desires?*

He had plans. Three more semesters until graduation and then he would go overseas and do mission work for a few years. Afterwards, return to the States, maybe Tennessee, and teach in a high school and coach basketball. Wherever he ended up, he would do all he could to make a difference in people's lives, especially the lives of young people. He wanted to get married, have kids, play drums in a church, speak and do mission work in the summers. Real mission work, not baby-sitting spoiled American kids. He had already put in his time with the youth groups of two churches in the area, churches whose members were well off and whose children knew it. The last thing they seemed to understand was their need for the Lord. Could he really handle this?

All the doubts he dealt with year after year were with him once again. *Here you are, this leader on campus, someone everybody looks up to, and really you're just a spiritual wimp, a phony with so much sin in your life.* An all too familiar voice reminded him he was just living a lie. But someone did believe in him. Richard had said he was the only one who could handle it. *If he only knew,* John thought.

Not wanting to listen anymore to the discouragement coming from within and ignoring the urge to pray, John picked Bill's guitar up from its stand. He liked to strum on it whenever he needed to think. Putting his thoughts to music always made them sound a little more positive. Bill had introduced John to the guitar, and he found it to be as addicting as the drums and a lot easier to take with you. To say the least, that guitar had taken the place of many hours of studying for the both of them. He knew one would come in handy if he took the job because nothing communicated to children and teenagers like music. Suddenly another wave of thoughts and ideas came rushing through his mind. These were followed by questions and, once again, more doubts. Frustrated, he finally put the guitar down and sat still. He knew he should pray. Felt he should pray. Wanted to pray, but for some reason stalled. Finally, realizing his pride was close to hardening his heart, he forced himself up onto his knees, closed his eyes and mumbled, "God, forgive me for my stubbornness…"

10 THE PEACE

The next few days seemed to last a lifetime as John went through the motions of daily classes, basketball practices, assignments and social gatherings. And although he was constantly surrounded by classmates, teammates and friends, he was often alone in his thoughts. Thoughts about his pending future, away from basketball. He told no one. He was waiting for a clear answer from the Lord. This was not something easily done and he often found himself longing to share his secret with his closest friends and most of all with Rachel. He stuck to his convictions, however, and didn't say a word. This was a decision he had to make for himself without being influenced by the opinions and plans of others. Besides, he knew exactly what those opinions would be.

Thursday began with an important nudge and ended with a lightning bolt. Bill often wrote Bible verses or inspirational quotes on his mirror at the start of the day, for himself, for John and for other visitors to their room. That morning when John climbed out of bed and looked in the mirror he saw a message written with a red marker in large block letters:

* * *

"Do not wait; the time will never be 'just right.' Start where you stand, and work with whatever tools you may have at your command, and better tools will be found as you go along." - George Hubert

* * *

He didn't know who George Hubert was, but his words gripped John's heart and were seared into his memory. They whispered to him all day long.

That night, at *Focus,* the weekly Bible study hosted by the Baptist Student Union, the scheduled thirty minutes of praise and worship stretched into almost an hour. No one wanted to stop, especially John who just kept the drums rolling as the Spirit kept flowing. They ended with an acapella version of "Here am I" and as the hundred plus voices filled the room, John stood and looked out over the crowd of students. It brought him joy to see so many of the athletes on campus there with hands lifted and eyes closed, singing to the Lord. For so long, the athletes, most of whom came to the school because of their scholarships, not for spiritual reasons, avoided participating in activities such as these. As an athlete himself, John knew God was calling him to reach out to the others on campus. It hadn't been easy. Especially at first, as the majority of those he invited, including his own teammates, would tell him not to waste his time. But he never gave up and with the prayers of many on the campus and in the churches, slowly but surely athletes from every sport began to show up at not only *Focus,* but other Bible studies and ministry events as well. There was nothing like having a bunch of jocks around to help paint a house or perform other manual labor. Now when the new recruits came in every year, more and more of the upperclassmen took the initiative to share their faith and the burden of ministry with John and others who had been involved from the beginning.

Strong, passionate voices sang out the final chorus. John came out of his thoughts and joined back in, at first not fully aware of the words he sang. Then it hit him…

Here am I Lord. Is it I, Lord?
I have heard You calling in the night.
I will go Lord, if You lead me.
I will hold Your people in my heart.

He sang the words slowly and loud, causing members of the praise team to look at him strangely. *I will go Lord!* That was the answer of his heart, soul, and mind. A wave of relief flooded through his whole being as he released his own will and enthusiastically embraced his Maker's.

Your will be done in my life Lord! How faithful you are God! Tears of joy rolled down John's cheeks and off his chin. He always led the group in a closing prayer at the end of worship time, but he was lost in the moment, kneeling in the presence of His Lord, worshipping at the feet of his Savior. Steve, the leader of the praise team, noticed John's attention was elsewhere and closed the worship time in his place.

During the message time, John snuck out the door and found a quiet place outside to pray. He returned long after the meeting was over and everyone had gone. All the musical equipment, except for his drums, had been put away. It took a while to disassemble and move all the pieces. As he walked out of the storage closet and back into the room to get his last cymbal, he found Rachel standing there alone. She was leaning against the inside of the doorframe with her feet crossed and her hands locked together at her waist. She was dressed in one of her tennis jogging suits with her racket bag strapped over her shoulder. Her straight auburn hair was pulled back in a ponytail, and there was a light glisten of sweat on her forehead. Even after hours of tennis practice she still looked radiant to John. As soon as their eyes met, his heart stopped beating for a few seconds.

"Hey stranger." Her voice seemed less confident to John than usual. "You've seemed to disappear lately, and we both know that's somethin' not easily done around here. I'd congratulate you for the accomplishment except that I kind of missed you so I don't want to encourage it."

"Yeah, I kind of needed some time to myself these past few days...I missed you too." John was immediately aware that was the first time they had spoken in such a way to one another and he liked it. "I'm glad you're here."

"Well, I'm glad the drums take so long to put away. We just finished practice and I saw the lights on in here. I wish I could've come tonight. Was it good?"

"Yeah, it was great." John wondered if he should just get straight to the point. He hesitated.

"You want to get that last one then take me for a stroll?"

Rachel's soft brown eyes seemed to sparkle and her smile put John at ease like it always did.

"I'd be delighted," he said, carrying his cymbal and locking it in the closet. He then escorted Rachel out into the cool night and onto their favorite campus trail, with her arm surprisingly yet naturally wrapped around his.

11 THE FRESHMAN

The winds picked up and Rachel walked closer by John's side, sometimes ducking her face into his chest when it blew. For a while they walked with no words, both content and comfortable just to be together. They had never spoken about what they were to each other, never defined where they were headed together. They had just been friends since almost the first day she had arrived on campus only months before. On that annual day when all the freshmen arrive with mom and dad and all the upperclass guys make their big appearance, helping the new "fish" move all of their furniture and belongings into the dorms – the perfect chance to be a gentlemen and meet the folks all at once.

* * *

John was part of a team responsible for welcoming the new class of '98 students onto campus and helping them get moved in and situated. He loved it. It gave him the perfect opportunity to meet the new students first hand, learn their names, and begin friendships that would grow throughout the year.

It didn't take John long to realize that even at a Christian university, high school games of popularity, acceptance and rejection were still being played. The lobbies of the dorms and the parking lots were the hot spots where groups of the recently admitted socially elite joined up with the veterans of the field to begin another semester of who can impress who the most. During those days when most were completely goofing off as well as showing off, John's focus was intense and his objective extremely clear. His vision was far more penetrating than most of his friends as he would watch closely for any students who seemed to be having trouble with their new environment or who were a little less noticeable – less noticeable at first, neglected later, and then gone. They were easy to spot if your heart was looking. They would walk by the groups and kind of duck their heads or just avoid them completely, zigzagging in between the cars or walking in large circles around them. John hated how they went unnoticed as if they somehow didn't belong. He would hunt them down, catch them by surprise, take the heavy suitcases they were dragging out from their hands, and practically force his love on them. Then they would walk by the mingling crowds and when John's teammates and friends called him over to meet some of the new students they were talking to, he would reply he was busy helping his new friend and then share the name of the new student he was with. This always made his companion smile, the girls sometimes blush, and then begin to trust and share their lives with him. But there were so many lonely faces, or faces trying their best to hide the loneliness inside and though he was not the only one to care, nor the only servant at his school, still many – far too many – were blind.

When Rachel arrived, she found about three or four tall, strong looking guys carrying her stuff before she could even consent. An athlete herself, she knew too well the egos that accompanied her that first day and was rather amused to see such shallow motivated servanthood in action. "If they only knew they didn't have a chance," she whispered to her mother and they giggled together, then she flirted and egged the young men on. Her father, knowing the boys were being played for fools, could only watch in pity.

John had actually welcomed Rachel and her family into the lobby of her dorm, introducing himself and carrying on with the usual chit-chat, before quickly disappearing. Though Rachel had thought he was handsome, there seemed to be no end to the attractive guys offering assistance. Even his politeness, which had impressed both her parents, was a characteristic too much on display to be trusted as genuine. For the time being, she didn't think much else about John Parker. However, off and on, over the next few days, as new students continued to move in and Rachel continued to get acquainted and be noticed – it seemed by all the wrong guys – she noticed John. The tall, athletic upperclassman was always smiling and talking with one or two students – students not many other people were hanging out with. Every day he was carrying bags, desks, shelves, TVs or just walking and talking with people of every size, shape, color, and nationality.

Then one afternoon, after trying to convince herself day after day that it wasn't her responsibility, the conviction of God hit her hard - *You know better.* Immediately, she began to reach out, welcome and befriend other new students who weren't very familiar or comfortable with their new surroundings. Two days later, after giving herself completely to the task, she found herself sprawled out on one of her dorm lobby sofas with her eyes closed, longing for sleep. She heard another body fall onto the couch next to hers with the same thud and peeked over to see John lying on his back with his hands locked behind his head and eyes closed.

"You've been busy lately." He said without looking at her. He had passed her many times and seen her with other new students who really needed her. "Good work."

"You too," she answered back. "Good pay too, huh?"

"Yeah, lots of benefits."

"Great boss."

"Amen." They both fell asleep.

* * *

The next thing John knew, he was wiping shaving cream off his face with his shirt while a lobby full of female students laughed around him. Susan, one of John's close friends and a complete clown, stood only a few feet away with a can of shaving cream in one hand, a feather in the other and a huge grin on her face.

"Good morning, John!" She said, "You're all ready for a shave now!"

He should have known better than to fall asleep in a female dorm lobby! He stood up with his hands in the air in a pose of surrender and began walking towards the front door. In a flash, John spun around, rushed Susan and before she could finish her scream or take a step, he had her in his arms and was rubbing his face all over hers. Next, he grabbed the half empty can of shaving cream from her hands and emptied it out all over her head. By this time the lobby was packed full of hysterical females and Rachel stood right in the middle with her jaws open, a hand over her mouth and a look of hilarious shock on her face.

John gave Susan a final squeeze and then turned to face Rachel.

"It wasn't me?" She pleaded.

"Well, thanks for your protection!" John thought she deserved a hug as well, but just then the Resident Assistant stepped between them and reminded everyone it was past curfew. She then proceeded to shoo a very messy John Parker out the front doors like a fly. Rachel walked up to the glass doors and caught John's backward glance and waved. Both went to sleep with smiles on their faces.

Over the next few days, they talked more and ate lunch with each other occasionally. Soon they began to run together in the mornings and exercise at night. John didn't really think of Rachel in any way other than a friend, kind of like a young sister, and he did his best to introduce and get her acquainted with everyone, especially the faculty and staff. He also challenged her to keep focused on spiritual things. To his delight, he found she was equally challenging and seemed to hold him accountable in ways that no other girl had before. A week never passed without her questioning his walk with the Lord and what he had experienced and learned or helped him to see as gently as possible what he may have failed to learn.

"You sure you're a freshman?" He would jokingly ask her. In a month's time they were already close friends, and from there they never looked back. Now they both felt as if they had known each other for years.

* * *

They had walked a dirt trail down to the edge of the school's pond. A large fountain in the middle sent a spray of water a dozen feet into the air. Large spotlights at the base of the fountain illuminated the spray in red, white and blue colors.

"So what's been keeping you so secluded lately?" Rachel asked, as she picked up a rock and tossed it into the dark water. "Unless it's something you don't want to talk about."

"No, I was going to tell you, but I had to wait. Some things have been happening that have required a lot of prayer and discernment. I had to make some decisions and I wanted to make them with the Lord's influence alone. You know how easily I share stuff with people. Remember how I practically told you my whole life story the first time we attempted studying together, you hardly got a word in?"

"Yeah, you're quite a talker. I finally met my match."

"So you can imagine how hard it's been to hold all this in, but I was determined to keep to myself until I knew, and tonight I got the answer." John suddenly felt a little scared to go on. What was it? He was going to have to say goodbye to her. *So soon,* he thought.

"Before you tell me the answer," Rachel said softly, looking up at the stars and then directly into his eyes, "What was the question?"

"I'll start from the beginning."

"That's a good idea," she replied, looking more anxious than John had ever seen her before. John was relieved he could work his way up to the hard part. They sat down on a picnic table at the water's edge. John retold the events of the past few days again, and it took Rachel no time at all to figure out where John's story was heading. After he finally announced he was leaving to spend a semester in Venezuela, no one spoke for a full 30 seconds. John wondered if Rachel could hear his heart thumping inside his chest. Rachel stared up at the stars again and cleared her throat.

"What an awesome God we serve."

John looked up at the stars as well and smiled weakly.

"I'm proud of you, John. I've never met anyone like you and this decision just proves you're one of a kind."

John wasn't sure how to respond so he just said the first thing that popped into his head. "I'm gonna miss you, Rachel Nix."

Rachel looked over at him and smiled and then took his hand in hers. "I'll be here waiting for you, John Parker."

She scooted closer to him and as she did so John wrapped his arm around her shoulders. They sat for a while longer just listening to the wind. Eventually her head rested against his chest and he was sure she could hear his heart thumping wildly. The silence was cover for a tempest of emotions and thoughts stirring within them both. Emotions and thoughts they dare not give voice to. An hour later, a campus security guard woke them both with his flashlight in their faces and a stern warning that it was way past curfew. He tagged along a dozen feet behind as John walked Rachel back to her dorm building and said goodnight.

12 THE AFFIRMATION

The following evening, John sat alone in his truck, parked outside his house. Talking with Rachel had been more difficult than he had wanted. The most frustrating aspect of all was that while the decision to go had sort of forced their feelings for one another to the surface, it also made discussing those feelings unnecessary for the time being. He pushed all thoughts of Rachel out of his mind and focused on the task at hand. It was time to tell his parents…something he dreaded even more.

He walked into his house and found his mother where he always did at this time in the evening, in the kitchen preparing dinner. It was wonderful being able to get good home cooking whenever he pleased, something his friends – especially those who came from out of state – never forgave him for. He invited them over often. His mom loved the extra guests and treated each one the way she would want her own children cared for far from home. In fact, many of John's friends had become such good friends with his parents that they sometimes even came without him. This night he made sure no one would be there, just in case things got ugly. He walked over to his mom and kissed her on the cheek as his father came in from the backyard. John could tell by the look on Mr. Parker's face that he was a little frustrated.

"The mower," Mrs. Parker whispered, causing John to chuckle.

The Mower was like a family heirloom. In fact, John was pretty sure it had been around long before his birth. Early on it must have been an impressive piece of machinery, but as far back as John could remember the metal contraption was nothing but a coughing, wheezing, fire hazard on wheels. It had broken down and been fixed by Mr. Parker more times than anyone could count, but getting rid of the mower just wasn't an option. John's mom was afraid it might someday suddenly appear in the house as decoration.

"Dad. Maybe it's time…"

"Don't say it John," Mr. Parker answered back while washing his hands in the sink. "Believe me. I know," he quickly added, grinning at his wife and son as they carried the food to the dining room.

Megan was called downstairs and soon they all sat down to eat. Over dinner they talked about the usual things. Megan was in her first year of middle school, and that day she had been asked to be the girlfriend of Billy Rumbley, a red haired, freckle-faced boy who, just the year before, thought he would surely catch a disease by having to sit next to her in class. John made sure that she warn her new suitor of her over protective big brother. She giggled. John was her hero.

After dinner, the brother and sister washed the dishes and John whispered to her to pray for the talk he was about to have with mom and dad. She asked what it was going to be about and he assured her she would find out soon enough. When they were through, Megan took her cue to leave and went back upstairs to her room. John went and joined his parents in the living room where they were sitting and reading. They both looked up as he sat down across from them.

"I need to talk to you two about something."

"That's what we're here for," his mom answered back, smiling.

"So what's up son?"

"Well, before I even begin, I just want to ask you to first hear me out, okay? I have a lot to say, and you're going to want to jump in, but just let me finish first."

"Okay," they both answered, nodding their heads.

John swallowed. "You know how sometimes you hear a message or sermon or go to a concert or something and it's so incredible that all you can think about while you're there is wishing that the people you know and care about could be there and experience it with you?" His parents grinned at each other and then him, obviously having felt the same way many times before. "Well, Monday in chapel we had a speaker come...now that I think about it I never even got his name. I wasn't paying much attention at first..." he had decided to leave his last minute test preparation out of the story, but now changed his mind. He wanted them to know everything.

As John shared, he found himself reliving it all over again. He was back in the gym reading his book. Then came the startling question from the podium, a question addressed to him, but then directed to everyone in the audience. The message, as much as he could recall, was repeated. The challenge echoed. And as he remembered and shared, the thrill also returned. The Parkers listened attentively, both very aware of a change in their son's countenance. John went on to dramatically describe how he had sat and prayed after the service, asking God what he could do to make a difference. From there the subject turned to basketball and it caught his parents a little off guard. His mother looked over at his father who only stared ahead and continued listening intently. John shared about his struggles with fame and popularity. He described experiences and expressed emotions that he had never told them about before.

Somewhat assuming where this was all headed, his mother began to fidget nervously in her chair.

All the temptations and frustrations poured from John's heart, and he was relieved to see his father slowly nodding his head in understanding. Then John spoke of how the idea of quitting the team came to him. His mother began to speak, but before she could complete her sentence, he asked her to please let him finish and she grew silent. He took a deep breath. He was half way through and finished with the hardest part. From here he told them how he had asked God to show or tell him exactly what to do – either play or not – and he would do it. His voice grew louder and his words came faster as he laid out the events of the previous days: the offer from Richard, his struggle to find an answer, the debating of reason and emotion, even the quote from George Hubert which he had memorized…all of these John described in detail, sometimes repeating himself. Finally, he concluded with the Thursday night Bible study and the way God had spoken to him during the music and his realization that all the reasoning in the world would never produce an answer, only a step of faith and when that step was taken he had known it was the right one. He could see God's hand leading him through it all.

"And so I've decided to quit the basketball team and go to Venezuela to serve as a youth pastor for a semester." He was through. Silence. For almost a minute no one said a word. His mother, after waiting for his father to speak first, but fearing he might not say anything at all, quickly began with the line of reasoning John had expected.

"John, what about your responsibilities here? We know you want to do what God has planned for you. That's the most important thing to us as well. Never doubt that. God will show you what He has planned. Right now He's preparing you for those plans. That's what your education is for, and He's provided you with a full scholarship to receive that preparation."

He understood his mother's concern. If anyone knew his personality, temperament, and all too often hasty decision making, it was his mother. He had inherited it all from her side of the family. While his dad was the rational and level headed one, John found himself getting emotional and teary-eyed alongside his mom during all those tragic classic movies she loved to watch. But she could never know the complete assurance he felt in his heart that the decision he had made was the right one. Finally his father spoke.

"Son, we can't tell you what to do. It's up to you and you know that. We'll support you whatever you decide. But I just want to remind you that God is first and foremost concerned about your relationship with Him, much more so than what you do for Him. He wants to build character in you that is a reflection of the character of Christ. No doubt God has blessed you with a talent to play ball – more so than anyone in our family before you. You have grown and matured a lot through it all. I know how you feel. I felt the same way myself when I played. Basketball is not your life, but everyone likes to make you think it is. There's no easy solution. If you're quitting because it's getting too hard to handle the pressures and temptations involved, I've got to tell you that nothing else you ever do will be without these things. In fact, only more temptations and struggles will await you in Venezuela. The important thing is that you quit because you're obeying God…and it sounds to me like that's exactly what you're doing."

John felt a tear roll down his cheek, then noticed his mother wiping her eyes as well. They looked at each other and laughed at their pitiful appearances. His mother stood up and walked over to him with her arms open. John stood and received her embrace.

"You know I get this from you Mom."

"Sorry, son. Too bad you can't share some of it with your father."

They laughed again as Mr. Parker stood and put his arms around both of them.

"You know we'll support you just like your father said."

"Thanks. I could never tell you how much I love you both."

"We know," his father said. "We know. Honey, how about we pray over this special boy of ours?"

Mrs. Parker nodded in agreement and they all closed their eyes as he began to lift up words of thanksgiving, protection and hope for their son. Soon two more hands joined in their circle. All eyes briefly opened to see Megan standing silently with her eyes already closed and a big smile on her face. John had never expected such support from them, never in a million years, but he was just learning more and more to expect the unexpected from His God, Who was showing him more and more every minute that he was on a well chosen path.

John drove back to his dorm that night with visions of his family huddled together in prayer playing over and over in his mind. He had almost been sure that he had seen tears in his father's eyes when they had hugged afterwards.

"Thank you God," John whispered. "Now for the final test." The next day he had to tell his coach and team. His father's final words of advice echoed inside: "Just do what you have to do and remember what God says…if He is for you, who can be against you?" His father had been as calm and collected as usual, but John had also sensed a fire right under the surface.

* * *

"Am I missing something, Todd?" Linda Parker asked her husband as they laid in bed in the dark, both staring at the ceiling above them. "You don't think this is a mistake?"

"Linda, remember when I went on that mission trip to Mexico? That trip changed my life and I would love for John to experience that for himself."

"I know dear, but that was for three weeks, not an entire semester and that was after you graduated. John is sacrificing a lot more than you did."

"And I believe the Lord will honor him for it."

"I thought for sure you'd at least give him the pros and cons assignment!"

In the dark, she couldn't see her husband smiling, but she felt his soft pinch. "Stop! I'm serious! Where did all this peace come from? We're talking about our son giving up a semester of school and maybe his scholarship to go to Venezuela. Am I just being too rational here? Am I lacking faith? Why are you so calm?!"

Her husband reached over and turned on the table lamp, picked up his Bible, flipped through the pages, then stopped and read.

"'And they began bringing children to him so that he might touch them and the disciples rebuked them, but when Jesus saw this he was indignant and said to them, 'Permit the children to come to me. Do not hinder them for the kingdom of God belongs to such as these.'" I read this verse this morning in my quiet time, and, as I prayed afterwards, God seemed to speak to me, asking me if I was willing to let our children come. I didn't understand what He meant or wanted at the time, but all day long

Christ's words have echoed in my mind, 'Let your children come.' Even before John began tonight, I knew he was going to ask for something that was going to send him away from us and closer to God, I just knew..." his voice shook and he stopped. Linda reached over and wrapped her arms around him.

"Linda, I'm scared to lose our son. I'm scared to tell him he can go, but I'm more scared to keep him from what God has for him. That's where I've found my peace - in God's will and protection."

His wife now found her peace there also. She stared into her husband's eyes and caught a glimpse of her son's as well. She was so proud of the men in her life.

13 THE CAMPUS

John parked his car and sat still in his seat. He still couldn't believe his parents' response. He pulled a folded up piece of paper out from his pocket and opened it. He had been so sure his father would ask for a list of pros and cons that he had written them out in advance. On the right side of the paper, a long list of "Cons" stretched down the page. On the left side, under "Pros", there was only one: "Obey God". With his parents support, John was more sure than ever that he was on the right path. He closed his door and was just beginning to walk towards his dorm building when headlights blinded him and stopped him dead in his tracks. A Jeep CJ7 skidded to a halt and a familiar face appeared above the front windshield.

"Get in, roomie!" Bill shouted in as soft a voice as possible while beckoning John over with a wave. He glanced quickly around the parking lot. "And hurry!"

John climbed into the Jeep which was completely free of doors and missing a roof. Bill was still standing tall and looking all around. He dropped into his seat and then scooted down low as if hiding from someone.

"You being stalked again?" John asked, with a smile on his face. "Remember good ol' Monica? How she…"

"Tell me it's not true," Bill interrupted. He wasn't smiling.

"What's not true?"

"I think you know brother. Actually you have something to tell me, right? I mean it's not like I would've expected you to tell me first or anything, but hey, no biggie, a guy sometimes has to hear something from the rest of the world before his own roommate and best friend tells him!"

John knew the cat was out of the bag. "Listen Bill, I was gonna talk to ya, but I had to talk to my parents first."

"Well then how does the entire campus know already?"

Rachel, John thought. *No, she wouldn't have told everyone. But she might have told her roommate, Jennifer. And Jennifer would tell…everyone.*

"I told Rachel last night and then my family tonight. You were next, I promise."

"So it's true?"

"It's true." John started to open his door. "Come on."

"Close the door! I've been swamped with visitors and phone calls all night! You don't understand, this is for your own safety."

"What are you talking about?"

"Listen. Sam and Eric and Jackson and Eddie, heck the whole team has been calling every five minutes. Coach McKenrick has probably hired a bounty hunter to find you!"

John laughed and shook his head. Bill always had a flair for the dramatic.

"I'm telling you John. Before you even get to our lobby, you're gonna be surrounded. And you can expect a long and busy night."

John looked in the direction of their dorm building. His roommate probably wasn't exaggerating this time.

"Let's go grab a bite," John proposed.

"My thoughts exactly."

* * *

They drove to Taco Bell and ordered from the drive-thru. According to Bill, eating inside was not an option. John was beginning to feel like a fugitive on the run. After receiving their food, Bill drove them out of town and up some dirt roads to a secluded spot on a hill that slightly overlooked their campus. They had been here countless times before, hanging out with friends, talking and laughing long into the night. The current mood was a bit unfamiliar for them both.

"So you're really leaving?"

"I am."

"And where are you going?"

"Venezuela."

"Seriously?"

John felt that he owed his best friend the full story so he started from the beginning, repeating everything he had shared with his parents. This time he included more details about his recent walk and conversation with Rachel. Bill listened attentively and didn't interrupt once which was unusual for him. John knew his roommate was struggling to come to terms with these sudden and unexpected plans. After a full minute of silently staring up at the stars, Bill put a hand on John's shoulder.

"I can't say I'm 100% on board with this brother, but I'm willing to admit that may be due to some selfishness on my part. It just won't be the same around here without you."

John nodded, but didn't say anything.

"But I promise I will pray for you everyday while you're on this adventure…and that starts now."

Bill gave John's shoulder a squeeze, and the two closed their eyes. It was over half an hour later when they finished covering one another in fervent, soul-stirring prayer and opened their eyes.

* * *

"So who is George Hubert?" John asked.

"You saw that, huh? Great quote, right?"

"That quote messed me up brother. In a good way!"

"He was a 17th century Welsh priest and poet. My Theology professor introduced us to some of his works and those lines really stuck!"

"So it's your fault I'm going to Venezuela!"

* * *

They talked more about John's plans and his expectations for life in South America, but he didn't really have much to share. He was taking everything one day at a time.

It was getting late. Bill looked at his watch and gave John a weak smile.

"Well, brother. I can't say I envy you. It's time to face the lights." The Jeep's tires spun out, throwing dirt and rocks into the air behind them.

"Sorry to drag you into this roomie!" John shouted as the wind blew through the Jeep. "I guess our room will be bombarded, huh?"

"You have no idea."

* * *

As expected, Bill's Jeep was swarming with students and even a few staffers and security officers before it could park. Everyone wanted to know one thing.

"Is it true?"

John's affirmative answer led to another question - "Why?"

As much as he wanted everyone to understand his decision, he felt deep down that he didn't owe them all an explanation. As John pushed his way through the gathering crowd, one of his teammates ran up and told John to come with him. John followed and found most of the basketball team waiting in the gym locker room. They had called an unofficial team meeting. John had escaped one mob only to find himself surrounded by a much taller and stronger one. The questions and rumors began flying around the room. Finally, John got them to quiet down. It would be easier to just tell them everything, so he did. Some held his steady gaze, others stared at the floor or played with their shoes. Everyone was uncomfortable. He finished the entire story, ending it almost five times before finally realizing there was nothing more he could say. He knew he couldn't make them understand.

"So are you gonna to keep playing until you leave?"

"Are you playing against Belmont tomorrow?

"Will you play in the Winter Classic?"

"You think coach is going to let you?"

These questions and others flew at him from all around the room.

"I want to play and help the team until the winter break, but after that I gotta get ready for Venezuela. I'll know soon enough whether or not Coach is going to keep me around until then."

Everyone knew that was not going to happen, but no one said it. Coach McKenrick had kicked many players off his teams over the years, but no player, especially not a starter and captain with a full scholarship, had ever walked out on him!

* * *

A few of John's closest teammates went back with him to his dorm room where they talked more. Others stopped by and the phone continued to ring. Bill helped juggled conversations and calls all through the night. Long after midnight, with the ringer turned off and the door locked, as most of the campus slept, John's closest friends laid hands on their brother and prayed for his peace, for his strength, for his calling…and for his survival. They all knew coach was coming for him.

14 THE COACH

Someone knocked on the door – lightly at first, then louder and louder. John opened his eyes and looked over at his clock. It was 7:00 am. He looked over at Bill who was wrapped up in his covers like a cocoon. John cleared his throat. "It's true, I'm leaving...come back later."

"John! Hey punk! Your stupid coach called my room and woke me up and told me to tell you to turn your phone on!"

It was Steve, their neighbor.

"All right, sorry bud!" John said sincerely.

"Yeah, tell him he can eat his championship rings!"

"Sorry! Dangit Coach..." John mumbled as he turned the ringer switch on. The phone rang before he removed his finger.

"John, be in my office in five."

"Alright coach."

Click.

* * *

Coach McKenrick didn't have the most amiable personality or social skills. You either hated the guy or loved him, depending on your ability of loving unconditionally. He'd made a lot of enemies over the years at the university. He was a basketball coach and that was it. Basketball was the first and last thing in his life. All else and others didn't really have a place. Professors had their bones to pick, other coaches and players did as well, even the students had a few. The chief complaint usually revolved around McKenrick's rule that NO ONE could step foot on the gym floor for any reason during the basketball season. It was his gym, not the school's, or so he thought. The students tried to remind the board that it was actually their tuition which helped pay for it, not to mention McKenrick's salary. But in the end, he had built a winning program, which deafened ears to all complaints. He knew how to win, and that allowed Coach McKenrick to just continue being his same old self, a self which others wondered how even *he* could live with.

McKenrick's players quickly learned how to survive. Be on time. Work hard. Don't complain. They also knew that under his tough exterior, he had a soft side. They had seen him shed a few tears after their championship victory last season, although some joked it was because he hated seeing so many students spilling onto the gym floor and hanging from the goals in celebration.

Though he had never expressed words of affection or appreciation to his players, he did call them "his boys", and they knew this was his own way of showing he cared. They were the only family he had. He never had children with his wife of twenty years who passed away from cancer long before he became the Lumberjacks coach. Everyone wondered about the amazing woman she must have been. Her illness and death had no doubt affected him, but he never spoke about it. He was a man of few words even with his players, but what he lacked in conversation, he made up for in volume. His temper-tantrums came to be known as "The Volcano" and occurred any time someone or something got in his way or irked him to a point of no return – a few wrong calls by a referee being the most common cause. The students, seeing it coming long before the refs themselves, would begin softly chanting "Volcano, Volcano" growing louder and louder until, like clockwork…BOOM! Rumor had it that officiating teams began demanding a pay increase for calling TCU games or else a boycott was on the horizon. McKenrick drove them all crazy, but always with acceptable speech. He had a gift for using ordinary and innocent words in such a way as to completely humiliate you. The rest he kept under his breath.

Coach McKenrick professed to be a Christian, at least someone said they'd heard from someone that he had at one time or another professed something to that affect. Still, he was definitely a popular prayer target for the weekly groups meeting all over campus. John and the coach had actually hit it off from the beginning. McKenrick had watched John play in high school and knew the outstanding athlete he was soon to get. Everyone knew John was going to TCU to follow in his father's footsteps, but that didn't stop other schools from trying to get him to look their way. John actually played along with them all for a little while just to keep Coach McKenrick on his toes. It worked, and McKenrick did his thing, threatening the competition away and offering John a full scholarship to play ball. John knew his coach wanted one thing from his players and one thing only – 110% effort all the time. For an athlete as driven as John, this was never a problem. John respected his new coach and the old crank in turn respected him. After two years of working together, John had won a lot of trust and freedom from the man who supposedly trusted no one. This allowed John to be more involved with music and other things on the campus. Now in his 3rd year under Coach McKenrick, John's role as captain and team leader was unquestionable and unchallenged. His plan had been to finally take the opportunity to share the gospel with his coach during the season, just in case.

He's not going to be happy, John thought as he entered the athletic office. *Well Lord, this is the final battle…go with me.*

Betty, Coach McKenrick's veteran secretary, smiled at John, but nervously, he noticed. *You too?* He thought.

"Hi Betty, how are ya?

"Good, John. So it's true, huh?"

"Yeah, it's true."

"Even coach can't stop you I guess."

"Not unless he's got great influence with the Almighty."

"I guess not then," she said, winking and smiling.

John returned the smile. "How's Dave and Sam? They still fighting over who's taller?" John had coached her twin boys two summers in a row at basketball camp. Two years in which they both went from 13 to 15 years old and 5' to 6' tall.

"Now it's about shoe sizes. Coach is ready for you. Go on in…and good luck."

* * *

John stuck his head in the door, and Coach McKenrick, without even looking up from his desk, motioned with his hand for John to come in. John sat down in the chair in front of his desk and the coach lifted his head and stared at John in silence for what seemed like an eternity. They both knew before saying a word that John's decision had already been made, but McKenrick wasn't one to fold without a fight.

"Well son, it seems you've got this town in a pickle, and all because of a game." McKenrick spoke slowly and direct. "You've got me in a bind, you've got the other players in a fuss, and all because of a game. Does that seem strange to you?"

John really had no idea where his coach was going with this.

"Basketball is just a game. At least that's what so many people tell me. But is it? I mean it gets kids off the streets and out of trouble. It gets high school graduates to college with money for tuition. It gives adults who work all day and would otherwise sit at home doing nothing, a way to entertain themselves and stay in shape. It teaches, disciplines, and brings satisfaction. I'd say it's much more than a game. And I know you would too. I know you see more in the sport than just competition. Its purpose goes beyond that."

John was beginning to get the idea.

"I know basketball's been more to you than just a game. It's been your passion and your expression. You've used it to succeed in life and you've used it to touch kids' lives. It's made you a role model and it's given you the opportunity to be a leader. That's something not many people get to be. So the question now is, is it over? Is this it? Have you worked this hard just to give up now? Are you satisfied with what you've accomplished? I know you've had some struggles, son. You've told me your frustrations with being so well known for just the game and the temptations of pride. But, just because it gets hard doesn't mean it's time to throw in the towel. You've worked hard, but God has blessed. Now you've reached a level where people can see and hear everything you say. You can let that beat you or you can let God really begin to use you to help others."

John had never heard the coach speak so many consecutive words and was a bit shocked. He also thought the coach's sudden interest in the spiritual side of basketball was strange, but he did have a point and it was one that had given John the most trouble. He wasn't a quitter.

"John, if you can beat this now, there's no telling where your God given talents can take you."

John had never heard coach call them "God given" before.

"You stop now and you may never know. I know you'll tell me that you'll just be gone a semester and that you've still got another season, but John you really don't know. You go now and you may not have the chance again."

John recognized the subtle threat and wasn't surprised at all.

"You've got a lot of potential, son. The pros are a realistic possibility for you. Once there, having beaten your weaknesses..." John shuddered at the phrase – the coach was getting to him. "God could use you to speak to the world. Do you understand? You could go to Jamaica, or wherever it is..."

"Venezuela."

"Venezuela then, and have crowds in every city. Don't let basketball beat you, John. Master it and then use it the way God wants you to. Don't run away from it scared."

That was all he could take. He was angry.

"Coach, are you finished yet? I'm thankful that you're suddenly concerned with my potential to be the next NBA Billy Graham, but you and I both know that's not what you care about. Next season is all that's on your mind. If I'm here you'll use me and if I'm not you'll replace me and probably never give me another thought. Coach, if you read the Bible you'll find that God's word doesn't change. I listened to no one on this one, not even myself. God alone told me to go, therefore you telling me to stay – no matter how much you try to speak on God's behalf – can't change what He's told me or what I've decided."

The coach's face changed, it seemed darker now. He looked the same way he did after they lost a game. He hated to lose. John suddenly felt sorry. Sorry for the way he'd responded to the coach, letting his anger control him. He wanted so much for his coach to know God and let Him change his heart.

"Coach, there's one thing about basketball that'll never change. Every game has an end. When players go to the locker room, coaches go back to their offices, and fans go home, they find the same problems waiting for them. The game doesn't solve them, it just makes them forget for a little while. Maybe if people stopped playing so many games they would get serious about the important questions of life and they could finally find the answer they're looking for: peace in their hearts. You can look forward to the next game, but one day that game will never come. And Coach, you can win a thousand more championships but even that won't bring you peace. You need Jesus Christ."

"Get the hell out of my office." John was startled, but didn't move.

"Coach, God loves you."

McKenrick stood up and pointed to the door. "Get out of my office, clean out your locker, and don't come back!"

"Thanks for the chance to play, Coach," John said as he slowly walked out the door.

"Shut up, you quitter."

John heard McKenrick mumble the words, just like he did on the sidelines after a bad call. John stopped and closed his eyes, he turned around as Betty stood up from her chair and said, "No John!"

"Coach, the only thing I've quit doing is respecting you!"
Betty rushed past John and quickly closed McKenrick's door.
"John you need to go." There was no trace of a smile on her face.

* * *

John felt hot as he exited the building. He was burning up and his eyes were moist. He had failed. He cursed under his breath as he stomped up the sidewalk towards the gym to clean out his basketball locker for maybe the very last time. *God, I blew it! Why do I get so angry?! Why can't I handle that? They're only words...*

* * *

Coach McKenrick was also livid. Chad, one of the players trying to work his way up the coach's favor ladder, had come by early that morning and told the coach everything John had shared with them the night before. McKenrick couldn't believe this was all a result of that crazy sermon in chapel. John was letting his emotions get the best of him. McKenrick grinned. Perhaps he'd just done the same. He imagined John was already on his way to clean out his locker. They had both over reacted. John's feistiness had actually surprised him. He knew he'd get under John's skin by calling him a quitter and all, but he never knew it would upset the boy *that* much. John was a fighter. Which is why they had to have him on the team. The championship depended on it. Belmont was non-conference so he would make John sweat out one game, but only one. No matter what John said, there wasn't anyone who could fill his position. They needed him to go all the way again. With John it was almost a guarantee, without him it was left to chance. Coaches don't like chances. First, he called Betty into his office and asked her to hunt down Eric Williams, the team's other captain and 6'10" center, and set up an appointment for that afternoon. Next, he picked up the phone and called the only other man who had as much at stake with John's going away. The President of TCU, Dr. Kyle G. Pierson, also liked guarantees.

15 THE BIGGER PICTURE

The following afternoon, John's absence at the Lumberjacks' sold-out match against Belmont sent shockwaves through the community. Not only was John Parker not playing, he wasn't even on the bench. According to quickly spreading rumors, he was temporarily off the Lumberjacks team.

Throughout the following days, all over campus and all over town, people talked and groups discussed the big news. In every circle voices spoke of stupidity and absurdity, but in every crowd there was often at least one voice of defense reminding everyone that there was more to life than sports. That voice was mostly ignored.

John's family was spared no attack. From the grocery store to the mall, from work to the gas station – people seemed to come out of the cracks with their comments. Their favorite question:

"Are you sure your son's doing the right thing?"

"As sure as there's a God," Mrs. Parker learned to reply without hesitation. These instances were sporadic but annoying. However, it was on Sunday morning when the town gathered for worship that the Parker family faced their greatest trial. The irony of those in God's house having the most difficulty recognizing God's will was the topic of many Parker family dinner discussions.

Grandma and Grandpa Parker were informed of their grandson's new plans the day after John had told his parents. Meemaw and Peepaw, as their grandkids called them, weren't too thrilled with the idea. Even though they were people of great faith, their concept of missions was donating clothes and food to the local homeless shelter. Yes, they remembered how much their own son's life had been changed during his mission trip to Mexico, but that had all been *after* college.

"Take care of what's first, first", was the way Peepaw had put it. Still, they knew John's life was his to live, and he wouldn't be the first Parker to do something on his own and to the scoffing of others. They would respect his decision and support him. They would also be praying for him more than he would ever know. They were great to have on your side when the battle lines were drawn and no way was anyone in that town going to talk bad about their grandkid, if they could do anything to help it. As such longtime respected members of the community, people were careful not to talk of John's strange decision in their presence…but not careful enough.

One Sunday, Meemaw and Peepaw had had enough, so Elder Richard Parker, after arranging to be asked to pray for the offering, used the time instead to remind the congregation that their grandson's life was God's, their family's, and his own business – nobody else's. John and his father had to laugh while Mrs. Parker, fed up herself, cried with pride and new respect for her father-in-law. The grandparents never heard another derogatory remark. At lunch that Sunday, the whole family treated Peepaw like a hero. He didn't really know what the big deal was; he had just said what needed to be said. He and Meemaw were just enjoying the best kept secret of their age – being able to get away with saying whatever you wanted as directly as you wanted – a privilege they enjoyed using often.

But nothing could stop the masses from asking the "Are you sure?" question. John finally wrote, "I'm sure" on the front and back of a T-shirt and wore it almost daily. Even Megan had to defend her brother from would-be slanderers. Her classmates, many of whom were junior ballplayers, often repeated at school what they'd picked up at home from upset fathers – fans of TCU who weren't thrilled at all about losing their star shooting guard for the season. What John was doing seemed mighty selfish to most – giving up his obvious "God given" talents and being so irresponsible with his scholarship! Now John couldn't wait to leave, but this is not how he'd wanted to say goodbye. However, it was the article in the newspaper that drew the last straw, at least for Mrs. Parker. The Parker men had actually been expecting it, had even begun wondering what was taking so long…especially after Peepaw's church-wide threat. The men could ignore the hurting words easier than Mom, who couldn't help but take it all personally. There it sat on the front page, bottom right corner of Sunday's "Sports" section:

* * *

-- Local basketball star, team captain and 1994 MVP for the Tennessee Christian Lumberjacks, John L. Parker, has voluntarily forfeited his scholarship and starting position to take a trip that will keep him away from college basketball for the remainder of the '94-'95 season. Coach McKenrick is left with some difficult decisions about who will fill the abandoned position. Both students and citizens alike wonder what will become of the nationally ranked team. The reasons behind Mr. Parker's decision are not clear.

* * *

She could only stare in disbelief. Take a trip. A trip! They were making it sound like a vacation or something. Nothing about Venezuela. Nothing about God. Only basketball.

John just smiled as he listened to his mother read the article.

"Poor abandoned position," he said, as if describing some stray animal.

"Some difficult decisions Coach has, huh son?" John's dad asked mockingly. "Town shocked! Citizens wonder! Sounds like a new movie coming out. 'Ball Boy!' coming to theaters everywhere."

John and Megan laughed.

"Starring Leonardo Di Caprio," John whispered to his sister. She punched him in the arm.

"It's not funny, Todd." Mrs. Parker said, looking up from the article in her hands which she kept reading over and over again. Her face looked tired and her eyes sad.

"Mom, it's okay," John said assuringly. "Don't worry, they're not getting to me. You know it's actually rather sad, really. I never dreamed so many people could be so mixed up. I mean if this is how it is with God's will in other areas of people's lives then just think how much of His will people are missing out on."

"Son that was pretty deep." Dad was still in a joking mood. Mom put an end to it with one look.

"Yeah? Thanks Pop. I get it from you."

"What did you mean? Say it..." Megan tried to ask, but mom wasn't finished,

"It's these crazy sports, they've got everybody obsessed."

John walked over and massaged his mother's shoulders. He smiled at his father who gave him a quick wink. They had heard the "Sports are from Satan" speech before. They knew she was probably right and didn't want to argue with a prophet, so they kept quiet.

"Honey, it seems God's got our son on a quick mission here before he goes to Venezuela," Mr. Parker said, walking over and taking his son's place, he knew just how she liked it.

The idea that maybe God did have him on a quick assignment right here at home excited John. If God wanted to use him to shake things up in his town, he was willing. And if somehow, through it all, folks began to recognize their obsession with sports and it's priority over the things of God, then for that alone the questioning looks, disappointed stares, and derogatory remarks would all be worth it.

"Now I'm sure John made the right choice!" Mrs. Parker said defiantly, hitting the table with her fist. The others looked at each other, then at her. They wanted to laugh, but had to wait. She gazed upward sternly. Then her frown melted into a smile that finally became laughter. They quickly joined her. She was calming down, but when the family left for church, she stayed home, still too upset to face everyone. She had to write a letter while the feelings were flooding through her.

16 THE PRESSURE

That morning after church, Pastor Larry asked John if he could speak with him in his office. Upon entering, John was surprised to find President Pierson, also a member of the church, already seated. He quickly stood up smiling and extended his hand to John.

"Hello, John."

"Hello, Dr. Pierson." They shook hands firmly.

"Have a seat, son. We want to talk to you for a moment."

John took a seat at Pastor Larry's round study table with both men on either side of him.

"John, I just want to say that I'm proud of what you are doing and for the way you are standing up for what you believe."

"Thank you Dr. Pierson. It hasn't been that easy. Not many are standing with me on this."

"John, I know how hard it is to stand alone. But you just have to be careful that you don't start to think you always have to stand that way. There are people here to help."

"Thanks. That's good to know."

"The reason Brother Larry and I asked you to come is because we want to pray for you and with you. The Bible says that it's good for the young to seek the counsel of elders, and we want to help you make the best decisions. We've got a lot of experience, and sometimes, believe it or not, we actually do know what's best."

John was suddenly afraid of where this conversation might be headed. He felt himself melting inside to the same heat that had overtaken him in his coach's office. *Not again*, he thought. *Stay calm! Holy Spirit, please help me to stay calm.*

"John." Brother Larry took over. This was a tag team effort. "There's no doubt the hand of God is on your life. You have never looked back after the decision you made to follow Christ in high school. You have grown into a mature man of God. If God wants you to go to Venezuela, then you must go, but timing is important. Patience is a difficult virtue, especially when it comes to doing good. Of course, it will be good for you to go and help those kids and of course God will use you. But remember, there is a good way, and there is also a best way and that's what we want for you. We want to ask God to help you know not only what to do, but when to do it."

He was on the ropes. Tag! Dr. Pierson jumped back in.

"John, the school's helped you every way it can and you've given back even more. Our goal is for all of our students to go out into the world and change it with the love of Jesus Christ, but first we must be about the business of preparing them. You are being prepared right now for the task ahead. Don't jump ahead like Brother Larry said. You have to be patient. You have vision, now timing is everything."

John had been nodding his head so much that it felt like it was about to fall off. He hadn't really heard much they had said because he'd been too busy telling himself to remain calm, but he got their point. Why not wait, graduate and then go? As both men pointed out, he would only be more mature and more prepared. In the meantime, he could lead the team to another championship, continue ministering at school and in the town, hang-out with friends, watch his little sister grow, take more moonlit walks with Rachel and in the end, still go help the kids in Venezuela just the same – perhaps even more. But he *was* sure of God's answer…well, almost sure.

"Let's pray," John said, wanting only to end the meeting.

"Good idea," Dr. Pierson said as he and the pastor stood up and laid their hands on John's shoulders. They prayed and prayed. John listened as they over and over again asked God to give him discernment for making the right decision. John's thoughts took him across the ocean to a far away place. As the two men prayed for timing, John prayed for the children and the people who needed him and God reminded him – they needed him *now*. Pastor Larry and President Pierson said "Amen" and John echoed. Smiles and handshakes were again exchanged. John said goodbye and left the men alone to discuss the success of their influence. He drove back to his dorm feeling sick.

* * *

He walked into his room and immediately noticed two things. First, his small desk lamp was on, and the room was softly lit. Second, there was a large dark figure sitting on his small sofa against the wall. There was only one person on campus who could own a shape that size.

"Hey Eric."

Eric Williams slowly stood to his feet and his head almost hit the ceiling. They shook hands, pulling each other in for the standard chest and shoulder bump.

"Bill let me in." As expected from an abnormally tall human being, his voice was deep and penetrating. "I asked him if I could speak with you alone, so he'll be back later."

John imagined his roommate didn't argue about being kicked out of his own room. Eric was intimidating even when asleep, but John knew he was a softy at heart.

"Sit back down and I'll pull up a chair."

Once they were both seated, Eric didn't waste any time, but got right to the point.

"I'm sure you know about the beating we took from Belmont."

"Are they that good this year?"

"No. We're just that bad without you."

"Seriously? Phil played that bad?"

"John. Phil hasn't prepared mentally or physically for starting or even playing for that matter. You know your minutes over the past two seasons. You hardly get tired, and Coach rarely takes you out. So Phil is out of shape. Combine that with the pressure he's under to fill your shoes, and it was a catastrophe in the making."

"He'll get better."

"We don't have time for that brother."

"Eric. What do you want me to do? I've made my decision."

"John. I know you stick to your convictions. I know your faith is real and that's why so many respect you and why some of us gave our lives to Christ, because of your leadership and example. I'll never forget the day you baptized me in the pool. I owe you much, but I'm asking you now to think about what you owe your team, your school, your community? I can't think of a single story in the Bible when God asked one of His chosen leaders to walk away from his responsibilities. To quit. This is what everyone thinks you're doing. Quitting. This will be your testimony. Your witness. Maybe even your legacy at TCU. Is that what you want?"

Eric's words were hitting him hard. Was he misrepresenting Christ to his team? Didn't he owe them his loyalty? Proverbs 18:24 came into his mind. "A real friend sticks closer than a brother". John quickly and silently prayed for God to help him respond. Immediately, he received a message in his heart: *He's looking at this thing from one side, but there are always more sides to a story. Help him see your side.*

"Eric. This is what I feel certain the Lord is calling me to do…walk away from what has always been most important to me, to do something very important for Him."

"Why would He ask you to do that? And what about us? Your team?"

The word "team" clicked in John's head and he thought about the stories he had recently been reading in the book of Acts. He continued speaking from his heart.

"Here's what I've been learning lately. After Jesus rose from the dead, his followers must have been ecstatic, right? They had their leader, their star player back on their team. They were probably ready to follow Him anywhere and then within 40 days, He was gone again. He left them and returned to heaven after telling them to go and take the good news to every nation and make disciples of all peoples. He also promised the Holy Spirit would come and be with them always. God knew there were many other star players on that team, and now that Jesus was gone, and with the Holy Spirit's help, they would step up. And that's what happened. Peter begins to preach boldly. Stephen gives his life evangelizing an angry mob. Philip is sent into the desert for an encounter with ONE lost person, and right after that he's whisked away to another location where he keeps on preaching. Persecution comes, they are all scattered, and as they go, the gospel spreads and the kingdom grows. You and I are here today, members of this tribe, because those first followers left everything to take the good news where God led them. And now I find myself on a similar path. God is telling me to go. From one angle it could look like I'm being selfish and irresponsible, but from another angle - what I believe is the right angle - God is sending me to do something very important for Him. He's still scattering the tribe because there are people in Venezuela who need to hear the good news…from me."

John paused to let Eric respond, but his teammate remained silent.

"Eric. Part of me wants to stay man. Keep playing the game I love. Win games. Be celebrated. Help the team win another championship. Hang with my friends. See my family. Get closer to Rachel…why in the world would I want to give all that up? I'm telling you brother, it's because I hear God calling me to go and I have to obey Him. I have to."

Eric stood, brushed past John on his way to the door and opened it. He stooped down to walk out. "I knew that would be your answer." And he was gone.

John continued to sit in the dark. His heart was broken and his spirit crushed. The last thing he wanted was to come across as "holier than thou", but he imagined that was how many were looking at him. Even his close friends and teammates. *Lord, please help my friends understand my heart in this.* He suddenly realized he may not see his teammates again. Their Christmas break officially started the next day, and the campus would be almost empty. The team would practice a few times after Christmas for the Winter Classic game on January 2 - the day he would fly to Venezuela and leave behind everything and everyone he knew.

* * *

He felt exhausted. He left the desk lamp on, climbed into bed fully dressed, and was asleep within minutes. He awoke later to the sound of Bill strumming softly on his guitar and practically whispering the final verse of a familiar tune.

Though none go with me, still I will follow.
Though none go with me, still I will follow.
Though none go with me, still I will follow.
No turning back. No turning back.

Under his covers, and with eyes closed, John smiled as a weight lifted from his heart. *No turning back Lord.*

17 THE EDITORIAL

The following week a letter was printed in the "Editorial" section of the *Lewisville Gazette.* A letter that would change the course of a town's thinking about a game.

* * *

To the Editor:

When Jesus walked the earth, he had a very specific, unique, and special task for his life. We find that when he was just over thirty years old and just beginning his public ministry, he also began to tell those closest to him about his approaching death. Those who heard couldn't understand. It was impossible, absurd, so much so that they couldn't even comprehend his words, though they were simple. His death just wasn't an option. One follower named Peter was even rebuked by Jesus for telling him that he wouldn't die. Jesus knew it was God's will – the others did not. So as they time and again failed to recognize God's plan being unveiled, they also missed opportunities to share with their Lord. Share their love, support, and understanding which he so dearly longed for. And on his final night on earth, as he prayed for his life, they slept.

I had always thought I understood Jesus' frustration before. Now I find I'm learning to understand it for myself in a new way. You see, my son has also been created by God to fulfill a specific and unique plan in his life. At this moment he is in the very midst of making decisions and seeking the Lord's guidance to help him in this special plan. As those around him listen to him speak, they don't seem to hear. They, too, don't seem to comprehend his words, even though they are simple. It's absurd, impossible, they think. My son is a basketball player. Many say he's a phenomenon. God's blessed him with wonderful and amazing talent and the best thing for him to do is to use it to lead his team to another winning season, or so his fans and followers tell him. That makes sense, right? The King of Kings on a cross? That doesn't make sense. A basketball star quitting the team in the prime of his career, sacrificing his scholarship and fame to go live in Venezuela and help some kids? That doesn't either.

Praise God for ways that are higher than man's! Ways that place people before sports. Ways that allow sinners to find forgiveness through the death of a man on a cross. To the soul that has found freedom and the heart that has found peace, Christ's unique and special plan makes perfect sense. I hope and pray that the children and people in Venezuela for whom my son is being sent will see the purpose for his coming even if the town that knows him best can't see the purpose for his going.

And so, while John L. Parker prepares to leave, everyone sleeps, unaware of his need for their love, support, and understanding.

I'm awake son and I'm proud of you. Love, Mom

18 THE CHRISTMAS FELLOWSHIP

Mrs. Parker knocked on the bathroom door. "Your father and sister are in the Suburban and everyone else is already on their way."

"One second, Mom." John looked his clean-shaven face over once more in the mirror. The nick on his chin was still bleeding. *Always on an important day.* He joined his family in the car, and they headed to church for the evening Christmas fellowship as a light snow continued to fall.

It had been a wonderful white Christmas day full of all their family traditions: big breakfast, reading through the Christmas story, opening presents and then welcoming grandparents, uncles, aunts and cousins for an afternoon feast and card game marathon. Everyone made it clear they were not going to take it easy on John just because he was leaving. Not much else was said about his departure. Everyone just wanted to enjoy being together. This year their Crazy Eights marathon ended early so they could attend a rare Christmas Night fellowship at church. John was just about to finally walk away with a victory when his dad, sensing imminent defeat, looked at his watch and said "Okay. Time to go! I win!" and grabbed John's cards and threw them down on the table with his own. Everyone else shouted and laughed and tossed their cards at him.

As Mr. Parker drove along, following behind the rest of their family, John looked at his dad's reflection in the rear view mirror and shook his head.

"That was bellow the belt Dad. Just wait. Holy Spirit's gonna get you tonight at church." John pointed at his father with his long index finger, "Conviction and repentance are coming!" Laughter filled the car.

Things had reached a climax with the letter his mother had written and afterwards exploded into a war with letters to the Editor flooding in expressing people's opinions on both sides. "Basketball is here to stay!" Some wrote. "Don't be so extreme!" But for every person who expressed such a view, a few more denounced the hold that sports had on society. It seemed there were more out there who, even though still not completely satisfied with John's reason for leaving, at least agreed that sports and basketball in particular had moved into sacred territory pushing out things that had once been important. Many had just been waiting for someone to speak out and now that the first voice had been heard, others found the courage to follow. Most who wrote were women, but slowly and surely some male figures began to join in as well. Of course, most of the children and even teenagers didn't understand what all the hoopla was about. They found themselves more confused than ever as convicted fathers and over-competitive parents who had always pushed their kids to win, now started reminding them there was more to life than sports and winning. "Okay, whatever," was the usual response, but it was a start.

Besides letters to the paper, many wrote directly and personally to Mrs. Parker herself. Some even stopped by in person to apologize for their behavior and comments to her and her family. Sports in Lewisville were beginning to be looked at in a new light. Sermons began to deal with the issue, as preachers who had themselves given in before to the Sunday Super Bowl pressure, now found the pressure from the Holy Spirit even greater. Bible studies discussed the topic, offices chatted over the debate, and even casual conversations at the pubs and coffee shops focused on the pros and cons. Most agreed that people's obsession with games had gotten carried away, but not many knew of a solution. It was part of society, part of who we are as Americans. "We should be proud of our sports," the veteran jocks clamored, "as athletes have played just as big a role in shaping the country as politicians, teachers, and all other professionals and laymen alike."

It was never Mrs. Parker's intention – nor anyone else in the Parker family – to shape peoples' convictions, but she was pleased to have helped them start to think. Perhaps by thinking, they would turn their focus more inward and off of her son and family. All she had really hoped was for everyone to get at least a glimpse of why her son was going and what that really meant. Meant for those he was going to serve, but even more for those he was leaving behind. Many in the town finally began to understand. Instead of wasting time asking the "how" and "why" questions, people began to share their support and encouragement with the young man who was so important to them, both on and off the basketball court.

John's closest friends and classmates were affected the deepest, those who would miss his presence everyday on campus. He received so many letters and verses in his mailbox that he felt overwhelmed about how to write them all back. He read many of them to Rachel over the phone and she assured him it wasn't necessary, that they weren't meant to get a response, just encourage. It worked both for and against his going. He was ready for the adventure that lay ahead, but dreading the reality of leaving so many he loved and cared about.

* * *

On this Christmas night, his church was throwing him a farewell party after the Sunday evening service. John secretly hated these kinds of things because he felt so uncomfortable knowing everyone was there for him. He never knew what to say to people.

"This is going to be a long night," he said out loud to no one in particular, but hoping someone might offer encouragement. True to her colors, his mom's reassuring voice responded.

"Son, just relax and enjoy it."

"Don't worry son, just stay close to your mom and grandpa and everyone will keep their distance."

His dad looked in the rear view mirror and winked at him as him mom playfully punched her husband in the shoulder.

* * *

At church, things went pretty much as expected, though for a Sunday evening service the sanctuary was unusually full. As he looked over the crowd from behind his pulpit, Pastor Larry thought he should have more farewell parties. The sermon that night was on sacrifice, and the words and verses all seemed to speak clearer to everyone, now that one of their own was going in obedience. John listened, challenged by the words. In conclusion, Brother Larry cleared his throat and reminded everyone that John's going was not *their* going. His sacrifice was not theirs. Everyone had their own part to play. And there was much to be done right in their own town. John nodded his head in appreciation for the words he was hearing. After the closing prayer, everyone headed to the fellowship hall where the food and desserts awaited. It took John half an hour just to make it to the room because of all the people who gathered around him. *There won't be any food left!* was all he kept thinking. With the same thought in mind, Mrs. Parker fixed an extra heaping plate to take home for him. While Dad discussed politics, mom expounded on her letter, and Megan played tag with boys she supposedly couldn't stand, John finally made it to the food tables. Then he felt a hand on his shoulder and turned to find Pastor Larry standing outside of the line.

"John, could I see you for a moment?"

"Sure," John answered, exiting the line and following behind him, but glancing back one last time at the food, a look of longing in his eyes. He'd almost made it.

Pastor Larry held the door open for John who entered the office to find Dr. Pierson once again standing with his hand extended, saying "Hello John. Merry Christmas!"

Deja vu, John thought. *What this time?*

The two men wasted no words, but proceeded to take turns apologizing for their behavior and inferences the time before. John was totally caught off guard and blown away. He didn't know what to say when they were finished. Here were two of the most influential and respected men in his life asking him for forgiveness. John wracked his brain for something that he should apologize for, but found only peace.

John, forgive them and learn from it, the Lord whispered to him. *Learn how to be a leader by admitting when you're wrong.*

John voiced his forgiveness, still finding the whole sentence strangely out of place, but he *would* learn from it. And he would never forget the humility he discovered that day in his pastor and president.

"John, when Coach McKenrick told me you were leaving, I was really surprised, and then also upset. Of course, coach talked about how important you are to the team and for another championship. Listening to him made me focus momentarily on that as well. But I want to assure you; we will miss you for what you do off the court, not on. You are such an example of servant leadership on our campus. People like you are hard to come by, and I for one did not want you to go – honestly, even if the Lord did. But one night it hit me. Your going is just another step in your learning to be like Christ and just one more way that the Lord is going to use you to lead others by example. Once again your sacrifice will benefit our campus by challenging the students, by increasing their level of commitment to the Lord. For that I want to thank you. So now Pastor Larry and I want to pray for you again. This time, not for the timing of God's will, but for obedience to what He's called us to."

Once again they laid their hands on their younger brother in Christ. The heaviness that was present before was now replaced by an overwhelming sense of strength, determination, and joy in John's heart. They said "Amen", stood and hugged one another, then left the room together to once again join in the fellowship. Instead of sickness, this time

John felt blessed. Brother Larry announced a time of prayer for John and different elders all came to the front and laid their hands on the young man as the entire church lifted his life up before the Lord. John was touched beyond description, but felt guilty for being unable to stop peeping at the table every time his stomach growled. Afterwards, the crowds gathered around once again and voiced their love and affirmation. John did notice the crowds backing away as he talked with Meemaw and Peepaw for a few minutes. He couldn't thank God enough for their presence in his life. There were many tears, handshakes with all the men, and hugs and kisses on the cheeks from all the women – especially the mothers who as a result of the letter, now felt like they were saying goodbye to their own son.

The walk from the church doors to the car took another half-hour. Then with the last "Goodbye" and "Thank you" crawling from his lips, John plopped down into the front seat of the Suburban and let out a breath of exhaustion. Mr. Parker scared away any final would be greeters by immediately revving the engine and throwing the vehicle into reverse. The men whooped and hollered and the girls screamed as the Suburban's tires spun out, leaving a wake of dust, smoke, and high pitched ringing in the air. John was still laughing as his mother handed him two plates of food.

"Merry Christmas son."

"You're too good, Mom," he said.

She only smiled and then sat back and began stroking her daughter's hair. They were all too tired of talking. John's mouth was too full of food. The plates were empty by the time they reached their driveway.

19 THE FAREWELLS

John's final week of '94 was set aside for family. They shopped and planned, prayed and packed, and shopped and planned some more. John had to reorganize his luggage every time his mother tried to squeeze in "Just one more thing!" The weather was her main concern. She couldn't have her son getting sick so far away from home. John felt like he was 13 going away to camp again. Mr. Parker had to remind his wife that their son wasn't their little boy any more. She knew this, but couldn't help it. This was a new frontier for all of them.

* * *

John took Megan roller-skating, bowling and to a movie on Friday. During their big brother-little sister date, they joked and laughed a lot and didn't talk much about his leaving, but near the end of the comedic movie John heard a sniffling sound and looked down to see a tear roll down his sister's cheek. He took her hand in his and forced a smile that she did her best to return. There was a sudden knot in John's throat. This was going to be the hardest part of leaving. Megan was his princess and he was her prince. Friends, teammates, parents and older relatives, even Rachel...he would miss them, but not necessarily worry about them like he would his little sister. She had just started middle school, the beginning of the craziest years of a person's life. Puberty, peer pressure, social cliques...puberty. *God please watch over my sister and help her understand and know who she is in you.*

On the drive home John brought up the subject that was most on his mind, "Remember what I told you about guys?"

"Yes, guys are like gorillas."

"How so?"

"They can be funny and entertaining from a distance, but dangerous up close."

John smiled. "Exactly. And don't forget that a guy who likes you will treat you like a queen to impress you so the only way to know what he's really like is to watch how he treats everyone else."

"Got it."

"Always remember that it doesn't matter what people think about you. Mom and Dad love you and I love you and most important of all God loves you for who you are...everything about you Megan. Don't ever change or do anything to try and make people like you more. Those are not true friends."

"Okay, I'll remember."

John could go on and on. Soon he wouldn't be around to watch over his little sister and it was weighing heavy on his heart.

"John, we've been talking about missionaries this month in Sunday School and we read a verse last Sunday that I thought sounded pretty sad at first. Jesus told his disciples they had to love him more than their own families and then one of the disciples, Peter, I think, told Jesus that they had given up everything to follow him and Jesus said everyone who leaves their mom and dad or brother and sister will get one hundred times as many moms and dads and brothers and sisters in this life and in the life to come. I'm not really sure what that means, but I think it means that God wants you to be a brother and maybe a son to more people who need you."

John felt the lump in his throat return. He stared at his amazing sister and nodded his head.

"But don't forget I'm your FIRST little sister!"

"No one could ever replace you Meg!"

"I'll love you forever John."

"Forever and a day."

They drove the rest of the way home in silence. Megan, with her head on John's shoulder while tears streamed down his cheeks. Tears of sadness and thanksgiving.

* * *

Over the next two days, John received or made phone calls to every relative on the family tree. They all promised to be praying for his journey. Grandma Wiley was last. Grandpa Wiley had passed away three years earlier, leaving Grandma alone in their lake Michigan home, which they'd lived in for over thirty five years. She refused to give in to her eldest daughter's request that she move to Tennessee so they could be closer together – especially in case of an emergency. She couldn't leave. Besides, she still had all her animals to keep her company. Mrs. Parker knew it was only a matter of time before her mother would have no choice. Her mind just wasn't as clear as it used to be. John spoke slowly and loud into the receiver. She wondered how he was doing and how was the weather. She was making her famous bread. The dogs and cats were good. He could hear the birds chirping in the background. He and Megan loved to visit that house. It always smelled like a bakery and sounded like a forest. He mentioned about his leaving for Venezuela. She'd been told, but forgotten. After John repeated the sentence for the third time, she finally understood. She would be praying for him.

"Trust the Lord," she reminded him over and over. "Only God will be with you 'til the end and He'll always take care of you, just like He did your grandpa and I."

John had heard all the stories before, but he always let her tell them again. They took her back to places and times she loved and they taught him about the Lord's faithfulness. John promised to write, knowing that saying so was half the battle to doing so. They both said goodbye, and John told her how much he loved her.

"Those are a grandma's favorite words to hear," she said, like she always did and then carefully hung up the phone. It would be a week later, when her daughter called to say "hello", that Grandma Wiley would come to understand her grandson had actually left the country. Though surprised, it didn't cause much change in her prayer life. She lifted her family up one by one, name by name, everyday, regardless of where they were or what they were doing. She just hoped he would have enough to eat.

* * *

A blizzard hit on New Year's eve, putting a damper on everyone's plans. John was happy for an excuse to stay home and go to bed early. He fell asleep wondering what all the American kids were doing in Venezuela at that very moment. One thing he had learned about his soon-to-be new home and was excited about, it was summer time there.

20 THE DATE

John and Bill went fishing on New Year's day. The storm had ended as quickly as it had come. Ice-fishing was an annual tradition they had kept up since Bill's dad first took them back in middle school. They didn't catch a thing, but didn't really notice or care. They passed the time swapping memories of all their adventures and laughing until their sides hurt. Afterwards, they grabbed one more lunch together. John's roommate was taking it all in stride. Bill promised to keep a special eye out for the castaways on campus while John was away.

* * *

That evening, after his last piece of luggage had been zipped shut, and while Mrs. Parker was double checking the inventory in her mind, John kissed her goodbye and headed to campus to pick up Rachel. This would be their last dinner together for a while. Thankfully, Rachel had returned early for a tennis tournament, although John would have gladly driven to her hometown four hours away.

She was waiting in her dorm lobby in a dress and with a hairstyle John had never seen before. She looked radiant. Her coat and a scarf were draped over her arm. John suddenly felt a little underdressed. He stopped a few feet away and stared. Her hair, usually long and straight, was now full of long perfect curls. John had never been nervous around Rachel before, but suddenly and for the first time, he felt his palms begin to sweat. There was a long silence until Rachel, feeling more and more awkward by the second, finally asked "What is it?"

"Um, nothing. I mean…"

"Do I look *that* weird?"

"No! No, definitely not. It's just different, but in a very good way. I mean...you look…beautiful." John said the words and then felt a little awkward himself. That was the first time he'd said anything to her about her appearance. *You always look beautiful*, he wanted to add, but held his tongue as Richard's voice echoed in his head, *friendship is the key to lasting love!*

Rachel blushed and let out a sigh of relief. She hardly ever dressed up. The athlete in her preferred sweats over skirts, but this was a special occasion and now she was glad she'd made the extra effort. John's compliment put a big smile on her face.

John helped her put on her full-length winter coat and wrap herself up in her scarf. “Well,” he said, extending his hand, "Reservations are for seven. Shall we?”

“We shall.” She placed her hand in his. As soon as they exited the building into the bitterly cold outside air, John’s arms wrapped around her and pulled her close.

The conversation in the car was light and humorous while both of them wondered how long they could put off the inevitable. After dinner and another half hour of chitchat, John finally put down his fork and cleared his throat as Rachel picked at her chocolate cake.

“Rachel.”

She lifted her eyes to his.

“I just want you to know that I’m so glad we met and became friends this semester.”

“Me too, John,” she said, with the warm, soft smile that melted his heart like butter.

Friends, friends, he repeated to himself.

“John,” now it was Rachel's turn. “It’s been a long time since I’ve gotten so close to a guy. Really, I didn’t want it to happen again, not yet, but I just can’t seem to help it with you. I just really like to be with you.”

John nodded his head. He stopped repeating Richard's phrase.

“Me too,” he responded, then slowly added, “but…sometimes I get tired of hanging out with myself. You know what I mean?" Rachel was so caught off guard by John's asinine joke that it didn't fully register until a huge smile had already spread across his face.

“John, you’re terrible!” she said, pretending to slap his face. “I was trying to get serious, you goofball.” But now they were both laughing. “Maybe that’s why I like you so much, because sometimes you’re sooooo…I don’t know what to call it.”

“Wonderful?” John offered the word only to have it rejected.

“Nope.”

“Sweet?”

“No, that’s not it either. Maybe hopeless.”

Now it was John's turn to shadow punch her. But he was breathing easy again.

That was too close, he thought. Only fear had made him say something as idiotic as he had, but he couldn't let them go to the next level one day before he had to leave! All John could think about now was Rachel's previous remark. She had said she liked him so much. *Yes!*

The rest of the night only continued in humor and laughter as they shared all the funny memories they had made in such a short time. Before they knew it, it was time for John to say goodbye once again, but he couldn't rush it. They stood on the patio of her dorm building and looked into each other's eyes. John had to let her know as well.

"Rachel, I really like you a lot and I'm going to miss you, but the most important thing to me is that whatever happens in the future, we'll always be friends and we'll always be comfortable together and you'll always know you can trust me."

"I know, John. That's my prayer as well. Guess what? I memorized a verse to share with you, "The Lord Himself goes before you and will be with you; He will never leave you nor forsake you. Do not be afraid; do not be discouraged." As she said the verse, she stuck a small piece of folded up paper in John's shirt pocket. "That's Deuteronomy 31:8. I wrote it down for you to keep close to your heart, okay?"

John felt the warmest sensation rush from the top of his head down to his toes. This girl was the bomb! She loved God's word as much as he did. She suddenly seemed more beautiful to him than anyone he had ever met or known in his whole life. *Oh boy.*

"Always trust Him, John. I'll be here when you get back, ready to hear all about your adventure. You're gonna be changed - that I know for sure."

"And I'll be praying for God to continue doing His own number on you and when I get back I'm sure we'll both have some adventures to share…we'll both be changed."

"I'll be waiting," Rachel said softly.

"I'll be running," John said, and they both giggled. Then they moved into each other's arms for one final embrace.

"Take care," he whispered.

"You too, big boy."

John backed away, staring at her one last time. He gazed over her dress, curls, and face and then shook his head with the sound "Mmm. Mmm." escaping from his mouth.

“Get out of here,” she said, threatening him jokingly with her purse.

“I still can’t believe Rachel Nix actually got dressed up to go out with a guy like me!” he said, walking backwards down the ramp. “No one will believe me!” At that moment he bumped into the short cement wall at the bottom of the ramp, almost tumbled over the side, but grabbed the wall with both hands and caught himself.

Rachel laughed as John stood back to his feet and placed both hands on his heart.

“See what you do to me!” He said, then leaped over the wall and trotted across the parking lot to ol’ Bess. Rachel turned and entered her lobby. She looked back out the glass doors and waved one last time as John did the same while climbing into his truck. After he drove away she quickly ran to her room before anyone could see her.

That night, two hearts ready to burst with new emotions and two souls overflowing with delight in the Lord, prayed from their beds for God to safeguard their feelings for one another. They both knew a lot could happen in one semester. The last thought that entertained them both before falling asleep was how worthwhile it had already been.

21 THE SEND OFF

John woke up two hours before his alarm was set to go off and was unable to go back to sleep. Finally, after staring at the ceiling for half an hour, he decided to get up and get the day going. He went for a walk around the neighborhood, taking in the houses and yards, the trees and flowers, all the neighborly pets, one last time. This was also a part of "home" he would miss and hoped to take with him. He returned to his house to find his dad reading the newspaper and his mother in the kitchen preparing him an omelet, his favorite.

"Well son, today's the big day. How you feelin'?" Mr. Parker glanced up from his reading as John took a seat beside him on the sofa.

"I'm ready to get this adventure started. Honestly, I think it's going to fly by. Six months isn't all that long."

His father lowered the newspaper. "Yeah that's what I think. Don't rush it. My trip to Mexico went by so fast. All the friends I made there were back out of my life before I even knew it. Yet, those friendships were some of the closest I've ever known. God's gonna bless you son, and your mom and I are both excited to see what He's got in store."

John couldn't even respond. The thoughts in his mind overwhelmed him. Megan came down the stairs still sleepy-eyed and in her pajamas just as their mom called everyone into the kitchen for breakfast. They took their time eating and talking. There was no reason to rush. John was packed and ready to go. A few hours remained before they would drive him to the Nashville airport 100 miles away, so they all just sat at the table and continued to talk long after the food was gone. No one wanted the moment to end.

* * *

Meemaw and Peepaw arrived ready to see their grandson off. They stuffed John's things in the back of the Suburban and left for the airport. It was a nice drive and a nice chance for the Tennessee countryside to leave a lasting impression. The conversation focused mostly on all the events of the last few months, events that had strengthened a family and tested a town.

As the trees flashed by outside, so did faces and voices. All those who had said goodbye were doing so again in John's mind. With all the parties and dinners, letters and phone calls, it had seemed like there was no one he had failed to tell goodbye, but now many came to mind. The most disturbing was Coach McKenrick. John had visited his office again, hoping to apologize and leave on better terms, but the coach had been out and Betty didn't know when he would return. She promised to tell the coach that he had come by and John had no doubt that she had. It was McKenrick who didn't want to talk to him again. John called one last time to find him out of the office again.

"Betty, just tell coach I said goodbye and good luck this season."

"I will John. You take care of yourself and get back to us safely."

"God willing, that's just what I plan to do."

McKenrick didn't call back, proving to be one of the last to hold out with the thought that John was making the biggest mistake of his life.

* * *

As they pulled into the airport parking lot, John was wondering if he'd ever play basketball for Coach McKenrick again. The question returned, *Are you sure you know what you're doing?*

Once inside, they had to hurry as usual because Mr. Parker had taken a supposed short cut that only he knew about, and that caused them to be later than planned. John's ticket and passport were cleared and his luggage checked in as his father and grandfather continued to argue over the route Mr. Parker had taken. Soon it was time to say goodbye and the women shushed their adolescent behaving husbands. Even though they were announcing for passengers to begin boarding, John's father wasn't letting him go anywhere without a time of prayer. John didn't argue. His father kept them short and to the point. His mother on the other hand would have caused him to miss the flight. They all held hands. A minute later, as Mr. Parker said "Amen", there was not a dry eye in the circle though Mrs. Parker had them all beat with tears running down her cheeks and her make-up smearing. She laughed as John wiped her face and then kissed her on the cheek.

"Son, you better get going." His father was not one for long farewells.

"Bye Dad." They shook hands firmly then hugged tightly.

"Go with God," his father said into his ears.

"I will." John hugged the others then picked up his backpack and backed away, waving goodbye and blowing kisses.

"Grandpa, you better drive back!"

The females burst into laughter as Mr. Parker and Peepaw started arguing again.

* * *

Even from his seat on the plane, John could see them standing at the window waving. Soon the plane taxied away and his family faded out of sight, but not out of mind. Their faces and smiles and words would remain his constant companions.

22 THE FLIGHT

John had a short flight to Miami where he was quickly ushered to his connecting flight to Caracas. Staring out the window at the approaching runway, John knew there was no going back now. He was on his way to an uncertain future, but in the hands of a most certain God. As the plane taxied for take off, a large overweight man, followed by what appeared to be the entire flight crew, took a seat next to John forcing him to squeeze even tighter against the wall and making his cramped surroundings even worse.

"They really should make a plane for the big and tall!" the man joked gruffly as he tried to get comfortable.

John smiled back and replied, "Or at least keep us on opposite sides of the plane to keep it balanced."

"Now that's an idea." The man's hair was dark, curly, and somewhat out of place – a little too dark and curly for a man his age. It was tilted just enough for John to notice and understand he was covering something. His face was red and flustered and dripping with sweat. A barrage of odors arrived with the man and none of them pleasant. That he was a smoker was immediately obvious. After shooing away the flight attendants like flies, he looked over at John and finally introduced himself.

"Howdy. My name's Frank Logan. Call me Frank. I always like to argue with these pretty girls and see how sassy they can get." Not even giving John the opportunity to make an introduction, Frank Logan went on to tell of the time he had almost been thrown off a plane for refusing to wear his seat belt during take off. John's new acquaintance already held him captivated. He wore a huge pair of dark sunglasses. A style, John thought, that hadn't been seen since the early 70's. He was dressed in a western style, blue polyester suit, halfway-unbuttoned black collared shirt with no tie, and shiny tan ostrich-skinned boots. A thick braided gold necklace matched the gold-nugget rings on each hand. The lower buttons on his shirt were stretched to their popping point and it was obvious his suit jacket couldn't close. However, unlike Frank Logan's plump upper torso, his legs appeared long and scrawny. John wondered how two sticks like those could hold up such weight. Frank Logan reminded John of his Little League coaches back in Tennessee. Fathers who somehow managed to only grow larger and wider in and around their mid-section. Every one of them wore the gray polyester "Bike" coaching shorts and knee-high athletic socks, exposing skinny and sun-starved legs in between. The perfect embodiment of fitness! John pictured Frank Logan in such an outfit and shuddered. Frank Logan's face was large and chubby. His cheeks sagged a bit and John thought he could see large rings under his eyes, even through the tinted lenses of his glasses. His nose was long with a crooked section in the middle and large nostrils at the bottom. A few dark hairs peeked out in different directions. John noticed a few matching hairs pointing out from his ears as well. Each time Frank opened his mouth to speak, two rows of crooked, smoke stained teeth appeared along with an upper left incisor encased in glittering gold. John realized Frank Logan was proud of that tooth as he always managed to let it show, even when he wasn't talking.

"What was your name again?" Frank Logan finally asked.

"John Parker."

"Nice to meet ya, John Parker. So whereabouts you from?"

"Tennessee."

"Oh, southern boy like myself. Glad to hear it. I'm from Texas – Abilene to be precise. So whata ya doin' headin' to Venezuela?"

John thought he'd never ask. He explained to Mr. Logan about his faith in Jesus and the position he would be taking as a youth pastor.

"Well, that's mighty damn good, son. You're gonna make the good Lord proud." John thought he sounded about as sincere as if he was talking to a brick wall.

"What about you Frank? Do you believe that God sent His son Jesus to die on a cross for your sins?"

John had learned that asking someone if they believed in God was too easy. A person could answer "yes" and still not have a clue about Jesus' redemptive work on the cross. Even in Lewisville, Tennessee, there was a growing trend toward spiritual relativism and the belief that all religious roads lead to heaven. "Belief in god" was becoming more and more a description of new age philosophy in which one's search for God could lead to anywhere, including the god within one's self. To avoid all confusion, John simply liked to ask people if they believed in Jesus Christ as Lord and Savior. *Even the demons believe in God,* John thought, staring at the back of Frank Logan's head as the Texan quickly called to an attendant standing nearby and asked her to bring him a glass of wine. Then he turned to face John and began talking about his hometown again as if he hadn't heard

John's question.

"It sure has been hot down in Abilene. Ya know they say it's that damn ozone layer that's disappearing."

John couldn't help but smile. Every opportunity to talk with someone was a God ordained moment to share about His love. Some needed encouragement, some advice. Others needed nothing but good old confrontation. John however, knew when to quit and wasn't for shoving the good news down anybody's throat. As he watched his seat-mate pull out a handkerchief and wipe the sweat from his forehead, John sensed in his spirit that Mr. Logan was a very lonely man running from God. John's dread of the long flight quickly disappeared. What was 3-4 hours between two eternal souls?

"So do you go to church Frank?"

Mr. Logan shifted in his seat. "Well, son, I stay so busy these days. You know I run businesses all over the world, and there's just never any time."

"So what about when time runs out?" John decided to be as blunt as necessary.

"Well, I suppose I'll just have to deal with that when it comes."

The flight attendant returned with the wine and gave John a sympathetic stare as Frank took the glass.

"Thank you, cutie," he smirked as she walked briskly away, shaking her head.

"Well I guess I won't look at my girlie magazines since I'm sitting next to a preacher boy."

"That's real considerate of ya, Frank. You wouldn't want to tempt me, right?"

Frank nodded his head and smiled. His gold tooth sparkled.

"So let me just ask you once again Frank, do you believe God sent His son Jesus to die on a cross for your sin and mine?"

Frank was quiet for a moment, and John was beginning to think he was going to avoid the question again, when the cowboy slowly turned his face toward John and answered.

"Son, I don't believe in much of nothin' at all, except having a good time while I can, but since I can tell that you're genuinely concerned about my soul, I'll be completely honest. Sometimes I believe there must be a God out there somewhere, but before I think too long I start having a good time again."

"I respect your honesty..." John paused and gazed out the window at the clouds and sky. He silently prayed for the right words to share and then continued, "Here's the last thing I'll say about it Frank. Let me be one person you will remember as telling you that no amount of good times can compare with the goodness of God nor can any amount of earthly pleasure and riches compare with what God has planned for those who love Him and spend eternity with Him in heaven. But here's the catch - there's only ONE way in, and that is through Jesus Christ. He is the door and you gotta go through Him. Don't spend all your short days down here thinking only about life on earth when the reality is that we will all one day stand before God and have to give account for everything we've ever said and done. Truth is that moment could be today...even before the end of this flight." *Nothing like the thought of a plane crash to get someone's attention!*

"You gotta be f-ing kidding me", Frank Logan mumbled gruffly as he shook his head, pulled out a Playboy magazine and began reading or at least looking at the photos.

John, understanding the conversation was over, took out his *Sports Illustrated.* As John read, Frank lowered his seat back and pull the bill of his cowboy hat down over his face. Soon John was lost in his thoughts and the pages of his magazine were ignored for the view of the clouds and sky outside the window. He still couldn't believe he was really on his way to Venezuela. From the moment he'd made his decision to go, he had fought to keep all the noise and arguments behind him and not look back. There had been few doubts that he was doing the right thing, but now that he was all alone, with no chance of turning back, he suddenly began to wonder if he really knew what he was getting into. *What are you going to accomplish with these kids? What do you have to offer them? What if there's no change?!* With these questions pounding in his head, John reached into his shirt pocket and pulled out the slip of folded paper Rachel had given him the night before.

* * *

"The LORD himself goes before you and will be with you; he will never leave you nor forsake you. Do not be afraid; do not be discouraged."
Deuteronomy 31:8

I can't go with you John...this time :) But you don't go alone!

John's eyes were glued to the paper. He read Rachel's short message at the bottom over and over again and each time the smile on his face grew bigger. There was no missing her intended meaning...*maybe one day we will go on mission together.* He looked out the window, but instead of blue sky and clouds, all he saw was Rachel's face and smile. *Okay, God. You obviously brought Rachel into my life for a reason, right? Please help me to wait on your plans and your will for me and for us...if there is an us!* Part of John suddenly wanted to turn the plane around and fly back to Lewisville, find Rachel and take her in his arms and profess his affection. *Easy now. God please keep me focused on what you need me to do now!* Just as John finished praying these words, Frank Logan let out a low, but prolonged belch that caused most of the nearby passengers to look his way in disgust.

Gotcha. Thank you Lord. For my life...for Rachel. John smiled at the overbearing, rude and obnoxious man next to him, now quiet and sleeping like a baby. *And for Frank Logan.*

Somewhere over the Caribbean Sea John fell asleep and awoke later only because of the movie that began playing. He looked over at Mr. Logan who appeared to be sleeping, but in reality was just pretending, hoping to avoid any more discussion with this Jesus freak kid sitting beside him.

Frank Logan had run into all sorts of religious people in his time and he actually enjoyed the opportunity to let them know how stupid and gullible he thought they were, but this boy was different. Not only had the young man not given him the opportunity to do his dirty work, he had actually gotten him to start feeling guilty for it! John Parker had succeeded where all others had failed, causing him to think seriously about God and eternity, and he didn't like it at all. He had decided the more talk of Jesus he could avoid from now on, the better. But he also didn't like to run from a fight and the fact that he had to pretend to be asleep because of some spiritual threat he felt from John, embarrassed and angered him. For the first time he admitted he was a coward, scared of the things John spoke of, things he really knew nothing about.

* * *

The movie ended and John realized they would be arriving in less than an hour. He wanted to talk some more with Frank, and he thought he would get the chance when the flight attendants began to serve the final snack, but his hopes were dashed when Frank refused to budge. The attendant refused to wake him; she wasn't stupid – the trip had been peaceful and quiet for everyone since he'd closed his eyes. Another flight attendant returned to collect the trash as the captain announced the landing time to be twenty minutes away and requested that chairs be returned upright and seat belts fastened. John gently tapped Frank's shoulder and whispered his name, until the large man in perfect Academy Award form pretended to wake up from a long and satisfying sleep.

"Frank, we'll be landing in about twenty minutes and the captain asked everyone to buckle up."

"Okay, okay son."

Another flight attendant appeared and reluctantly asked Mr. Logan to move his seat to its full upright position and fasten his seat belt, to which he responded sarcastically, "This is a new procedure, right? Honey, your captain just told me what I need to do and I think I've been flying since you were in diapers so I know the rules."

"Sir. Just please sit up and buckle your seat belt," she repeated again and briskly walked away.

"And tell the captain, with twenty minutes to go, this is hog wash!" All eyes turned on him and a few women let out exasperated sighs.

"Was I talking to you?" he asked the entire plane's population. Eyes rolled, heads shook in disapproval, and John just smiled. Inside he was still laughing at the "hog wash!" phrase. He'd only heard that on "The Dukes of Hazard", never in real life conversation.

"Well, Frank, you shouldn't need any rest for a while."

"Yeah, I don't know what hit me. I guess I was more tired than I thought." Frank Logan was seething and hating every second of his lying.

"Maybe the flight attendants drugged your wine," John said, chuckling.

At this even Frank had to smile. "Wouldn't surprise me the least bit."

"Well at least your trip went by fast."

Frank wanted to yell, "Are you crazy! That was the longest trip of my life preacher boy! I couldn't read my magazines. I couldn't watch the movie. All I could do was think, and I hate thinking!" But he didn't yell and he had a feeling it wouldn't have accomplished anything. He expected John would have only smiled back and said, "God loves you, Frank, and so do I!" Frank Logan finally had to admit that he had been licked.

"Almost there," John said to no one in particular.

"Thank God," Frank mumbled just a little too loudly. Then as if realizing the hypocrisy of such a statement, he added, "Or whoever!"

John grinned as the flustered Texan got up and went to the restroom before John could say another word.

Well God. He's running all right. I hope I can run into Frank Logan again someday or someone else can take up the task. John smiled and glanced upwards. *Whoever it is, give them an extra dose of your blessing!*

* * *

Not until the landing gear was deployed did Frank Logan return to his seat and buckle up, to the angry protests of the entire flight crew. After the plane came to a stop and the passengers began to disembark, Frank, not able to think of anything else to say, asked John what city he'd be living in. Upon hearing it was Jajo, one of many destinations he would also be visiting, he suddenly had an idea.

"Well son, I guess this is where we say goodbye. It was sure nice to ride with ya."

They shook hands as John replied, "Same to you Frank." Then John took a small booklet out of his pocket. "Frank, I want to give you this to read."

Frank took the small tract, recognizing immediately what it was. He had thrown many away over the years.

"Thank you John," he said, trying to sound as sincere as possible. "And I want to give you my business card. I'll be in Jajo for a time as well, so maybe we could get together." John was surprised at Frank's invitation and took the card gladly. Then the two shook hands again and said goodbye. John hurried to his next and final connecting flight to Merida's Alberto Carnevalli Airport. After storing his backpack in the overhead compartment and taking a seat, John pulled Logan's business card out of his pocket. "Logan's Gentlemen's Club / Exotic Dancers / World Wide Chain" – John smiled and looked up. *No wonder, Lord. Poor guy must have gotten no sleep. He's in Your hands.*

* * *

In the back seat of a taxi, Frank Logan already had a cigarette lit and dangling from his lips as he stared down at the Christian tract in his hand. "Do You Know Where You'll Go When You Die? YOU CAN!" He wasn't going to read it, but instead of throwing it out the window, he stuffed it into his suit pocket. "I'll whip this John Parker yet," he mumbled to himself. If he could just get the Parker boy to his club then he'd have him. No healthy young man could resist his girls. Compared to old Father Ramirez, this preacher boy would be easy! The memory of Father Ramirez sneaking in through his backdoor twice a week made Logan chuckle. It was so sad the day he finally let the priest know he had over 10 hours of videotape of him with his favorite girl. The priest's dark skin had turned ghost white! Father Ramirez skipped town the very next day and was never heard from or seen again. Of course, getting rid of the shepherd was satisfying, but it was the flock that Logan was interested in all along. Soon he let a copy of the videotape out and just as he guessed, it turned the town upside down! His plan couldn't have worked out better. A few were sent to replace Father Ramirez, but the parishioners just ran them out of town one after the other. The people of Jajo were fed up with religious hypocrisy. It didn't take long for the church to all but disappear and as the faithful diminished, Frank's customer base grew…just as he had planned all along. Now he would have the chance to make it happen all over again. He laughed out loud at the prospect of watching the new preacher boy fall to the oldest temptation known to man.

23 THE DRIVE

John followed the crowd to the luggage pick-up area, which consisted of one long conveyer belt circling a large auditorium-size room. It was full of people and loud. It was also warm. It was hard to believe he had started the day surrounded by snow.

* * *

John waited for any sight of his bags and guitar. He was glad he had listened to his father and packed light. Well, somewhat light. If his mother had had her way, his whole armoire would be sitting on the conveyer belt now. In a matter of minutes all of his things arrived and with nothing to declare to the customs officer, John quickly walked out into another large room filled with eagerly waiting friends and families. Dark skin and dark hair dotted his view. The room was loud with conversation, but John recognized none of what was being said. He was definitely far from Lewisville, Tennessee. Immediately he spotted a tall, attractive, brunette woman standing to the side, holding up a sign that read "JOHN PARKER". She saw him a second later, but waited for him to approach. John walked up and somehow managed to extend a free hand through his luggage.

"Maggie Stevens?"

"Yes, and you must be John Parker?"

"Yes ma'am. Nice to meet you…and Happy New Year!"

They shook hands.

"Happy New Year and welcome to Venezuela! Here let me help you with that."

"That's okay, I got it."

"I insist." She practically took his guitar case from his hand.

"Yes ma'am."

They began walking out of the terminal.

"Well," Maggie said, glancing over, "It's a good thing you arrived when you did. I had one John and two Juans approach me and I was about to just go with the next one."

"I'm glad you waited."

"Actually, Richard told me you were quite a tall fella and now I see what he means. You're a basketball player right?"

"Yes ma'am."

And that was the end of that. No follow up questions. No quizzing on personal stats, team schedule, team ranking or anything that had mattered most to folks back in Lewisville. *Strange, but nice*, John thought. *No one here knows anything.* John smiled. All that mattered now was the kids he had come for.

* * *

Richard had explained John's situation to Maggie. She knew what he had given up to come live with them. Even before meeting him she was already impressed with his sacrificing so much for the chance to help her kids. "So how was your flight?"

"Not bad," John answered, "but my seat partner might not agree." John went on to tell Maggie about Frank Logan and some of what had taken place on the plane.

"So you were unfortunate enough to meet Mr. Logan. We hear about him all the time, but have never actually seen him. His name travels through all the circles and depending on who you're talking with, he's either admired or hated. Admired by the macho patrons of his sleazy club and hated by their wives and families who can't bear to watch them destroy themselves."

"So is he around a lot? He gave me his business card and it says world wide chain."

"Ha!" Maggie exclaimed, "World wide chain, huh? He wishes. From what I've heard, he owns about three or four dumps in the Trujillo State, which includes Jajo and some other small towns and that's about the extent of his empire."

John grinned, remembering the air of importance the slick Texan had put on when he handed John his card. "How did he end up here?"

"I have no idea, but I can promise you we don't consider ourselves blessed to have him."

"Are they *just* strip clubs?"

"What do you think?" Maggie asked in a flat voice. "There's definitely prostitution going on, but sadly it's ignored by everyone. It might as well be legal."

"That's hard to fight."

"It sure is, but thankfully Jajo has a new mayor who's doing a lot to clean it up." With that said, Maggie pulled a set of keys out of her pocket and aimed them in the direction of a new shiny black Range Rover. A loud chirping sound echoed in the parking lot, the front lights on the vehicle flashed, and the locks on all the doors clicked opened.

Yes, the oil business seems to be treating them pretty well, John mused, but imagined he had seen nothing yet.

"We've got about an hour and a half drive ahead of us, but you'll enjoy it." As they drove away from the airport the sudden thought that it would be six months before he saw the terminal again came buzzing into his head like an annoying insect. He lowered his window to breathe the outside air and let the thought fly out. He smiled as a sense of peace engulfed him.

A ringing sound cut through the silence and John turned to see Maggie pull a large handheld phone receiver out from under her seat. He had only seen one of these new car phones in a magazine.

"Hi honey. Yes, he's safe and sound and we're heading home now. We've still got a long drive. Okay. See you in a bit."

Maggie placed the phone back under her seat and looked over at John.

"Okay. That was pretty cool." He said.

"What? The phone? I thought it was the dumbest thing in the world when Paul first brought it home, but he was right. It comes in handy...no pun intended."

John liked Maggie. She was obviously rich, but down to earth and funny.

"So how were your good-byes?" Maggie asked, glancing over at John through her Ray Ban shades.

"Pretty tough," He answered, "But it helps when you *know* God's involved. More peace, less apprehension. That's how my mom put it. What about you? How hard was it to say goodbye and move your family here?"

Maggie thought for a moment. "Wow, that was about about four year ago. I can't believe it's been that long." She grew quiet again and John was happy to let her silently reminisce. She finally continued, "Well, it was hard to say goodbye, especially to my family. We're all very close. But at the time we all thought we'd be back again after a year or two. No one had any idea we'd still be here. But I was married with two kids, so I wasn't coming alone like you. The hardest part was not knowing how life here would affect our two sons. There was so much in the US that I wanted them to have and experience, but they have done great here..." Maggie paused, realizing there was no need to sugar coat the truth. John had come to solve some problems and she was sure he had already been filled in on some details. "Well, at times it's been difficult and to be honest lately things have gotten worse, but I'm still glad our sons have had this experience. Plus we travel to the States a lot so they get to see their grandparents, uncles, aunts and cousins about twice a year.

"That's good," John replied. He wasn't sure if he should make his "Here's what I hope to accomplish" speech then or wait for a larger crowd. He decided to save it for later and let Maggie lead the conversation. She wanted to know more about his relationship with her old friend Richard. They swapped one humorous story after another and laughed until their sides hurt.

* * *

As they left the busy city of Merida behind, the talk turned to more pressing matters. Maggie briefly described the events planned for the next few days. From there she launched into an emotional speech about all that God could and would do through John's leadership. *No pressure,* he thought to himself. He definitely shared in her enthusiasm, but at the same time, couldn't help noticing there had been no mention of what God *had* been doing in their lives. He wondered just how much the money had affected them all. He remembered Richard describing Maggie as "on fire for the Lord during college."

That they both equally enjoyed talking was obvious. John appreciated Maggie's openness and she was delighted with his sense of humor and easygoing style.

"The kids are gonna love you," she said smiling and nodding her head.

"I hope so," he replied.

* * *

They had driven over an hour and their conversation had been non-stop, but John had still managed to take in the views of the Venezuelan landscape outside his window. The Range Rover seemed to constantly climb higher and higher. Soon the mountain road took a sharp turn around a corner which seemed to suspend them over the very edge of the earth. Green covered the land as far as John could see. The road suddenly began descending into a wide valley, twisting and turning then finally straightened out as one last hill brought them down into a town and within minutes, the middle of a market and plaza.

"This is Jajo," Maggie began, "it's the closest town to where we live. This is the main part of the town, but it actually spreads out quite a ways. Some want to say it's a city, but I don't go that far. Right now we are driving through Plaza Bolivar."

"It's beautiful," John replied. The whole scene before him was picturesque, like something out of a magazine. The plaza consisted of an assortment of colored bricks laid down in a circular design with a four-foot high stonewall wrapped around its perimeter. The area was dotted with statues of military heroes and bubbling fountains. Everywhere were trees, bushes, and flowers. On a hilltop to the North of the plaza, a blanket of green grass invited many to enjoy a picnic, game of soccer, or barefoot stroll. Everything that had been made by human hands appeared ancient and worn down, with some of the statues way past the point of needing repair, but it was exactly this aged characteristic that made Jajo so appealing and genuine.

John remembered Mr. Logan and began looking for his club, half expecting to see some crazy Vegas style sign with a big picture of Mr. Logan himself in lights, but he saw nothing. He decided it smarter if he didn't ask Mrs. Stevens about the club's location. There were hundreds, if not thousands, of people walking around selling, buying, and trading goods.

"You can come here and do some shopping and find some pretty neat souvenirs. Be sure to bargain. We bring the kids here every other week so they can run around and play with friends at the park." Maggie maneuvered the SUV slowly through the crowds who filled the narrow streets. Many stopped and stared at the vehicle and children ran beside them and waved, though they couldn't see in through the dark tinted windows which John assumed correctly, were bullet proof. He sat still and silent, staring at the faces outside. He was amazed at all the children he saw. Most of them wore few clothes while some of the smallest children wore none on at all. Feet and legs and even some faces were covered in dirt. Dirt and smiles. John wondered what kind of pain, fear and despair was hiding behind all the smiles. He assumed the majority of Jajo's population were Catholic, and he began looking for signs of religious life in the city. After a few minutes he still hadn't seen one statue of a saint, crucifix, or church building.

"Where is Jajo's church?" John asked, glancing over at Maggie.

Maggie just shook her head and let out a brief, but meaningful, sigh.

"Remember your new friend Logan?"

John nodded his head silently.

"Well, Jajo was the home of Father Ramirez, a sweet and dear priest who had lived and served here faithfully for over 20 years…he was the backbone of all the good things that happened in this city. He ministered to the sick, he took in abandoned children, fed the poor and homeless, and most important of all, he had a way of involving everyone in his work. He was truly a joy to be around; I don't know when or how it started, but somehow he got mixed up in Logan's club…"

John had been afraid that was coming.

"What I'm sure happened," Maggie continued, "but no one's ever proven, is that Logan blackmailed Father Ramirez and he just disappeared…leaving behind a spiritual vacuum that's never been filled. Soon after Father Ramirez went missing, a videotape of him was discovered that, from what I've heard, is unbelievable and horrible. Some of his parishioners went on a rampage destroying the church building, knocking over statues, and vandalizing shops that sold anything religious, but did anything happen to Logan's? Not a thing. Not a single person spoke up against him or his club. Everyone was so busy raging against the missing priest and false religion that no one saw the truth of what had really happened…that Father Ramirez was just another victim of the deadly perversion that Logan deals out. This was just over a year ago, and since that time this town has come more and more under Logan's control…his place is just pure evil."

John looked into the faces of a few more people passing by on the street and realized there was brokenness behind the smiles. With a heavy heart and troubled spirit, John stared out the window, silently praying again for Frank Logan. The Range Rover climbed a dirt road up into the hills above the town and wound its way around and around through the thick jungle. As shades of green and brown swirled around him, a memory of Rachel came upon him and quickly lifted his soul. She was leaning over a pile of maps they had spread out on a table in the university library. She looked at him and smiled and then pointed out that the town of Jajo was located on the northern edge of the Andes Mountains. "Sounds so adventurous!" she exclaimed. The memory began to sparkle, and then John found himself staring into a forest that was aglow with glittering light. The setting sun's rays filtered through the trees making the spaces in between catch fire. *If only Rachel could be here with me right now.* John knew he'd have to get control of this thought or it would torture him.

As if reading his mind, Maggie asked, "So is there someone special back home you're missing like crazy?

John glanced at Maggie in disbelief.

"Are you a mind reader?"

"Trust me. I know the look. You'll get through this, John, and hopefully come out stronger and closer on the other end."

John smiled. Maggie was cool. He liked her already and knew he could learn a lot from her.

They continued to wind their way up the mountain, turning off the dirt road onto an even smaller one. After a few hundred feet the road suddenly widened and became paved in dark black asphalt. Another hundred feet and the Range Rover slowed to a stop before a massive iron gate with a large brick security booth beside it. Lights shone down onto the vehicle as a guard inside the room pushed a button opening the gates and waved them through.

Maggie rolled her window down.

"John, this is one of our guards, Fernando."

"Hola, Fernando!" John said and waved to a friendly middle-aged Venezuelan man dressed in uniform.

"Hola, Senor Juan. Nice to meet you."

"El placer es todo mio" (the pleasure is all mine), John answered back to the surprise of both Maggie and Fernando.

"Woah!" Fernando exclaimed and then quickly added "You speak Espanol muy bien. Very good!"

"Gracias!" John replied as they drove past the smiling guard and through the gates. John noticed what appeared to be ten or twelve small black and white monitors stacked against one wall in the guard house. His eyes followed the tall wrought iron fence, which extended from both sides of the gate and guard house and disappeared into the woods. Out of the corner of his eye he caught sight of a wire running parallel with the fence below. It stretched through multiple treetops and then ended at a bundle of mounted security cameras high in the trees.

John hadn't spent much time thinking about safety. He was much too concerned with plans for managing the children. Strangely no one, not even his mother, had brought the topic up to any serious degree. Suddenly the reality of his new surroundings were beginning to register. He was moving in with millionaires in an impoverished area of the country. He wondered just how safe they really were.

"We have two more guards named Diego and Ricardo. They rotate between guardhouse duty and patrolling the fence...which is electric, by the way, and turned on at night. Two guards are on duty at all times."

He still wondered.

"Sounds like you brushed yourself up on the language a little."

"Well that special person we were talking about, whose name is Rachel by the way, gave me a crash course in Spanish before I left."

"I'm sure you were really focused," Maggie said smiling.

As they drove up the blacktop road, beautiful Victorian light posts lit the way. Soon houses began to pass them by.

"All of these homes belong to the different families who are involved in the corporation that my husband works with. Instead of all buying homes on the market, we decided to just purchase land together and make our own little neighborhood, especially so all the kids could stay near each other."

Maggie drove slowly through the neighborhood, pointing and telling John which family owned which house. The homes were huge and modern, with immaculate landscaping. Similar to those belonging to the wealthiest families back in his hometown. There were no fences so he could see into all the backyards. There were large decks, playground sets and a few fancy gazebos. Two homes had swimming pools with slides, diving boards and elaborate waterfalls cascading down from rock formations. Here and there, John's eyes noticed the tall iron fence in the distance, tracing out a large perimeter of their exclusive and secluded neighborhood.

This is money central.

Another Range Rover, a Land Cruiser, and a Suburban much like his father's, sat in the driveways. Inside the garages he would later discover a Mercedes, a Porche, and a Jaguar.

"Is that a shuttle bus?" He asked, pointing to an enormous white vehicle parked in the distance. It was long, tall and covered in dark tinted windows. John could make out a set of folding doors at the front.

"Yes," Maggie chuckled. "Mr. Childress picked up The Swan, as he likes to call her, just a few months ago so we could transport all our kids together when they go on field trips or if we all want to go to town together. The first time we showed up some locals tried to board thinking it would take them to the next town."

"I bet."

As they continued past the houses, the road began to slope and the trees grew dense. John looked off into the distance and saw a huge gray circle at the bottom of one hill. It appeared to be made of stone or cement and looked like a driveway with nowhere to drive. There were red circles painted on it – large circles that grew smaller towards the middle. *A giant bulls-eye*, John mused, then asked Maggie about it.

She stopped her vehicle and looked where he was pointing. "That's the helicopter landing pad," she answered flatly, as if everyday homeowner property.

"Really?" John mumbled, trying not to sound surprised. *That's the helicopter landing pad*, he told himself again with a smile on his face.

"The men fly out two to three days a week to inspect the oil rigs. It's about a 30 minute flight to Lake Maracaibo where the rigs are."

"They're in a lake?" This time John didn't hide his surprise.

"A very large lake, connected to the Gulf of Venezuela in the Caribbean Sea."

"How many rigs are there?"

"Three at the moment, with two more in construction. Sometime you can go with Paul to inspect them."

"That would be sweet," John answered. He'd never flown in a helicopter before. Maggie went on explaining about the corporation that her husband and the other father's were involved in. "The oil industry here has been under government control for decades, but a rare opportunity opened up a few years ago when the Venezuelan Supreme Court changed the laws in favor of a new policy called Apertura which allows international corporations like ours to partner with the PDVSA or Petroleos De Venezuela…the name of Veneuela's state-owned oil and natural gas company. This new partnership allows us to split extraction rights and profits."

John was impressed. Maggie knew her stuff. "Are you on staff?"

"Me? I run things from behind the scenes."

They shared a smile as Maggie took her foot off the brake and the SUV began to roll forward. Maggie wasn't through yet. John learned that Paul was in charge of operations for all of the rigs in Venezuela. The other fathers were even higher up in the company and responsible for all of South America. Many of them took monthly trips to Caracas, Bogota and Rio De Janeiro. They also took monthly trips to their US headquarters in Houston, Texas. There was little cash to be found in their neighborhood. Property was the only valuable thing they possessed. This, Maggie explained, was for their protection. As John looked around, he couldn't help but think their property was as good as gold itself. And though he hated to contemplate the possibility, the children were definitely at risk. One ransom would be all it would take and there were nine to choose from. Had the parents even thought of that? How much had increasing wealth blinded considerations of safety? It sounded as if the fathers were hardly ever around. If something bad did happen, he doubted Fernando, Diego and Ricardo could handle it by themselves and the police were a long way down the mountain.

"You're probably thinking it's dangerous for us to live here."

John looked at her and silently nodded. She smiled faintly.

"I can't tell you how terrified I was the first year. The kids were practically never allowed to go outside the fence and I had nightmares they were somehow kidnapped right from under us."

Maybe he had judged too soon.

"After a while, my fear reached a point of almost paranoia, but the problem wasn't so much a growing threat as it was a growing reclusiveness on my part. See, I rarely went to town and had no knowledge of the people there. No friends or even acquaintances. I was actually convinced everyone despised us because of our wealth. But finally, after listening to the kids complain every day for an entire month about being kept prisoner in their own neighborhood, we couldn't take it anymore. So all the parents agreed to take the kids for an all day excursion to Jajo. To be honest I wondered what in the world we were going to do there all day, but you know what? That day was probably the first real fun time we experienced in our new home – parents and kids alike. We shopped and ate the local food. We played in the park and in the square. We must have been quite a sight! Here were all these white foreigners playing freeze tag, running and screaming in their strange language. The people seemed amused and even eager to join us. Most importantly, that day we began to make many new friends. Everyone was so kind and giving. God used that day to open my eyes..."

Maggie was staring out into the woods. The vehicle had come to a complete stop without either John or her noticing. She brushed her cheek as if wiping away a tear then continued, "Yes, it's still dangerous for us here and, yes, as much as I hate to think about it, there is still a very real threat to our children, but I've learned you just can't live in fear of the unknown. I've given it up to the Lord, and in return He's shown us that we're not alone. Jajo has become our town and the people, many of whom we know by name, are our neighbors. They have sort of adopted our kids as their own and feel a sense of responsibility for their safety. And even though the kids still aren't allowed to go out by themselves, we probably make two to three trips to town a week. I'm finally able to live without fear because I know hundreds of eyes are helping me watch over them."

She pressed on the gas and they began to move again. "You might find yourself being invited to town quite often. I hope you don't mind the exercise?"

"Not at all."

"Well Fernando will be glad to hear it. He's been the official chaperone off and on."

"So that's why he was so glad to see me, huh?" They both smiled.

* * *

Their vehicle continued slowly along the road, passing by a row of elegant apartments that sat a little ways down a hill and partly in the woods.

"Those are for guests, both business and friends and family. There are three of them, all exactly alike. One of them will be yours. You can fix it up in whatever way you want."

"Fix it up?" John asked incredulously.

"Decorate it or do whatever. It's your home. We want you to feel comfortable."

John chuckled.

"What is it?" Maggie asked.

"Well, let's just say I won't be sending any pictures of this place back to my prayer partners in Tennessee. So much for being a missionary."

Maggie objected, "John, you are a missionary and your mission is our kids. Believe me you'll need this refuge after a day with them. You'll earn your keep."

"Well, it's going to be hard going back to dorm life, that's for sure."

24 THE WELCOME

Across the road and down the other side of the hill, a medium sized one story building passed by with the lights inside turned on. A few children were spotted running around outside. John's stomach fluttered a bit.

"That's the recreation room, better known as the Rec. All the kids hang out there and play their games and "chill out" as they like to call it. That will be your room to have meetings and do whatever you want. The kids should all be there waiting to meet you, so we'll walk over and you can say hi. Then you can eat at our place, and afterwards we'll help you get your things moved in. Tomorrow you'll get to meet the parents." As she finished the sentence, the road split forming a circle drive in front of what was obviously the final house. "Well, here we are."

"So this is home?" John asked as he peered out the window, his eyes following a walkway that led up to the front door of a mansion he thought belonged in both "Architectural Digest" and "Better Homes and Gardens." The house was a gray brick with dark wood beams running across the top. Half of the house was one story with a flat roof, the other half was two stories with the dark beams rising diagonally. There were large windows on all sides and beautiful plants and flowers decorated the landscape.

"You can just leave your things in the car for now," Maggie told him.

John climbed out of the Range Rover and stretched for a moment, gazing around at his new surroundings. Maggie waited patiently, letting him take it all in. Soon they were walking the trail towards the Rec. It was so green. He took a deep breath of the fresh air, heavy with moisture. Birds were calling to one another overhead and crickets were in chorus all around.

"I love to just sit outside and breathe the air and listen to the birds."

"I bet," John replied. "The air is so fresh."

As they neared the Rec building, the children noticed them coming and quickly ran inside. John smiled, thinking to himself, *they're probably as nervous as me.*

* * *

The Rec looked liked the entertainment center of some ritzy resort. There was a full-sized paved basketball court with high quality professional goals to one side of the building and on the other a sand volleyball court. Inside he discovered a pool table, ping pong table, karaoke machine, state of the art stereo system with four mounted speakers around the room, and a large TV in a corner cabinet. Cables poured out of the cabinet, running to a pile of video game controllers on the floor. There were two large sofas, five beanbags and a large dining table with chairs in one corner of the room. There were also "girls" and "boys" restrooms and a large kitchen with a full size refrigerator. Soft, plush carpet stretched from wall to wall. John couldn't imagine what his condo would be like.

Maggie switched off the TV and stood in front of it. "Kids, I want to introduce you to John Parker."

Nothing but silence.

"How's it going, guys and girls?" John smiled at all the young faces staring at him.

Still silence.

John saw Maggie's face turn red as she gave a tall boy sitting on the pool table a stern glance.

"It's okay," John said to her and then turned to face the group. "Well, let's see..."

Then from the middle of the group out squirmed a small boy with blonde hair hanging in his eyes. Eyes as blue as the ocean. He walked right up to John.

"Did God send you here?"

John thought for a moment at all the different ways he could answer and then just simply said, "Yes...yes, He did. Is that okay with you?"

"Yep, cause I asked Him to."

John peeked over at Maggie. Her face was still red, but now a large smile had replaced her previous frown. John guessed this was her youngest son. "Well, thank you for requesting me. What's your name?"

"Wobert," he answered back.

John assumed that was spelled with an R and not a W.

"Well Robert, just be sure to let me know if you ever ask God to send me somewhere else, okay?"

"Okay." Robert smiled and some of the other kids giggled.

John turned back to Maggie, who looked more relieved now. "Maggie, just let me chat with them for a while, and then we'll come eat."

"Alright, but I know you're tired and you still need to get moved in, so don't feel like you have to get to know everyone tonight." As she left the room, John noticed her give the teenage boy on the pool table one more motherly glance. *That must be the other one.* John looked out over the faces of the group and took a deep breath. *Where to begin?*

"Well, I guess we should start with everyones' names. So I want each of you to stand up and..." a couple of the older boys groaned, John ignored them, "and tell me your name, your age, and your favorite...music group." For a moment no one volunteered then Robert stood again. John liked this little guy already.

"I'm Wobert Stevens and I'm six years old."

"Do you have a favorite music group Robert?" John asked.

"Yeah, I like Hanson." There were moans from the older boys and girls and a few excited claps from the younger girls.

"Hanson, huh?" John knew the group. Three adolescent brothers famous for their long hair and high voices.

Robert nodded his head smiling.

"That's all he listens too!" chimed one of the older girls.

"*Mmmbop*," John said, remembering the name of the band's claim to fame. A catchy tune that was a #1 hit in over 27 countries at the same time.

"Not you, too!" the same girl responded.

"Who doesn't know Hanson? They're such cute little girls."

Before John could even finish his sentence all of the younger children were screaming at him, "They're not girls! They're boys! They're brothers!"

The older kids were laughing and John just smiled and said, "Oh, sorry." He couldn't resist. "Are you sure they're not girls?"

"Yes!"

"Okay, well, I know a lot about Robert, including his direct prayer line with the Lord. So who's next? How about you?" John pointed to the girl who had spoken earlier. She didn't even hesitate, but stood up straight and tall and looked John directly in his eyes. She was taller than John had expected. John looked down at her feet and saw a pair of platform sandals adding about 4 inches to her height. Just from her posture alone John could tell she was confident and sure of herself. She wore short khaki shorts and a white frilly halter-top shirt. A diamond stud earring sparkled from her bellybutton. Red lipstick and blue eye shadow added unnecessary color to a naturally attractive face. Sandy blonde hair fell straight and to her shoulders. John imagined this girl had recently experienced a growth spurt of some sort. John also noticed the guys on the pool table had given her, or her figure, their full attention. This girl was a distraction.

"I'm Susan Childress. I'm 16 years old and…I don't know...I like..."

"The Chipmunks," one of the other boys said teasingly, no one laughed.

"Shut up, Brad," Susan said, rolling her eyes.

A red-haired stocky fellow sitting on the pool table ducked his head in silence. It looked to John like Susan could handle things herself. She was still trying to think of an answer.

"No favorites? Maybe you just like a lot of different styles?"

"Yeah," she said, nodding her head.

"Kind of depends on the mood you're in?"

"Exactly." She smiled and sat down.

The youth were warming up to John's relaxed personality, at least some of them. There were others, four boys to be exact, sitting together on the pool table behind the rest, who didn't even pretend to pay attention. They just talked amongst themselves. John had seen this attitude before and knew it was going to be a challenge. He decided to wait for another time to deal with them. Meanwhile, one by one, the rest of the girls stood and introduced themselves. Robyn and Jamie Cook, 14 and 11 year old sisters, took turns telling John and the rest of the crowd everything from their favorite music group (along with every detail about each member of the band) to their favorite line of brand name clothes, to their favorite toothpaste and how it actually whitens teeth as it cleans.

"See?" Robyn asked, spreading her lips wide open.

"See?" Jamie repeated in the same pose.

Appearance wise, John saw little resemblance between the two sisters. Robyn had straight black hair, brown eyes, olive skin, and lots of freckles all over her cheeks. She was average height, but a bit overweight. Jamie had short brown hair, like it had been trimmed with a deep bowl around her head, blue eyes, and dark tan skin. She was already as tall as her older sister, but as thin as a stick. However, once they opened their mouths to speak, it was easy to recognize their sibling relationship. Every gesture, expression, and tone that Robyn demonstrated, Jamie mimicked and echoed beside her. Even though he wasn't exactly seeing double, John decided he *was* hearing double.

After the talking twins finished their exhaustive introductions, the final female in the group quickly stood up and introduced herself as Stephanie

Rollins, age 13. She hesitated for moment, looked back at the guys, then turned and smiled at John. Her face was flush red. John noticed her hands shaking and surmised from her previous backwards glance and her curly strawberry hair that she was most likely related to the red haired brute sitting and fuming on the pool table behind her. At that moment, Stephanie Rollins became precious to John. Her blue eyes sparkled and something about her expression pierced John's soul; it seemed to be silently screaming, "you have no idea what's going on inside"! John felt a lump in his throat. Stephanie's tight lipped grin separated just enough for her to whisper "Sorry" and quickly take a seat again.

"Stephanie's kind of shy," Susan said, taking hold of Stephanie's hand and giving it a squeeze.

"That's okay, Stephanie," John said softly. He hoped she could read the message behind his smile: *I'm here for you.*

Now that all the girls had volunteered, it was the boys' turn.

"Alright men," John said, giving the four boys on the pool table a look far sterner than he realized. "We've saved the best for last. Who's it gonna be?"

Nothing but silence. Minutes passed and John waited. Some of the girls started complaining.

"Taylor, quit being stupid." Susan knew what they were trying to do. Still no one stood.

"You guys are so immature," Robyn said, followed by a "yeah" from her sister.

* * *

What nobody knew, except the four guys themselves, was that before the meeting they had all agreed not to say a word to this new lame youth leader their parents had hired for them. Taylor was still in shock. He couldn't believe they'd done it. They hadn't even talked to him about it. All he and the others wanted was to go back to the States, and instead their parents kept trying harder and harder to bring the States to them. He was pissed. This John guy, whoever he was, would be on the next plane home if *he* could do anything about it.

"Tommy, I'm gonna tell Mom and Dad!" Jamie yelled, feeling safe sitting between her older sister and Susan.

John saw a tall and lanky, curly brown-haired boy stick his tongue out at Jamie. *Another brother/sister puzzle solved*, John mused. Although he was getting hungry, John was rather enjoying the scene unfolding before him. If the guys were testing to see how patient he could be, he was going to surprise them. Meanwhile, the girls were making it easy.

"Quit acting like babies!"

"Yeah!"

Feeling the pressure getting too heavy, the youngest of the group of boys quickly got to his feet. The other boys shook their heads and whispered something derogatory, or so John assumed by the look on their faces.

"I'm Mike Littleton, I'm twelve years old and I like U2 and basketball." He quickly sat down and was frogged in the arm by one of the boys beside him.

"Thanks for being brave there, Mike," John said. "U2 is a great band and Larry Mullen Jr. is a solid drummer, and what's the guitarist name?

"The Edge," Mike answered.

"Yeah, the Edge, and Bono's voice is powerful. Do you have, 'Under A Blood Red Sky'?"

"Yeah, I have them all."

"That's one of my all-time favorite albums."

Mike smiled, impressed with John's knowledge of the band.

"Basketball is my favorite sport, too. We'll have to shoot together sometime." That was all John would say about his illustrious career.

"How tall are you?" Jamie asked.

"Last time I checked I was around six foot five inches."

Some of the youth looked at one another in astonishment. Things got quiet again. Everyone waited.

"We still have a few more to go," John said.

No movement. The three remaining boys sat stone faced and still. Two, three, five, then ten minutes passed. John began short conversations with the girls and Robert about things like the food, weather, and culture in Venezuela. They all gathered closer and chatted with him. Mike Littleton wanted to join in the conversations, but he was stuck.

The three boys continued to just sit still.

"How long are we going to sit here?" Tommy whispered.

"Just shut up. We'll stay all night if we have to." Brad whispered back.

Taylor didn't say anything, but he was thinking. He knew his mother would be calling them for dinner any moment. They were supposed to have finished quickly and then gone home. Now she would probably come to get them and once she did, John would tell her what was going on and they would get it good. But he had to stand firm. He kind of wanted a confrontation with his mom anyway. Then he'd have the chance to tell her how wrong this was. Besides, his dad wouldn't be getting home until the next afternoon, so he'd have enough time to butter her up again before then.

John was just about to let the rest of the youth go while he stayed behind with his three little rebels, when the door opened and Maggie walked in.

"You guys hungry or what? Dinner's getting cold. The rest of you need to get home. Your parents have called me wondering where you are. I take it you're still getting to know each other." She smiled at the children and then looked at John. So did everyone else. They all held their breath, even Taylor, who knew what was coming.

"Yep," John replied, smiling back. "Just been chatting with my new friends here. They've been filling me in on how to survive in Jajo."

Tommy let out a sigh of relief. Brad looked even angrier and Taylor didn't change his blank expression in the slightest. The girls all smiled and Susan shook her head looking in the boys' direction, thinking how lucky they were.

"Well," Maggie continued, "if anybody knows how to survive this place, it's these kids. They'll show you around."

"I hope so," John said, followed with "Let's eat!"

Robert and the girls stood up and raced out the door, causing Maggie to move quickly, shrieking as she did so. Next, Mike Littleton made a quick escape. Maggie and John followed behind. Tommy, Brad, and Taylor eventually exited the Rec in silence. Tommy and Brad walked off in the direction of their homes without saying a word. The girls said goodbye to John, offering to take him to town the next day if he wanted. He took them up on their offer. John, Maggie, and Robert walked the trail toward the Steven's home. Taylor followed far behind. He could hear them laughing. John was supposed to be miserable at this point, not himself. He watched John put Robert up on his shoulders to the thrill of his little brother. It was going to be a long night. This tough guy act was tiring him out.

25 THE WALK

The next morning John woke to the sound of knocking on his door. He looked at his watch. It was 10:30 a.m. He had been up late unpacking things and getting situated. Although there really wasn't much to do but just decide how to hang up his clothes and where to put his few books and pictures. The place was fully furnished, complete with all the pots, pans, plates, cups, and silverware he could possibly need. The bathroom had matching towels, washcloths, a rug, and curtains and the cabinets were already stocked with the basic essential toiletries. The condo had a master bedroom downstairs with a full sized bathroom, a full sized kitchen, and living room with a sofa, love seat, small coffee table, large screen TV and VHS player, as well as a large CD stereo system. A sliding glass door and large windows surrounded the living room allowing for an excellent outside view. Upstairs was another room and smaller bathroom. John decided he would use this as a study and exercise room, if only just to have a reason to move things around and do something himself.

* * *

Stumbling out of bed, John forgot for a moment where he was and walked into the closet instead of the bathroom. Someone knocked at the door again. He quickly put on sweatpants and a t- shirt and walked the hallway to the front door. He opened it to find Maggie standing with her hands resting on the shoulders of a short, smiling Venezuelan woman in front of her.

"Good morning, John. Hope we didn't wake you."

"No," John said, running his hands through his uncombed hair, "Well kind of, but I'm glad you did. I might have slept through the day."

"Well, you're free to do so if you want. I know it will take a few days to get your energy up to par so just relax and take your time."

"Thanks."

"John, this is Rosarita."

"So *this* is the famous Rosarita," John said, referring to the excellent dinner he had eaten the night before that had been prepared by her. She had already gone home before they finished the meeting. She looked at Maggie, then back at John, smiling and nodding her head.

"Nice to meet you," John said, smiling and extending his hand, wondering if she could understand him.

She smiled back, her white teeth glowing against her dark skin, and took his large hand in her tiny one.

"Hola, señor Juan. Mucho gusto en conocerle," she answered back, wondering the same thing.

Both continued smiling.

"Rosarita does everything." Maggie began, "The washing, cleaning, and the cooking. She'll come by here once a week and clean up your place as well as pick up your dirty clothes to wash and dry. Most likely it will be on Saturdays. She has a key so don't worry about letting her in. She'll vacuum, dust, and clean your bathroom. But as you can probably tell, she doesn't speak any English."

John and Rosarita continued to smile and nod their heads at one another. John was feeling more and more useless every minute.

"You know, Maggie, it's really not necessary. I can take care of this place."

"John, don't worry about it. Rosarita loves her work. It makes her proud to earn her paycheck and support her family. If we told her not to clean she wouldn't understand."

John wanted to say that it would make him proud to earn a little too, but one more look at the smiling, little old lady beneath him, and he decided to hold his tongue.

"Okay," John replied then added, "Thank you, gracias," and shook Rosarita's tiny hands again. She giggled and repeated the words to him.

"She'll start this Saturday."

"Great."

"Well, is everything satisfactory so far?"

"Maggie, come on, this is too much. I feel useless already. Which reminds me, would it be all right if I moved the desk upstairs and kind of rearranged the room into a study of some sort?"

"Anything you want John, this place is yours. Also just give me a list of things you want from town to eat and snack on. You can cook here or join us anytime at our place. Rosarita could even come here and cook for..."

"Maggie, that's okay. I'll come up to your place, but I'll also cook some things myself."

"Alright. Just give me a list of things you want Rosarita to get."

John said "Okay" but had already decided he could go to town himself and pick up whatever he needed.

The women said goodbye and after closing the door, John sat down on the sofa. John couldn't stop thinking about the life Maggie Stevens had created for herself and her family. He wondered if Richard would believe it or still recognize her. John had nothing against wealth, especially when a person works hard for it, as Maggie's husband probably did. But it was strange and a bit scary for him to see luxury replacing the menial tasks of daily life. He would just have to keep his place so clean that Rosarita could only look around before moving on to her next task.

John found milk and orange juice in the refrigerator along with bread for the toaster and cereal in the cupboard. He half expected someone to walk in any minute and say that he was in their home. Everything was too neat and tidy. He ate breakfast then read a few chapters in his Bible followed with a time of prayer. There was so much to think about, so many things to plan and get started with the kids. Ideas had begun rolling long before he left Tennessee, but now he needed to clarify and even get them down on paper. He decided that night he would rearrange the room upstairs and spend time doing just that. After showering, he went to Maggie's house and had a quick sandwich to eat, one that he made himself as Rosarita watched in horror, not believing her skills were being neglected right before her eyes. John could only laugh as she mumbled in her native tongue. He would have to tell Maggie to explain to Rosarita that he didn't mean to disrespect her, just take care of himself a little.

After lunch, the girls were waiting outside just as planned and they all headed for town with their new leader and friend. The kids were nearing the end of their summer vacation. There was only a week or two left before school would start up for them. School, meaning home-school lessons with the kids meeting in a different house each week under the direction of Mrs. Cook, a certified and experienced teacher. The other mothers took turns each week serving as her assistant. The girls said it was rather easy and they liked it all right. They would often go on field trips and visit museums and other historical landmarks.

That would be a fun job, John thought sarcastically to himself, feeling pity for Mrs. Cook. He hoped he would never be asked to fill in as a substitute teacher for the day!

* * *

Jajo sat at the bottom of the mountain on which the American families lived. It took them all of one and half hours to reach the town by walking the road. The girls promised to show him a shortcut on the way back, a trail through the woods that took around 45 minutes. As they approached from the high road above, John could see all of Jajo spread out before him. The large town resembled a spider web with tons of paved and dirt roads running in circles and intersecting with a handful of larger roads leading inward towards the middle. Beginning at the edge of the mountainside woods, these roads were lined with one and two story brown and white adobe brick homes. About a mile away from the the center of town, all the homes were replaced by hundreds of shops and booths belonging to the day and night markets. The main roads finally converged at the expansive and captivating Plaza Bolivar.

Their descent complete, the girls proceeded to show John the town from top to bottom, leaving nothing uncovered. Everywhere they went, local eyes quickly focused on this new giant foreigner in their midst. The girls giggled and laughed, full of pride as if showing off their new boyfriend. John just smiled and said "Hola" over a thousand times. Children gathered around him and he played with them, made faces, and even chased a few which sent running, screaming, and laughing all at the same time. He spent almost an hour at the park alone meeting new people and playing with kids. Before long, he was worn out. A few stares held mistrust and fear, but most sensed his kindness and the mothers and fathers of the children he played with objected none at all to the entertainment he provided.

The girls introduced him to everyone they knew, but soon John was introducing them to new friends as well. They showed him the school, the police station and jail, the movie house and video store, and the supermarket – inside of which he discovered sandwich bread, peanut butter and jelly, Doritos, and even Pop Tarts, not to mention a few other American items. He loaded up and the supermarket owners, a short and jolly looking husband and wife pair, welcomed his business gladly. On their way home, the girls took John by the town's large sports park which had a soccer field, baseball field and four basketball courts. A lot of kids were kicking a soccer ball around and a few were throwing a baseball back and forth. Dozens of kids, teenagers and young men were playing on the basketball courts. When some of them noticed John walking by, they started to yell and point his way. Almost everyone stopped playing. Some of the older and obviously talented players stared at John with a look of defiance. One of them motioned for John to play, but he only smiled and shook his head. As if not understanding, the guy continued to beckon him over. Finally John spoke over his shoulder, "Not today, next time." Another guy just waved him off, while the first one mumbled something that caused the rest to start laughing.

"I think he called you a chicken," Susan informed him.

"Really?" John asked, trying to sound surprised.

"My dad said you're a basketball player. Is that why you're so tall?" Jamie Childress asked.

"Well, Jamie, I don't know if playing basketball made me tall, or if it's the other way around."

The older girls laughed and Jamie turned red, then mumbled, "Oh yeah."

"But yeah, I grew a lot in high school and that's when I started playing ball a lot."

"Are you good?" Robyn asked

"Depends on who you ask." Which was the truth since most of the players on their arch rival team from Tennessee Sate just considered him lucky. "My mom thinks I'm pretty good," he said smiling.

"That really tells us a lot," Susan replied sarcastically.

"Are you gonna go back and show those guys how to play?" Stephanie chimed in.

"Only if you promise to cheer for me and you can't stop even if I'm losing."

"It's a deal!" she said. By this point all the girls were wondering if he was really any good. He didn't sound too convincing. They walked the trail home as evening came on the mountain. The girls, now completely comfortable with their new youth leader and not caring much for why he had come, just happy to have someone from the States to keep them company, began to share things from their heart that John never expected to hear so soon.

"John, you know we hate it here? And I mean really hate it…all of us do. All we do is beg our parents to move back to the States."

"Really?" John asked.

They all nodded their heads in agreement.

"You mean you didn't know?" Robyn asked.

"No, not really. I mean I knew that you probably missed the States and your friends and...yeah I can see why you might hate it here."

"It sucks," Susan began. "All we do is live in this tiny miniature American neighborhood away from everything, it's so boring. Our parents know it too. That's why they brought you over I guess, to keep our minds off of it. We didn't even know you were coming until the day before you got here."

"You're kidding?" John asked, genuinely surprised by the revelation.

"Nope," she answered, "but we knew something was up for a couple of weeks, cause our parents started meeting together a lot. Something they hadn't done in a while."

"Some of us thought they were about to let us go back to the States," Stephanie said. "Especially Taylor, he was sure of it. Then they let us know you were coming and Taylor was so mad."

John was beginning to understand more and more, but not wanting to sound too inquisitive or worried, he continued with a new question.

"So what would you be doing if you were in America?"

"I'd be hanging out with friends, shopping, going to movies and out to eat..."

"I'd be going to the lake and swimming and skiing."

"I'd be riding horses."

Well that question didn't work, John mused. He had expected to point out that their lives weren't really all that different here in Jajo. He was reminded again that these kids had pretty lavish lives back in the States.

"Yeah, I see what you mean, but…"

"There's always a but," Susan interrupted and as soon as the words were out of her mouth, they all started giggling.

John didn't understand why until he responded with, "Of course there's always a but." Which caused them all to break into hysterical laughter and John, with red cheeks, joined them. Teenagers!

"Okay, let me say it this way...theirs always a choice. Situations are rarely going to be exactly what you want. That's part of life, right?"

No one answered.

"Think about all the kids we saw today. Have any of you ever been inside one of their homes?"

"I have," Stephanie said.

"What was it like?"

"It was pretty small and there was only one big bed and my friend told me they all sleep on it together. And there were no toys or video games...she didn't even have a TV."

"Has your friend ever been to your house Stephanie?"

"No, our parents don't really want us bringing our local friends home." It was hard not to notice how prejudice her response sounded. John wondered if any of the older girls recognized it as well.

"Well, if you could bring your friend to your house, what do you think her response would be?"

Stephanie didn't respond. Susan answered instead. "Our Venezuelan friends would be speechless. They wouldn't believe how big our houses are and how much stuff we have."

The conversation was turning pretty serious and John was happy to let it play out.

"Now, did any of the local kids here have any choice in where and to whom they were born?"

"Nope."

"No."

"No one does."

"Exactly. No one has control over where they are born or who their parents are. Only God does. Every person on earth has to deal with the circumstances they are born into. Comparing your circumstances with those of the locals, do you think you should complain?"

It was a hard and slightly offensive question to ask these wealthy young girls, but John wanted to know who might already be sensitive to Christ's call of putting others' needs before their own.

This time no one said anything. It took a full minute before Susan responded. "But it's not our fault they were born poor and we were born rich."

"You're exactly right Susan. But I'm not talking about them right now. If you compare your life to theirs, do you think you have a right to complain?"

"No." All the other girls shook their heads in agreement.

John had their full attention. He knew the real answer to their problem was getting them to stop focusing on themselves. All he could think about while walking through the town and in the parks seeing all those people, was how much of a difference these kids could make if they could just start to care. If they could let God use them to love others. That was the vision he had: his kids serving and ministering to the people of Jajo. He didn't know how it would happen, but he was going to pray and leave the rest up to God.

26 THE SHOCK

John wasn't finished yet. "Girls, do you ever think about the people in Jajo needing to know about Jesus and God's love?"

"A lot of them know about Jesus, I think," Stephanie answered.

Susan elaborated. "There was a priest here for a long time and he had a church and I think a lot of people went, but now he's gone."

"Well," John wanted them to think a little bit harder on his question, "do you ever think God would want *you* to tell people about Jesus?"

"How could we do that? We can barely have conversations with them," Robyn answered. She still saw little point in learning a language that she'd never use with her friends back in the States.

"I don't think our parents would want us going to town and doing that," Jamie added.

John didn't want to push it right then, but that wouldn't be the last they'd hear him talk about sharing the good news.

"Well, here's the last thing I'll say about it. I think God has you here for a reason. Actually, I know He does, because everything God does is for a reason. Just like I'm here for a reason too."

"Yeah, Robert prayed you over," Stephanie said smiling.

"Right!" John said and they all laughed again, "God wants to use you wherever you are."

The girls were all quiet. John wondered if they had ever heard that before. He imagined they were wondering what in the world he was talking about. *One step at a time,* John reminded himself as they walked up the last hill behind his condo, stopping at the tall iron fence.

"Um, shouldn't we be going through the front gate?" He asked, looking around at all their smiling faces.

"Watch and learn big guy." Susan lifted up on her tiptoes, placed her fingers on the top edge of the fence and pulled herself up. She threw one leg over and then the other. She paused, sitting on the top edge, looked back at the others and said "Adiós, amigos!"

John heard her land on the other side with a thud. He was impressed and certain that no one else could pull off the same maneuver. To his surprise, one after the other, all the girls scaled the fence. Jamie got a boost from her big sister.

"Okay, so you girls have had a lot of practice! I'm not so sure about this!"

"Come on! You're tall enough to step over this thing!" Robyn taunted.

"I heard this thing can give you a shock."

"A big one, but it's always turned off until six o'clock," Stephanie answered.

Jamie quickly piped in, "Because her brother got fried so many times trying to go over it!" The girls laughed, even Stephanie, whom John was realizing wasn't so fond of her brother.

John handed the bags of food over the fence to the girls and placed his hands on the top edge. He jumped and pulled himself up, and his knees banged against the side of the fence like a gong. He got one leg over and then the other and sat on the top edge.

"See John." Jamie exclaimed. "Piece of cake!"

John was just about to launch himself off when a sudden bolt of heat ripped through his buttocks and hands. His palms felt as if they were on fire. A white-hot vibration shot through his arms and legs, jolting his body, but also paralyzing it. He shouted and fell from the top edge, landing with a crash on the ground below. The girls laughed, thinking that he was only playing, but as he continued to lie still, panting heavily, they began to wonder whether it was a joke or not. Walking closer and seeing dark red marks on the palms of his hands confirmed otherwise.

"Are you okay?" Stephanie asked, quickly sitting down and taking his hands in her own.

Jamie was beside her. Susan and Robyn ran off in the direction of the guardhouse, cursing as they went. They both had the same thought running through their minds. At the guardhouse, they found Fernando asleep in his chair as usual. Behind him on the opposite wall, the switch to the electric fence was turned on.

"Fernando! Wake up!" Susan yelled, tapping him on the shoulder

"Oh! Yes! Yes! ¡Por favor! Que paso, miss Susan?!"

"Fernando, did you see anyone or hear anyone around here a few minutes ago?"

"No, there was nobody! I promise, I see and hear no one. I sure."

"Then why is the electricity turned on Fernando? It's not 6:00 yet?"

Fernando stared at the switch on the wall and then looked at the two girls. "No lo sé. I don't turn it on."

"Susan, come here." The tone of Robyn's voice hinted to some discovery. Susan walked outside and stood beside Robyn who was pointing at the ground. "Look."

There were footprints in the dirt. They counted four sets.

* * *

Susan and Robyn found the other girls with John back at his condo. He was sitting on the couch with bags of ice in his hands and they were all laughing.

"What's so funny?" Robyn asked as they sat down.

"I'm just trying to imagine what I looked like flying through the air like a rag doll. If my friends had seen that!" John laughed out loud again. None of the girls could believe he was in such a good mood after what had just happened.

John's initial embarrassment was gone. "Where's a video camera when you need one. I'm definitely winning $10,000 on 'America's Funniest Home Video' with that one."

"Yeah, but they always choose the dumbest one to win," Jamie added.

"Believe me," he replied, "that would be the dumbest one."

"John," Susan said, her expression very serious, "that was pretty dangerous and I'm afraid it wasn't an accident."

John didn't wait for her explanation. "Susan, don't worry, I know the boys did it."

She looked at Robyn then back at John.

"Surprised? Believe me, there is nothing these guys can pull on me that I haven't done before. You know, one summer at camp we put dog poop in our counselor's shoes, the ones he always wore with no socks on. I'll never forget watching his face as he slipped his feet into those. We ran out of our cabin before he even stood up because of the look of pure rage that came over him. But he had the last laugh, and you know why?"

They all shook their heads.

"Because he never chased us. He never even came out of the cabin. So we were too scared to go back. We slept out in the woods that night, with no pillows, no sleeping bags, and in our clothes. Mosquitoes and ants tore us up, strange noises kept us awake, and it was the longest and worst night of our lives. The next day the whole camp was waiting for us in the cafeteria and they all laughed at us. We looked, smelled, and felt like dog crap.

Anyway, there is this saying that 'what goes around comes around'."

"You're not even angry?" Stephanie asked.

"Well, I could get angry and stay angry, but what good is that going to do me? It feels better to laugh about it instead."

"But they need to pay for what they did," Robin demanded.

"Yeah, Tommy will get his butt whooped after we tell Mom and Dad, right, Sis?" Jamie looked up at her sister.

"How about we don't rat out the boys just yet, okay?" John looked all of them in the eye. They didn't appear persuaded. "Don't worry girls, I have a plan. Remember, what comes around goes around. They'll be expecting something so let them suffer in anxiety for awhile. The longer I wait, the more nervous they're going to get."

The girls smiled with understanding and then continued to whisper and giggle as they said goodbye and went home. None of them could wait to see what John had in store.

* * *

John sat on his couch wondering what in the world he was going to do. For now he had to keep the girls quiet and patient. He didn't want them telling their parents. Honestly, he was more worried about looking like a wimp and failure than anything else. How could he get those boys to like him and teach them a lesson at the same time? He wanted to email his folks, knowing they'd have the perfect parental advice, but this was something he had to do alone. He had to show these boys who was boss, but at the same time not ruin all chances of being their friend. At least after his conversation with the girls he had a better idea of what all the rebellion was about. His coming had been a surprise to all the kids. He couldn't believe their parents hadn't told them. Actually he could believe it. The parents had only wanted to avoid upsetting their kids and now he was left to deal with it. *So they all hate Venezuela and want to go home, but instead of getting America…they get me.* He stared at his hands and sank back into the sofa. He was suddenly glad for his comfortable apartment. Maggie was right, he was earning it.

27 THE PARENTS

At 7:30 p.m. John walked the black top road to the third and largest house in the neighborhood. The Rollins estate consisted of two stories as well as a basement bar and game room. A tennis and basketball court sat on either side with a par three, 120-yard, golf hole with a full-sized green in the back.

Brad sure has it tough, John thought as he knocked on the door.

Mrs. Rollins had made sure the welcome party was held at her place. She didn't have many chances to show it off anymore. Mr. Rollins was away on business, something he conveniently kept up almost year round, excluding Christmas and a few other holidays. It was widely known that the marriage was over and that Mr. Rollins had taken up permanent residence in their villa in Spain. Rumors of mistresses had been swirling for years. Mrs. Rollins however, had nothing in the States to return to except haunting memories of the life of poverty and misery she had escaped from. She had been a young cocktail waitress in Reno when she discovered her supposed gold mine romance. Now all the money in the world couldn't buy her the one thing she longed for – love from her husband. She also knew that the others were aware of her predicament and for this she resented everybody and everything, even her kids. She was the last one to see any point in bringing John over, even though it was her son who was having the most problems and worrying everyone else. In America, the other parents would have made sure their own kids didn't hang out with someone like Brad, but here that was impossible. Mrs. Rollins hated to admit he was a problem child, but given the circumstances, she had little choice.

Stephanie answered the door smiling.

"Hi John! Come in."

"Hey Stephanie." John walked in and immediately wrapped his hand around her tiny little outstretched one. "Are you going to give me the tour?"

"No, I think Mom wants to do that."

She led John through a hallway covered in portraits and then onto a spiraling, descending staircase, but halfway down Mrs. Rollins came running up, took John's arm in hers and proceeded to show him all around her house. Brad was sitting in the kitchen eating a sandwich at the counter.

He fidgeted nervously as John and his mother passed by. John smiled and said “Hello.” Stephanie, who was following behind, smiled at her brother as well, she couldn’t wait for what John had planned. Mrs. Rollins – Regina, as she asked John to call her – showed him every room in the house. As she talked and pointed, all John could think about was the excessive amount of make-up, perfume and hairspray she had used.

Twenty-five minutes later, John finally made it to the basement where all the parents were waiting. They took turns shaking John’s hand, introducing themselves, and reminding him exactly whose parents they were. John spent half an hour introducing himself, telling about his family and life as well as his future plans. Later the mothers asked questions and the men returned to their business discussions, feeling content with their brief but sincere interest in his presence. John asked to go to the bathroom, then snuck upstairs to escape the interrogation. He found Brad still sitting in the kitchen watching a small TV that sat on the counter. Brad didn’t look up as John opened the refrigerator. It was almost completely empty.

“Um Brad, did you just eat everything in here?”

No answer.

John walked over beside him, “Hey where did you get that sandwich? I can’t eat those strange vegetable kabob things downstairs.”

“Are you raggin’ on my mom’s cooking?” Brad’s voice matched his irritated expression.

John had to be careful with this kid, but he wasn’t backing off. “Where’s the sandwich stuff?”

“There is no stuff.”

“Look, I just saw you stuffing your face with a sandwich the size of a football and you’re gonna tell me that everything’s gone?” John opened the refrigerator again. Some cokes, a gallon of milk, and a few eggs were all that sat inside.

“Houdini, are you gonna help me eat or what?”

“Open the freezer,” Brad mumbled. John opened the door and as he did a pile of frozen boxes spilled onto the floor.

“Woah!” John yelled as Brad began to chuckle. John chuckled too and Brad immediately stopped. “Thanks for the warning.” John picked up the boxes and read each one before shoving it back into the freezer. He had never seen anything like it before. In front of him sat frozen boxes containing every food imaginable. From chicken legs to hamburgers, burritos to grill cheese sandwiches, submarine sandwiches to last but not least, vegetable kabobs. Mrs. Rollins obviously wasn't in the mood to cook these days. John didn't know if he should feel sorry for Brad or relieved. He placed the sandwich inside the microwave, set the appropriate time, and pushed start. "Well, this is definitely convenient."

"And safe," Brad mumbled.

He speaks! John whispered then turned to the young boy at the counter.

"Mom's cooking kind of scary, huh?"

"Just be glad those kabobs came from a box."

John sat down to eat and as he did, Brad stood up and walked away.

"Come over sometime and I'll whip up some spaghetti for ya."

Brad disappeared around the corner without responding.

Getting closer, John mused, smiling. He knew that the way to a growing boys' heart, just like a man's, was through his stomach.

28 THE CONNECTION

After eating, John went back downstairs to find all of the parents on their way out. They shook hands again and told him how glad they were he had come. They all invited him to come to their house to visit and eat any time. Maggie's husband, Paul, offered to walk John back to his place. John thanked Mrs. Rollins for her hospitality and wonderful kabobs and then said goodnight to Stephanie. Maggie stayed behind to help clean up.

The night was cool and beams from a full moon filtered down through the trees, glittering on the dark paved road.

Paul Stevens was only an inch or two shorter than John and though a little thinner, very chiseled and very fit. John could tell at once that he was an athletic person. Ruggedly handsome, he and Maggie made quite an attractive couple. Richard had left that part out. Perhaps there had been a little rivalry back in the day. John was sure Maggie could tell him all about it.

"Well John, I have to admit I did a little background check on ya."

"Is that right?" John replied, wondering where this was leading. "Hope you had a reliable source."

"Well, I don't know if the Lewisville Gazette is tabloid material, but thanks to the internet, I checked out your university's web page and came across some articles about the basketball team and last year's MVP John L. Parker. It seems you're quite the basketball star. All National team, leading scorer, second in assists and rebounds, quite impressive. I didn't know we'd have a star among us."

"In the flesh," John said sarcastically. He knew it would catch up with him sooner or later. "Actually my being here is part of an attempt to leave that status behind."

Paul was listening. Here was a young man who had sacrificed success for service. He'd been faced with that choice too before. "I don't know if I understand. Was it too much for you?"

"You know at first, that question, which I often asked myself, always ticked me off. I thought if I said "yes" then I was giving up. I was a quitter. But now I'm starting to see that, yeah, maybe it was too much for me. All I know is that the attention and the people who were putting me up on a pedestal fed my ego in ways that I hated. Somewhere I felt that John Parker the person got lost in the hype of John Parker the athlete. Whether it got too much or not I really don't know. I was willing to stay if I thought that's what God wanted, but He opened the door for me to come here and I chose to walk through it. Perhaps it's time I admit my weakness, to admit I needed to run away from it for awhile. Whatever I'm doing, it feels good and I know God's with me."

"I bet you made quite a few people upset."

"If you only knew." John said, smiling. "Check that website again and you'll probably find a few more articles about my "irresponsible and selfish" decision to leave. But it was good. All the stuff I went through back home only helped confirm I was doing the right thing. You know my mom even wrote the newspaper and blasted the town about people's obsession with sports. Things got pretty hot in little ol' Lewisville."

Paul laughed just thinking about John's mom taking all the people in the sports community to task.

"I'll have to let you read it sometime. I brought it with me of course – my mom's the celebrity now."

"I bet."

"So what about you? Did you play any sports? You seem to be in good shape."

"Well, I've always loved sports and I played just about everything growing up. I did the basketball and football thing in junior high, but from childhood all the way through college my whole world revolved around the baseball diamond. I played until my junior year at Birmingham Christian before giving it up to focus on my degree. I knew I really didn't have a chance to go to the Bigs…not quite enough speed on the bases."

John had enough friends on the baseball team at TCU to know that when draft time came, a tenth of a second could be the difference between going and staying.

"Any regrets for not trying?" John asked.

"No, no regrets there."

John wanted to ask "Honestly?" but held back. Instead he found a different question coming off his lips before he even knew it. It had been the one thing he'd wanted to ask Paul and Maggie ever since Richard had explained their situation to him. "Any regrets about coming here?"

They had reached John's front porch. Paul was quiet for a moment. "You know to be honest, I kind of had the opposite experience from you. I was never the best at anything really, just an average athlete and even student. You could count on me to be consistent perhaps, but never outstanding. I wanted more than anything to play pro ball, that was my lifelong dream and giving that up was hard, but once I did it, I put all of my focus into my career. When I graduated and started working, it seemed in business I could do nothing wrong. In fact, I quickly found myself climbing the corporate ladder. Though unexpected, it was exhilarating. I was having more than just average success. As a result, the money rolled in. In my mind I thought I was finally showing everyone – friends, family, and the world – that I had made it. Coming here was just another step, a big step in becoming independently powerful and more successful. That's why I came, to build my ego, not run from it. Now it doesn't satisfy me anymore. In fact, there is no business deal or money making venture that I can see ever satisfying me. It's an old game and you know what the funny thing is?"

"What?" John asked, completely absorbed in Paul's words.

"I do still miss the diamond." After finishing his sentence, Paul started to chuckle. "Sorry, I guess I lied a second ago. Truth be known, I have regrets."

John understood completely.

"In fact," Paul added, "I think I might give it all up to go back and just play minor league." He continued to chuckle, then quickly grew serious again. "But then there's the whole spiritual side to all of this. I don't even know where to begin with that. You know John, when Maggie and I graduated, we also had the chance to become missionaries."

Now we're getting to the good stuff, John thought then asked "Really?" as if hearing this for the first time.

"I became a Christian my Sophomore year in college after going to BCU strictly to play ball on a scholarship and then finding myself following this tall, gorgeous brunette student to chapel and every Bible study on campus. Of course, she wouldn't give me the time of day until I gave the Lord my life, but I honestly had no clue what it was all about. Then one night as I sat in my room reading a borrowed Bible, trying to understand why so many people wanted me to believe what it said and seemed to be so concerned for my soul, I came across Romans 5:8. God allowed me to understand, to see the truth, and I suddenly found myself face to face with my sin. Then and there God broke me, and I pleaded for His forgiveness and salvation and found it. That year was the hardest yet most thrilling of my life as relationships not pleasing to the Lord were torn away from me and I learned to stand firm in my new walk. Talk about persecution! Most of my ball buddies ridiculed me night and day. They all thought I was just trying to get Maggie. Well, I did, but not before getting Jesus first. When graduation time came, Maggie and I both thought about going to China. Can you believe that? Man, I can't imagine what our lives would be like…but I followed my professional aspirations instead and took a job offer and the rest, as they say, is history. The most tragic part is what I've put Maggie through. It's one thing for you to choose to run from the Lord, but it's even worse when you drag your wife with you. I know she wants to leave, John. I know Taylor hates it here and Robert, well, Robert is happy anywhere and with anyone."

John smiled, but felt Paul's pain.

"Well listen," Paul suddenly felt like he had talked too much and shared too much as well. "I'd better be getting back to the house."

John didn't really know what to say. He put his hand on Paul's shoulder.

"Paul, can I pray for you?"

Paul hesitated, wondering how in the world he had ended up in this awkward situation. He had only meant to walk this young guy home and make him feel welcome and now he was spilling his guts and receiving prayer. Paul thought about refusing but something inside him, long forgotten yet familiar, surrendered.

"Okay, sure John."

John closed his eyes and Paul followed. John's grip remained firmly in place. He would keep it short like his dad.

"Father God, I just want to begin by thanking you for the life you give. I thank you that in both of the lives represented here you brought salvation and change. God, whether it was yesterday or twenty years ago, it's just as much a reality today. Thank you that the salvation we have is everlasting and the changing is constant because You are never finished with us nor tired of us and it's never too late to know You more. Strengthen Paul with your might and fill him again with your peace. I know that both he and I are not here by accident or of our own accord, for You always have a purpose for our lives. Use us where we are, Lord. Thank you for a brother in Venezuela. Thank you for a friend."

After John said “amen”, Paul looked him straight in the eye. “Thank you.”

“No problem.” John slapped Paul’s shoulder then added, “I forgot all you baseball players slap each other on the rear end.”

“Don't even think about it.” They were laughing again as Paul shook John’s hand and said “Goodnight.”

* * *

Paul walked home feeling lighter, freer, yet a little strange. What was it? What had he just experienced that he had missed for so long? After getting home and checking on the boys asleep in their beds, Paul went upstairs and joined his wife in their bedroom.

“That was some walk home,” Maggie commented, looking up from the book she was reading in bed as Paul began to undress.

“Yeah, no kidding. You’ll never guess what just happened.”

“What?”

“John and I just prayed. Well, actually he prayed for us, I guess.”

“Really? That’s great.”

“Yeah, but,” he sat down on the bed with his T-shirt pulled halfway over his head. “It was so strange. I mean, I haven’t done that since...I can’t even remember.”

Maggie helped him finish pulling off his shirt. “Doesn't matter honey. All that matters is tonight you prayed with a friend.”

“And God reminded me of a lot of things.”

Maggie remained silent, but began to scratch his back. Paul looked back at her and recognized the look immediately: she wanted to know everything on his mind.

29 THE LESSON

John spent the next day walking around with the girls once again. From early morning until after dark, they showed him all the trails around their area and took him to a beautiful waterfall higher up in the mountains. Once again, the boys were nowhere to be seen. All along the trail John was anxious they would pull another trick on him, but he tried not to look it and the girls didn't notice.

After returning home, he ate a snack and then went to his room to read awhile and relax. While eating, he thought his kitchen smelled funny with a faint, rotten scent lingering in the air, but it was so faint that he ignored it for the time being. He showered then climbed in bed to read, but his eyes had plans of their own. He fell asleep after dropping his book a few times and didn't wake again until the next morning.

* * *

Even before opening his eyes, John knew something was wrong. His nostrils were burning. He suddenly sat up in his bed with his eyes blinking and quickly covered his nose and mouth with his hand. An extremely foul odor permeated every inch of his bedroom, smothering him. It was strong and putrid and a few times he almost gagged as he climbed out of bed and began searching through his place for the source of the smell. It was everywhere, but strongest in the kitchen, near the refrigerator. John searched through the appliance from top to bottom, emptying shelves and cleaning off racks, but he found nothing. He closed the door, perplexed and nauseous, and leaned against the counter top. A fly buzzed in front of him and John swatted it away. Then another fly and another followed in the same route, disappearing behind the refrigerator. John walked over to the wall and peered down into the shadows behind the refrigerators' backside. He saw something dark and bulky on the floor. John yanked the refrigerator away from the wall and out buzzed a swarm of flies. A brown paper bag lay silent and still. John reached down to open it as the smell of rotten flesh wafted into his nostrils and sent him stumbling backwards a few feet. Desperate to rid his home of the smell, he quickly bent over, grabbed the bag, ran out the front door and shook it with it's open side facing the ground. Immediately an object fell to the ground with a soft thud. John quickly tossed the bag and wiped his contaminated fingers on his boxers. He stared down at a dead, rotten squirrel, or what was left of one. One side of its body was missing; its innards were oozing out and maggots were feasting on the carcass. It didn't take long for John to put it all together. He wasn't sure how the boys had gotten into his condo, but guessed they probably had access to a key. It was time they had a talk.

* * *

On Wednesday night, when the youth were all supposed to come to the weekly meeting in the Rec, only the girls and Robert were there. For the first time John thought about going to Maggie and letting her know what was going on, but he didn't. Instead they sang some songs and talked about what it means to be a Christian and then briefly discussed some of John's plans for their group, but his heart and mind were hardly in it. Even Robert's smile brought little satisfaction.

That night, back at his place, after checking all his appliances for booby traps, John decided to remove his TV and put it in the upstairs closet. He then dedicated himself to praying for the group of kids until there was a breakthrough. Perhaps the TV removal was unnecessary, but desperate situations called for extreme measures. He prayed long and hard, day and night, but still no boys on Sunday or the next Wednesday. A set of drums were delivered the following week, thanks to the Littleton family who'd learned of John's playing ability and hoped their son Mike could learn from him. Only the girls and Robert were there to watch John set them up and perform a demonstration. John went from house to house informing all the boys of lessons he would be offering on Thursday nights. They all pretended to be interested while in the presence of their smiling parents, but come Thursday, once again only Robert and the girls were there. John also began to play basketball every afternoon next to the youth room drawing a crowd of spectators, all of them female, except for Robert. It was getting ridiculous. John couldn't believe how bad things were going, but they were soon to take a turn for the worse.

* * *

The girls – John's faithful friends to the end – continued to invite him for walks and visit his place daily. He was happy to spend time with them, as it was the only time he really felt needed. As they hung out more, the girls opened up more. Once John learned about Stephanie's philandering and absentee father, he went out of his way to shower the young girl with care and encouragement. She really loved to talk, more than the rest combined, and John was happy to listen and share thoughts and words of encouragement. But it was Susan who began to bring new worries for him. He couldn't help but notice the frequency of her visits to his place increasing. Visits she sometimes made alone. On top of that, it seemed that the outfits she wore, which consisted mainly of cut off jean shorts and tanks tops, were getting, if possible, even shorter and smaller. One day she left him a note saying the girls were all going to the waterfall with Robert and they wanted him to join them. Once there, he found Susan alone sitting on a rock. She said the others had gotten scared and left. John, knowing better, quickly headed back home saying he'd better make sure they made it all right. Susan followed behind, protesting his worries. He had a big problem on his hands. The next day Stephanie confirmed his fears by confessing Susan's secret crush. Later, on schedule, Susan showed up at his place alone and John, with no idea how to correctly handle the situation, told Susan directly that she shouldn't come to his place alone anymore. He assured her that he wanted to be her friend, her close and good friend, but nothing more. Embarrassed, ashamed, and angry with Stephanie for telling him – though John never mentioned her name – Susan ran away in tears. The following night only Robert showed up for their meeting. Susan had told all the girls that John had been rude to her so they were upset as well. Plus Susan and the other girls were angry at Stephanie for abusing their trust. Stephanie on the other hand was upset at John for obviously telling Susan she had told him. John was ready to throw in the towel.

When Robert alone walked through the Rec door that night, John didn't know if he should laugh or cry. For almost a month he had been fooling everyone – fooling the parents that he was having a successful start, fooling everyone back home with letters and emails that said the same thing, fooling himself that he could handle this. But he'd also been praying and he didn't understand why God wasn't answering. He showed Robert a few simple beats on the drums, then handed the sticks over to the small, eager boy and lifted him up onto his lap. John controlled the foot pedals while Robert proceeded to beat on every drum with every rhythmic style

John had ever heard. The little guy especially appreciated the thunderous crash of the cymbals and it didn't take him long to figure out the relationship between the force of his swing and the volume produced. John wished he'd brought his earplugs. At times however, it actually all came together and Robert would turn to look at John with a victorious smile on his face causing him to lose his place and begin striking the sides of the drum cases or even John's knee. In the end, the fun was worth all the pain. Later, John walked him home. At the door, Maggie asked him to come inside but he refused, saying he needed to get some things done. *More lying,* he said to himself. She asked how he was doing. "Fine," he answered. "Everything's fine." Dishonesty was eating at his soul. She asked how things were going with the kids. "Good. They're just running around somewhere." If she asked one more question he would collapse under the weight of guilt. *Please shut up, Maggie!* he begged in his mind. She finally said "Goodnight" and closed the door as he walked away with sweat trickling down his forehead.

He didn't want to go home. He returned instead to the youth room and with the lights off, took the drum sticks in his hands and released all his emotions onto the five piece set. Finally, after ten minutes of intense and exhaustive playing, one stick snapped on a rim shot, sending half of it flying across the room. He fell forward resting on the drums, soaked in sweat and panting. He suddenly missed chapel, missed basketball, and missed his friends and the fun and laughter they brought to his life. What was he doing? In just over four weeks time he had succeeded in getting everyone to hate him, except of course, Robert. *Hmmm.* Maybe he was only there for Robert. The little guy *was* the only one who'd actually asked God to send him over. John wanted to forget the rest of them, it would be their loss, not his. *God, why haven't you answered my prayers?!*

Just then he heard the door open and saw a shadow appear in the doorway. A voice filled the silence.

"John, is that you?" It was a boy's voice, but John hadn't talked to them in so long he couldn't recognize it.

"Yeah, it's me. Come in and turn on the light."

Light quickly filled the room and exposed the visitor. Mike Littleton, the one in whom John had at first seen signs of acceptance, was standing nervously just inside the door.

"Mike, it's good to see you. You know these drums your parents bought are really sweet."

"Really? They're really a good kind."

"Yeah, Tama is a great brand and these Ziljian cymbals are amazing."

John struck the crash cymbal and the explosive sound reverberated through the room.

"Come take a look."

Mike walked closer as John continued to talk. "I guess since your parents bought these, they're really yours. Man if you don't play these it's going to be the biggest waste I've ever seen. I would've loved to have a set like this when I first started."

"Really? I don't even know how to play at all."

"That's okay, everyone has to start somewhere. Even Larry Mullen Jr. had to pick up sticks for the first time." John hoped an allusion to Mike's favorite band, U2, would help. "The most important thing is to take a seat."

Opening a pack of new sticks, John once again, as he had done with Robert and the girls, showed Mike how to hold them, where to place his hands and feet and how to begin playing simple beats. Mike picked it up quickly, and John told him he was a natural, honestly meaning it. Mike was immediately excited. They played for almost an hour that night. John would show off a lick until Mike, fidgeting in anticipation and unable to wait another second, would finally shove John out of the seat so he could have a go at it. They worked on simple things like gripping the sticks and counting beats in your head. John smiled at Mike's frustration with his feet, remembering his own experience, and assured the boy it just took time. Mike smiled, and John began to see the easygoing manner and gentle spirit that the boy possessed. Mike was the kind of student teachers dream about. By the time they said goodbye, a bond, though small, had begun to form. As they walked away from each other, Mike stopped and called after John who turned to face him.

"John, I'm sorry for all the bad things we've been..."

"Mike, it's okay."

"But I want to say I'm sorry. Those guys told me not to talk to you, but I don't care. They don't really like me anyway."

"Well, I'm glad you talked to me. You know I've done so much with the girls; I've kind of missed hanging out with the guys. Hopefully the others will come around too."

"You know they just want you to go."

"Well, before I go we gotta get you jammin' on those drums, but that won't take too long."

Mike smiled, excited by John's compliment.

"Thanks John. Good night!" Mike ran home, jumping imaginary hurdles.

John watched him go.

"Good night Mike. Thanks. And thank You," he said, lifting his face to the sky.

30 THE CHANGE

The following week, school started and not surprisingly, John found himself filling a new job position: PE and exercise coach. He was actually glad to do it. Unlike their youth group Bible studies, which he had unintentionally given the kids the choice of attending, PE was mandatory. He would finally have all the kids together at once and all he had to do was play games and get them in shape. *How hard could it be?* That was the question on his mind when he told Maggie he'd do it. Now every afternoon at 1:30 they were his for an hour, but the new responsibility turned out to be another curse. No one participated except for Mike who was now ready and willing to show his support and of course there was always faithful Robert. The girls were still upset, something John couldn't fathom. And the boys, more determined than he had assumed, continued with their boycott of his leadership. Except now Taylor had a new irritation for John. The conniving teen decided to only speak to him in Spanish, something the other kids found quite amusing. John finally decided their liking him would have to be none of his concern. One afternoon as all the kids sat down in a muddled circle on the basketball court, John cracked down and cracked down hard.

"Alright, listen boys and girls. I'm tired of playing games with you all. It's time I got honest. If I hurt your feelings, I'm sorry, it's not like you've been too concerned with mine these last few weeks. At no time was it an easy decision for me to leave America to come and be with you all. I don't need to experience a new culture, I don't need your parents' money, I don't need a job, and I don't need any new friends or enemies for that matter."

The girls, Mike, and Robert had given him their full attention. The others pretended not to listen.

"Guys, look at me when I'm talking to you! You can pull your disrespectful crap on your other teachers and your parents, but not with me. Tommy, look at me when I talk to you!"

Tommy quickly looked up. Even his father had never yelled at him like that. And John was twice the size of his father.

"Taylor, are you scared of me?!"

"I'm not scared of you," Taylor mumbled to the grass.

"Then look at me, you big chicken!"

Taylor looked John directly in the eyes. John had everyone's participation except one.

"Brad, what's it going to take for you to listen to me?!"

"You can't make me do anything!" Brad yelled, continuing to avoid John's stare.

"I can make you get out of my sight. You have a choice. Either I escort you home and we sit down with your mom for a nice revealing chat or you can leave on your own. Either way, you're out of my class."

As John spoke, he walked towards Brad and never broke eye contract. When he came within a few feet, Brad stood up quickly, and backed away. The startled teenager looked around at the others, and then smiled.

"Fine. Thanks for the free pass." He trotted off into the woods and disappeared. Taylor and Tommy stood up and were about to follow.

"If you go, then both of your fathers and I will have a talk and we all know I have a lot of information to share. Now sit down!" he yelled. "You're all going to listen to what I have to say. This isn't a Wednesday night meeting that you can just skip out on if you want. Which, I might add, is over. From now on, if you don't show up, your parents will know about it." His free choice option was out the window. "If you don't come, I'll just lock the room up. I'm sure you'll love the chance to spend more time at home. Don't fool yourselves anymore. The Rec is mine now and I can do with it as I see fit." John took a deep breath and silently told himself to calm down. "You know it's sad it had to come to this. If you had just been cool and semi-polite people, we'd be having the time of our lives by now. But for some reason you've had to pull this macho baloney on me. Taylor, nothing you can ever do to me is going to make me leave, so just give it up. All you're going to do is make this 6 months of misery for us both and if that's what you want to do just because you're angry at me for coming to hang out with you, then you're more of a jerk than I thought. Understand something…even if I wasn't here, you still would be. You wouldn't be in America. I didn't make you come here, so quit blaming your unhappy lives on me. The reason I left all my friends and family and gave up school and basketball and my whole life to come and live with some spoiled rich kids in another country was because I hoped I could make your lives a little more interesting and fun. It's the best I can do. But Taylor..."

John hesitated, letting his gaze penetrate even deeper. He had realized early on Taylor was the rock that had to be broken and so most of everything he was saying was directed to him and everyone knew it. Tommy scooted a little farther away from his brave leader.

"God brought me here and He, only He, can get me to leave, do you understand?" John didn't give him time to respond, but turned his attention to the others, "And girls, you've got to just let everything go. If you want to stay mad at me and each other forever, then I can't stop you, but it will be a waste of time, I promise. All I want is for us to hang out again and talk like we used to. I've missed you all."

John noticed Robyn put her arms around her sister Jamie and console her as if she was crying.

Oh great, John thought, *now you've really done it.*

Then Susan stood up and walked over to Stephanie and they hugged and began to cry and apologize to one another. Soon all the girls were in a big huddle talking and crying, laughing and consoling.

The scene reminded John of the Christian teen camps he had attended, where the annual forgiveness sermon always resulted in a mass of wailing adolescent girls and a few tear-streaked boys, but mostly a bunch of confused ones. Soon the huddle made its way over to John. Susan stepped forward.

"John…I'm sorry for the way…I started acting." Her cheeks were flushed and John sensed her nervousness. She was still embarrassed about the whole episode. John wanted her to know it was okay.

"Susan, I'm sorry you felt hurt by what I said, but I never wanted you to stop being my friend." Susan walked over to John and hugged him, the other girls followed.

Now it was Stephanie's turn, "John, I'm sorry for thinking you told on me, even though I'm the one who told you Susan's secret."

"Stephanie, I've missed talking with you. How about no more secrets from now on?" John looked at all of the girls. "Deal?"

"Deal!" they all answered.

"Group Hug!" John yelled and they all squeezed together tightly. Mike and Robert attached themselves to the outside. Taylor and Tommy remained sitting on the ground, too cool to join in. After the last person returned to their seat on the pavement, John continued.

"Don't think you're going to get off this easy. Everybody on your feet! Now!"

They all jumped up. In perfect Coach McKenrick form, John started them running and didn't let them stop until the end of the class. He warned they would repeat this activity everyday until they all began participating in his games and exercises. They continuously promised to do so, but he pretended not to hear them. Brad watched and laughed mockingly from the nearby woods.

31 THE MESSAGE

John walked up the hill to the Steven's house for his weekly email check. He was just over two months into his stay and already this ritual was the highlight of his week. He unlocked the Steven's front door with the extra key they had lent him. He entered, climbed the spiral staircase, and walked into Paul's study where he quickly took a seat at the computer. There was a note on the monitor screen that read "Be back in a while. Help yourself to the fridge - easy on the fingers tonight! Maggie" He removed the note and turned on the computer. As it warmed up he went back downstairs and took a Coke and a few Snickers from the refrigerator. He paused with the door open, debating whether or not to stay and make a sandwich and pig out on all the goodies they had, but he was in a hurry to get started. Soon he was sitting in front of the computer with his shoes off. As usual, he planned on being there for a while. Finally he could write home about some honest success he was experiencing. He had decided it was time for him to come clean with everyone and just admit he *really* needed their prayers.

Perhaps a prayer chain could help Brad, he thought as the Yahoo Mail homepage uploaded before his eyes. He typed in his user name and password, hit "enter", and waited…slightly holding his breath.

Spiritually, things were up and down. John knew he needed a charge, but was unaware of the fact that time spent doing things like writing on the computer and even hanging out with the kids was replacing his time with the Lord and the reason for the spiritual roller-coaster ride he was on. He was too absorbed in his activities and neglecting the relationship that mattered most. At that moment, only one relationship seemed to matter. The screen lit up and at the top it read "New Messages." John clicked the mouse and a list of names appeared, but one caught his attention before any other…the name of the one person he was coming to miss most, whose messages sometimes tempted him to take the next plane home just to see her face. Their time together had been short, and their goodbye borderline plutonic, the thought of which made John smile to himself. How in control of his heart he had been at that time! Now he was turning into a sick puppy. His eyes glowed as they scanned over the contents of the message. His stomach slowly turned to knots.

* * *

John, Hey there big boy! How's your week going? You whipped those kids into shape yet? Tell your little friend Wobert "hello" for me. You go easy on them! Remember this isn't Coach McKenrick's basketball camp! John...I want to tell you something and it's not going to be easy for me...I wish we could be face to face and walk and talk around here the way we used to at night. John, I was up very late last night, doing a lot of thinking – about my life, what God has planned for me, for you, for us both. All I could think of was…I DON'T KNOW and that's what has me troubled – because I can't see where this, where we, are going. I don't have a peace. John, my feelings for you are real and I miss you very much, perhaps too much. I don't want to feel this way for another 4 months, this sense of longing for something that I can't have right now. I think we should define our relationship as one of only friendship until further notice, notice based on time spent together. It's got to be this way for me...I'll keep in touch, but probably slack off on the emails for a while. Please don't take your friendship away. Your friend and sister in Jesus. Rachel

* * *

Your friend and sister in Jesus…friend and sister?! John sat and stared at that last line, trying to make sense of those final six words. Of course, Rachel's meaning was crystal clear, but John didn't want to admit it.

"Really Lord?" John asked the emptiness around him. He turned off the computer and just sat for a moment in the dark. He definitely had not seen that coming. He wanted to go back and read her previous message again, but he didn't need to because he had basically memorized it. "I miss you dearly…I miss our walks and praying together….I can't wait for you to come back." Apparently she meant that last line literally. She didn't want to wait. John's heart was aching now. Just minutes before he could have sworn he was falling in love. At least one area of his life was headed in a direction he could clearly see and now…it was over.

Could he just be Rachel's friend? Their relationship hadn't even gone to the next level yet. At least not in practice, but his heart had definitely crossed a line. Could he go back to the way it was when they first met? What had really changed since then anyway? They had never said they loved each other, they had never promised one another anything, so why this pain!?

Because you got dumped! He heard a voice inside him scream. *By an underclassmen and everyone at school's gonna hear about it!* That complaint just made him even more frustrated. Now he was sounding like a middle schooler.

"This is ridiculous!" he said, standing up from his chair. He had to go somewhere. He had to get out of the house, to go do something, anything. As he left the Stevens' house, he thought about playing the drums. That was always a good release. *Too close to here,* he decided. He passed by the Rec and then the other houses and finally arrived at the gate. He waited as Diego pushed the button that automatically caused the massive wall of ornate iron to swing open. Diego waved and said something to John through the security room window, but John ignored him and struck out immediately towards the one place he was certain there would be *something* going on: something to get his mind off her.

All down the trail every step jolted his frame. He wasn't walking, but stomping. Cool breezes pushed him along, but he felt extremely hot. He wasn't so much angry as he was disgusted with his heart for having fallen so quickly.

"Why did you have to go and fall so hard!" he said out loud as the sky in front of him began to brighten from the town lights below. He concluded that it wouldn't do any good to write her back about it. What would he say? He definitely wasn't going to beg her to wait for him to come back. Wow! He was sounding like his friends that he had laughed at after they got dumped and moped around their dorm rooms feeling sorry for themselves. Good thing they couldn't see him now! But they'd know soon enough...probably already did. He walked on, accompanied by a chorus of self-pity.

* * *

John abandoned his usual habit of taking his burdens immediately and desperately to the Lord. Not that the idea to pray never crossed his mind, but he ignored it and instead gave his bitterness full reign. Besides, praying about this, meant admitting it was a problem, that it bothered him. His pride wouldn't allow *her* the satisfaction. Rejection could be rejected too!

32 THE CLUB

If John *had* prayed that night instead of charging off with his pride leading the way, he would've probably never left Paul's study. He definitely would have gone to town under better control of his emotions. For certain, he would never have found himself standing outside the front door of Mr. Logan's Gentleman's Club.

He had walked through the square chatting with familiar faces and playing with the kids he saw. He had bought some fried snacks from a vender then washed them down with a Coke. Eventually he had found himself mingling with some older teenagers at the basketball courts, trying to be funny and though he didn't notice it, cool. He was trying to impress. He had seen a few beautiful faces, some of whose eyes had met his.

I could have any girl here, he thought to himself.

The rain of rejection was flooding the pride of his heart, causing the currents of the once small stream to overflow their banks and rush ahead out of control.

I'll show Rachel.

It was just as this thought came to him and he turned the corner on one of the last dirt roads, that his eyes noticed the flickering neon sign at the end of the street: LOGAN'S "Más Finas Del Mundo (The Finest In The World)". Immediately John grew hot. He watched a few men stumble, obviously drunk, up the front steps and into the club, as a few stumbled out laughing and swearing.

Probably all married, he speculated.

He wanted to burn the building down. He reached for his wallet, pulled out the business card Mr. Logan had given him and scanned the bottom. "The *Finest* in the World". So this was the place. John felt a righteous indignation welling up within him. Frank Logan needed to be confronted with the truth and called out for his evil ways and John was the messenger God was sending to do it. He would walk right into Mr. Logan's office and speak words of condemnation and warning to the owner's face causing him to fall on the ground right then and there in repentance and find salvation. Then the spiritually newborn Texan would close down his business, the city would be cleansed, the girls would be saved, men would be kept from sin, and families would be healed all because of John. And of course Rachel would somehow hear about it.

His pride was an ocean now.

So what are you going do? The hero in him asked, just as a large hand fell on his shoulder and a voice shattered the silence.

"Well, I'll be damned!"

"Speak of the devil," John mumbled, immediately recognizing the only possible owner of the thick Texan accent. John turned, smiling, and took Mr. Logan's extended hand in his own, squeezing long and hard.

"Mr. Logan, what a surprise."

"I'll say! John, right? John Parker?" John nodded his head.

"I was just on my way to my club. Come and join me in my office and let's have a chat. I want to hear how your work is going with the kids."

Yeah right, John thought. He knew the last thing Mr. Logan cared about was his ministry, but he was about to let the godless man know all about it. Feeling too cocky to consider the costs and with visions of John Parker Crusades still in his mind, John agreed.

* * *

"Quite a place you've got here," John said as they neared the front steps, hoping Mr. Logan noticed the sarcasm in his tone. Worried that he didn't, he quickly added, "Could use a new paint job don't ya think?

"It's the beauty on the inside that counts, my friend," Mr. Logan said smiling.

John tried to think of something smart to say in response, but nothing came. He hated getting one-upped by this cocky pervert. Mr. Logan opened the front door and the two stepped through into a small dark lobby filled with smoke, loud outdated disco music, and the stench of cigars and cheap beer. Colored flashing lights reflected off the wooden plank floor beneath two saloon-style swinging doors. A large, husky man with more hair on his face and arms than his head, nodded to Mr. Logan and then stood toe to toe and eye to eye with John. One eye was covered with a black patch, and John had the impression that he had finally met a real life pirate. He glanced down at the hands to see if there was a hook.

"Hola," John said smiling. No smile or even nod was returned. John noticed the large knife the man, or beast, had strapped to his hip.

"John, this is Rico. He's my security man. Sometimes things get out of hand around here. He's quick to solve the problem. He's a little on the unfriendly side, but you get used to it. Rico, John and I will be going up to my office. Have Lenora bring us some drinks."

"Coke for me," John said quickly.

"Make that two," Mr. Logan added, chuckling, then led the way through the swinging doors and into a large room filled for the most part with empty tables and seats. About five men in all could be seen sitting close to a small stage, yelling and whistling at a full figured half dressed woman, trying her best to move seductively to a fast disco beat.

"A little slow today huh?"

"Things pick up around 10:00 o'clock when my best dancers take the stage. I've got three stages and all of them are occupied and surrounded by 11:00."

John actually found his head nodding in understanding. *Great John. Now you're talking business with a pimp. Where's the fire and brimstone? Get to God. Get to Jesus.*

They walked along the bar counter. The bartenders greeted their boss as they passed. A small older man with a mop approached Mr. Logan talking to him quickly in Spanish. Mr. Logan responded back fluently.

He's got me beat there, John thought.

Mr. Logan turned from the small man. "John, I'll be right back. Got a little problem with the plumbing, always a little problem first, then a disaster if not taken care of. Just wait here." Before John could say a word he was left standing all alone. He tried his hardest to avoid looking toward the stage across the room. He turned and pretended to be interested in some pictures of supposedly famous people who had visited Mr. Logan's club and had their photo taken with him. He studied the wood floors, furnishings, ceilings, and the architecture of the room, but eventually his gaze returned to her. He looked at her face and her eyes. Behind the tired smile that she wore like a mask, he could see she was..."full of hurt, and empty of hope." John suddenly remembered the words of the chapel speaker. Words that had challenged John and changed him and brought him here.

* * *

He walked quickly up to the front, shoving patrons out of his way. He leaped up onto the stage, took his jacket off, and wrapped it around the naked chest of the dancer. Then he grabbed her hand and led her off the platform to the screaming and cursing of all the men. One charged at him and he quickly kicked a chair in the man's way causing him to trip over it and fall on his face. "I'm going to get you out of here!" John said to the woman who clung to his arms, not resisting the rescue. Rico suddenly filled the doorway, his broad shoulders rubbing both sides of the frame, the only obstacle between them and freedom. Rico's hand was on his knife. The bouncer pointed back to the stage and spoke sternly to the woman in Spanish. John let the Spirit speak. "Rico, God will not stand for this, this is wrong." Perfect Spanish rolled from John's tongue to the amazement of everyone. "Let us go, Rico. God loves you. Give him your life." Rico's hand dropped slowly from beside his knife and he stepped away from the revolving doors. John and the dancer were on their way out. God had saved them...

"John! John!" The vision dissipated like a mist over his eyes and John found himself standing only feet away from the stage. Mr. Logan stood at the back of the room next to some stairs. "You can look, but don't touch!" He yelled playfully, followed by explosive laughter.

John couldn't move. The woman stood directly before him dancing and smiling down at this new handsome foreign customer obviously drooling over her body. "Money Men" the dancers liked to call them. Imagining this could be her lucky night; she did her best to seduce and tempt him on the spot. She knew what all men liked.

John's heart was crushed – crushed beneath an unbearable weight of guilt and fear. He felt as if someone had just punched him in his gut, knocking all the air out of his lungs. His strong healthy body almost collapsed to the floor from weakness. He grabbed a chair and caught himself. He hadn't saved her. He couldn't. *Jesus loves you,* his heart cried, but his mouth remained shut.

"Come on son, let's go up to my office!"

A dry burning sensation caused his eyes to close shut and when he opened them again, she answered his gaze with a kiss to the air. John turned abruptly, slamming into a table and chairs, sending them tumbling and sliding in every direction. He stumbled forward, then regained his balance and stood up straight. He rushed towards the swinging doors. Suddenly a small female figure crossed his path and before he could stop he collided with the woman, sending her onto the floor and the two Cokes she was carrying, into the air. As the bottles struck the ground and shattered around them, John pulled the woman – a young girl actually – back to her feet, mumbling "sorry." over and over. Then he ran out of the room, but not before the image of another face and eyes, hurting and empty, left their impression forever. As John busted through the revolving doors, Rico was rushing in, alarmed by all the noise. The two giants struck shoulders and Rico went flying back against the wall. Finally, John crashed through a crowd of men coming through the front door, sending two of them onto the ground. They swung out and cursed at him as he ran away down the street. Mr. Logan, who had remained still, watching the whole scene with an amusing grin, now began to laugh and clap his hands. Everyone else in the room seemed paralyzed with confusion.

"Whew! What a show!" Logan bellowed out. His obvious delight seemed to melt everyone's apprehension. "I apologize to everyone for the chaos. Nothing to worry about…a round of beers on the house!" That helped get things back to normal in a hurry.

* * *

John ran and ran and ran. Sweat poured down his face, neck, and body. Some went into his eyes and burned them. He could barely see on the dark trail and kept running into branches that scratched and bruised him. He felt nothing. He wanted to hurt, wanted the pain to register, wanted to suffer, but his emotions had erupted like a volcano and now they oozed through his veins like burning lava, melting away his ability to feel…anything. He had the sense of being in the middle of some surreal out of body experience. It was as if he was floating above himself, watching himself crashing through the jungle, watching himself run, wondering how he could be so stupid, so gutless, so worthless.

John skirted the road that led into the American neighborhood and instead of returning, he passed by the entrance gate and continued up the mountain deeper into the darkness. He couldn't face them now…maybe ever again. John thought of Father Ramirez and understood clearly why the pastor had run away never to be seen or heard from again. John now longed for the same escape. How could he look the youth in the eyes and challenge them to love God more, to make a difference, to live for Christ? He ran far up the mountainside and finally came to a clearing where a small waterfall cascaded down from above, first striking some rocks then collecting in a shallow pool. He couldn't run any longer. He took off his shirt and collapsed on a large rock next to the water's edge. He lay there, gasping for air. He wanted to keep running away from himself. *You really screwed up this time! What the hell was that?!*

John realized that his pride and arrogance had kept him from asking the Lord for help. He had headed to town feeling rejected. Now he felt repulsive.

You're such a fool and you're gonna pay big for this one...

He knelt over the water's edge, splashed some onto his face to wash the sweat away and then sat on the ground. Discouragement took a seat on the rock above and shared its thoughts long into the night, reminding John about all his problems and shortcomings, his weaknesses and his many sins. The voice gladly proposed that what John hoped to accomplish was simply impossible. He was running out of time and wasting it too. Why had he even come? John didn't say a word.

* * *

Later that night, with Rico standing beside him on the front steps, Mr. Logan stared down his dusty street and up into the darkness of the mountains. He still wore the silly grin. Rico, missing the humor, was stone faced as always. Mr. Logan knew his deadly servant was itching for the order to pursue. He turned and patted Rico on his massive bicep.

"Not today, my friend. Not today." As he walked back inside, his cowboy boots noisy on the wood planks below, he spoke over his shoulder,

"That may be the last we see of John Parker, but I kinda hope not."

33 THE THREATS

John was struggling. A full week after his venture into the seedy world of exotic dancing, and he was still avoiding God. Instead of confessing his sin and seeking God's forgiveness, he continued to dwell on his weaknesses and try to somehow correct them in his own strength. The irony of it all escaped him. Not surprisingly, Satan's foothold on John's heart and mind increased, but John took all the blame. It was a spiritual battle he chose to fight against himself. Satan was delighted. The result was increasing sin and increasing frustration. The sin being an old temptation he had long before defeated that was now returning to haunt him. He had sacrificed lust on the altar many times in his Christian walk. At first only to find it lingering closely behind, always ready to entertain him once more if he would but offer a glance. But over time, through countless hours spent together with the Author of his faith, John cultivated a will and discipline against such flirtations. Now those hours had diminished and his discipline along with it.

She kept appearing in his dreams at night, in his thoughts all hours of the day. Again and again he watched her dancing on the stage, but now his focus was no longer her eyes. He saw her nakedness. And his purpose was no longer her rescue. He dreamed they were together. She took him to some hidden, dark room in the club and they indulged in pleasure. Her need of salvation was replaced with his need of physical gratification. She was no longer a person with a soul, just a body…an object of desire. John's guilt compounded. But still, it was *he* who had made the mistake of going in and it was *he* who would have to overcome this struggle. He would show God he still had the strength. That God was near, only waiting and longing to help, John failed to consider.

* * *

Other problems surfaced as well. With school having begun and the youth busy with their classes and studies, there was less and less for John to do during the days. He began running and exercising more…and playing ball. Soon he started going to town to play with the locals, many of whom didn't go to school. He didn't go to minister, but to compete…and to win. They quickly regretted having called him a chicken before. He proved his skills, but not his faith. On top of that, the TV came out of the closet and thanks to the state of the art satellite dish hooked up outside, John found enough sports channels to occupy all his free time. Just as the youth were ready to start getting together regularly with John, the idea of meeting with them every week seemed more of a burden than a delight. Now that the opportunity for growth was upon them, the last place John longed to be was in their presence, where his every effort at prayer, worship, and teaching piled on heaps of guilt and shame. The hypocrisy of those moments tortured his soul. As a result, less and less of his time and effort went into preparation. Of course he justified this with the thought that the youth were very well capable of growing in their faith on their own. Besides, he wouldn't be around forever. This line of reasoning allowed John to spend one night playing basketball in town with somewhat of a clear conscience, while the youth waited in the Rec for him to show up. They finally left in their small segregated groups. The next day he hit rock bottom when an email from Bill arrived with news that Rachel had been spotted out and about with Roger Harris for three nights in a row and word was they were hooking up. The email ended with the question, "What's going on?"

If you only knew!

John actually wasn't surprised by the news of Rachel's moving on. His heart, bathed in pessimism for days, had been expecting it. At least now he could say to himself "I told you so!" Besides, it didn't really matter anymore. He no longer felt worthy of her anyway. If she knew what he'd done and what he'd been thinking lately, she'd never want to talk to him again. Perhaps she did know. Maybe God had told her in a dream or showed her in a vision or something.

I don't care who knows! The declaration reverberated off the walls of John's mind as one last rush of pride swelled through. He wouldn't be hurt! He decided to feel sorry for Rachel instead. She would probably just end up following in the TCU tradition of "marry and mate before you graduate". Rachel Harris…it had a ring to it. He was thankful to be single and free! In truth, he was wounded and lonely.

* * *

Then something strange started happening. In the course of a week, the Rec was vandalized three times with messages written on the outside walls threatening to harm, even kill the Americans. The messages always included crude drawings of satanic symbols. The most shocking detail however, was not in the messages or artwork, but in the substance used to write the messages. At first it appeared to be a simple red paint, but upon further investigation, blood – animal's blood – turned out to be the vandal's ink. The video recorders along the perimeter ran non-stop and the tapes were checked over and over, but no footage of anyone coming or going was found. This detail alone caused a few sleepless nights for the parents. To the youth it added little suspense; they all knew a dozen different locations where one could slip in or out without being caught by one of the "All Seeing Eyes" as they called them.

The threats continued for a second week. Diego and Ricardo stood guard one night to no avail. They were the most baffled of all the following morning until Taylor translated the newest message in English that read, "We culd hav kiled you sleepin pigs!" The two men began arguing and pointing fingers and continued until running out of breath. With red faces, they apologized to the parents. The fact that all the messages were written in sloppy English with many misspellings had everyone guessing the vandals were young and Venezuelan. That left them with a few thousand suspects.

The police did nothing, said it was just a prank, nothing serious. Those were not the words the mothers wanted to hear. Their husbands were given an ultimatum, put a stop to it or we're all leaving! Robyn overheard her mother make just such a threat one night when her parents were arguing and she was supposed to be asleep. It didn't take long to get the news out and soon the kids were praying for more threats. Taylor even began packing his suitcases. He also made it a point to inform his father daily how scared he and Robert were.

"Scared of blowing this chance to go home!" he later yelled to everyone gathered in the Rec while demonstrating the look of panic and utter fear he had displayed to his father. They laughed and shared similar experiences. Whatever danger the threatening messages truly represented, the youth no longer cared – going home would be worth a few more days of terror.

Over the weekend, one of the police officer's daughters – a friend of Susan's – overheard her father mention to her mother about finding a chicken with it's head cut off outside the perimeter of the American neighborhood. But that wasn't all. There had been several discoveries of headless chickens in the jungle over the past months. And in one instance, in an area where a large fire had burned and much blood had been spilt, another item was recovered by a passerby and taken to the police station – a severed human ear. The girl shared this information with Susan, and soon nine American teenagers had plenty to talk about. Four boys in particular were especially freaked out. Suddenly, Taylor was no longer performing for his father.

* * *

John knew his time might soon be up, but first he had a hunch to follow. Even though things had improved between he and the older boys, they were still far from friends and Brad was more an enemy than ever before. John had heard how Mrs. Rollins reacted to his tactics in PE.

"He had no right to kick my boy out of class!" She took turns complaining to each of the mothers. It was either blame John or herself and she had enough emotional issues to deal with already without adding responsibility for her son's behavior. As long as she didn't confront John, he would just avoid her. That had been Maggie's advice as well.

As John inspected the Rec building he couldn't shake the feeling that the American boys might be behind it all. Getting back to the US was all they ever thought and talked about and this sure looked like the perfect play to scare the moms, pressure the dads and pack their bags. If the boys were behind the threats, John would be impressed at just how far they were willing to go, but not impressed enough to give them a free pass from the whooping that was sure to follow after their scheme was revealed to the parents. For their sake, John hoped he was wrong. He would soon find out.

34 THE RIGS

On Wednesday night nobody showed up for the meeting. John waited inside, not really wanting to be there himself. Suddenly the door opened and Paul Stevens stuck his head inside.

"You busy?"

John looked around the empty room, "Not exactly."

"Ever been in a helicopter before?"

The unexpected question caused John to hesitate and then smile.

"Nope."

"Come on." Paul motioned for John to follow him and they walked briskly down the hill towards the helicopter.

"One of my main responsibilities is to check our rigs on a weekly basis."

"You sure you can fly this thing?"

"Just finished reading the manual tonight. Piece of cake."

John climbed in and already felt claustrophobic.

"You couldn't have gotten a big and tall model?"

"Tight budget."

"Right."

John was happy for this distraction. He buckled in and put on the headset Paul handed to him. Paul checked a few gauges, flipped a few switches and then pointed to a large button.

"Push that please."

John did so and the engine came to life. The blades above them began to whirl faster and faster. The entire cockpit seemed to be swaying beneath the force of the blades.

"So you're clear to just lift off and fly this thing all over Venezuela any time you want?" John practically shouted.

Paul pointed to the headset and said, "I know you think you need to yell, but you don't. Try that question again with your inside voice." Paul's voice was crystal clear inside John's headphones.

John nodded. "Got it. Sorry. So you're clear to fly all over Venezuela whenever you want?"

"Why? You want to go to the beach sometime?" Paul responded with a glance and a grin.

John chuckled and Paul continued, "I'm clear to fly on three specific days each week at three specific times on one specific route between here and our three rigs on Lake Maracaibo, which is about thirty minutes away as the crow flies...this is Crow by the way," Paul said, patting the dashboard that was covered in blinking lights, gauges and switches. The sleek helicopter was jet black in color, so the name fit.

"Hold on!" And with those words, Paul pulled back on the control stick, and up they went. As they did, John's hand instantly went up against the large plexiglass window to his right. His heart was thumping in his chest.

The Crow leveled off and then dipped a little in the front and started moving forward. John noticed Paul's feet working some pedals in the floorboard.

John pointed to the pedals. "Gas and break?"

"Not exactly. These pedals control the rotor blade on the back tail which basically keeps us level."

"Level is good!" John exclaimed as the helicopter shot forward and he flew back against his seat.

It was dark outside, but John could see the silhouettes of trees passing beneath them. Occasionally they would fly over a small town or village, full of lit up houses and shops, but the longer they flew, the higher they climbed and the darker it got below them. The sky was midnight blue. Behind them the moon shone bright without a cloud to interfere.

"Perfect flying conditions tonight. Remind me to drag you along during the next typhoon."

"No thanks."

* * *

They held a steady northwest course. The magnetic compass on the dashboard in front of John was the only instrument he could read. Occasionally, Paul would dip the helicopter to a lower altitude to point out some important landmark or town, but for the most part they travelled at a constant 9000 feet above the earth below. That is until the earth below turned black and disappeared altogether and all at once. They arrived over the dark and empty blackness of Lake Maracaibo so suddenly that John turned left and right in his seat looking for some familiar landmark to help get his bearings.

"Welcome to Lake Maracaibo," Paul announced. "the largest body of water in South America." Paul tilted his control stick forward and they descended to 5000 feet above the black waters. "This is actually not a lake, but a bay connected to the Caribbean Sea…roughly 5000 square miles in size, but only 200 feet deep."

John was only half listening. He was more focused on trying to figure out where the sky ended and the water began. He finally located the moon reflecting on the water behind them and was able to gain his bearings. What a strange sensation to momentarily have no idea where the earth was!

As they flew closer to the water's surface, the moon's reflection grew brighter and the water all around danced in its light.

"It's unusually clear tonight which is why I asked you to tag along. There's something I want to show you that you can only fully appreciate at night. I usually only fly during the daytime." Paul intentionally emphasized the word "only" and looked at John to see if he would take the bait.

"Okay. Why is that?" John looked amused.

"Because at this very moment, you are flying over the most electrified location on planet earth."

Paul had John's full attention.

"What does that even mean?"

"That means lightning storms occur over Lake Maracaibo nearly 300 nights a year…but tonight looks to be one of the other 65."

John stared out the large plexiglass windows in all directions. Countless stars were visible in almost 360 degrees of vision. He started to relax.

"At least for now." Paul added, grinning to himself.

"Something tells me you're not entirely joking."

"Don't worry. This is a short trip tonight. I won't be landing on any platforms, just giving you a quick tour of the area and then heading home. If a storm rolls in we'll make a quick exit."

"I'm thinking lightning and helicopters don't mix very well."

"That would be correct thinking."

"Have you ever been hit?"

Paul looked over at John with his eyebrows raised. "Do you really want to know the answer to that question?"

"Never mind. So do you ever have issues with your platforms? Any oil spills?"

"No spills or major catastrophes. We run rigorous checks and protocols to avoid any news headlines. Just to give you some perspective, the United

States currently has around 1000 operating rigs around the world so when you hear of a spill in the news, it's a rarity."

"But a costly one."

"True."

In case Paul misunderstood his implication, John added, "For the local environment more than the oil company."

"Yes, I hear ya John."

* * *

Soon tiny white and red blinking lights appeared on the horizon as if they were floating in mid air. As they flew closer a large dark shape took form behind the lights. Suddenly they were circling a huge structure of steel and metal. It was hard to make out an exact shape at night, but John could see multiple platforms, large tanks, cranes sticking out in all directions and a circle platform extending out over the water which was obviously the helicopter landing pad. There was also a single metal tower that rose up high above everything else. John didn't know much about oil drilling, but he knew that tall part was called a derrick thanks to his relatives in East Texas where oil derricks were as common as pine trees. Just to be sure, he pointed to the tall tower, "That's the derrick, right?"

"That's right, and this derrick is our tallest one at 160 feet. This kind of rig is called a Jack-up rig because the three legs are buried deep into the lake's floor and then the hull or platform is jacked out of the water."

They were now hovering directly over the top of the circular platform. A voice suddenly cackled through both of their headsets.

"Nest One to Crow. You setting down?"

"Negative Nest One, just passing by."

"10/4."

Immediately Paul pulled back and away from the platform and then descended towards the water.

"Let's do a quick flyover of Nest Two and Three and then there's one more thing I want to show you before heading back home."

On their way to the other platforms, it was impossible to miss the dozens and dozens of other similar and smaller platforms and pumps that were lit up with all manner of blinking lights above the water. John's curiosity got the best of him, "So do you know how many companies are drilling this lake and how many rigs are out here?"

"Hard to say for sure, but at least a dozen international companies are drilling for oil and gas with hundreds of platforms and pumps."

They approached and circled the other two rigs in similar fashion and Paul had the same simple and quick conversation with each radio handler.

"There's one more thing I want to show you," Paul said, then turned the Crow away from Nest Three and set a northwest course towards the nearest coastline.

* * *

John's mind was full of questions. "How many people work on your platforms?"

"Each rig has just over 100 beds."

"American workers?"

"Almost entirely. We do train a few locals to help with maintenance and operations, but most are seasoned veterans from the States with some new recruits and trainees mixed in."

Within minutes the Crow reached the coast line and dropped and banked left at the same time. John felt his stomach almost come out of his throat and he loved it.

"Woohoo!"

Paul laughed. "That's the most excitement we're going to have tonight."

Now the Crow was hugging the coastline at just over 3000 feet above the shore. John stared at the narrow and dark beach passing beneath them in a blur. Then something ahead caught his attention.

"What in the world?" John said, staring intently ahead at what looked like a glowing giant snake slithering out of the woods. John looked over at Paul, with a look that said, "Well?!"

Paul just motioned with his chin for John to keep his attention on the scene unfolding in front of and below them.

A line of hundreds of lights grew brighter and brighter until they were directly below them. Now John could make out dark wooden boats with poles sticking up in the middle with a single large kerosene lantern hanging from the pole. Two or three human figures were standing or sitting in each long wooden canoe. The boats were entering into the lake from one lone tributary that disappeared into thick trees. As the boats hit the open water of the lake, they fanned out and their collective shape changed from a long snake into slowly exploding fireworks. It was quite an amazing scene, and John gazed down silently as Paul circled overhead.

"These fisherman belong to the Guajiro tribe which are scattered throughout the mountains and rainforests between here and Colombia. Every night they travel down the Catatumbo river in their homemade wooden canoes with their lanterns lit and come and fish along the shores of Lake Maracaibo. At sunrise they turn their lanterns off and head back for home…paddling upstream."

"Amazing." John said.

"They've been doing this for hundreds of years, if not longer."

"And all this drilling hasn't had any side-effects on the fish population?"

John's question hung in the air for a few seconds until Paul cleared his throat. John had his cheek pressed up against the side window trying to get a good view of the scene below, but now he turned and looked directly at Paul, who met his gaze.

"I'm not gonna lie to you John. The drilling is not good for the fish or the fishermen or their people. My job is to make sure our equipment doesn't malfunction and cause a macro-level catastrophe, but there is no way to avoid environmental damage on a micro-level."

The Crow banked right, heading back towards deeper and darker waters and the firework show below them slowly faded out of sight.

As one blinking drilling rig after another passed by beneath them, the gravity of Lake Maracabo's situation really began to sink in to John.

He decided to keep sharing his thoughts. "So it's a numbers game. If your company, as careful as it is, can't help pollute on a micro-level then consider all these dozens and dozens of other rigs which might or might not be as careful and advanced as yours. Add it all up and it's not a good situation."

"No, it's not."

And that doesn't bother you?! John wanted to ask, but he kept quiet. Paul had invited him on this little excursion and it wasn't his place to give the guy a grilling. John knew his direct question had caught Paul off guard and caused him some discomfort and embarrassment. That was enough for now. John admitted to himself that it was hard to find any modern day convenience that didn't negatively impact the environment in some small way. Ultimately, it was the Venezuelan government who was authorizing all these oil platforms and basically flushing their own natural resources down the drain for a quick and temporary profit.

* * *

It was a quiet ride home. Paul kept the Crow high above the hilltops and trees. It was easy to spot their approaching neighborhood which was more lit up with electricity that any of the towns and villages they had passed. The Crow slowed to a complete stop above the landing pad, and Paul sat her down onto the concrete surface more gently than John had thought possible. There was nothing gentle, however, about the force of wind thrashing the branches and leaves on the trees circling the landing pad, but it grew calmer as the rotor blades slowed and then came to a complete stop.

"You're pretty good at this Paul. I'm impressed."

"Well, it definitely helped to read the manual today." Paul winked and John just shook his head and laughed. He really enjoyed Paul's sense of humor, and he was relieved that their somewhat tense conversation hadn't completely ruined the fun mood of their trip.

John opened his door and climbed out. He had to place one hand on the helicopter to steady himself.

Paul came around to John's side and put a hand on his shoulder. "You've heard of sea legs right?"

John nodded.

"Welcome to air legs. Don't be surprised if you experience more flying in your dreams tonight. Let me walk you home."

Paul continued to grip John's shoulder for support as they walked the trail over to John's condo.

"That was very cool Paul. Thanks for the invitation."

"The pleasure was all mine. It's usually a quiet trip both ways."

They stopped a few yards away from John's front door.

"There's something I need to share with you before I go. Earlier today all the fathers met together and decided we'll be sending our families back to the States for an indefinite vacation if the vandals aren't caught and stopped by the end of the week. The idea wasn't mine and it's a little drastic if you ask me, but this is one of those situations where it's better to be safe than sorry."

"I understand."

"If we do end up flying our families back to the States then you're welcome to travel home with them or you can hang around here longer and return home whenever you want. I encourage you to travel around South America since you're over here and I'll cover your expenses. Consider it a going away gift from all the families for the great work you've done with our children."

John felt a queasiness in his stomach at the thought of his work coming to such a sudden and premature end. "I appreciate your generous offer Paul, and I might just take you up on it, but I hope and pray it doesn't come to that. I'm not ready to say goodbye to your kids yet."

"We're hoping and praying the same thing."

The men shook hands, said goodnight and parted ways.

35 THE TRAP

On Friday afternoon John stopped by the Stevens' home for a visit, and Maggie informed him that floodlights and video cameras would be installed around the Rec the following morning. He didn't have much time.

In the Stevens' living room John found Taylor, Robert and all the girls sitting around the TV watching a movie.

"You guys watching Friday the 13th?"

"Very funny John," Stephanie replied looking up and grinning.

"Where's Brad?"

"At home," she answered, this time without looking up.

"And Tommy?"

"He's at home too," Robyn replied.

"Probably packing his bags," Taylor added, causing everyone to smile.

"Any of you want to go for a walk? It's nice out." John knew Maggie wouldn't allow it, but he was just going for a response.

"Are you crazy?" Jamie asked without looking away from the TV screen. "Tommy said whoever is writing the stuff is probably watching us from the woods all day."

"He won't leave the house," Robyn added.

"Are you scared, John?" Robert asked, standing up and motioning for John to lift him up into his arms. John let him climb up on his back.

"Well, it is a bit creepy...but I'm guessing whoever's writing that stuff doesn't plan on doing much more."

"How do you know?" Susan asked.

"I don't know for sure, but they haven't done anything to any of us yet…and they had the perfect chance when Diego and Ricardo fell asleep. I think someone's getting their kicks out of scaring us."

"If I caught whoever's doing this I'd kick their butt," Taylor mumbled boldly, looking over at the girls as he did so.

John called his bluff. "Taylor, I need to chat with you alone for a second. Follow me."

Taylor looked around at everyone else, but none of them moved their gaze from the TV. Slowly, he stood up and followed John out onto the front porch. Taylor was wondering if John was finally about to let him have it for all the previous pranks and his bad attitude.

"Okay Taylor, I've got a plan. How about joining me for an all-nighter in the Rec? See if we can't catch some butt for you to kick."

"Tonight?"

"Yeah, tonight."

"Aren't they putting up lights and security stuff tomorrow?"

John nodded. "Exactly, that's why we've got to get them tonight. After tonight they may not come any more. They might hear about the beefed up security or even watch it get installed and that will be the end of it. I know you want to catch these suckers as bad as I do."

Taylor shifted nervously on his toes.

Gotcha! John was enjoying this.

Taylor hesitated and was about to refuse with "I'm too tired" as his excuse, but he knew how chicken that would sound, especially after the heroic statement he had just made.

"Okay," he finally mumbled.

* * *

John asked Maggie if Taylor could sleep over at his apartment, saying they had a lot to talk about. She agreed, delighted to give John an opportunity to have some one on one time with her son. Maggie already knew that if they did leave for the States in a few days, her biggest regret would be not giving John enough time with their children. She immediately lifted up a silent prayer for the Holy Spirit to use John to do something special in her son's life that very night.

John followed Taylor to his room and watched him pack his things. Next, they returned to the den and finished watching the movie with the others. Afterwards, the two of them walked everyone else home. John was sure not to let Taylor out of his sight for even one second. The boy couldn't have an opportunity to call his partners in crime. John was betting on Brad and Tommy's ignorance as well as their determination to get back to America. Everyone knew one more night of threats would be the icing on the cake. Interestingly, Taylor didn't make things very difficult for John. They returned to John's condo for a few hours of chit-chat, nachos, and card games and all the while Taylor seemed to have only one question on his mind…

"What are we gonna do if we catch them?"

"We'll just have to wait and see." John repeated each time, thoroughly amused at Taylor's performance. There was one brief moment of confusion however when the teenage boy asked whether or not John was going to pray to God for their protection. John obliged Taylor's request and took the opportunity to label their attackers as "cowards and criminals" and beg God's help in "capturing and punishing these losers!" Afterwards, John thought he'd recognize at least a hint of regret or guilt on Taylor's face, but the boy's expression was no different than it had been all night and the question remained…

"What are we gonna do if we catch them!?"

"Just get your dark clothes on and let's go."

Soon they had changed and headed out John's front door, blending into the darkness.

This has been too easy, John thought, as he and Taylor crept into the Rec, keeping the lights off. He wondered if the boys were aware of his plans or if Taylor had finally found himself stuck. They would all soon find out.

They sat alone in the darkest corner of the room. There was no talking, just waiting. 30 minutes passed. One hour. Two.

John had recognized from day one that Taylor was the key to his success with the group and that if he could get Taylor to accept and trust him, then the teen's influence would lead the others. It hadn't taken long, however, before John decided it wasn't worth the effort.

After tonight it won't matter anymore. He was about to bust Taylor and the others once and for all for the crap they'd given him. Taylor was just about to nod off for the fifth time when he heard some talking outside.

"John!" Taylor whispered frantically, his eyes immediately wide open, "I think they're here!"

"I hear them." John wondered how long Taylor would act ignorant.

"What are we going to do?!"

"Go outside and see who it is." John just wanted to hear Taylor's response.

"No way! Are you crazy!"

"Look, your own friends won't kill you."

"What are you talking about, my own friends?" Taylor looked as scared and confused as John had ever seen any kid. It was time to bring this all to an end.

"Okay, just wait here."

"John, are you sure you wanna do that? They could kill you or something."

"Taylor if it's my time to go then so be it. I don't think God's ready to take me out of here yet." John said the words then wondered if he really believed them himself. "Just wait here."

"No, I'm coming with you," Taylor whispered, thinking John was crazier than he had imagined, but he was also big and that was important now.

"Just stay behind me."

"Trust me. I will." They crawled on their hands and knees through the kitchen and slowly opened the back door. The outside voices became louder, right around the corner.

"Let's write…the youngest will die first." Others joined in muffled laughter.

Both John and Taylor recognized the voice at the same time. John turned around to finally let Taylor have it, when the teenager suddenly charged around the corner before John could stop him. John heard the sound of someone being tackled and others running away and by the time he came around the corner himself, two figures were rolling around in the dirt. All the others, as much as John could tell having only seen their backsides, were locals. He chased after them briefly, not really trying to catch them, but wanting them to think he was. Then he quickly ran back to the other two who were still on the ground. Finally, Taylor managed to climb on top of the person and started punching him in the face uncontrollably.

"Taylor, stop!" John repeated the command again before finally grabbing Taylor by the shirt, throwing him off, and ending his assault on Brad who was now laying on his back with his face covered in blood. Brad began to laugh. John had an uneasy feeling. Something was not right about the teenager sneering up at him.

"Are you psycho!? Are you sick!?" Taylor growled, climbing back to his feet. Brad just continued to laugh. Taylor lunged again, "I'll kick your…!"

"Taylor, be quiet!" John said and grabbed Taylor's shirt and jerked the teen towards him. Taylor's lips clamped shut and he stared up at John with eyes full of pain and hatred. "Go and get the others, all of them and don't wake up the parents." John would have thought such a request impossible if he hadn't learned of their monthly secret meetings in the Rec after the parents were asleep. Taylor ran off and John just stood over Brad.

"You can't have him," a voice snarled, "he belongs to us."

John didn't say a word. He just waited and silently prayed over what to do next.

36 THE SCREAM

As John stood over the teenage boy, Brad's eyes began blinking, then shutting for seconds at a time, and finally closed completely. John picked him up, carried him into the Rec and laid him down on one of the sofas. He began walking towards the kitchen to get a wet towel to clean the blood from Brad's face when through a passing window, he caught sight of a bouncing light in the distance. Curious, John stepped outside and waited. The zig-zagging light drew closer until finally revealing Paul Stevens and Ricardo, with flashlight in hand, jogging towards the Rec. They were out of breath when they stopped a few feet from where John was standing.

"What in the world is going on John?" Paul managed to ask between gasps.

"First off, Taylor's okay in case you and Maggie are worried."

"Maggie heard shouting, woke me up and I called Ricardo. Where is Taylor?"

"He'll be here in a minute. So I decided to lay a little trap for our vandals and Taylor wanted to help. Turns out Brad was involved."

"Brad? You can't be serious."

"I had a hunch and Brad and some locals were just about to paint some new messages when we surprised them."

"So where are they?"

"The locals got away, but your son and Brad got into a little wrestling match until I pulled them apart. I sent Taylor to go get all the kids and Brad is just worn out and sleeping on a sofa in the Rec." John stepped aside and pointed over his shoulder at the door behind him which was still open. Paul asked Ricardo for his flashlight and then stepped into the doorway and scanned the room with the bright white beam. It came to rest on the back of a teenage body stretched out on a sofa. Brad's bushy red hair was unmistakable.

"I don't think he's been getting much sleep lately and Taylor kind of finished him off."

Paul switched off the flashlight and turned around. "So why are the kids coming here? *How* are the kids coming here at two in the morning?"

"I've got a plan Paul…I want all the kids to pray with me for Brad."

Paul was silent for a few seconds, searching for the right response. John waited, sensing that his plans were about to be put on hold.

"John, I'm not sure this is a good idea. I know prayer is important, but can't this wait until morning? Besides, there's no way Taylor can get all the kids here without waking up our entire neighborhood!"

Before Paul finished his sentence, the sound of children's voices quickly approached. The entire group of nine children came around the corner and one by one said "hello" to Mr. Stevens, John and Ricardo and then disappeared into the Rec as if nothing was out of the ordinary and they were just showing up for class…at two in the morning. Taylor and Robert brought up the rear of the group.

"Hi Dad." Robert chirped before disappearing through the Rec door.

"Don't worry Dad." Taylor said as he passed by, "None of the parents are awake."

Paul looked at Ricardo and then at John with a bemused expression. "I stand corrected."

"Paul, I'm asking you to trust me on this one. And you're welcome to stay and join us."

"No, I better get back and let Maggie know everything's okay…everything is okay, right?"

John nodded.

"And how long do you think this is going to take?"

John shrugged and spread out his palms.

Paul couldn't believe he was about to go along with this insane plan. When the other parents got word of it, which they certainly would, *he* would be help accountable. Despite the objections in his head, his heart trusted John and his spirit felt peace. "Okay John. Do what you feel is best and take care of our kids."

"Thank you."

"I'm going to have Ricardo patrol the fence line and just keep his eyes open, but it sounds like you've put an end to our vandals."

"I promise it's over." John turned and headed into the Rec as Paul and Ricardo went their separate ways.

This might be a colossal mistake, John thought as he stepped through the doorway. *What if they aren't ready for this, Lord?* But it was too late. This was it, the future of the group and especially his employment, all hung in the balance of the next few moments. *Lord, please give them all courage.*

John closed the door and then suddenly the ceiling light turned on. Robyn had flipped the switch. After a short gasp from all the girls, everyone stood still and quiet, staring at Brad's silent and still body on the sofa.

"That's Brad?" Jamie asked.

"Robyn. How about turning on a lamp or two instead of the main light?" Robyn quickly turned the light off and then two lamps on opposite sides of the room were turned on and a much softer glow enveloped the room. John took a seat on the sofa and lifted Brad's head, resting it on his thigh.

"Susan, can you go to the kitchen and bring me a wet towel with warm water?"

As Susan headed to the kitchen, the others approached the sofa and stared down at Brad's face, which was covered in dry blood. Stephanie stared quietly at her brother from across the room.

"It's okay, Stephanie, he's all right," John assured her, hoping she wouldn't panic. Susan handed John the towel and then walked over to Stephanie and put her arm around her shoulder.

"He's all right," she repeated.

John slowly and gently wiped at the blood around Brad's nose and lips until it was all cleaned away. He used the other end of the towel to dry Brad's face. When he was finished, John looked around the room at all the kids. Robert was standing in front of Taylor, whose hands were resting firmly on his tiny shoulders. The little boy's eyes and mouth were wide open.

"Come sit around us."

After everyone sat down, John continued. "Brad's had a really long night. He's probably had a lot of them lately. He needs our prayers, but first I want to explain to you what's happened tonight." John went through the whole story pausing to let Taylor put in his own version of certain events. It didn't take long. John left out what had happened after Taylor left, they were confused enough already.

"If any of you know something about what Brad's been up to lately, don't be afraid to share it. No one's going to be mad at you, but it's important that I know what's been going on with him."

No one said a word.

Tommy shuffled in his seat and glanced quickly over at Taylor who was still on edge and angry.

"Okay. Well, what I want to do is have everyone circle around Brad and pray for him." John had spent many nights at his university praying for friends and being prayed over, but he knew this was something totally foreign to these kids and even he had never come face to face with a demon before, at least not one manifested in another person. All he had to go on were the handful of stories in the New Testament describing different people being afflicted and possessed by demons, and he was silently reviewing all of them in his mind. All the while he knew the filthy creature was still inside watching and waiting. "All we're going to do is pray. Whatever you want to say to God on behalf of your friend Brad, just say it."

Taylor didn't want to pray for Brad. He wanted to pound his head in. The jerk didn't deserve prayer. He stood to his feet and spoke without realizing it.

"I'm not praying for him!"

All eyes turned to Taylor. John's were the last.

"He's been threatening to kill us, John! He's crazy! He needs to go to a psycho ward or to jail or something. You heard what he was going to write tonight, 'the youngest one will die first!'"

Robert's face turned pale. He was already scared enough of Brad. Robyn pulled Robert into her lap and wrapped her arms tightly around him.

John was about to lose them. "Alright Taylor, that's enough. I know you're angry and you want to make him pay for this, but have you ever thought *why* Brad's been doing this? For one second have you stopped and wondered what's caused him to act this way? Don't turn your back on your friend so easily."

"I can't pray for him," Taylor mumbled, turning away.

"Then your heart's colder than I thought."

Taylor walked towards the door. His hand turned the knob when suddenly a scream ripped through the room.

37 THE BREAKTHROUGH

To everyone's horror, Brad flew off the sofa and began screaming and flopping all over the floor the same way he had that night by the fire. This sent the girls into hysterics, colliding and falling over one another as they frantically cleared the room. John threw himself onto Brad's body, and it took all his weight and strength to pin the boy down. Meanwhile, everyone was screaming or shouting or crying, except for John and except for Taylor who just stood still and watched.

"Tell him Taylor! Tell John what happened. You know what's wrong just like I do!" Tommy yelled, then began crying.

"Tell John," Robert echoed.

Taylor slowly walked over to John's side and gazed down at Brad's contorted figure. Everyone else stood with their backs against the wall.

"In the name of Jesus Christ I command you to name yourself!" John's voice boomed with authority. There was another scream that seemed to almost fade away within Brad's body then the same sneering scratchy voice that had spoken to John earlier returned.

"Witchcraft. And he's mine. You can't have Him!"

"He's not yours, he belongs to the most High God!"

"NO!!!" the voice yelled.

"In the name of Jesus Christ I command you to leave this body now!"

"No! Please no!"

Looking into the eyes of the helpless tiny figure below him, John could see an evil, yet frightened, presence gazing back and it angered him that something so filthy had control of something so young and helpless.

"I bind you in the name of Christ Jesus, powerless to stay in this body. Leave now!"

The demonic voice let out one final scream as if it were being ripped and torn away from inside. Brad's body writhed and twisted violently, actually knocking John off, then went completely limp.

Total silence.

John crawled back to Brad's side and placed his hands on the boy's shoulders. Brad blinked his eyes and slowly sat up and stared around the room.

"It's gone," he whispered.

"Yes, it's gone Brad and you're going to be okay."

"The voice is gone too."

"What voice?"

"The one that's been telling me again and again to hurt all of you. I didn't want to…I'm so sorry everyone." Everyone was still speechless from everything they had seen and heard, but a calm had come over the room and now everyone gathered close around John and Brad.

"It's okay Brad. It's over." As John spoke, Taylor knelt down beside John, put his hand on Brad's shoulder, and began to sob uncontrollably. Taylor tried to speak, but his words were all muddled and slurred. John spoke softly, hoping to calm him down, "Taylor, he's all right, it's over."

"I'm…I'm…I'm sorry. I never meant to…to let it happen."

"What are you talking about Taylor?" Susan asked.

"I saw it happen," Robert said.

"We were there." Tommy added.

"But we didn't know what was happening." Taylor was finally calming down.

Brad lifted himself up onto his knees. He placed his hand on Taylor's shoulder and squeezed. "You know it wasn't your fault."

"Taylor, are you ready to talk?" John looked him straight in the eyes. Taylor nodded his head.

"Take a deep breath and relax."

Taylor did so then began, "We had all been smoking marijuana for a couple of months, not a lot, just every now and then when we were bored and really hating it here. It made us feel like we could escape for a little while. A friend of mine, Manuel, would always get the stuff then meet us in town and we would pay him and then go smoke somewhere in the woods. One night he took us into the woods, deep into the woods, and then we came out into this clearing where there was a big fire going. Well, Brad and Tommy had gotten there before us."

"Us, being you and Mike?" John asked, afraid to hear his answer.

Taylor knew how bad it would sound, but didn't care, he had to come clean, "And Robert."

Susan and Robyn began a verbal assault…

"You stupid jerk!"

"I can't believe you, Taylor!"

"You took Robert with you?"

"Did you actually give him Marijuana?"

"Girls calm down!" John spoke forcefully. Inside, he was also seething.

"He never smoked anything. I wouldn't ever let him," Taylor answered, staring down at the floor.

"I didn't want that stuff," Robert exclaimed, looking at John and then the girls. "I just wanted to go with them."

Taylor looked up, "I didn't have a choice. Robert was having nightmares and sleeping in my…"

John wasn't in the mood for excuses, "You had a choice Taylor. You made the wrong choice. Just finish the story."

Taylor's face turned red. He wanted to run away from everyone and just cry all night, but he couldn't. He knew he owed them all the truth. After another deep breath he continued. "There were these two men there with Brad and Tommy when we got there. They were smoking this pipe and then they let us smoke it with them. We weren't sure what was in it, Peyote I think, but we didn't even care. It didn't take long before we were all *really* high. Whatever it was, it was strong. Then this guy leaves and comes back with a chicken and cuts off its head and pours some blood in a bowl and drinks it. We were so messed up we didn't know what was going on and then he offered the bowl to us and we all took a drink."

The younger girls gagged and shook their heads in disgust, the older girls in disbelief.

"Tommy, is this true?" Robyn yelled. He nodded his head without looking up. He couldn't face her. "You're all psycho!" she yelled. John decided to just let the girls have their say. It would save him the trouble.

"What's wrong with you guys?!" Susan asked. "Are you complete idiots? You actually drank blood! And with Robert with you! I cannot freaking believe this!"

"Susan, I know." Taylor started to choke up and tears rolled down his cheeks.

"Mike, where were you?" John asked, unable to believe that such a gentle kid could've had a part in it.

Mike knew anything he said would only make everyone angrier with Taylor and the others. He figured Taylor was already getting all he deserved. Of course, he'd dreamed of the chance to get even with Tommy and Brad, but now all bitterness was gone. "I left before all this started," he simply answered.

"Smart move, Mike," John said, winking his way. The girls echoed their agreement. All eyes zoomed in on Taylor once more and he continued the story,

"That stuff was so strong, it really messed us up. I couldn't think. I forgot all about Robert...I didn't even know..." at this point Taylor started to lose it again and after finishing with, "he ran away," began bawling like a baby. He reached over and grabbed Robert and pulled him into his arms, squeezing him tightly against his body.

Robert took over the narration. "I didn't run yet, I watched first." The little boy smiled, happy that the truth was finally coming out.

Tommy decided to join the conversation, but made sure to avoid his sisters' glares. "Then one of the men, who turned out to be a witch doctor or something, started dancing and chanting these words over and over again and we all mumbled along with him just having fun and playing around. Brad started to dance in circles around the fire with the guy. We all knew Brad was just making fun of him so we were laughing really hard. Then all of a sudden the witch dude yelled something at Brad really loud and Brad fell onto the ground shaking just like he was doing tonight."

Brad spoke up. "I remember thinking how cool all this voodoo stuff is and finally being glad I wasn't back in the States and then the witchdoctor looked at me and yelled something and pointed his fingers and I felt something take control of my body. It was like I could see what was happening, but I had no control to stop it. I thought I was going to die…"

No one said a word. Brad's story was still sinking in.

"That's when I ran!" Robert exclaimed dramatically.

"And we all started freaking out!" Tommy yelled in similar fashion.

His composure regained, Taylor spoke up, "I fell onto Brad trying to hold him still, and when I yelled for help I looked up to see the crazy witch doctor dude standing over me with his machete raised above his head. I thought we were dead for sure and then he was suddenly tackled by the older man. Manuel was gone and so was Tommy."

"I ran home!" Tommy blurted out.

"So I dragged Brad, who looked like he was dead, into the woods and practically carried him to my house and put him in my bed and that's when I remembered Robert. I had totally forgotten about my little brother…" Taylor had to take a deep breath to keep from losing it again. Robert was still smiling. This was his favorite part of the story.

"He wasn't in my room. He wasn't in his room. I've never been more scared in my life. I felt so sick I threw up…"

"Good!" Robyn interjected, expressing her continued frustration.

Taylor was quiet for a moment, staring at the floor. "Then I remembered seeing him run off into the woods and I was about to go back and look for him, when my mom stuck her head into my room and whispered that Robert was sleeping in their bed for the rest of the night. She noticed Brad in my bed, but didn't say anything. I had already put my sleeping bag on the floor and was lying on it when she came in. Only my closet light was on so she didn't notice the complete mess we were in. I held my breath until she left and then buried my face in my sleeping bag and cried all night. I didn't sleep. All I could think about was how Robert had gotten home, how he had gotten into their bed, and what he had told them? They obviously didn't know anything yet or both my Mom and Dad would have killed me right away. Still, I just knew Robert would have a nightmare and everything would come out. The next morning Robert told me that he hadn't said anything and I could finally breath again. Brad went home that morning and it was as if nothing had happened to him. His mom didn't question him at all about spending the night and my mom didn't say anything either. Somehow we got away with it. Then a few days later Manuel found me and I told him to stay away from me. He begged me to listen to him. He was scared. He said he had no idea that was going to happen and that he was in trouble. He said that he found out later that the witch doctor wanted to sacrifice one of us that night, but that the other man knew what kind of trouble they would be in if they killed an American kid and so he stopped him, but not without losing his ear in the fight. Manuel said that now the witch doctor was after him. I was still so mad that all I said was 'good' and walked off." Taylor grew quiet, thinking to himself.

John was thinking the same thing and offered the suggestion to everyone,

"Manuel needs our help."

They all agreed.

Now it was Robert's turn again. "I ran into the woods and just kept running. I got so lost. Finally I laid down under some bushes and that's when I prayed to God and asked him to save my brother and Tommy and Brad. I had left them and was so scared. I was not a good brother." Taylor squeezed Robert in his arms and now the only dry eyes in the room were Robert's. "But after I prayed and prayed, I wasn't scared anymore and I just followed this bright star out of the woods and back to our house. God sent me that star to help me and he sent you John just like I asked, to help save my brother and Brad and all of us."

"Come here little buddy," John said to Robert, opening his arms.

Taylor released him and Robert walked over to John and gave him a hug. "Robert Stevens, for acts of bravery and extreme faith in the face of danger, I officially appoint you Prayer Warrior Captain of this group." John saluted Robert and the little soldier snapped to attention and saluted back. Giggling rippled through the room. Suddenly Taylor yelled "Group hug!" and everyone leaped into the air, dog piling on top of John. Brad tried to roll away, but John made sure to grab and hold him so that he got buried right along with him. Laughter replaced tears as siblings and friends asked forgiveness and old grudges and jealousies were released. One by one the youth apologized to their leader for their bad attitudes and rude treatment, some for the first time, others again, just to be sure he knew they really meant it. They all settled down and began sharing things that were going on in their lives. Brad described in more detail the increasing inner struggle he had after that night with anger and the subtle voice that urged on his rage. Susan confessed to trying some marijuana. Most of them voiced the same frustration with their parents and with having to leave their homes and friends back in the US. John didn't pretend to understand how they felt, but he wanted to, so he listened and learned as they talked. He also continuously thanked his Heavenly Father for the breakthrough that had occurred, one he had begun praying for back in his dorm room at TCU, but had recently given up on.

* * *

With the first rays of early dawn peeking through the Rec windows, John played his guitar and they sang songs like they had never sung before. They learned the words and lifted them up to the Lord with a gratitude they had never before felt. Joy was in their hearts and they laughed and sang in true delight for the first time since moving to Jajo. And for the first time, they really saw each other clearly, accepted one another, and enjoyed being together. A transformation had begun.

38 THE LIVING WORD

The next night, at exactly 2am, John walked into the Rec and found everyone already sitting around the room with Bibles in hand. Brad and Stephanie had been the first to arrive. Somehow they had all convinced John to let them sneak out and meet *one more time* in the middle of the night. John had shared their secret plans with Paul and Maggie who requested that this *please* be their last clandestine meeting. John promised it would and that they would not regret it. They hoped he was right, but weren't so sure. The other parents still knew nothing.

* * *

John took a seat at the front. "Looks like you guys are ready." Heads nodded in agreement. Brad raised his Bible in the air, "Let's do this!" Everyone was smiled, just as eager to get started. John asked everyone to bow their heads and said a quick prayer for God to open eyes and ears to His truth. He ended with a hearty "Amen".

"We're going to start at the gospels…in the book of Matthew." John opened his Bible to Matthew chapter one and then helped everyone find the right page in their own Bibles. Once they were all on the right page, John began to read. The kids followed along as he led them through stories of Jesus' birth, calling his first followers, healing the sick, feeding five thousand, raising the dead to life, and rebuking the demons. Suddenly they all understood the reality of the Bible. They wanted to know more, to understand more. They listened to Christ's words about sin and the enemy and understood more clearly the reality of Satan's grip on a fallen world. Tommy shared a thought.

"Just think…that same demon we told to leave Brad could've been one that Jesus talked to a long time ago."

Susan jumped in. "It just goes to show you the devil never changes. He'll always try to hurt us."

"Where did Satan come from?" Robert asked. All eyes turned to John. He had everyone's full attention and he couldn't have asked for a better opportunity to start from the beginning and tell them everything he could about God and His creation and plans. He began with Lucifer's rebellion in heaven and banishment to earth, followed with Adam and Eve in the Garden of Eden, Cain spilling Abel's blood, and then the Tower of Babel. Next came Noah and the giant ark with the animals two by two. Then Joseph, Moses and Joshua. The children's mouths hung open as darkness covered the land of Egypt and their eyes were wide with excitement as the walls of Jericho came crashing down. When John described the incident of Balaam and his donkey and their encounter with an "angel of the Lord" the kids couldn't help laughing at the thought of a talking donkey and then Jamie piped in, "Can an angel get in your body, too?"

Robyn rolled her eyes at her little sister's foolish question as John thought for a moment about how to answer it.

"You see Jamie, when a demon goes into your body it's because it wants to control you, cause you to suffer and turn from God. Angels would never want to take away your freedom and God wouldn't let an angel do that. According to the Bible, angels basically do two things when it comes to people: deliver messages to us and guard and protect us, and I believe they're busy doing that every second of every day. But here's the most important thing: the Bible says that when you believe in Jesus Christ, the Holy Spirit, the Spirit of God, comes to live inside you and give you a new life. God *Himself* makes His home in your heart and gives you all you need to live for Him. His power and wisdom and love becomes yours. It's amazing! There's a reason God sent the devil down to earth – maybe so that we would have to make a choice between good and evil – I don't know for sure, but I do know that the devil's time will soon come to an end and one of the coolest verses in the Bible says that when Jesus Christ comes back he will overthrow Satan with just the breath of His mouth!"

Taylor liked hearing that. "Ha! So the devil's a wimp compared to God."

"That's right, and some day when we all go to heaven, God is going to send the devil and all his demons to Hell for all the evil they've done. Listen everybody, I haven't even begun to tell you all the stories in the Bible. There are so many, and they are so cool. That's why we've got to start reading more. The Bible is what God uses to teach us how to live for Him. If we're gonna know God, we've got to read His word." And then John stopped. He slowly looked down at the pages that were open before him. A voice inside told him to read.

"Ephesians chapter six, verse ten. 'Finally, be strong in the Lord and in His mighty power. Put on the full armor of God so that you can take your stand against the devil's schemes. For our struggle is not against flesh and blood, but against the rulers, against the authorities, against the powers of this dark world and against the spiritual forces of evil in the heavenly realms'." As John read, the kids "oohed and ahhhed" at the words of the verse. Although they had never heard them before, they understood them completely because of what they had witnessed and experienced the night before. John finished reading and was silent. For more than a minute it was completely quiet. Quiet, except for the voice that was speaking loud and clear to his heart. A voice that reminded him the battle wasn't his to fight alone, that actually the battle had been won already on the cross. The words came like a piercing arrow:

Why did you decide to leave Me that night, John? Why? I'll never leave you. Why have you avoided Me? My words? My presence? My power? Don't you know Rachel is mine? Be content her life is in My hands. You have been jealous. Now understand, I am a jealous God. I have longed for your return. Listen to the words you've spoken tonight to these children. They are the same words I've been speaking to you.

Forgive me Father, John prayed.

I already have.

The youth stared at John as he, with eyes cloudy and moist, gazed straight ahead at the wall.

"What's wrong, John?" Susan asked, bringing him back to the room and the moment.

"I'm sorry everyone. I'm so sorry."

"What is it John?" Taylor asked, wanting to understand what was troubling his leader.

"Listen everybody. I haven't been completely honest with you. Tonight I've shared everything I could about God and how wonderful and awesome He is, but I haven't been believing it myself lately. I've asked you to get to know God and spend time with Him, but I haven't been wanting to, in fact I've been running from Him."

"Why?" Robert asked.

"That's a good question Robert. It's really stupid when you stop to think about it. You see, when you do something wrong you feel guilty. And when you feel guilty you want to hide from God because you know you messed up. This is how Satan keeps Christians from living the lives that

God wants them to. If Satan can keep us feeling too guilty to go to God, then he's happy enough. This isn't easy for me to tell you, but last week I made a mistake and went to town after reading an email that really upset me. When I got to town I wasn't thinking like a Christian, but like a fool. I ran into a guy I'd met on the plane flying over here who was not a Christian and who runs a club with women dancers."

"Are you talking about Logan's?" Taylor asked. Looking around at the other guys.

Of course, they know the place, John thought. "Yes."

Tommy stood to his feet. "Man, they don't wear any clothes in there!"

"How do you know?" Stephanie asked accusingly, standing to her feet.

"Uh...I..." Tommy felt stuck then quickly answered, "Because Manuel told us. His father goes there all the time."

"That's gross," Stephanie remarked, hoping Tommy would agree, which he did by nodding his head. He wasn't stupid.

"That's a bad place," Robert said.

John felt like an idiot. "You're right Robert. That's a bad place."

"You know Manuel told me his father saw you come out of that place," Taylor said, "but I didn't believe him."

Tears fell from John's eyes. He was paying a price.

"I'm sorry to let you down Taylor, but it's true."

"Why did you do it?" Taylor asked, upset more than anything else because he had been wrong in defending John to Manuel and the other locals who had talked bad about him.

"Well, it all started when I flew over here. I met Mr. Logan…in fact, I sat beside him on the plane."

"Really, you sat beside Mr. Logan?" Robyn asked. "Was he mean?"

"Was he scary?" her sister added.

Stephanie had to put her two cents in, "I've heard he's dirty and greasy!"

John laughed, thinking she was almost right on that one.

"Well, I don't know about all that. He was a pretty normal guy on the plane, a little rude and rough around the edges, but not scary. Most of all, he really didn't want to talk about God."

"Of course not! Why would you want to talk to him about God?" Tommy asked.

"Listen Tommy, who does a doctor help, healthy people or sick people?"

"Sick people." Tommy answered quickly, but he still didn't get it.

"It might surprise some of you, but God loves Mr. Logan just as much as he loves you and I. And when Jesus died on the cross, He died for Mr. Logan just like he did for you and I. Mr. Logan needs to know this, so I wanted to tell him. But like I said, he didn't want to listen. After we landed, he gave me his business card and that's when I realized he sometimes lives here. After we said goodbye, I had a feeling we would meet again and that God wanted me to share more. So the other night when I went to town, I ran into him on the street and he invited me to come and chat in his office. Of course by then I knew he had the club with dancers, but I didn't even think about it. All I wanted to do was talk to him about God and Jesus and make him feel bad for what he was doing, then save the girls in there and get the people out and be a big hero. It was stupid thinking, but I was full of pride. I convinced myself what I was doing was right, but when I went inside all my courage disappeared. I saw the girls dancing and it broke my heart, but I didn't do anything. I didn't help them or say anything to Mr. Logan. I just ran out. I felt terrible, but I didn't ask God to forgive me or help me. But tonight while we were studying and talking, God spoke to my heart and reminded me of His love and mercy and kindness. That in spite of all I've done to push Him away, He still pursues me and calls us all closer to Him. I asked God to forgive me, and now I need to ask you to forgive me too."

"Manuel's dad did say you came running out of there and even knocked some of his friends on their butts," Taylor said, followed with a grin. There were some giggles and John even chuckled. He was ready to continue with the joking, but suddenly caught sight of Brad's tear-streaked face. Before he could ask what was wrong, Brad spoke.

"John. I've never asked Jesus into my heart…I don't want to die and go to Hell." Another tear rolled down the teen's swollen cheek.

"Listen Brad and everyone else, too. The Bible says in John chapter three, verse sixteen that God loved the world so much that He gave His one and only Son, Jesus Christ, to die on the cross for us, and that whoever believes in Him shall not die, but have eternal life. All you have to do to be saved is believe in Jesus. Believe that He is the Son of God and that He died for your sins. Ask Him to forgive you for your sinful ways and invite Him into your heart to be the Lord of your life. He'll never leave you or let you down. I can promise you that."

Robyn's hand slowly lifted up into the air.

"What is it, Robyn?"

Everyone turned to look at her.

"Jamie and I both went to a Christian summer camp the year before we came to live here. We both heard about God's love and Jesus and the last night we were there, both of us prayed to ask Jesus into our hearts..."

Robyn stared down at the floor and when she continued, her voice quivered. "When I got here and met the others, I decided not to tell anyone I was a Christian. I didn't want them to think I was weird or different. I was...embarrassed..." She began to sob.

"I was too, a little," Jamie added, "but I kept praying to God, asking Him to help me stay close."

"Jamie always told me to read my Bible and pray, and my parents did too, but over time I grew further and further away from God. Now I don't feel like a Christian at all."

"Sometimes I don't either, John." Jamie echoed.

"I understand exactly what you're talking about, girls. Every Christian struggles with staying close to God. That's why being a Christian is not about feelings, but about fact. The fact is that God forgives us once and for all when we accept Christ's death for our sins. Nothing can change that fact. Now, we can waste a lot of time focusing on feelings and fear and doubt, but the truth is we are eternally secure. And for every child of God who has ever found him or herself far away from where they know God wants them, all they have to do is turn around and run towards Him and He will run towards you and take you into His arms and restore you completely. There's a story in the Bible about just such a young man, and it's a wonderful story of God's patient love for us...I think I'll save that one for our next Bible study."

John smiled at the sisters as they wiped their cheeks and they nodded their heads in understanding.

"I'm not going to mislead any of you and say that being a Christian is easy. It's not. In fact, it's the hardest thing in the world...denying your own flesh to follow and obey a God that you can't physically see or hear. That's tough. You've got to see it as a journey. God is going to use your whole life, and I mean your *whole* life, to teach you and show you how to be His child. You'll crawl through valleys and sprint on mountaintops. The most important thing, what God is most pleased with, is a heart that's committed to live for Him in all circumstances. When things are good, praise Him. When things are tough and hard...praise Him even more, trusting and relying on Him to get you through. The last thing Jesus said before he went up into heaven was that He would never leave or forsake us."

John let Christ's promise settle in their minds for a moment. As he waited, he had a sudden flashback to his days with Scott. So much of what he had just shared with these kids, he had heard and learned from his Christian brother and mentor. With a rejuvenated soul, John smiled and asked the question everyone in that room needed to be asked. "So, what's keeping you from giving your life to God?" John's eyes scanned all the faces. "Now's the time guys and girls. God's got an adventure in store for each of you. Things you cannot imagine. It's time to give Him your life. Or I should say give Him back your life, since He's the one who gave it to you in the first place. If you're ready to follow Him, close your eyes and let's tell Him."

* * *

As a new day dawned, nine young voices prayed out for repentance and salvation, seven for the first time and two once again, caught up in the moment. John couldn't hold back the tears as he listened to his prayers being answered. One thought reverberated through his entire being...*I love you God!*

When everyone's eyes opened again, they were taken aback by the sudden glow of sunlight in the room. Many wiped tears away, smiling as they did so. John knew he looked like a mess.

"These tears..." he said, pointing to his face, "are tears of joy. We are brothers and sisters in Jesus now!"

Robert stood to his feet, but didn't say anything. His face was completely serious. Everyone grew quiet and still.

"Dog pile!" Robert yelled and then threw himself onto John's back as everyone stood to their feet in laughter and followed his lead. Once again John was buried beneath an avalanche of bodies. He assumed this meant they had forgiven him. They were finally a group, and whatever they were going to face in the future they would face together. God's Spirit had them bound.

39 THE COMMISSION

The nightlong revival service in the Rec was followed by an unexpected knock on John's front door only hours after everyone had gone home. John hoped he was dreaming, but reality came splashing in on him.

"Wake up!"

John recognized each and every one of the nine voices yelling at him and then his eyes opened wide just as a wave of shimmering liquid came flying at him. The ice cold water hit him head on, sending every inch of his comatose body into immediate shock.

Worse than the dorms! John thought as he yelled and leaped out through the door, chasing everyone in a hundred different directions. He ran and grabbed the water hose behind the front bushes, turned on the pressure, and sent a stream in the direction of his attackers. Water guns shot back from all sides. Water balloons came crashing down upon him. He was doomed! He quickly turned the water off, ducked back into his condo and locked the door. He went to the bathroom and after drying off, carefully opened the front door and shook his white towel in surrender. *I surrender, Lord.*

* * *

Soon all the youth had piled into John's living room, sitting on his sofa and on the floor. John handed out towels, thinking at the same time he should give them all a good pop with the end of one.

"Am I the only one who needed to catch up on some sleep?" he asked, truly bewildered.

"We were all out like a light," Taylor said eagerly.

"Then I woke up," Robyn jumped in, "with a crazy urge to get my Bible and read. I wanted to look again at the last words that Jesus' said to his disciples. I kept thinking how sad and even scary that must have been for them to watch Jesus leave…so I opened my Bible and found the book of Matthew and then turned to the last page and read His last words…"

John began to move towards his kitchen counter to grab his Bible and hand it to Robyn, but he froze in mid-step…

"All authority in heaven and on earth has been given to me," Robyn continued with her eyes closed. "Therefore go and make disciples of all nations, baptizing them in the name of the Father and of the Son and of the Holy Spirit, and teaching them everything I have commanded you. And surely I am with you always, to the very end of the age."

Robyn's eyes opened, full of bright hope and glowing conviction. "First. We need to get baptized. Second. We need to obey Jesus and go and make more disciples. Jesus said all nations! The lost are here all around us!"

Jamie gripped her sister's shoulder and looked at John. "Robyn woke me up and read Jesus' words to me. We're disciples of Jesus now so that means we have been commanded to teach the world about Him!"

"Then they came and told me!" Tommy shouted. "And then we went and got everyone else and read to them what Jesus wants us to do."

"We've got to tell the people of Jajo about Jesus," Stephanie said, balling her hands up into tight fists.

"There's no time to waste," Mike added.

"The harvest is ready," Susan stated emphatically, "and we are the workers that Jesus is sending out."

Taylor looked around at them all and then rested his gaze on John. "John…of all the people God could have brought here to do His work…he chose us."

"And you John!" Robert gushed with a bright smile.

The growing lump in John's throat and the tightening in his chest made him momentarily unable to respond. He put his hand on his chest and took a long slow breath.

"What is it John?"

Without answering, John knelt down onto his knees, closed his eyes and raised his hands into the air. "O Lord God…You are awesome and wonderful! Lead us Christ Jesus! We are your disciples. We will follow you anywhere you tell us to go…we will do and say whatever you command!"

Nine other bodies fell to their knees in prayer. Nine other hearts were broken and stripped of self-glory. Nine other minds were filled with wisdom from on high. Nine other souls were set aflame for the salvation of all mankind.

* * *

That afternoon, nine youth were baptized by John in the shallow end of Mike Littleton's swimming pool. John had suggested they tell their parents first and invite them to come and watch. Robert's response captured their unified sentiment "We can't wait."

"And besides," Taylor chimed in "They're next!"

40 THE VISION

From that day on, the lives of the youth were marked by a common focus and ambition: to know God and make Him known. They had been witnesses and partakers of the power and reality of God Himself. How could they go back to Sega and ping pong when there was so much more to discover in His word, so much praise and worship to be sung, and so much prayer to be offered? Even more, how could they keep these new wonderful things closed behind the Rec's door when there was a lost world right outside?

John's role began to resemble more of an overseer than leader. The youth were so hungry and thirsty for the things of God that it was nothing for them to sit for hours discussing and dissecting Scriptures, praying, singing, and then discussing some more. Everyone brought a different perspective to the conversation, which made for a well-rounded - at times hilarious - discourse. There were the occasional rabbit trails and John was always there to get things back on track, but he loved to let them debate with one another and wrestle with topics that were difficult to understand. In truth, John was blown away by the intensity with which the youth were studying God's word. He had yet to experience anything like it in all his years of high school and college. He had the feeling he was in the midst of something special and not of this world. With each passing day, the youth found themselves praying more and more for hearts and minds willing and capable to share the good news with all the people of Jajo. Everyone had ideas, but they needed a plan…a plan from God. A day was set-aside for prayer and fasting. Parents didn't see their children at all that morning or afternoon as sons and daughters remained behind bedroom doors searching the Scriptures for wisdom and pleading for God to give them a vision. Rosarita could only sit in the Stevens' kitchen all day feeling useless. That evening Taylor came exploding out of his room, dragging his little brother down the stairs behind him.

"Are you boys ready for dinner?" Maggie asked as they headed for the front door.

"We're fasting today Mom! And God answered my prayers!" and with that they were out the door.

Seconds later Paul came walking into the kitchen with the newspaper open in his hands, "did I just hear Taylor say they are fasting?"

"I uh…I believe so."

Paul kissed his wife on the cheek then laughed out loud as he turned and headed back to his favorite reading chair.

Maggie looked up at the ceiling "Lord? You hear that?"

"They're fasting!" Paul said from the den followed with another round of chuckles.

Maggie giggled and continued to smile as she put some of the table settings back into the cupboard.

* * *

The Stevens brothers quickly spread the word: everyone was immediately needed for an emergency meeting in the Rec. In minutes, all the other youth, along with John, sat in anticipation waiting for Taylor to share what was on his mind. Growling stomachs were ignored completely. This was a group of young people whose boredom and apathy had been swallowed up in new passion and purpose for life. Their business was now to be about God's business. There was no more time to waste. There was so much to be done!

"I just want all of you to know that I unpacked my suitcases today." The importance of Taylor's words weren't missed by anyone in the room, John included. "The other night we talked about Manuel and how we needed to help him. Truth is we know a lot of people who need help. We know a lot of people who need Jesus to save them."

All heads nodded in agreement.

"If we go back to the States we may never have another chance. Our parents have to be sure that it's safe for us here so I have an idea. First we invite our closest friends from around here, like Manuel and Raul and Pedro. And Susan, you girls can invite Daniela and Angela..."

"And Carlita," Robyn blurted.

"And Liliana," Susan added.

It was Jamie's turn, "Don't forget Rena."

Taylor interrupted before Stephanie opened her mouth. He knew the girls could go on forever.

"Okay, you get my point. Each of us can invite someone or a few, but not everybody, just those we know best."

"Invite them to what?" Tommy asked, unable to wait any longer.

"We invite everyone here for a party on Saturday night. We can have a cook-out and play basketball and other games and then come inside for some music and then John can speak about Jesus to everyone." It sounded wonderful. The idea had everyone's support. "Here are some things we need to do."

John sat quietly and listened, offering advice only when they asked or really needed it. Everything was set. They had a few days to prepare. Before the meeting ended, a hand silently raised.

"What is it Jamie?" Taylor asked.

Jamie looked around the room then slowly lowered her arm, shaking her head. Robyn shrugged her shoulders, just as confused as everyone else with her sister's odd behavior.

"Anything you want to say?" Taylor asked again.

Jamie shook her head "no" once more.

John was watching the young girl closely and could tell she definitely had something on her mind. By the look on her face it was something troubling.

"Jamie," John spoke gently, "if there's something we need to all talk about. Don't be afraid to tell us."

Everyone waited patiently. Finally the young girl found courage and stood to her feet. She spoke slowly.

"Is he still out there?"

"Who?" Tommy asked.

John, Taylor, and everyone else knew exactly who she meant. All eyes looked to John. After one more "Who?" Tommy finally caught on and grew silent as well.

"Well, I suppose he is out there somewhere." The kids didn't like that answer and John knew it. "But remember, even though *we* don't know where he is, God does know. God knows *exactly* where the man is and we've got to trust God to take care of us." One by one, John looked them all in their eyes. "You're all through with the drug junk right?"

Every head nodded "yes."

"You're ready to let God use you here, right?" Same response. "So the last question is – are you gonna trust God completely?" This time he got a vocal response.

"Yes!" Taylor declared boldly, followed by "I am's" and "Me too's" from all the others.

"Then let's get busy and leave the witch doctor to God."

* * *

After everyone left, John sat alone trying to figure out if he was making the right decision. He would keep the kids' story a secret for the time being. The parents didn't need any more stress and the police would possibly find this witch doctor man on their own. Then again, maybe they wouldn't. He bowed his head in prayer, asking God for one thing only…wisdom.

41 THE GUESTS

The rest of the week passed quickly for everyone. With the new surveillance equipment installed and no recent intruders, the parents began to return to their usual busy-ness. However, they did notice another strange phenomenon occurring around them, their children were busy as well. For the first time in a long time, moms and dads didn't hear any complaining from their kids about the miserable lives they were living. For the first time in a while, they didn't have to beg their children to turn off the TV, get up from the couch, and go find something to do. Most surprisingly of all, they didn't have to break up the constant arguments between their sons and daughters. Something had definitely happened, but none dared ask, too scared to ruin a good thing.

* * *

On Saturday night, phones rang all along the street as parents tried to figure out what was going on over at the Rec. What looked like around twenty Venezuelan kids had gathered at the basketball court. Scared that a mob of locals had come to attack their kids, perhaps the vandals themselves, the parents hurried over after calling Fernando in the security booth for his assistance. He wasn't there.

Paul arrived first, followed by Maggie and Regina Rollins, then the Cooks and Mrs. Childress. Lastly, the Littletons made the parental group complete. Mr. Childress was too busy reading the newspaper to join them. They stood and watched bewildered, as their children ran around in circles with around twenty local boys and girls and John yelled out some words they couldn't understand.

"Is that Fernando and Diego?" Mrs. Childress asked, pointing to two dark skinned, dark haired men dressed in blue uniforms, one of whom suddenly began running across the basketball court and towards a line of kids whose arms were outstretched and hands clasped together. As he crashed into the line they all fell to the ground and on top of him laughing hysterically.

"I think so," Maggie replied, unable to believe what she was seeing, but liking it.

"That's why Fernando didn't answer his phone!" Regina blurted out, still nervous.

"What are they doing?" Mr. Cook asked, looking around at the other parents.

"I don't know."

"Beats me."

Paul, who had been silent up to that point finally said, "I think it's a game."

His wife quickly agreed. "You're right honey, they're playing Red Rover, Red Rover!"

"You're right, Maggie!" Mrs. Cook exclaimed, "I remember that game!"

"Sure is," Mr. Cook added.

"Are you sure?" Regina asked, not yet convinced and still expecting the worst.

"Regina, don't you know Red Rover, Red Rover?" Mrs. Littleton asked. Regina shook her head slowly from side to side. "See watch...the kids from one team call out the name of someone from the other team and then they have to run over and try to break through their line." As Mrs. Littleton explained the game they all watched as Robert took off running across the court and crashed into the other line only to be lifted up into the air on the arms of John and Fernando. All the parents laughed at Robert's hopeless and failed attempt. Regina had one last worry, "But why are these kids here?

"I don't know, but it looks like they're having fun," Mr. Littleton said smiling, happy to see his son enjoying himself.

"Did any of you know about this?" Paul asked everyone.

They all answered, "No."

Paul continued, "Well, has anyone noticed their kids acting a little strange the past few days?"

"What do you mean by strange?" Mrs. Childress asked.

"More...*agreeable* is the only way I can think to describe it."

"Exactly," Mr. Cook said, winking at Paul and nodding his head.

They had all noticed the same thing, even Regina.

"You won't believe this, but Stephanie and Brad haven't fought one time in the last five days."

"Neither have Tommy and the girls, and I haven't heard the letters U S A in over three days. I believe that's a new record!" Mrs. Cook said, looking at her husband.

He looked at her then the others. "Do you think he's finally done it?" he asked.

"It could be," Paul said smiling.

"So what's going on out here?" Mr. Childress asked approaching from behind, his newspaper still in his hands. Mrs. Childress looked relieved.

"We think the kids might actually be enjoying themselves!" Paul answered back.

"Is that possible?" Mr. Childress joked, putting his arm around his wife and looking in the direction of their kids.

John suddenly appeared, startling the adults and interrupting their conversation. As they looked up they also saw Fernando walking quickly away towards the guardhouse. Diego had already disappeared. Fernando waved and yelled "Lo siento!", apologizing for being caught away from his post and behaving so immaturely. Maggie couldn't help laughing at him.

"No problema, Fernando!" she yelled back waving, as did the others. He was happy to hear it.

"Hello, parents!" John said while bending over trying to catch his breath. His clothes were pulled all out of place and his face flushed and shiny with sweat. "Well, as you can see we're having a little party this evening!"

"This is a good idea," Mrs. Cook said nodding her head.

"Well it wasn't mine, your kids came up with this one."

"Impossible," Mr. Childress replied.

"Nope, there's a few things going on that we need to talk about and so your kids want you to join us for our Bible study tomorrow night so we can share about it."

No one spoke for a few seconds.

"Okay," Paul answered first, followed one after another by the rest.

"Um..." John felt a little out of order saying what he needed to next, but he knew their success with the local kids depended on it, "I think the local kids might feel a little strange if you stand here for too long watching us."

The parents looked at their kids who had all stopped playing the game and were staring back. A few kids waved and their folks did the same though one or two failed to respond, still in shock from the transformation they were witnessing. The local kids looked a little nervous. They all realized John knew what he was talking about. Mr. Childress broke the silence, "Well John, have fun and we'll see you tomorrow night at what time?"

"Six o'clock."

"Alright, six it is."

Mrs. Childress shook John's hand and said "Thank you John." John just smiled. The others all dispersed in similar fashion. Maggie invited Mrs. Rollins to their home for coffee. She knew Regina would need an ear to listen to her thoughts about what was going on. Maggie was one of the few who still didn't mind spending time with her. God loved Regina, how could she not? Paul lingered around a little longer. John started the game up again, then after a few minutes realized what he should do.

"Come and join us Mr. Stevens!" he yelled.

"Oh no, that's okay. I just wanted to watch for..."

"Come on! I know you want to play."

"Yeah, come on dad!" Robert yelled.

The others joined in, "Come on Mr. Stevens!"

When Paul saw Manuel, whom he knew from the boy's few visits to their house, wave for him to join, he finally gave in.

* * *

The rest of the night went smoothly. They played more games and then the kids ran around as John began to grill hamburgers and hot dogs. Paul stayed around to help out and soon took over the job. John knew little about grilling, so he was relieved and glad to hand Paul the spatula and tongs. Soon everyone was stuffing his or her face with meats charbroiled to juicy perfection.

* * *

Twenty minutes later, after the last empty plate was thrown away, John invited everyone into the Rec room where he took a seat at the front and lifted his guitar into his lap. Mike took a seat behind the drum set and the two kicked off the night of worship with a set of songs they had practiced for many hours. Mike played softly or laid out completely most of the time, but he was doing it – he was the drummer in a band! A week before, the American kids would have all laughed and made fun of him, but not anymore. He was working for the King of Kings and the others totally respected his efforts. Actually, he was now the coolest in the bunch. As

Taylor watched and listened to Mike play, he regretted not showing up for drum lessons when John had offered the chance. Susan and Jamie also stood at the front of the room and helped lead the singing. All the songs had been printed out on small sheets of paper that were passed throughout the room, but many of the local youth had trouble keeping up with the English lyrics. By the end of the worship time, every single one of the Americans had committed in his or her heart to learn more Spanish. Still, all the local kids were eager to try and at least hummed the melodies as John and the girls repeated them over and over again. Paul sat in the back, feeling as if he was finding his life again.

After worship, John invited Susan's friend Angela to come and sit with him at the front of the room. She had offered to translate his message into Spanish. Speaking slowly and taking turns with his young translator, John shared a short ten minute testimony that described his life before he knew Jesus and how it changed after putting his faith and trust in his Lord and Savior. He concluded with a short explanation of why he came to Venezuela...to tell them about the good news of God's love for them. Taylor closed with a simple prayer in English and Spanish. The locals were impressed and touched. Until then, Taylor had used his second language to show off and build his ego, now he felt humbled to offer it to God. Afterwards, the Americans escorted their friends back to the front gate where they said goodnight and goodbye.

* * *

Instead of going home, the nine new missionaries returned to the Rec for a time of prayer. They were so full of joy and gratitude they thought their hearts would burst! Before praying, everyone shared an idea or two of what they thought could be done better or differently. Susan suggested working with Angela to translate a few songs into Spanish and then teach them to the group. Tommy voiced his desire to play guitar at the next meeting. Robyn thought she might be able to play keyboard. Stephanie volunteered to be in charge of preparing the song sheets with Robert's help. Finally, Taylor, with no official duty yet, was voted the group's leader, under John of course. Even though no one said it, they all had the same feeling that Taylor would soon be the team's preacher of some sort. He was almost ready. Their final commitment was to feast on the word of God every day. They made an agreement to hold each other accountable to spending time alone with the Lord every day in prayer and Scripture reading. John mentioned the idea of reading the Bible through in one year and they all jumped on it. He promised to get copies of the daily reading schedule to everyone the next day.

* * *

By the time John crawled into his bed it was after midnight. In his mind, the events of the night replayed over and over again. He saw the faces of all the Venezuelan kids – smiling faces – delighted with the friendship being shown them and the chance to experience something new. The faces of his youth also flashed before him. They too were smiling, thrilled and overjoyed as they experienced God's love moving through them. And what a time of prayer it had been! Each of them had lifted up their own words of thankfulness and praise to their awesome God. Paul Stevens had also joined in. Things were working out better than John could have ever dreamed. In a few days time, his little group of rebels had become a family. He still couldn't believe it. So much weight was gone from inside. The peace had returned, and with it a renewed passion for loving and knowing his God.

"This has all been too good to be true," John whispered to the darkness around him and for a split second he worried that come morning, it was all going to be the same as before.

Nothing, the words came from within and yet all around him, *will ever be the same again.*

With no need or desire to look back any longer, John silently prayed for the meeting they would have with the parents the following night, then quickly fell asleep.

42 THE UNITY

The inside of the Rec looked oddly different. For the first time in three years it was full of families. Finally, the building was being used for its intended purpose, not as a place of escape, but of gathering. The youth, who were discovering more joy and contentment each time they met inside, now wanted to share that joy and contentment with their parents.

Each family sat together in a group on the floor. Every father and mother, except Mr. Rollins, was present, but he hadn't been seen or heard from by his family in months. Of course, the men kept up with their partner's business dealings on almost a daily basis. At first, Paul kept Maggie up-to-date on his whereabouts and activities and she in turn kept Regina Rollins informed. After awhile, however, Mrs. Rollins didn't want to know anymore – she needed to let go and stop wasting her life waiting and worrying. She smiled proudly as Brad walked to the front of the room and asked for everyone's attention.

"I'd like to start tonight's meeting with a Bible verse – Hebrews 10:25. 'Let us not neglect our church meetings, as some people do, but encourage and warn each other, especially now that the day of his coming back again in drawing near.' "

Brad closed his Bible and took a seat next to his mom, who began to clap. She was so overjoyed, and all the other parents understood how she was feeling. All their children were changing, and, even though they didn't fully understand it, they knew it was something real. Every parent was truly interested in seeing just how John Parker had pulled it off.

John sat at the front of the room with his guitar in his hands and Stephanie and Susan on either side of him. Mike took his seat behind the drums. They led everyone through a series of praise and worship songs and a few traditional hymns. Most of the songs were new to the adults, and they found the words comforting, honest, and intensely personal.

"As the deer panteth for the water,
so my soul longeth after Thee..."

The Cooks felt as if they were back in their home church in Alabama. They could envision the choir members swaying back and forth in their white gold trimmed robes…

"Then sings my soul, my Savior God to Thee,
how great Thou art, how great Thou art…"

Mr. Littleton was reminded of his few visits to church with his grandmother as a teenage boy. His grandmother had loved that song; he had also, but soon afterwards decided church wasn't the place for a "cool" kid to go – an excuse that easily stayed with him into adulthood. He couldn't help thinking now just how cool his son was on the drums. Mike smiled at his dad and Mr. Littleton winked back at his son, causing him to miss a beat. No one noticed.

"Father I adore You and I lay my life before You,
how I love You…"

The Childresses had never gone to church before in their lives except for the annual Christmas service. These definitely weren't the campy folk songs they had expected to hear their daughter singing. The depth of the lyrics stirred something within them.

"I could get used to this," Mr. Childress whispered to his wife. She agreed.

"You are my strength when I am weak,
You are the treasure that I seek,
You are my all in all…"

Maggie and Paul were miles and years away from the rest. The songs had taken them back to another time and place – a place where God had brought them together and a time when they had been challenged and inspired. It was all coming back, but things were different now. Somehow, they were different. Those wonderful days of college were far behind them. Could it ever be the same again? They could at least try, and their sons were showing them the way. *It's time*, Maggie thought as she looked around at all of the parents, some holding each other, and everyone trying their best to sing the songs before them. She would never have believed it if she weren't seeing it herself. It was truly a miracle. It was time to stop longing for the past and let God move in the present. As the others sang, Maggie prayed silently, *Thank you Father for never leaving us. We've run so far, and yet You've stayed with us, waiting for us to turn back to You. May the others in this room find You also.*

* * *

After singing, John asked them all to turn to the book of Philippians, chapter two. Everyone reached for their Bibles, most of which were shiny and stiff from little use. Paul and Maggie had brought two and now lent one to the Childresses, who didn't even own one. It took awhile for everyone to find the book of Philippians. Some had to check in their table of contents while others looked to their neighbor for help. Tommy momentarily confused everyone by declaring that Philippians started on page 1505…in *his* Bible. That got everyone shouting out different page numbers and cracking up. Eventually things calmed down as everyone began to focus on the words before them. John led off with verses one and two, and then Tommy followed with two more. Susan gave passionate voice to verses five and six, and then Stephanie, when she came to the last words of verse eight, read each one slowly, as if they stood alone on the page. This pattern continued until Robert finished with verses seventeen and eighteen. As his sweet, innocent voice declared the joy of being poured out like a drink offering on the sacrifice of faith, a profound conviction fell upon everyone. Mothers and fathers alike were wiping tears from their eyes as Taylor walked to the front of the room. He stood before them all completely confident and relaxed. They all recognized the natural leader within. Paul beamed with pride.

"First, I want all of the parents to know that there will be no more graffiti or threats on the Rec walls."

The parents looked around at one another as the kids held their breath. Taylor was betting on the hope they would take his word and leave it at that.

"You're sure of that?" Mr. Cook asked.

Taylor's heart sped up.

"Yes sir," he answered without a trace of doubt.

"Alright." Mr. Cook responded, looking at the other fathers and then nodding at Taylor. Every adult in the room believed him. And that was the end of it.

"The reason we wanted all of you to come tonight is because first of all you're our parents and the most important people in our lives."

There was not a parent in that room who didn't have the same thought – aliens had kidnapped their children and taken over their bodies.

"And secondly, because something has happened to all of us, which I'm sure you've all noticed, and the best way I can describe it is this: God has changed us from the inside out, and we want you to know how wonderful and real it is." Taylor opened his Bible. "God's Word says, 'Trust in the Lord with all your heart and lean not on your own understanding, in all your ways acknowledge Him and He will make your paths straight.'"

All the parents wondered how different their lives would be if they were to truly seek such a promise. Mr. Littleton suddenly felt like his ego had caused him to miss out on the things of God long enough. He hadn't been too cool, but too *scared*. Now his son was showing him what courage was all about. He could at least try.

* * *

Paul was so proud of his boys…but were they proud of him? It was time he fulfilled his role as father and husband. He had to have more of God so he could be more of the leader he was called to be.

* * *

"His will. His way. His glory. It's that simple for us now. God has our full attention." Taylor had everyone's full attention at that moment as well.

"Say it with me – His will. His way. His glory!" All the children and parents repeated the phrase. The youth put a little more gusto in it, but the parents were trying and gaining more enthusiasm with each passing second.

"Tonight," Taylor continued. "I just want to tell you some of the things that we want to see happen. We want to invite you to join us every Sunday night for a family time just like this. We'll sing, read and pray. We feel that not only do we need to all stick together, but also draw close to God together. We're going to start to do a lot of outreaches to the people in Jajo. We just want to let you know some of our ideas so you won't be surprised next time you see a bunch of our friends here. Susan's going to share about this." Taylor stepped back as Susan stood up in front and continued.

"On Wednesday nights we're going to invite our closest friends from town to come for games, music, and Bible study. We want to take God's love to the people in Jajo, but we're not sure yet how to do it. We've got to do some planning, but God has really given us a desire to share His love with the people. If we sit in here every night, we might as well be back in the States. We're here for a reason and now we know why."

Now we know why. Those words echoed through every parent's soul. The adults suddenly realized that the glue binding their children was "purpose". The kids had never stopped to think that their parents might actually be dealing with the same feelings and frustrations they were. The youth would've never guessed their folks also lay in bed at night asking the darkness why they were there. The men convinced themselves it was for work and success, but soon that wasn't enough to satisfy. At first, the women had been excited about starting a new life in a foreign land, but the longer they hid behind their tall electric fence, the more depressed and confined they felt. As the adults listened to their children speak about a newfound purpose, they longed to share in it.

"We want you to join us and be involved as much as you can. We know you're busy and don't have a lot of free time, so whenever any of you want to help out just tell us."

This was it; the parents were finally being offered a reason to live a thousand miles from everything they once held dear. Two mothers, eager to belong, raised their hands. Taylor thought they had a question.

"Yes, Mrs. Cook?" He asked stepping forward, ready to defend their cause to the death.

"Count me in."

"Me too!" echoed Mrs. Childress, followed by her husband.

"I'll be there!" Mr. Littleton spoke loudly, smiling at his wife and son. Maggie and Paul Stevens raised their hands, as did Mrs. Rollins, "Don't forget about me!" It was unanimous. The children had never felt prouder in their lives.

"Okay, well here are some of the things we want to do..."

* * *

John looked around the room with a huge smile spread across his face. Once again he didn't need to say a thing. He thanked his Father in Heaven wondering at the same time if he was still needed anymore.

You're not finished yet, was the answer given.

John was glad; things were just getting exciting.

43 THE GAME

The following Wednesday afternoon, over twenty kids showed up for games, snacks and Bible study. The mothers prepared cookies and drinks and were there to serve the kids after they played. Two of the fathers also came to join in the activities. The following Saturday morning, all the kids, along with Paul and Mr. Childress, went to town. The fathers talked with Mayor Velasquez, getting his permission to use the town's sports park to hold a basketball tournament in two weeks time. Then the youth handed out flyers to everyone in the area. The Americans would form their own team with Mr. Stevens, Mr. Cook, Mr. Littleton, Tommy, Brad, Mike and Taylor. John and Mr. Childress would be the referees. Seven more teams with no more than nine players each would be allowed to sign up. Only those 13 years and older could play. It would be a single elimination tournament with the first games starting at 10 a.m. and the final match planned for sometime around 5 p.m. Best of all, it was free, and the winners would each get new basketball shoes and a ball, and everyone who participated would get a T-shirt. The fathers had all the prizes planned and ready to order. The women, more concerned about safety and health than anyone else, planned to purchase first-aid kits, fruits, water, and sport drinks for everyone.

By late that Saturday afternoon, the sign up sheet was already full and the first round match-ups decided. The locals were thrilled. They were actually going to have a real life tournament with prizes and everything, just like the NBA! Of course, not everyone who wanted to participate got to sign up, but their disappointment was soon caught up in the excitement and anticipation of the others. Rumor spread that it was sure to become an annual event.

The American families spent the next two weeks getting things organized. Eighty T-shirts were ordered and delivered from Florida. Each team's shirts were a different color and displayed the words "Jajo Street Jam" with the image of a basketball on the front and John 3:16 in Spanish on the back. The winners would get to choose the ball and shoes of their choice from a major sports catalog.

"What if you win?" Maggie asked her husband one day, wondering if the locals would scream "unfair!"

Paul knew what she was thinking. "Honey, wait 'til you see me out there," He said, laughing. "You just make sure there's plenty of fruit and water and a stretcher ready for me."

"But it could happen and that would be kind of anticlimactic don't you think?"

"Maggie, all the teams who signed up know that we're playing and they expect us to try to win. If we didn't then they probably wouldn't even accept the prizes. So if we pull it off – thanks to our boys – then we earned it and I guess we'll save a little money cause there's no way Taylor's getting any more shoes. Besides, John's not playing so everyone has a chance to win."

* * *

During the second week the mayor had the park cleaned and even repainted the two basketball courts that would be used for the tournament. The kids stayed off those courts as if they were holy ground. The local newspaper wrote a short article about the event. The excitement spread up into the hills and reached a few surrounding towns. For the American youth, those two weeks passed by faster than any ever before. From morning to night, through school and free time, the kids worked hard to finish their studying and preparations for the big day. The real purpose of the basketball tournament was to open the door for the Americans to share the gospel with as many of the people of Jajo as possible. During the half time of the championship game, they planned to perform a simple drama and then John would share the good news of Jesus Christ.

On Friday night it was difficult for everyone, adult and child alike, to get any sleep. Early Saturday morning, with all of their vehicles packed full of tables, chairs, coolers, balls, T-shirts, and every other necessary item, and the kids all packed into the Childress' shuttle bus, the families started the journey to town. They arrived to find what appeared to be Jajo's entire population, including a group of police officers, waiting and strolling about. A large banner had been hung the night before by order of Mayor Velasquez, surprising even the Americans. It read "Primer Torneo de Basquetbol Anual de Jajo". Apparently the mayor had also caught on to the idea of a yearly event.

After parking, everyone worked together to get everything set up as fast as possible. Regina Rollins and Maggie took their seats behind the coordinators' table and checked off the player's names as they arrived. The other parents handed out the T-shirts to the players who put them on as fast as possible. The courts were soon a kaleidoscope of colors as shirts of light blue, red, green, purple, black, gray, brown, and pink moved about warming up. John set up a portable CD player with two large speakers, and soon the park was filled with the booming sound of upbeat hip-hop Christian music. Next, he walked to the center of the court in his homemade striped referee shirt and blew his whistle. As he watched the players of all the teams circle around him, he knew in his heart he wouldn't trade that moment and that day for all the MVP awards and championship rings in the world.

The teams were filled with many familiar faces. From young teenagers to young men and even a few fathers and single men in their 30s and 40s, the sight of whom made Paul and the other American fathers relax a little. Taylor stood next to John and translated the best he could.

"Well, guys are you ready to get started?"

The crowd of smiling faces erupted in one voice "¡Si!" "Yes!".

"Good! By the way, nice shirts everyone!"

The smiles grew even wider as everyone glanced around at the colorful array of team colors. John couldn't help laughing at the American team with their hot pink look. The shirt company had made a mistake and sent the wrong color. Knowing that no team would want to wear such a girly color, the Americans humbly decided to suffer. John was sure the Lord was involved in this lesson of humility. The wives and girls thought they looked cute.

John explained the few simple rules they were going to use — basically, no rough stuff. Any fighting or threatening or excessive cursing would mean immediate disqualification. More than anything, he wanted to keep order. There would be no shot clock, lane count, or things like that.

"Just have fun and remember it's just a game. Good luck to everyone. Now we're going to have a quick prayer to ask God to be with us today."

Taylor asked them all to close their eyes as he thanked God for the day and for the chance to have some fun and make new friends. The local players stood still and silent. They were also thankful and desired to express it along with the Americans.

After "Amen", John told the four teams who were playing in the first games to stay and shake hands. Then they headed off toward their benches. Suddenly Mrs. Childress came running up to John with a look of distress on her face.

"John, Larry had to leave for an emergency! He can't be the other referee!"

John tried to stop her from panicking but she kept talking, "I'm sorry, it's the stupid rig on the West coast, something's wrong and Larry's in charge of repairing…" as she spoke, a helicopter flew overhead then moved up the side of the mountain and disappeared. "I'm so sorry John, they're always needing him to..."

John knew she'd go on explaining forever so he put a hand on her shoulder and just interrupted her. "It's okay Mrs. Childress. Don't worry. We'll be alright."

"But how? Now we can't play two games. We'll never be able to finish."

John could tell she was truly upset; he assumed she felt responsible in some way.

"I promise everything will be alright. Don't worry." Just then a voice spoke from behind them.

"Hello, is there something wrong?" It was a deep and kind voice.

John and Mrs. Childress turned to see a tall strong looking Venezuelan man standing and smiling at them. His face and eyes were as gentle as his voice. He spoke again.

"My name is Hector."

John shook the Venezuelan's outstretched hand, followed by Mrs. Childress.

"Is there any way I can help you with the tournament?"

John and Mrs. Childress looked at one another and the worry on her face was quickly replaced with a smile.

"Well," John replied, "we seem to be in fast need of a referee. Could you be in charge of some games on that court over there?" John pointed to the nearby court where two teams in black and gray were warming up. Hector gazed in the court's direction then turned back to face them.

"I'd love too. It's been a while since I've played. I might be a little rusty."

"Well, you'll only need to watch for the basic stuff. Any fighting or threatening or excessive cursing means immediate disqualification. Here's your whistle."

"Sounds easy enough," Hector answered, taking the whistle and roping it around his neck.

John liked Hector immediately. He was certain that his new helper, with his broad shoulders and long arms, had been or still was a ball player, and probably a very good one. The two men said goodbye to Mrs. Childress and then walked over to Hector's court as John explained the details and rules of the tournament. Soon they were both blowing their whistles and tossing jump balls into the air. All the players who were on the other courts practicing soon quit and joined the crowds to watch the first games.

* * *

Into the day they played. The first two games went smoothly with little disruption and some very entertaining shots. The crowds grew as the minutes passed. Afterwards, the teams shook hands and went their separate ways – the winners relieved to be moving forward and the losers already thinking about next year.

The Americans played during the second round and managed to pull off a win with a last second shot by Taylor. The fathers were completely exhausted. Maggie thought maybe she *should* get a stretcher ready. By noon, the mothers had to send for more fruit and water.

John and Hector sat down and ate lunch together discussing some of the different calls they had made and shots they had seen. Hector was thrilled to be involved. Soon they were back on the courts blowing their whistles once again.

Only one game caused any trouble for the referees that day. Not surprisingly it was between the team of mostly high school players and mostly high school dropouts. An obvious foul was made and John's whistle blew but that didn't stop one player from throwing a punch that landed on the chin of Juan Lopez, one of the most talented and popular players in the area, who chose to demonstrate his skills on the public courts all day long rather than on the high school team. He took the hit and didn't retaliate. John could tell as he ran in between the circling teams that Juan was using all his strength to hold himself back. They had all heard John's warning – any fighting meant immediate disqualification. Juan's teammates were ready to pounce if he gave the word. He didn't. He wanted those shoes.

John told the player who had struck Juan that he and his team were out. They immediately yelled and protested and John was glad he couldn't understand them. Hector stopped his game and went over to assist John in quickly getting everyone calmed down. The disqualified team walked off cursing under their breath, mostly at their own player who had ruined their chances. They *had* been the favorites to win; now the other teams felt rejuvenated.

By four o' clock there were three teams left — the Americans, a team of thirteen and fourteen year old boys including Taylor's friend Manuel, and last but not least, Juan Lopez' team.

To everyone's relief, the sun, which had been shining brightly all day, finally began to disappear behind thickening clouds as the Americans and young Venezuelan boys began their match to see who would make it into the championship against Juan's team.

The Venezuelan youngsters ran circles around the Americans, especially the men. Luckily for the Americans, they couldn't get many to go in the net. The fathers then began to implement a new strategy. Their sons were sent driving through the lane for lay-ups while they sat at the perimeter and tried their luck at three pointers. Between the three of them, they went 7 for 11. The Americans won by nine points. The fathers were happy to have survived, but realized once they lost their touch from the outside it would be over. Their sons were excited. They had felt that if they made it to the finals it would make everyone listen more to what they would share at half time. They had all feared losing early on and then standing before the crowds and talking about victory in Jesus. John had reminded them that it was God's show, not theirs. They listened, but still worried. Now they could breathe easier, except for the fathers who sat exhausted on the bench barely able to breathe at all.

"You've got to find your second wind dad!" Taylor said to his father, as Mrs. Stevens wiped her husband's face with a cool, wet washcloth.

"Did you hear that men?" Mr. Stevens asked, looking in the direction of Mr. Cook and Mr. Littleton whose wives were also tending stiff necks and sore muscles.

"Did he say *second* wind?" Mr. Littleton asked.

"I'm on my 8th wind already." Paul said, winking at Taylor.

"What's the limit on winds anyway?" Mr. Cook asked

"I don't know, but I've passed it." Mr. Littleton replied.

"Dad, you're not *that* old!" Mike Littleton remarked as he sat next to his father.

"What about your mom?" Mr. Littleton asked, then squealed as his wife's fingers dug into the back of his neck. Everyone laughed out loud together. The families, though tired and worn out, were having the time of their lives.

44 THE HALFTIME

After a twenty-minute break, John blew the whistle. It was five o'clock. The fathers were gently helped to their feet, tenderly kissed, and then sent back out onto the court with a firm slap on their rear end and shouts of "Go get 'em!" and "Play ball!" erupting behind them. Wife sympathy time was over.

The sun was disappearing behind the mountains, the air was growing cool, and the crowds continued to increase. It was time for the final match. John and Hector would officiate together. The teams shook hands and took their places. Juan and his teammates were smiling and relaxed; too relaxed. From somewhere inside, perhaps an area reserved for such emergencies, the grown ups discovered a new spark to their game once the ball was tipped. The wives and children noticed, and their cheers increased in number and volume. The people of Jajo didn't really know who to cheer for — their own, or these crazy Americans who had given them all a chance to enjoy themselves. They decided to cheer for every player and every shot. The cheers energized the players. This was by far the biggest crowd most of them had ever played before and probably ever would. The result was non-stop action and noise. Even John's whistle was drowned out. The teams took turns taking the ball down the court and scoring. Back and forth they went. The men continued their strategy and it continued to work. They would sink two or three perimeter and three point shots, then throw the other team off by suddenly dishing it inside to one of their boys. For every score the locals made, the Americans answered with one of their own. It was turning into a dogfight. As the seconds ticked down before half time, the moms and girls were busy getting the speakers, microphone, instruments, and music ready. John blew the whistle and the players exited the court to get a drink and sit down. Soon John reappeared at center court with a microphone in his hand and Hector standing beside him. Taylor was glad to let Hector take over the translating so he could recuperate.

"Is everyone having a good time?" John asked excitingly. "We've had some good basketball today haven't we?"

As Hector translated, the crowd and all the players yelled and cheered in agreement.

"Now we want to ask everyone to just have a seat or stand quietly and listen to some songs and testimonies that we want to share with you. Today is a special day. Not because of basketball and not because of the fun we're having. It's a special day because God is with us in this place and His love is bringing us together. The Bible, God's word, says, 'Let all the peoples of the earth, from every tribe and tongue, praise His name.' We want to praise God together with you today."

John took a seat as Tommy, with his guitar strapped over his shoulder, and the rest of the music team walked out to center court. Mike, the group's official percussionist, carried some small bongos to beat on. The girls plugged in their microphones. Hector remained on the court with them.

Susan looked out over the crowd and spoke, "We're so glad all of you are here. We thank you for making us feel so welcome today. Now we want to sing and tell you about something that is very important to us, the most important thing in our lives. We want you to know God loves you. This first song is called "Lord I Lift Your Name On High."

Hector translated Susan's words and immediately the talking in the crowd ceased. Everyone wanted to hear.

Tommy began strumming the chords on his guitar, and Mike quickly joined in with the percussion. After a stanza of only instruments, the girls began singing the first verse in beautifully blended harmony. They had practiced long and hard.

After singing the song through in English, all the others stopped and Susan repeated the chorus in Spanish with Tommy strumming softly behind her. Everyone began clapping and cheering, proud of this American girl's enthusiasm for learning their language. Susan's eyes were closed. She felt her spirit being lifted up. A smile spread wide across her face. She was smiling at her Savior. Soon the applause died away as everyone listened intently to the words. She repeated the chorus three times, then ended slowly. Applause erupted again. The Americans smiled as Tommy counted off "Where Do I Go". The guitar sprang to life again in his hands as he slid them up and down the fret board – they were going to rock this one! Mike kept the tempo moving and with Robert's help, everyone's hands began to clap. Once again they sang the song in English twice then all the Americans attempted to repeat the chorus in Spanish. During practice in the Rec they had all followed Susan's lead, now it was impossible to hear her and some of them forgot exactly how to say the words. The crowd cheered again, but some leaned forward not clearly understanding exactly what the kids were singing. The song kind of ended on a dead note with all the kids mumbling a different word. Tommy let go of his guitar and shook his head at the others who were all red faced and embarrassed. The crowds however continued to cheer and clap. They were impressed. The Americans quickly ran off the court mumbling to each other. Hector spoke into the mic informing the crowd that a short drama was next. Off the court the youth huddled around John, their faces dejected.

"Guys, it's okay, you were awesome! Everyone loved it and most of all they listened."

Taylor joined them. "Awesome job, guys!" As their leader he only had encouragement to share. "Now let's do this drama for Jesus. Everyone get in your place."

"Okay go! I'll start the song," John shouted, winking at Taylor, proud of his positive attitude.

The four Americans in the drama took their places. John set the CD to the right track and hit play. The soft sound of violins and cellos filled the evening air. Everyone grew quiet and still. The music was intoxicating and stirring. The hint of a melody rolled along gently until finally a kettledrum rolled and Susan took her cue to begin slowly moving across the court with her arms out in front of her feeling the air and occasionally stumbling as if she were blind. Her body suddenly came to a complete stop. As she did so, Tommy began moving across the court in the opposite direction with a look of unbearable pain and agony etched on his face. He held and dragged his crippled leg behind him. Soon he froze in place, and as he did so Stephanie began walking between them both. She moved slowest of all, shaking with each step and holding two red folded up bandanas to her eyes. She halted and raised her sobbing face towards heaven with a look of confusion and despair, then buried it in her hands. She crouched down to her knees and went still. The music reached a crescendo then disappeared. No one in the giant crowd stirred. No voices could be heard. A soft piano began playing and Taylor, who was standing off to the side of them all, slowly began to walk around. He moved closer to them, observing them, almost touching them. They all remained frozen in place. Again the music grew louder and louder, then faded away. Taylor closed his eyes and lifted his hands toward heaven. Once more, the music disappeared. Soon a full orchestra began to repeat the melodies that had been introduced earlier in the piece. Taylor opened his eyes and walked over to Tommy. He ran his fingers down the cripple's leg. As Tommy came to life and began to leap for joy, Taylor moved his hand down his own leg and it went limp. Tommy ran off ecstatic and Taylor moved towards Stephanie dragging his crippled leg in pain. Upon reaching her, he touched her head and she looked up at him frightened. He gently removed the red cloths from her hands and wiped her face. She stood up in amazement, turning in circles, laughing and smiling and Taylor wiped his own eyes with the cloth and began to sob. Stephanie skipped away as Taylor, limping and shaking, made his way towards Susan. He moved his hands over her eyes and immediately they opened and she began to jump and run around excitedly in response to all that her eyes were taking in. Taylor wiped his hands over his eyes and then began to feel the air in front of him unable to see where he was going. He stumbled and sobbed and as he did so the other three formed a cross with their bodies. Tommy stood in the middle with his arms at his side. The two girls stood on either side of him with their arms extended outward. Taylor slowly backed himself up against the cross then proceeded to slam his own hands back against the girls' arms. His face twisted and contorted in pain. The music, building momentum by the second, reached a crescendo of full dramatic force then faded away. The kettledrum rolled as Taylor dropped his head, closed his eyes and let the red cloths he was holding slowly, but not completely, spill from his hands like blood. No one in the crowd whispered or even blinked and children who had climbed up onto the fences for a better view now hung completely motionless. Soft, high forlorn notes on a piano echoed throughout the park. Tommy walked out from behind Taylor's crucified body and one after the other pulled his hands away from the cross. Taylor fell forward into Tommy's arms, limp and lifeless. Tommy gently laid Taylor onto the ground then knelt down next to him. Susan and Stephanie walked around and knelt down as well. All three lowered their heads as if in regret and remorse. As they did so the orchestra began to softly join in with the leading piano.

Taylor stirred.

Just a twitch of his arm caused a shout of glee from someone in the crowd. The music began to build.

Next, he raised himself up onto his arms then pulled his knees up under his chest. The crowds began to clap in anticipation. The music grew stronger and louder, closing in on the climactic moment. Suddenly Taylor stood up tall and straight. The kettledrum rolled like thunder. The cymbals crashed! He threw the cloths out into the air as the full sound of the song's theme and emotion blasted out from the speakers. The three at Taylor's feet slowly lifted their faces with a look of amazement and joy spread across them. They raised themselves up onto their knees. Taylor reached out to them, smiling and even laughing. They took hold of his hands, smiling back. The music remained at the heightened pitch for many seconds as the crowd cheered, clapped, and whistled. Stephanie, Tommy, and Susan stood up and hugged Taylor, then the four of them walked off the court. John and Hector walked back out into the center. They waited for everyone to get quiet again. It took a moment. Many were discussing the powerful scenes they had just witnessed.

"First of all, thank you so much for letting us share our lives with you today…I want to start off by asking how many of you have heard of Jesus Christ?"

Hector repeated and hands all over the park shot up into the air. John continued.

"How many of you believe in Jesus and have given your life to Him?" About a quarter of the previous hands rose up into the air again. Many of these faces had tears streaming down their cheeks. It had been awhile since they had pondered what Christ had done for them.

"I just want everyone to know that what Jesus Christ did on the cross, he did for every person on the earth, for everyone here today…" John paused and Hector's booming voice repeated his words in Spanish. "He died for you and me because we have sin in our heart…When Jesus was on the cross, all the sin of the world was put on him…God says that whoever believes this will have all of their sins forgiven and will live forever with Him in heaven…Without Jesus, you will die in your sins and go to Hell. Most people don't like to talk about Hell, because it's such a horrible place…Well, it is horrible; it's bad because it's a place where souls will be separated from God forever. But God says it is real, and because I believe it's real and because these kids believe it's real and because we believe that you must have Jesus to get into heaven, we've come today to tell you about Him. We've come to tell you he loves you. We've come to tell you if you'll just believe what God says, He will save you and change your life. We want all of you to be in heaven and experience the joy of knowing God on earth and that's why we're here today." John hadn't planned on, it and none of the others had considered it, but he felt the Spirit leading and the question came naturally, "Does anyone here want to put their trust in Jesus today?" Even before Hector finished translating the question, hands went up all over. He and John both smiled and nodded their heads at one another.

Thank you, God, John whispered, glancing up at the sky. He looked over at the American families who were all staring back at him with wide grins stretched across their faces. Paul gave him a thumbs up.

"Okay!" He said, looking once again at the mass of people. "Okay," he repeated, wondering just how he was going to do this. He began ordering directions before he really knew what he was doing.

"If you want to find forgiveness from your sins and give your life to Jesus then please come forward. Please come here. Here onto the court." As John motioned with his hands, Hector looked at him with an expression that seemed to ask, "Are you sure about this?" then the Venezuelan repeated what John said and immediately people began to move forward. More directions followed.

"Everyone, please make room! Please back up if you can!"

It didn't take John long to realize the foolishness of his idea. Many near the court walked out and stood around him while others tried to move out of the way so that those behind could get through. The result was a collision of bodies. A human traffic jam seemed to be in the making. Aggravated voices began to fill the air. *Now what?* John wondered, a panic forming deep in his chest. The "altar call" technique had backfired. He needed to restore order and calm everyone down quickly. Where was Taylor? John suddenly wished more than ever that Jajo had a local church with a pastor…someone to help. A large hand fell on John's shoulder. John turned to see Hector still at his side.

"Brother John, do you have a plan?"

"Not really. I'm afraid that was a bad idea. I just wanted to lead everyone in a prayer of repentance and salvation but now we just really need to get everyone calmed down."

"Maybe I can help."

Hector raised his microphone and began to speak to the crowds. Soon they grew as still and quiet as they had been during the drama. Even those who hadn't tried to come forward listened quietly, interested in what was happening. As Hector spoke everyone suddenly closed their eyes and bowed their heads. Hector closed his as well. John watched as the man's face changed, a look of urgency appearing. His eyes were squeezed shut so tight that his cheeks had wrinkled up around them. John wondered what was happening. Hector had just proceeded to take over and John didn't even know who he was or if he was even a Christian. *Lord, I hope I didn't just blow this.*

Hector continued to speak slowly, his voice full of emotion. The crowd murmured along with him. John wondered what they were saying.

Hector paused then preceded to speak using short sentences, one after another, that everyone in the crowd repeated after him. John realized they were all praying. He tried to understand their words, but could only recognize one, "Jesús", which they repeated over and over. Soon Hector said "amen" and a loud "amen!" echoed from the crowd. All eyes opened. Hector suddenly raised his fist into the air and shouted more words. Everyone began to shout and yell with him, while at the same time smiling and laughing in joy. Hector repeated the yell over and over again and everyone began to hug one another and shake hands. John stared around in disbelief hoping that he knew what was happening. Someone grabbed John's arm from behind. He turned and was relieved to see Taylor's face.

John yelled down at him, "What's going on?"

"Can you believe it?!" Taylor yelled, grinning from ear to ear.

"What did Hector say?"

"He just led everyone in a simple prayer asking Jesus to forgive them and help them to follow and obey him forever and then he told them that Jesus is more powerful than any of their gods, more powerful than any evil spirit. Then he told the new Christians to read the Bible and pray and meet with one another…now he's saying something about starting a church and finding a pastor, that they should pray for this."

Hector pointed over to John and spoke. The crowds began to clap and cheer.

"He said God brought you here to help them."

John smiled at the mass of people. Hector spoke again and hands were raised all over the park.

"I think now he's telling those who were already Christians to meet with the new believers to talk and pray with them." Before Taylor finished his sentence, people began moving off of the courts, as those from outside came and took them by the hand or shoulder. Many came over to John and shook his hand whispering "Gracias, señor," and "Gracias, amigo." Manuel ran up and announced that he had become a Christian, and the three of them hugged and hopped around the court like kangaroos while the other Americans were swarmed with gratitude. Many of their local friends had echoed Hector's prayer and given their lives to Christ. The American youth were overjoyed and awestruck.

It took almost twenty minutes to get the court clear. Hector reminded John that it was getting dark and they should hurry to finish the tournament. John's mind was so preoccupied he barely heard him. There were so many things to plan now and to prepare, he didn't know if he could even finish the game. Hector blew the whistle and called the two teams back onto the court. As players took their positions, the thought struck John that without Hector, they wouldn't have been able to pull this off. As soon as it was all over, he and Hector had to have a talk.

45 THE FINAL WHISTLE

The championship game started again, but it wasn't the same game. All the players, American and Venezuelan alike, continuously glanced at all that was going on around them. People were sitting in small groups on the grass talking and praying. The American women and kids were scattered throughout the crowds talking and sharing as best they could. Three of the players on the local team failed to return to the court. Juan Lopez was one of them, and both teams immediately felt his absence. He was finally spotted in a circle of men sitting over on another court with their eyes closed and heads bowed. As the game continued on around him, John stared dumbfounded at all the spiritual activity taking place before his eyes. Some had come forward to find new and better seats to watch the game now that others were out of the way, but most, in fact almost all of the people, weren't really paying attention anymore. God had their attention. John noticed the mayor sitting with a group on the grass. Many police officers were sitting and praying as well. It was overwhelming. Tears of joy ran down John's face. If basketball had served any significant purpose in his life, it had just begun that day.

If only my teammates and classmates could see this, John thought. *If only Coach McKenrick could witness this! And I know you're loving this Scott!*

For the rest of the game Hector's whistle served two purposes; calling fouls and bringing John out of his daydreams and back to the game. Meanwhile, on the court, the Americans were off their mark. The fathers missed every shot they threw up and the boys mishandled the passes that the fathers dished inside to them. The other team didn't do much better, but managed to slowly even up the score. With only minutes left, Lopez reentered the game with a new spring in his step and look of peace on his face. He smiled at the Americans and patted them on the rear as he ran past. He also took the open lane to the basket before the others could blink and threw up swish after swish from every angle on the perimeter. He was on. His teammates knew it and gave him the ball every time. The Americans knew it and almost forgot they were playing against him, longing to just sit back and watch. Soon the people finished their talking and praying and walked back to the edge of the court to watch the final minutes of the game.

Taylor, sparked by Lopez' performance, began to find the basket himself on every drive. The two took turns answering each other's shot at both ends of the court. In the final minute, Taylor sank a three pointer, blocked a short sideline pass to Juan for an easy lay up, and tied the score. The crowd was going crazy again. Juan was having fun, and Taylor was focused on his opponent. With seconds left, the ball reached Juan's hands and the two moved down the court toe to toe. Juan dribbled in and out of his legs and Taylor slapped at the air only a split second too late every time. Juan stopped outside the three-point line and stood up tall, dribbling the ball slowly with his right hand on his right side. It was time for the final shot. The gifted Venezuelan player smiled at Taylor, who kept his eyes locked on the ball. The crowd let out a thankful roar of satisfaction to both teams for their entertaining efforts. The clock in John's hand was nearing ten seconds. He lifted the whistle to his mouth. Juan acted as if he had all the time in the world. He took one last deep breath, lifted his eyes to the sky, and then, as if knowing it was coming, deftly moved the ball behind his back to his left hand just as Taylor lunged forward. Immediately the American teenager knew he'd been beat. The dark skinned new child of God glided through the rest of the awestruck defense and lifted off the ground as the final whistle blew. He soared towards the basket for an easy lay up and victory. Paul, in his post position, jumped as high as his rubbery legs would allow and slapped down at the ball. He hit nothing but arm. Juan crashed down onto the concrete as the ball bounced off the court. Paul fell onto his knees beside the boy, apologizing over and over again in Spanish, "Lo siento! Lo siento!" It hadn't been intentional and everyone knew it, but still it looked bad and hurt a little. Paul lifted Juan to his feet at which point Juan suddenly wrapped his arms around Paul and hugged him. It caught everyone by surprise. When they parted, Juan's eyes were moist.

"Gracias hermano," he said. "Jesús está en mi corazón."

Paul felt his eyes watering up. "Yes," he said smiling, "Jesús está en tu corazón." He embraced the boy again. The crowds were cheering and clapping feverishly. They were already witnessing a change in a boy who had before always been the first to start trouble, not make peace.

Hector reminded everyone of the foul shots that Juan still had to shoot. The players took their places even though there would be no rebound. Juan was still smiling as he threw up the first shot. It bounced around the rim then rolled out and over the edge as the crowd "Oohed and ahhed." Juan, without hesitation or a care in the world, released the second shot…nothing but net.

His teammates ran to his side and lifted him up into the air yelling and chanting his name. He quickly asked them to put him down and started everyone yelling the name "Jesús, Jesús, Jesús!" They continued to yell, even after he walked away to shake hands with Taylor.

"You very good," Juan said smiling at his toughest opponent.

"You are very good Juan!" Taylor echoed.

"Thank you, thank you for Jesus."

"Thank God for Jesus," Taylor said in Spanish pointing to the sky. Juan shook his head in agreement.

All of the other players shook hands and talked on the court, which once again was swarmed with people. The American men collapsed on their bench as their wives poured water on their faces and into their mouths.

"Praise God it's over!" Paul said, lying on his back smiling up at Maggie. They all agreed. The women were so proud of their exhausted jocks.

John worked his way through the crowd talking with many, but mostly just smiling and shaking hands. He was searching for Hector, who was nowhere to be seen.

* * *

It was two hours later before the last items were loaded into their vehicles and the last "good-byes" and handshakes exchanged. The Americans had stayed around to talk and clean up, but the mayor assured them that he would take care of it all. He begged them to go home and rest.

The youth rode back together in the shuttle bus. They were hyper and loud and everyone, except Mrs. Childress, was glad not to be the one driving them home. She hated the Swan.

* * *

John sat in the front seat of Maggie's Range Rover as they waited for the other vehicles to pull out. Paul was sprawled out in the back.

"Guess what Susan told me guys?" Maggie asked.

John and Paul both opened their eyes, looking in her direction.

"Eleanor gave her life to Jesus today! She prayed during the halftime invitation. And Susan and her mom are going to talk to Mr. Childress about becoming a Christian as soon as he gets home. His girls are very persuasive!"

Maggie laughed with joy and excitement in her voice as Paul shouted "Thank You Lord!" and John followed with a hearty "Amen!"

She slowly drove away from the basketball courts, following behind the shuttle bus in an awestruck daze. No one said a word until Maggie voiced the opinion of everyone. "Wow!"

"Wow!" John echoed, feeling the same awe himself.

"I couldn't say it better myself," Paul added.

"Who would have thought," John mumbled.

"Praise God for plans so much bigger than ours!" Maggie exclaimed.

"There must have been around two hundred and fifty people out on the court praying with Hector." Paul said.

Hearing that name reminded John of something.

"You know I tried to talk to him afterwards, but couldn't find him. Where does he live?

Paul and Maggie were quiet. John looked at Maggie, then back at Paul. "Where does he work?"

"I don't know," Maggie said looking in the rear view mirror at her husband, "today is the first time I've met him."

"What?" John asked, "Don't you know him?"

"Nope, I've never seen him before either," Paul said sitting up in the back.

"You acted like you knew him," John said turning to Paul.

"We thought you knew him."

"No, he just asked me if he could be the other referee, said he knew a thing or to about basketball."

"Everyone seemed to know him," Maggie commented. "I'm sure he lives somewhere around here. You'll run into him again soon."

"Yeah, I'm sure," John answered, but he didn't feel so sure.

"Well, I'm going to sleep for a week, then we've got to get busy," Paul said, then fell over sideways back onto the seat.

"Yep, I think just about the whole town will be here Wednesday night," John said, as a big smile spread across his face. The same smile appeared on Maggie's and Paul's as they all repeated the word again.

"Wow!"

They were back to awestruck.

46 THE OUTPOURING

As expected, on Wednesday night most of the faces that had walked out onto the court Saturday to give their lives to Christ, now stood outside the Rec. Young and old alike had made the journey up the mountain to the American neighborhood. There was no way they could all fit inside the youth room. John and the kids decided to hold the meeting outside on the basketball court, and most of the people had to sit on the grass. Juan Lopez and his teammates looked through a sports catalog and told Paul which balls and shoes they wanted. Juan asked for size six shoes and Paul had to make sure he had heard him correctly then pointed out that they would be too small. Taylor translated Lopez' response.

"He say's he's going to give them to his eight year old cousin. He's crippled, Dad."

Paul filled out the order form and added an extra pair of shoes after learning Juan's size from one of his teammates. The young man had earned them.

That night everyone gathered around for an unforgettable time of fellowship, singing praises to God, and listening to testimonies of what God had done and was doing in the lives of so many. There were many shouts of "amen" and "hallelujah". There was also plenty of laughter and plenty of tears. When the meeting ended it almost felt like the Americans were saying goodbye to friends they'd known for years. It was the sweetest unity they had ever experienced.

* * *

By the next week, the shoes and balls had arrived and the champion team was awarded their prizes before a cheering and clapping Wednesday night crowd. All the American families were there to join in the celebration. Juan's cousin, a small boy named Emilio with frail legs, but a healthy wide smile, leaned on an old pair of wooden crutches surrounded by the team. The boy had also given his life to Jesus during the basketball half-time invitation. Juan put the shoes on his young cousin as everyone clapped and cheered. The players began to go back to their seats and Juan was helping

Emilio off the court when Mike stumbled out from the crowd onto the cement.

"Wait!" Mike exclaimed with a look of intensity and joy splashed across his face. He had a large leather bound book in one hand and his fingers were tucked inside the pages.

Juan stopped and looked at Mike, wondering, along with everyone else, what he was going to say or do.

"Please," Mike said, smiling and motioning with his hand for Juan and Emilio to come back to where he was standing.

Juan looked down at Emilio and then the young boy began to hobble slowly towards the center of the basketball court.

John was standing off to one side in the grass behind a group of local youth. Although curious to know what Mike was up to, he didn't budge from his spot. Many of the parents looked over at him and he smiled and gave them the okay sign with his hand. He felt a strong assurance that whatever was about to happen, it was something God was orchestrating. This revelation sent a pulse of excitement through him and he immediately began to pray.

Mike called the rest of the American youth over to him and they huddled together, forming a circle around Juan and his cousin. By then all of the American kids had figured out what Mike and the Holy Spirit were up to. The moment Emilio began limping back onto the court it was as if scales fell from their eyes and they saw things not as they appeared, but as they really were. They saw what needed to be done, what was supposed to be done.

"You know what we have to do…" Mike said, lifting his Bible up into the air before them all. All heads nodded.

For the past three weeks all of them had been reading the same stories of Jesus performing miracle after miracle on the sick and suffering around Him. Then the day came when they read about Jesus sending out seventy of his followers to perform the same miracles in His name. Immediately the youth had gathered together to discuss and pray over the amazing revelation that those verses provided. From then on, a new level of excitement and expectation took hold. Finally, on this very morning each of them had come across the most amazing and unbelievable promise from Christ Himself. A promise that Mike now read out loud to each of them once again: "I tell you the truth, anyone who has faith in me will do what I have been doing. He will do even greater things than these, because I am going to the Father.

And I will do whatever you ask in my name, so that the Son may bring glory to the Father. You may ask me for anything in my name, and I will do it."

The words overwhelmed and silenced them all once again. Then Taylor opened his Spanish Bible to the same verse in the book of Luke and read it again, loud and clear to everyone. There was a murmur in the crowd as many began to lift up praises and prayers to God. Some whistled and clapped. Some stood to their feet and lifted their hands to the heavens. Half of the American parents closed their eyes and began to pray while the other half had their eyes glued to the scene unfolding before them. A few, especially Mr. and Mrs. Littleton, felt their hearts crawling up their throats.

"Manuel, please tell Emilio that we want to pray for him, for his leg." Manuel translated Mike's words and Juan moved over behind his cousin and put his hands on his shoulders. Both of them had their eyes fixed on Mike.

"Tell him that in the Bible Jesus healed many people who were crippled, blind, and sick. He even brought dead people back to life. He had the power to do this because he was the Son of God." Mike paused to let Manuel translate and then continued.

"Tell him that Jesus told his followers they would have the authority to do this, as well, through His Spirit. God's Spirit is here with us now, and we believe God wants us to pray for Emilio to be healed. Will he believe with us?"

After Manuel finished translating, Emilio smiled up at them all and answered, "Si." Juan's eyes were already closed and his lips moving silently.

* * *

The youth closed their eyes. Susan and Stephanie went down onto their knees. All of the others raised their hands up into the air. Mike's voice, stronger than anyone had ever heard it before, cut through the silence.

"Father God, it is in the name of Jesus Christ that we pray for our brother Emilio to be healed. You are the Healer God. Please..." Mike bent down and laid both of his hands on Emilio's crippled leg, touching the skin with his small fingers..."touch this leg and make it complete...for Your Glory, Lord. For Your Name to be praised!

As Mike's voice grew in volume, many other voices also joined in, praying out loud for Emilio's healing and lifting up praises to God.

"We worship you God. We Bless your name. You are forever to be praised! It's in Jesus' name that we pray…Amen!"

For one brief second, as all eyes opened and heads lifted up, something like a white glow seemed to pass over Mike's figure. It caused all those around him to step back suddenly. John saw it too and felt his heart melt within him, but it wasn't fear that suddenly gripped his entire body. It was awe. He fell onto his knees and began to weep, for he had dreamed his whole life of tasting things not of this world, of witnessing first hand the miraculous work of the Holy Spirit. It never crossed John's mind, nor any other of the American kids', that Emilio would not be able walk for the first time without his crutches. John didn't even have to look. And when he heard the cheers and shouts of joy go up from every person around him, he could only whisper his own. His soul was completely overwhelmed by the goodness and love of God.

Emilio simply let go of his crutches, removed Juan's fingers from his shoulder and took one sturdy step, followed by another, then another. Next he jumped and leaped into the air and then began to run with clumsy, yet confident steps in circles, all along laughing and shouting out "¡Gloria a Dios! ¡Gloria a Dios!"

"Glory to God! Glory to God!" Manuel translated excitedly as Emilio ran around them all. Juan also began to run and shout alongside his cousin and soon the entire basketball team swamped the court.

47 THE HEAVENLY INVASION

Not surprisingly, from this point on, the ministry of the American youth was never the same. Things quickly intensified. In a matter of hours, word of Emilio's healing had spread not only through Jajo, but surrounding towns as well. Early the very next morning, Fernando called the American parents to let them know that a large crowd was gathering outside the front gate. A crowd filled with the crippled, disabled, and sick. An emergency meeting was immediately called.

Mr. Littleton welcomed everyone into the Rec and asked for quiet.

"First, I want to let everyone know that Sue and I decided to put our full trust and faith in our Lord and Savior Jesus Christ last night...and Mike led us in the prayer." Shouting, whistling and clapping erupted all over the room.

"And I did the same thing!" Mr. Childress proclaimed. More shouts and praises followed. His wife and daughter were beaming.

For everyone, the sight of little Emilio suddenly walking and dancing for joy confirmed what they knew in their heart was true. Jesus is real, and they needed Him.

Sue Littleton was holding Mike in her arms and smiling. "I'm sure none of you are surprised after what we witnessed yesterday!"

More shouts of "Amen!" followed.

Mr. Littleton continued. "Now. We need a plan going forward. We simply can't have people coming here at all hours of the day and night!" Even with his newfound faith, he couldn't help feeling anxious about all that was going on...and the most responsible. His own son was the catalyst of all the healings and now all the crowds.

"We also," Mrs. Cook started in immediately after Mr. Littleton, "can't turn people away who need what only God can give them...I mean we ALL agree that God is using our children right now in a supernatural spectacular way, right?"

Every head nodded.

Paul fought his natural instinct to serve as CEO of the meeting and make a decision based on his own wisdom.

"We need to pray," He said. "We need to pray now."

Without hesitation and like eager children, all the parents bowed their heads and closed their eyes. They prayed with desperation and longing, pleading for God to speak to them and give them wisdom. They fell onto their knees and lifted their hands. Then something totally unexpected happened. Mr. Childress suddenly raised himself high up on his knees and began to speak words that no one could understand. The words seemed to roll off his tongue like pouring water. They were fluid and free and totally incomprehensible to everyone around him. Something like a cool breeze filled the room and many of the parents gasped in delight. Then Maggie stood to her feet and spoke with authority.

"In the last days, God says, I will pour out my Spirit on all people. Your sons and daughters will prophesy, your young men will see visions, your old men will dream dreams. Even on my servants, both men and women, I will pour out my Spirit in those days, and they will prophesy."

Mr. Childress continued to speak and as soon as he finished, Maggie followed.

"Among the gods there is none like you, O Lord; no deeds can compare with yours. All the nations you have made will come and worship before you, O Lord; they will bring glory to your name. For you are great and do marvelous deed; you alone are God!"

Mr. Childress spoke in the heavenly language for another five minutes with Maggie interpreting his words and every time it was literal verses from Scripture. Then just as quickly as he had begun, Mr. Childress lowered himself prostrate and began to pray in English as if he had been doing so all along.

Paul stood up next and swayed from side to side. He nodded his head and answered over and over again, "Yes Lord" as if in deep in conversation with a presence unseen. Eventually his voice raised above all the others.

"We thank you Lord for blowing us away, for being true, for revealing your amazing will to us. Who are we, God, that you consider us worthy of such a privilege? We thank you God!"

Every parent echoed the words loudly. "We thank you God! We thank you God!"

Paul repeated the phrase once more and then concluded with a solid, "Amen."

Eyes slowing opened and blinked. The parents gazed around the room at one another without saying a word. Everything was the same and yet everything was different. Hearts continued to beat wildly and minds continued to reel. Whatever the adults in that room had previously thought about the power, presence, and reality of God, it had now been swallowed up like a drop of rain falling into the ocean. Husbands and wives fell into each other's arms. Laughter filled the room. Words like "awesome" and "wow" and "incredible" were spoken with teenage enthusiasm.

Paul, grinning from ear to ear, gazed around at the group. "God wants us to reach these people with His love. Our children are going to be the voice of Jesus. Our children are going to be the hands of Jesus…" Everyone held their breath. "The Holy Spirit revealed to me that all of this will take place in an orderly way. Our main responsibility as the parents of our children is to set boundaries in place that protect them and maintain order at all times. I'm going to go and tell the crowd that on Wednesday night they are all welcome here."

It was the hardest speech Paul had ever made, but he knew it was necessary and right. He was relieved to find everyone leaving without complaint, though many held their heads low. The sight of so many suffering people walking away was almost too much for his heart to take. *God I trust you, I trust you…show yourself true and bring every one of these people back Wednesday night.*

Afterwards, Maggie and Paul visited John at his apartment and shared everything that had happened that morning. Then John opened his Bible and showed them what he had read in his morning devotional.

"The Spirit of the Lord is upon me, because the Lord has anointed me to preach good news to the poor. He has sent me to bind up the brokenhearted, to proclaim freedom for the captives and release from darkness for the prisoners, to proclaim the year of the Lord's favor and the day of vengeance of our God, to comfort all who mourn, and provide for those who grieve in Zion – to bestow on them a crown of beauty instead of ashes, the oil of gladness instead of mourning, and a garment of praise instead of a spirit of despair. They will be called oaks of righteousness, a planting of the Lord for the display of his splendor." With each new word from Isaiah chapter 61, John's voice grew louder and louder until finally cracking. He choked back tears and continued in a whisper, "I delight greatly in the Lord; my soul rejoices in my God. For he has clothed me with garments of salvation and arrayed me in a robe of righteousness, as a bridegroom adorns his head like a priest, and as a bride adorns herself with her jewels. For as the soil makes the sprout come up and as a garden causes seeds to grow, so the Sovereign Lord will make righteousness and praise spring up before all nations!" As soon as John finished, reading he began to laugh and couldn't stop. He laughed so hard that he fell off his couch and onto the floor. His face was aglow with indescribable joy. Maggie and Paul joined him. They all laughed and whooped and hollered until their voices began to go hoarse.

"God is alive!" John said, trying to catch his breath and finally getting control of himself again. "And we are tasting and seeing His goodness!"

"John, this is something we never even dared to dream about God," Maggie exclaimed. "That He's so...*involved* and *intimate* with us."

"He has taken our breath away," Paul added. "I wish I'd discovered this kind of fellowship with Him earlier."

John looked up at them and smiled. "What matters, Paul and Maggie, is that right now the Spirit of the Living God is being poured out on this place."

* * *

On Sunday night, their family worship meeting began in the Littleton's backyard where Mr. and Mrs. Littleton and Mr. Childress were baptized in their swimming pool. Paul, Maggie and John took turns baptizing one after the other. The remaining adults and children stood around and celebrated with each dunking. Mr. Childress decided to have a little fun and grabbed his wife and pulled her into the water. She was horrified, but the sight and sounds of her daughter and all the others laughing hysterically, brought her to joyous tears of her own. When she asked everyone to help throw her daughter in, no one hesitated and Susan only made it a few steps before she was picked up and tossed into the water with her parents. All the laughing and shouting brought their security guard to the scene. Fernando wasn't exactly sure what was going on, but he knew a celebration when he saw one. He quickly returned to the front gate smiling and thinking to himself that life in the American neighborhood was getting stranger by the minute.

* * *

After drying off, those who had participated in the baptisms returned home to change clothes while the others headed to the Rec. On their way through the woods, Taylor gave John a nudge.

"I told you they were next."

John winked back. "We're just getting started my friend."

Eventually everyone was gathered back together in the Rec, sitting around the room, still laughing and giggling about the Childress family's hilarious skirmish in the pool. John asked Mrs. Littleton to open the meeting in prayer. Eyes closed and the room grew quiet. Mrs. Littleton cleared her throat, but remained silent. Waiting. Listening. She began to speak in a heavenly language and her husband interpreted, phrase by phrase, quoting the first seven verses of Psalm 105:

"Give praise to the Lord, proclaim his name;
make known among the nations what he has done.
Sing to him, sing praise to him; tell of all his wonderful acts.
Glory in his holy name;
let the hearts of those who seek the Lord rejoice.
Look to the Lord and his strength; seek his face always.
Remember the wonders he has done,
his miracles, and the judgments he pronounced,
you his servants, the descendants of Abraham,
his chosen ones, the children of Jacob.
He is the Lord our God; his judgments are in all the earth."

Tommy followed with a word of prophecy over Jajo and beyond, declaring a new dawn of salvation that will shatter the darkness for generations. Taylor opened his Bible and taught about the gifts of the Holy Spirit. God gave him insight and application that held everyone captivated. When he concluded his message, Mike stood up and prayed for Regina's chronic cough and as he spoke, she literally felt the phlegm and mucus in her throat and chest loosen and vanish. She began to cry and confess that she had been full of doubts all along. She declared over and over again that she wasn't worthy of God's touch. No one even noticed Robert until he was standing right beside her. His little fingers rested firmly on her shaking shoulder.

"'I will love you with an everlasting love,' says the Lord God Almighty. 'I am the Touch that restores and renews. I am faithful beyond your comprehension and I am with you always, even until the end of the world.'"

The room was so silent that Robert's breathing echoed off the walls. He smiled and walked back to his parents' open arms.

Stephanie's voice floated up in song and spread out over the room. "Spirit of the Living God, fall fresh on me." When she began the verse for the second time, all the voices in the room joined with hers…

"Spirit of the Living God, fall fresh on me. Break me. Mold me. Fill me. Use me. Spirit of the Living God, fall fresh on me."

* * *

That night, in an ordinary building tucked away in the mountains of Venezuela, five families and a young missionary fully committed to the Lord, experienced heaven and earth collide.

48 THE ANNOUNCEMENT

On Wednesday night there was simply no way to fit all of the people in or even around the Rec building. After Ricardo had opened the front gate for the fifth time to let more people into the neighborhood, he just decided to leave it open. There were young people sitting on the branches of trees around the basketball court. John figured the number of people crowded around to be close to 300.

A good beginning number for a new church, John thought, smiling to himself.

* * *

Earlier that afternoon, as the American families prepared for the evening outreach, they read in Acts where 3000 and then 5000 people were added to the number of believers and they prayed for God to move in the same way and expected it. As if confirming their expectations, the Lord sent them a surprise. Mr. Guzman, a local rancher, farmer and believer, delivered a new metal watering trough, ten feet in diameter and four feet deep. He parked his truck and trailer outside the front gate, and Ricardo scratched his head as he stared at the trough and listened to the rancher explain how Lord had told him that morning to drop it off for the Wednesday night meeting.

The families were overjoyed with the delivery! The Lord's message was obvious — new believers are coming, baptisms must follow. They placed the trough to the side of the basketball court. Paul built some simple wooden steps and placed them on the outside of the trough. Maggie had a small step ladder that they placed on the inside. Finally, they placed a water hose over the side and turned it on. It took hours to fill up.

* * *

All of the disabled, crippled, and sick who had come days earlier were now gathered around the basketball court along with many others who were there for the first time. The sight of the water trough filled to the brim was causing a lot of excited talk and speculation. Paul walked to the middle of the basketball court with Taylor at his side. There were tears in Paul's eyes. God had answered his prayer, and he knew that the Lord of all creation was about to answer many, many more.

Paul opened his Bible. Taylor stood beside his father with his own Spanish Bible open, ready to translate. Just before speaking, Paul noticed a familiar friendly face standing off to one side of the crowd.

"Bienvenidos Mayor Velasquez! Good to see you." Many in the crowd turned and looked in his direction, smiling and even clapping. The mayor just smiled and waved quickly.

Paul, with a quick prayer of thanks to God, looked down at his open Bible and began to read:

"Now when he saw the crowds, he went up on a mountainside and sat down. His disciples came to him, and he began to teach them, saying: 'Blessed are the poor in spirit, for theirs is the kingdom of heaven. Blessed are those who mourn, for they will be comforted. Blessed are the meek, for they will inherit the earth. Blessed are those who hunger and thirst for righteousness, for they will be filled. Blessed are the merciful, for they will be shown mercy. Blessed are the pure in heart, for they will see God. Blessed are the peacemakers, for they will be called sons of God. Blessed are those who are persecuted because of righteousness, for theirs is the kingdom of heaven.'" Taylor translated Christ's words, and they hung in the air like a fragrance.

Paul continued. "God has a simple question for you, 'What does it profit a person if he gains the whole world, but loses his soul?' What does it profit a person to be famous on earth, but unknown in the Book of Life? What does it profit a person to be healthy and strong, but have a dead spirit inside? What does it profit a person to live in peace and comfort on earth, but then burn in the lake of fire for eternity? There is only one thing people need. Everything else, in the end, is irrelevant. People - all people - need Jesus to come into their hearts and wash their sin away, to make them new and fill them with the Holy Spirit. This is all we truly need!"

"Jesus longs to give us good temporal things here on earth, but first we must receive what we need for eternity from heaven; and that is simply Him. We need Him. That is why He left heaven and came to walk among us on the earth. That is why He sacrificed his perfect life for us on the cross. That is why He stands at the right hand of God on our behalf and why He is going to return with an army of angels as King of Kings and Lord of Lords!"

"Until a few weeks ago, none of us standing before you had ever experienced the power of God like we are experiencing it now. We had only read about miracles in the Bible and heard amazing stories from others in far away places. I cannot tell you how or why God is moving the way He is among us. What I can tell you is that our children are putting God first in their lives and they have challenged us to put Him first and God's word says that when we put Him first, He will do more than we could even ask or imagine."

Everyone needs to understand this…it's only by God's Spirit that these amazing and wonderful things are happening. We rejoice and celebrate when sick people are made well, lame people walk again, blind people see, and dead people come back to life, but all of these miracles - as amazing and wonderful as they are - cannot compare to the miracle of salvation. The miracle of being forgiven and being accepted by God for eternity and not because of what you do, but because of Who you believe in and Who you trust with everything…Jesus Christ. There is nothing special about us." Paul chuckled out loud. "In fact, we've spent the last few years putting God almost last in our lives…" now his voice broke. "Oh God forgive us! It's not because of us…don't for one second give us any credit for these miracles. God gets all the glory! God we give You all the glory! We worship You now wonderful Lord! If you came today not knowing about this God who gave everything for you. If you have never tasted His forgiveness and the new life He freely gives, then now is the moment for you to be set free from sin and death. Now is the moment for salvation! If you are ready to commit to follow and obey Jesus for the rest of your life on earth then raise your hands to heaven!"

Paul had never before experienced such beauty and joy wrapped up in a single moment of his existence. He smiled at the hands lifted into the air and then shared words that many eagerly repeated – confessing sin, begging forgiveness, declaring belief, and committing to trust and obey. His "amen" was smothered by a thunderous echo and then buried under an avalanche of joyous shouts and whistles.

"Now!" Paul said, grinning at the crowd with a twinkle in his eyes. "We have a perfect size pool of water over here because many of you need to get baptized. First, I want to read a story to you." Paul opened to Acts chapter 8 and read the story of Philip and the Ethiopian Eunuch. As he read about the new believer's immediate desire to get baptized in the nearest water available, many were nodding their heads.

"Baptism is a sign of a person's commitment to following Jesus. Jesus Himself was baptized, and He commanded us to follow His example and to baptize new believers around the world. If you are ready to publicly declare your allegiance to Jesus Christ, line up and let's get the party started!" Shouts and whistling, laughter and cheers erupted once more as dozens of people began to line up next to the trough. Taylor and John climbed in first and then began inviting one person at a time to get baptized. Taylor remained by the steps helping people in and out while John stood in the middle and asked each person if they were willing to live and die for Jesus before dunking them in the water and pulling them back up. It was a simple question he had spent the afternoon practicing and memorizing. The next part took longer to learn, but once the baptisms began, it wasn't long before he was declaring in perfect Spanish: "I baptize you in the name of the Father, and of the Son and of the Holy Spirit. Buried with Christ and raised to new life!" Each and every person came up out of the water smiling and laughing and gave him a hug. Many jumped and splashed around, too excited to leave. Whenever a local friend stepped into the water, one of the American youth took over John's role and did the honors for their new sister or brother. Susan, Robyn, Tommy, Mike and Taylor all had the privilege of baptizing a friend or two. None was more celebrated than Manuel. When he came up out of the water, half the Americans tackled him and Taylor together. So much water spilled out that Maggie had to turn on the hose and start refilling the trough. All-in-all, it was an hour-long, water-filled worship extravaganza with non-stop clapping, cheering, shouting, smiling and hugging. No one left early. They all knew there was still more to come.

After John coaxed the last person out of the water, and with many still standing around in wet clothes, Mike walked to the middle of the court and looked around. Taylor joined him to translate. Those closest to him began to hop up and down and lift their hands into the air in anticipation. Mike smiled.

"If any of you need prayer for physical, emotional, or spiritual healing then wherever you're lying, sitting, or standing, just lift up your hands towards heaven!"

Parents and youth, both American and Venezuelan, moved out among the crowd, kneeling and standing beside those whose hands were lifted up into the sky. A sea of voices flooded the area, praising God and asking Him to heal and restore those who had come to experience His miraculous touch.

* * *

Everyone involved in this new healing ministry didn't really have a clue how it worked other than what they saw in Scripture — when Christ had compassion on people he healed them and when the apostles saw that those who needed healing had the faith for it - even faith the size of a mustard seed - they called them out to be healed. For these reasons, the Americans, along with the Venezuelan believers who joined them for this specific ministry, decided that above all else they would pray to have compassion and discernment. More than anyone else, Mike Littleton seemed to possess the supernatural ability to gaze past the outer shell and see the hearts of those longing for healing. When he prayed, God answered and many times nothing happened until Mike made his way to someone whom others had been praying for already. It was a mystery to everyone, but a mystery they accepted and even thanked God for. There were also those who came for healing and nothing happened so far as anyone could tell, even when Mike prayed for them. As confusing as moments like this were, especially for the one desperate to receive healing, Mike challenged the person not to give up on trusting God and reminded them that God's will has no flaws – for whatever the reason – there was a purpose behind the situation God was holding them in. Then he would share Revelation 21:4 'He will wipe every tear from their eyes. There will be no more death' or mourning or crying or pain, for the old order of things has passed away.'

"One day," Mike would promise them, "God's word says your healing will be complete in Jesus Christ; it's guaranteed."

Near the end of the meeting, Mike told one woman she simply didn't believe, which caused her to shout and cry hysterically. Her tears, Mike later explained to the American families when they'd gathered afterwards to regroup and pray, were an expression of frustration at not receiving what she thought she deserved. Mike also tried to explain how he had actually been able to see the hardness of her heart…like a dark spot hovering there. His words left everyone speechless, especially his parents. None could fathom the maturity, wisdom, and calmness with which he went about the Lord's healing work. All were aware of an other-worldly quality that engulfed him. This particular instance with the sobbing woman was difficult and tense for everyone around. Eventually she yelled at her friends to get her out of there and proceeded, as she rolled away in her wheelchair, to call down curses and threats on the whole gathering. Unnerved, Mike retrieved his Bible, walked to the middle of the basketball court, and read from Isaiah chapter 55: "'For my thoughts are not your thoughts, neither are your ways my ways,' declares the Lord." As Mike spoke, the praise team moved to the center of the court behind him. "As the heavens are higher than the earth, so are my ways higher than your ways and my thoughts than your thoughts."

Mike shut his Bible and the praise team stepped forward and proclaimed it was now time to praise the Lord of heaven and earth for all He had done, was doing, and was going to do! The Venezuelan people responded enthusiastically, especially those who had been baptized and who had come lame and crippled, but were now running around in circles!

During the previous week the Americans decided it was time they began to learn some Spanish worship songs. They invited a handful of local believers, both young and old, to come and teach them some songs and rehearse together. Manuel proved to have a beautiful voice. Susan's friend Angela joined Tommy on guitar. Her skills on the classical guitar amazed everyone and added a Latin flavor they all enjoyed. On this unforgettable night, five Americans and five Venezuelans stood and swayed at the center of the basketball court, singing and bringing their musical instruments to life. The Venezuelans had a gift for rhythm and singing that quickly transformed an ordinary praise and worship set into an all-out musical party. No one contemplated sitting back down, especially those discovering their legs for the first time.

* * *

During the worship celebration, Paul had an idea and asked John and the mayor to join him in the Rec for a quick talk.

"Mayor, what do you think about Jajo hosting our next outreach? I don't think we'll be able to fit everyone here next week."

John was surprised that Paul was speaking to the mayor in English. The short, portly man scrunched up his milk chocolate face and his black bushy eyebrows lowered as he closed his eyes for a quick moment of contemplation or prayer. Then he spoke with his eyes still closed,

"Si, it would be more better…more people come and hear the good news."

Then his eyes suddenly opened. Dark and smoky, they peered intently into Paul's. "But Christ, when he is lifted up from the earth, will draw all men unto himself..." Though the small Venezuelan man was still staring directly at him, Paul had the feeling the mayor was conversing with another Presence in the room. It was silent for a few seconds and then as if coming out of a cloud, the mayor turned his neck and gazed out the window at the people singing and dancing. Next, as if a bolt of lightning struck him from above, he lifted off his feet and shouted, "Yes, Gracias Dios!"

Paul, startled, jumped right after him.

"¡Por supuesto! Of course! La Plaza Bolivar! We'll set up a stage! How about every other Saturday night?!"

Paul and John both stood stunned, but smiling from ear to ear. John clapped his large hands together and shouted "Perfecto!"

"¡Perfecto!" Paul echoed.

"¡Perfecto!" The mayor announced, clapping his hands as well and then trotted out of the Rec to join back in the festivities outside.

Paul looked over at John with a big grin on his face. "You didn't know our mayor is almost fluent in English, did you?"

"Had no idea. Big surprise."

"He has a son who studied in the States and became a doctor. The mayor and his wife have grandchildren in Texas."

"You learn something new every day — like our mayor is also full of the Holy Ghost!"

"Amen brother!" Paul grabbed John and gave him a manly, backslapping hug. They walked back to the meeting full of awe and wonder.

* * *

Mayor Velasquez stepped onto the basketball court, waved his hands and asked for the musicians and crowd to quiet themselves. As he addressed the crowd in Spanish, Taylor walked over to his dad and John with a look of amazement on his face.

"Mayor Velasquez just made an announcement, telling everyone to come to Plaza Bolivar next Saturday night."

As Taylor spoke, the crowd of locals erupted in applause and shouts of joy.

"He told everyone to bring friends and family to Jajo's new church in the plaza!"

The American parents breathed a sigh of relief.

49 THE FLYERS

With a two-week break in between outreaches, the Americans now had more time for fellowship and preparation. John and the youth met together on Wednesday nights for an intense and intimate time of discipleship. Sunday nights continued to bring the families closer together. Each family was assigned to lead the group a different week. Parents and children picked the songs to sing and the scriptures to share and teach on. The families also discovered that one night a week together wasn't enough. Like it had been during their first year together in their new country, different parents could once again be seen walking in the direction of a neighbor's house for a lengthy chat, to borrow some sugar or just to say hello. The women began walking together again every evening for half an hour and one night a week, just as they had done that first year, the families took turns meeting in a different home for dinner. They now regularly traveled to town together, sometimes the kids rode in the cars with their parents and sometimes the parents walked the trail to town with their kids. They ate and shopped in the markets, the men sometimes played sports with the locals, whom they now knew personally and they all walked around and talked with the people in broken English and with the best Spanish they knew how. All agreed it was time they learned something more than "Hola" and "Adiós." Taylor and Susan became their official language tutors. The families also decided to order gospel tracts in Spanish to give to the people as they walked and mingled. John was blown away by the evangelistic passion that had swept over them. He watched amazed as they passed the tracts out and tried to share with the people. Jajo was becoming home and the residents were becoming family.

* * *

One evening as John and some of the boys walked around the streets putting up flyers for the upcoming Saturday night outreach, they found themselves passing in front of Logan's Gentlemen's Club. John stopped and looked at the building. Taylor and Brad glanced at one another, but didn't say anything. Manuel and most of the locals backed farther away. For John, that horrible night returned. He remembered the darkness and stench inside; he could sense the oppression and bondage even more so than before.

It's up to you, God. Only you can remove this place. John found himself climbing the stairs to the front revolving doors, but this time he wouldn't be going inside. Instead, he took two Spanish flyers they had made and taped them up on both sides of the doorframe. He knew they wouldn't be there long. As he stuck the last strip of tape across the paper, the door swung open, and out stepped his old friend Rico looking as glad to see him as he had the first time they met. John turned to walk away.

"Mr. Logan want you!" Rico commanded gruffly.

John was surprised to hear English, but still ignored him.

"Mr. Logan want you now!" Rico repeated, even more forcefully than before.

"That's okay," John answered back, walking down the steps.

Rico ripped one of the flyers off the wall and followed after John.

"Gringo! I'm talking to you!"

He put his hand on John's shoulder and jerked him around. John felt the man's incredible strength moving him and didn't resist. He quickly turned and steadied himself in front of his assailant. Rico's upper body was thick and bulging out of a sleeveless jean jacket. Underneath, he wore no shirt at all. His neck sat like a tree trunk on broad shoulders and his massive arms hung at his sides with fists that looked like sledgehammers. John took in all these details within a fraction of a second. As they stood face to face, John was thankful he at least had a few inches of height on this muscular freak of nature standing before him..

"I said Mr. Logan want to see you. Comprende?"

"Amigo, I said that's okay. He can visit me at *my* place. Adiós."

John started to turn and Rico once again reached for his shoulder. This time John moved, turning before Rico had a solid grip and knocking his hand away with his own forearm. Rico fell forward off balance, stumbling a few steps before quickly standing up straight again. He drew a knife from its sheath and lowered his frame, ready to leap. All the boys gasped in fright. The locals backed farther away. Taylor was about to run and get the police when the doors opened again.

"Rico! Alto! Put your knife away!"

Rico hesitated, tempted to face his boss' wrath for just one cut on this American pretty boy.

"Ahora, Rico!"

Slowly the bouncer obeyed and then spoke some words in Spanish to Mr. Logan who turned and read the other flyer that was still taped to his doorframe.

"Hmmm." He read the paper and scratched his chin then turned to John.

"Howdy, John. Longtime no see."

John hardly felt grateful for Mr. Logan's heroic intervention.

"I see you're still in the exploitation business," John said dryly.

"Exploitation? John. I'm helping feed and clothe families. I'm paying the rent. My dancers can walk away any time they want. But they don't want to because I treat them right." Mr. Logan looked amused. "Anyway, if my memory serves me right, you weren't too shy to take a long look at my inventory." Frank Logan smiled at John, but there was no friendliness in his expression – it was a cold, calculating grin.

John was through with the conversation. He hadn't wanted to see or talk with Mr. Logan in the first place, and he surely didn't want the kids to see him rattled.

"Well, you can take down the flyer now. Just thought I'd try to bring something good to your place." John slowly backed away. A crowd of faces appeared in the doorway behind Mr. Logan. One face caused Manuel to quickly duck behind his friends.

"Actually, John, I think I'll leave it up. Besides, without me, you wouldn't have anyone to save. So we'll work together. I'll supply the sinners and you turn 'em into saints. See, look." Mr. Logan turned to the men inside and addressed them in their native tongue. They all stumbled out of the door and read the Spanish flyer together out loud. As John and the boys walked down the street they could hear the men laughing hysterically, Mr. Logan's voice booming above the rest.

* * *

A few days later, however, at the first Saturday night outreach, a few of the men did come. They had been pressured by wives and families and friends and couldn't say no.

50 THE OUTREACHES

The Saturday night outreach was much like the Wednesday night event, just much bigger. Mayor Velasquez had a large stage built on the northern edge of the plaza that allowed an enormous amount of people to hear and see everything going on. The music group now resembled a choir; there were so many musicians and singers. The families had pitched in and purchased a complete and costly sound system, including a 24-channel mixer, two monitors, two 1600 watt speakers that towered over the crowd from the edge of the stage and two smaller ones that stood on eight feet stands, and more microphones, music stands, cords, and wires than they knew what to do with. It had all been delivered from Caracas by a large delivery truck that no one could believe had been able to reach the small town. The mayor offered to let them store most of the equipment, including the big speakers, in the basement of the police station for convenience and safety, putting an end to Paul's biggest concern.

That first Saturday with the new equipment proved to be an educational and slightly frustrating one as they spent all morning and afternoon in the plaza and on the stage experimenting with machinery they had never touched before. As genetically programmed, the men skipped the operating manuals and went straight to the hands-on technique, which hours later had successfully produced a continuous low buzzing sound from all the speakers followed by an occasional high pitched scream of feedback. It was quite entertaining for the locals. John had the most experience with music and sound equipment and even he didn't really know where to begin with setting it all up. By evening, they were finally able to bring the guitars and keyboard to life along with a handful of microphones. Not quite Radio City Music Hall, but after a day such as that one, they were happy to have any sound at all. In time they would tap into the system's full potential – a potential that flooded not only the entire plaza, but also the surrounding streets and even mountain trails with clear, riveting sound.

Along with the sound equipment, another huge set of boxes was delivered. Inside was packed a state of the art remote control digital projector, a stainless steel cart, and a gigantic 12 X 12 foot portable movie screen. A laptop computer was hooked up to the projector and all the songs they could possibly type into powerpoint slides were sent in brilliant clarity and color onto the giant movie screen stretched out on the left side of the stage. Mrs. Childress and Mrs. Littleton volunteered to work the machinery. It was an exhilarating experience for them both and no husband was needed to show them how. They read the directions. In time, they figured out how to add font and background colors and images that held the crowd spellbound. The whole event was a total sensory adventure to the throne of God!

Mike, with his dad's help, loaded the drums into their suburban, drove them to town, and set them up on the stage just the way he liked them. The number of microphones that soon surrounded him momentarily caused a panic, but as he took his seat that night behind his "wall" and before a crowd too large to measure, he was filled with a peace and excitement he'd never dreamed possible. *Let me play like Larry Mullen, Lord.*

Before the American and Venezuelan outreach team took to the stage that night, they met in the back, locked hands together, and prayed that whatever happened, God would be glorified. Overwhelmed with gratitude and humility, they ran onto the stage to an uproarious applause.

Mayor Velasquez opened the evening with a prayer of thanksgiving and expectation. The praise band erupted in sound that flooded the night air and sent a pulse of electricity through the crowd. Each song carried the crowd further and further away from Plaza Bolivar and nearer to heaven itself. In between songs, different inspirational images and Bible verses were flashed up onto the movie screen keeping all eyes and hearts focused on the reason for worship. The music set, originally intended for 20 minutes, instead lasted 45 and still seemed too short.

John preached that night with Manuel translating beside him. He shared a simple message of Christ returning for His bride. He read from Acts chapter one, where Christ, just before ascending to heaven, promised His disciples that the Holy Spirit would come upon them in power and be their Guide and Comforter and how the angels then appeared and told them all that just as Christ had gone into heaven, he would also someday return. Then from Revelation 19 John narrated the events of Christ returning in glory and power to wage war against the kings of the earth and the godless. Finally, John described the great white throne judgment when the dead, both great and small, would be sent to their eternal destinations – heaven or hell. He offered the crowd an opportunity right then and there to seal their fate with Christ, to secure their eternal destiny with Him in the glory of heaven. Even as he spoke these final words, many began to cry and shout, fall onto their knees, and push their way towards the stage.

Manuel led hundreds that night in the reading of a prayer that appeared bright and bold on the movie screen. Behind the words, a dazzling image of a sky filled with sunshine and clouds beckoned souls upwards. As broken voices declared their need of Christ's forgiveness, belief in his death and resurrection, and commitment to follow Him always, John stared at all the faces crowded around the stage. He recognized some of those he had seen standing outside Logan's club days before. Here they were, with tears streaming down their cheeks and smiles on their lips, holding hands with wives and family members who had no doubt prayed them to the cross of Christ. John couldn't help but laugh. He and Mr. Logan *had* actually worked together, and now, God willing, Mr. Logan would never see these men again.

* * *

If the first Saturday outreach went beyond everyone's expectations, the second one went beyond believable. What made it so special was that it was led entirely by the youth. Not a single adult, including John, took to the stage that night. An all-youth team opened with prayer. An all-youth band got the plaza moving and swaying, clapping and singing – worshipping with unashamed passion. Then Taylor preached for the first time on his own in Spanish. Though not a soul in the crowd really believed the young boy was ever on his own. God spoke through his child that night, and the words that flowed from his tongue brought conviction and repentance. It seemed half the crowd lifted their hands and then voices to ask the Lord of the universe to save and lead them. Then with the music playing once again, person after person took turns coming onto the stage – some alone, some with friends and family, some in their own strength and some pushed and carried along – and as they came they were met not by the power of man, but the power of God's Spirit. The scene was surreal. Here was this handful of children laying hands on the sick, on the diseased, on the broken, and with every compassionate touch and heartfelt prayer, a second or two of anxious silence followed and then an ecstatic cry of joy…surreal.

Simply put, the Spirit of the Lord Almighty poured down onto the stage that night, and no one who stood, or even gazed upon it was left the same.

* * *

In response to the hundreds of new professions of faith that were taking place, Mayor Velaquez announced a city-wide baptism event to be held the next day at the city's reservoir. The American families chose not to attend with the purpose of stepping back and letting local believers, under the direction of Mayor Velasquez, plan, prepare and implement the baptism service. Their strategy resulted in the beginning of a new home-grown revival movement in the mountains of Trujillo State and even down into the state of Merida. News of hundreds of men, women and children becoming Christians, being baptized, being healed and being changed from the inside out, spread rapidly.

* * *

John continued to put flyers up all over town each week including Mr. Logan's street. He didn't put anymore on Logan's building, but anyone headed in that direction couldn't fail to see them all around. A few times Rico came outside and watched him, but Mr. Logan never showed his face. As John walked by, he envisioned the faces of Mr. Logan's former customers who were customers no longer. After giving their lives to the Lord, many of them had shared with John about what all they had done in that place. Many had wept and John along with them, but their final tears were tears of joy for their newfound freedom. Still, too many were trapped inside, spending their money and selling their souls. The dancers were especially on John's heart, but he didn't know how to get them to come to the outreach. They were never seen going in or coming out. He wondered if they were actually kept locked up somewhere. Perhaps they were even immigrants trafficked from other countries, literally slaves of the sex trade, all alone with no friends or family to help them. He knew such things existed, and that it wouldn't be below Mr. Logan's character. John's blood boiled every time he walked by.

* * *

Mr. Logan's blood boiled every time John walked by, as well. This young American punk was having the last laugh. In the last three weeks, Mr. Logan had lost five high paying customers. True, his clientele reached well over the century mark, or so he liked to brag to his friends, but still five lustful men had given up their natural urges for Jesus. As stupid and ridiculous as that sounded, it was true. Their absence represented a weekly portion of lost revenue. In time it could be more – he was sure it would be more. What could he do? More girls? Cheaper beer? That would mean spending more money. John Parker couldn't have the satisfaction of causing him to lose another dollar. Frank Logan didn't yet know what he would do, but he would do something. Meanwhile, everyone in the club noticed a change in Mr. Logan's demeanor. There were less and less rounds on the house. The regulars and the dancers were more cautious in his presence. Unlike so many others, including John, they truly knew just how dangerous he and his guard Rico could be. A few dancers and patrons alike had disappeared before, never to be seen or heard from again.

51 THE CONFRONTATION

One Wednesday afternoon, John returned home from his drum lesson with Mike and found Taylor sitting on the porch waiting for him. He looked troubled.

"Hey John, can we talk?"

"Sure, come in."

They went inside and Taylor took a seat on the sofa as John grabbed two Cokes out of the fridge. It was good to have someone in the house with him. Everyone was so busy they rarely had time to visit John at his place anymore.

"Mike's got a new funky beat for the worship team this weekend."

"Good," Taylor said, his face expressionless.

John could tell he wasn't interested in music at the moment.

"So what's on your mind?"

"I want to tell you something, but I don't know if I should or not."

"Is it about you or someone else?"

"Someone else."

"Hmm. Remember when the girls got mad at me because of all that secret mess and then I said from now on no more secrets and we all agreed?"

"Yeah I remember."

"Well, if the other person wouldn't want you to tell me, then don't. How's that?"

"But, it's not that simple. What if they're scared to talk about it and if you tell their secret it might help them?"

"What do you mean help them? How?"

"Help them to stop being hurt?"

John wondered what Taylor meant by the word hurt, and if this, once again, had to do with someone having a crush on someone else.

"Okay, tell me what's going on, but don't use any names."

"Alright. Someone's father is hitting them. Not just spanking them, but punching them. And hitting his mom, too."

John's brain automatically began thinking of all the possible people Taylor could be talking about, all of them American. Could it be Mike? He never appeared upset or abused. John felt sick. The no names idea had been a stupid one.

"You're absolutely positive there's abuse going on."

"John, Manuel told me himself, plus I've seen the bruises."

John had hunched over on the sofa staring at the floor, now he straightened himself up and let out a small sigh of relief. It lasted for only a second.

Manuel had been one of the first locals the American kids had befriended. He was Taylor's closest friend and had quickly become a good friend of John's as well. He was special to them all. John had also become good friends with everyone in Manuel's family, except his father, who refused to like him. Manuel's mother and grandmother had been coming to the outreaches and had given their lives to the Lord only weeks before. John had even prayed with Maggie and Mrs. Garcia for her husband and his drinking problems and unfaithfulness. Everyone knew about his addictions. Now John wondered how many knew about this. John remembered the words Mrs. Garcia had prayed that night, how she had spoken with dedication and love for her husband even after all the pain he had caused her. Her English was poor, but she had managed to say, "I love him" over and over again after begging her new Savior for her husband's deliverance.

"So Mr. Garcia is beating his family?"

"Yeah." Taylor sounded as sad as John had ever heard him, "I think he does it now even more than before."

"Why?"

"Because now they are Christians and he hates them for it. Manuel said he's angry because everyone's leaving Mr. Logan's place. He said it's our fault, and Manuel told me that his father said he'd beat Jesus out of him."

The same rage that took hold of John as he had looked upon Mr. Logan's club for the first time now returned. Immediately he stood up and walked towards the door once again determined to right the wrong. This time he was personally involved; Manuel was being hurt at his expense. He was part of the cause, and now he would be part of the solution. Taylor leaped up and followed after John then suddenly crashed into his back. John stood frozen in the doorway. He was quiet as if listening for something.

"What is it John?"

John remembered the last time he had felt this way. He remembered what had happened. He quickly turned and walked back to the couch.

"What are doing?" Taylor asked as John knelt down on his knees.

"I'm making sure I don't go alone, come pray with me."

Taylor copied John's position beside him and they both rested their elbows on the couch cushions and closed their eyes.

* * *

An hour later, John and Taylor walked down the trail that led to Manuel's house. His emotions in check, John felt confidant that they were doing the right thing. Mr. Garcia had to be confronted and told that he was accountable for his actions and that someone knew what he was doing. John still didn't know exactly what he was going to say, but their prayer had brought peace. He was still praying as they neared the Garcia's run-down adobe home.

"Are you ready?" John asked, raising his fist to knock on the old wooden door hanging in front of him. Taylor nodded his head wondering how they were going to do this; he would have to translate, and he would have to be fast. He was scared. John was the biggest guy around, but Manuel's father was crazy. John knocked hard and loud. They heard a grumbling and rustling inside, someone yelled, then footsteps.

"Here goes nothing," John whispered.

The door jerked wide open. Mr. Garcia stood blinking his eyes and scratching his hair, wearing nothing but dirty old shorts.

"Y tú, quién eres?" he mumbled angrily.

"Who are you?" Taylor translated quickly, but John already understood. He hesitated.

"¡Que quieres!?"

"He wants to know what we want," Taylor said nervously, stepping backwards.

John found his voice.

"I want you to know that the bruises on your son tell the world what kind of father you are."

Taylor quickly followed with as accurate a translation as he could. Mr. Garcia just stared John over until Taylor finished. Then he smiled mockingly and finally began to laugh. John saw into the house over his shoulder. Manuel was standing in the room behind him. Even in the darkness John could see swelling and discolor over one of his eyes. Suddenly Mrs. Garcia appeared in the room, took Manuel by the arm, and led him away.

John had to fight back the anger.

"Do you like to hit your son? Do you like to hit your wife?"

Taylor spoke with the same force; he too, had seen Manuel and was livid.

John wanted to ask Mr. Garcia if he knew what it felt like and slap him around a couple of times.

"Don't hit them because you don't like me! You can hit me!"

Taylor continued to translate while praying no one would get killed. John's words were a dare, and Mr. Garcia took them as one. His smile disappeared. They all three waited. He wanted to strike this American boy. John prepared for a blow. He couldn't strike back, he wouldn't. Mr. Garcia didn't move.

"You know it's sad how much your family still loves you after all you've done to them," John said, followed by Taylor, whose voice held the same pity.

Mr. Garcia suddenly stepped back slamming the door shut. John's foot shot in between the door and the frame, blocking it from closing completely. Then he lowered his face into the doorway eye level with Manuel's father. He saw the boiling rage inside the man.

"Your son and your wife love you more than you'll ever know, but they're scared of you..." Taylor translated slowly from behind, "I'm not. If you ever hit them again, I'll bring the police."

Taylor finished as John removed his foot and began to back away. He and Taylor both turned to hear the door slam shut behind them.

"Do you think he'll do it again, maybe even right now?" Taylor asked, immediately fearful for Manuel and his mother's safety. John felt the same fear.

"Pray that he doesn't. Inside his house, he's boss and he knows it. No one's ever told him he can't do it. Maybe now he'll think twice, but I don't know."

"Is that what you planned on saying?"

"I don't know."

The winds were picking up around them, and both John and Taylor were thinking to themselves how dark it had suddenly become. Within minutes, a light rain began to fall. They picked up their pace, but continued in silence, both praying for God to keep Manuel and his mother safe. They said goodbye and split ways at the end of the trail.

* * *

John turned on his stereo, dialed in a favorite classical station he had discovered after first arriving, then plopped down on his couch and stared into space. Maybe he'd done it again. He'd stopped and prayed, but he'd never really sought God's agenda because he had his own all along. He didn't know if what he'd said was right or wrong. Had he acted out of anger alone? Had he even considered the cost to Manuel and his mother? He was suddenly gripped with fear for their safety. He wanted to go back and make sure they were okay, but then he'd probably just make things worse. He had to wait. Tomorrow he would find Manuel. If there were any new marks, they would get the police. For now he was left with his frustration.

Lord, teach me to listen! To know Your voice and will.

In the moment, he had wanted to give Mr. Garcia some of his own medicine, but now he wondered what Jesus would have given the man. He knew the answer, but it only led to more questions. He finally closed his eyes. *Please forgive me Lord for always taking matters into my own hands and not putting them in Yours. Please keep Manuel and his mother safe and may Your will be done in spite of my uncertainty.*

John spent the next half-hour praying over and over again for Manuel, his family's safety, and Mr. Garcia's salvation. The winds and rain picked up outside, hitting his windows in sheets that sounded like a staccato drumlins he had played in high school. His mind wandered back to earlier times, to friends and family and memories he had buried deep within. Eventually, the sounds of the storm and the memories of life enticed him to sleep.

52 THE STORM

Thunder crashed, ripping through the walls and silence of John's living room. Even with his eyes shut he could sense the bright flash of light just outside. He blinked opened his eyes and sat up on the couch half expecting a tree to come crashing down on him. How long had he been asleep? The last thing he remembered was praying. Now he felt guilty. Why did prayer always knock him out? He wished God would give his guardian angel permission to thump him on the head every now and then. He wanted to get up and go to his bed, but was too lazy to move. Instead, he laid back on his side with his head resting comfortably on a sofa cushion and stared out the sliding glass door at the spectacle of nature before him. Back home, the storms were never so full of energy and power. Lightning flashed, dancing across the sky, followed by an occasional rumble of thunder that accompanied the soft orchestra music like a perfectly timed drum roll. The news had posted weather warnings about the storm that was now upon them, telling everyone to remain inside because of the threatening winds. The trees outside swayed back and forth, bending down almost to the ground.

A flash of brilliant light filled the room followed by a crack! Boom! John flinched at the sound. *So much unseen power*. It was strange that he could be looking out upon such force and destruction from inside a room that was completely quiet and still. *Just like life in You, Jesus. Only You provide peace and protection from all the storms and chaos of this world.*

John's thoughts returned to Manuel and his mother. They faced storms everyday, but they also had a refuge. John realized it was Mr. Garcia whose situation was the most tragic of all. The cheating and abusive husband and father was trapped in destruction with no haven for his soul. *Oh God, break through the hardness of his heart! You alone are able, Lord!*

John began to think back on all that had happened since the first day of his arrival. So many unbelievable things had taken place. *All those wasted moments early on doubting what you would do, Lord!* John felt embarrassed for his lack of trust. And to think he had almost given up. *I would have missed it all!* John closed his eyes as unforgettable scenes from the past few months began to replay in his mind. Eventually the scenes turned to dreams and the dreams, once again, into sleep.

* * *

Bam! Bam! Bam! Thunder crashed louder and louder, again and again. John woke up in time to see a flash of lightning fill the night sky and reflect on the whites of two eyes peering in at him…

* * *

Ricardo stood outside slamming his fists on the glass. John jumped off the couch, ran to the door and slid it open as the security guard was practically shoved inside by a gust of wind from behind. John caught him in his arms and kept him from falling to the ground. What was once a small umbrella, now bent and twisted, fell to the floor.

"Senor Juan! A girl has come to see you! Please follow me!" And with that, the man stood up straight, regained his footing, and charged back out into the frenzy of rain and wind.

John stood motionless for a second, wondering what in the world was happening. The idea that this was just a dream quickly vanished as a gust of wind drove a spray of rain against his face. Without waiting another second, he ran out the door and into the darkness. With each step a new question surfaced.

Who was the girl?

What in the world was she doing here?

Why had Ricardo come to him and not gone to any of the parents?

John hadn't gone far when he was met again by Ricardo and a small dark figure standing beside him. Ricardo had draped a pancho over the girl and was practically carrying her at a frantic pace. John stopped, and they walked right passed him.

"We must get her inside, John. She's hurt!"

"Okay, go to my place."

* * *

They arrived back inside John's living room, and as soon as the poncho was removed, John's stomach tightened. The first thing to register was her identity. Although he had only seen her face for a split second, he would never forget it. This was the young waitress at Mr. Logan's club. There were now painful differences in her appearance. A bruise stretched across her right cheek and blood oozed from a deep cut above her lip. Her wardrobe was reduced to a muddy pink mini skirt and a blouse torn and stretched out of shape. She wore no shoes. How she had made it up the mountain in the storm, he couldn't fathom. The thought of it sent a burning sensation through his body. Anger engulfed him.

John asked Ricardo to move the girl to his couch where she laid down and curled up in a fetal position, shaking more out of fright than from the rain and cold. John ran to the bathroom to get some towels and at the same time yelled for Ricardo to go and get Maggie and Paul. When he returned to the room, Ricardo had already gone. He sat down beside her and gently dried off her face. Next, he draped a few towels over her. She continued to shake.

"Do you speak English?" he asked slowly, trying to think how to ask the question in Spanish.

"Un poquito," she whispered back.

"A little." John echoed, smiling and nodding his head, happy to understand her simple sentence as well.

"My name is John. Meee...llaaamooo...es...Juaaan." He dragging out each syllable, forgetting it was he who knew little Spanish, not the girl. "Cuaaal…es...tuuu...nooombreee? Your name?"

Whether or not she decided it would be easier trying her English than his Spanish he would never know, but she answered back slowly and clearly,

"My name is Lenora."

"What happened, Lenora?"

"Mr. Logan get very drunk, he take me to room and I no kiss him, he get angry and hit me...I..." the girl stopped and clamped down her teeth again and again pointing at them with her finger,

"Bite? You bit him with your teeth?" John said pointing to his teeth and mimicking her actions.

"Si, yes, I b..." She looked at John again, hesitating,

"Bit"

"I bit him and run away into jungle and rain, I run and run, I..." she stopped again, pointing to her ears.

"Listen. Hear. You hear," John said quickly.

"Yes, I hear of you stay in this place, I hear you a good man. Nowhere I can go." She began to cry softly. John wiped away her tears.

"You're safe now, it will be alright." He spoke comfortingly while inside his blood boiled. Frank Logan was evil, and John knew it now more than ever. Though he had assured the girl of her safety, he knew Mr. Logan was capable of anything. She might not be safe anywhere, but he would do everything he could to protect her. God had brought her to his condo, and she was going to stay. She raised her hand to her mouth as if holding a cup or glass, paused, then finally remembered the word "Drink?"

"You want a drink. Okay, just relax, I'll be back in one second." He went to the kitchen and made her some warm tea, took her the glass, then went back and made himself a cup of coffee. It was going to be a long night. He sat down beside her again and watched her drink. She looked at him, smiled, and whispered, "Gracias."

"De nada," John answered back. She was so young and frail. How could Mr. Logan even think of hurting her? John knew she had to get away from that place. There was so much he wanted to ask her, but it could wait until tomorrow; she needed to rest.

"You can stay here tonight. Sleep here," John said, while tilting his head onto his pressed hands and closing his eyes. Their conversation was more like a game of charades. She nodded her head in understanding and smiled again. Actually, John expected Maggie to take her to their house or maybe they would call the police and she would go to the police station. He wasn't really sure what was going to happen, but for now, while she was with him, he wanted her to get comfortable and try to rest.

John left, then returned with a pair of shorts and a large T-shirt for her to wear. Next, he showed her the bathroom where she cleaned up her face, put some ointment on her cuts, and then changed. When she came out, he took her to his bedroom and tucked her into his bed. After saying goodnight, turning out the lights, and closing the door behind him, he went back and sat down on the couch, which was his bed for the night. He sipped his coffee, turning thoughts over and over in his mind. It seemed impossible — or a miracle — that she would find his place in that storm. Where was her family? Maybe she had none. Then he remembered Ricardo. Where were Maggie and Paul? He had to go and find them, but he was suddenly tired, too tired to go outside. In fact, too tired to even think anymore, he had to sleep. Dizzily he laid over onto the couch spilling his coffee onto his leg and burning it, but he felt nothing.

53 THE BURN

Many mornings of waking up late in his dorm had taught John how sunlight felt on tired eyes, and he knew it was there when he awoke that day without opening them to see. The next thing that came to his attention was a terrible aching in his skull. It throbbed, causing his hands to instinctively begin massaging his temples. He moaned out loud — this was the worst headache he had ever experienced, worse than all his high school hangovers combined. He slowly opened his eyes and realized two things. First, he was in his own bed and second, he was completely naked.

Before he had time to think, there was a fist slamming against his front door. *The girl!* John thought. *Had it all been a dream?* He jumped out of bed and threw on some shorts and a T-shirt, wondering if it was all happening again. Then he heard Maggie's voice yell, "John, I need to talk to you right now!"

John sighed in relief; perhaps she could help him sort all of this out. There was no sign of the girl. He opened the door as Maggie marched in, forcing him to stumble backwards out of her way. He still felt dizzy. She skipped "good morning".

"John, this morning when Rosarita," she spoke looking over her shoulder at the little woman still standing outside with a basket in her hands.

"Hola Rosarita," John interrupted, waving hello. She just stared back in silence.

"John listen," Maggie demanded, bringing his attention back to her. "Rosarita says that when she was on her way to clean your place this morning, a *very* young girl came tip toeing out shaking and crying and then ran into the woods. Rosarita says she's a prostitute from town."

John, realizing right away where this was all going and not believing it, spoke quickly, his voice just as tense as Maggie's. "Maggie, listen to me..."

She wasn't ready to.

"When Rosarita came and told me I didn't believe her. Then, not a minute later Ricardo calls to tell me that a girl ran out the front gate crying and screaming she was raped!"

John had heard enough.

"Maggie are you going to listen to me or just keep talking?"

She chose the latter.

"John how could you possibly have thought to get away with this? I can't even fathom it!"

"Stop!" John yelled, lifting and spreading out a large hand in her face. "Now calm down and listen to me!" Everything was silent, but her breathing. "Maggie, the girl came here last night in the storm after being attacked and beat up by Frank Logan. She was terrified, crying, drenched with rain, and bleeding. Ricardo's the one who found her and brought her to me. I told him to go and get you and Paul, but you never came. I dried her off, gave her something to drink, some clothes to change into, then put her to sleep in my bed while I slept..." John paused, realizing how little he actually remembered of when and where he did sleep. Why had he woken up in his bed? "Why didn't you ever come?"

"John, Ricardo never came to us. In fact, according to him *you* brought the girl in and told him *not* to tell anyone about her!"

"What? That's ridiculous! He's lying Maggie!" Now John's head was spinning. He couldn't comprehend what he was hearing.

"You expect me to believe that she just somehow found her way here?"

John didn't hear Maggie the first two times she asked the question. He was still concentrating on Ricardo's lies. Maggie repeated the question a third time, almost yelling it. John came out of his thoughts.

"Uh…I don't know Maggie. She said she'd heard I was someone she could trust. I guess people in town told her to come here and…" John was too upset to think, "I'd met her before." Immediately he regretted his last four words.

"Where?"

He paused, not wanting to answer, debating on whether or not to lie. No, he was not going to add lies to this mess — he had done nothing wrong and the reassurance of that allowed him to answer truthfully.

"I met her at Frank Logan's club when I..."

"You what!" Maggie yelled.

John let out a frustrated sigh, tired of the whole conversation, but knowing it wasn't close to being over. He had been right about one thing — that night had finally come back to haunt him.

"You've been to Logan's Club? That's it, John, I don't want to hear another detail of this!"

"Maggie this is wrong. You're not listening to me. You've got to hear this out. God knows I've done nothing wrong, and Ricardo has lied to you."

"Don't bring God into this! You've been telling our kids and all of us about God since the day you arrived and now you've proven yourself a liar and a hypocrite! How could you John?" She began to cry, but quickly wiped the tears away not wanting to give him the satisfaction, but the look of pain lingered. "You only have weeks left!" Then her face flushed red in anger as another thought came to her mind, "How long has this been going on?"

"Forget this!" John yelled, feeling his frustration turning to anger. He quickly turned and walked towards his room. He knew he had to get away before he said something he would regret.

"We'll all be meeting in an hour!" she yelled after him.

He turned back around. "You know out of everyone, I thought I could always count on you, Maggie. This is bull-crap! I know it doesn't look good, and I don't know how I ended up in my bed, or why my head feels like it's going to explode, but I do know that I didn't touch her. If you're not going to believe me and help me, then go! And yes I am a hypocrite just like you and every other human on the planet, but I'm not a pervert or a rapist!" His last words only trailed after Maggie, who had already begun walking back to her house. Halfway up the hill she found her composure, stopped and turned to wait on Rosarita who was following some distance behind.

"Rosarita, please go back to our house and finish your work for the morning. If the police come they will probably want to question you." Maggie turned away and began walking towards the Rec room where she planned to do some praying before calling everyone to an emergency meeting. After a few steps, she stopped and looked back at Rosarita who just stood in her same spot looking bewildered. Maggie knew Rosarita didn't understand more than a dozen English words and immediately felt ashamed, frustrated and impatient all at the same time. She blurted out her orders again in broken Spanish. Rosarita nodded her head and marched off towards the Stephens' house, muttering to herself and wondering if everyone was going mad.

Maggie's walk turned into a run. Paul had left for town early that morning and didn't know anything yet. She had to call him now! What if the police came for John? Or should *they* call the police and turn him in? She only made it a dozen more steps before breaking down into sobs. *How could John do this?!* It didn't make any sense. This was so unlike the John she had come to know and love. She knew his walk with the Lord had been genuine — it had to have been for him to change the lives of their children and their entire families the way he had. It had to have been the Holy Spirit working in and through him! But that was all in the past now. The present only brought the reality of his humanity and tragic fall. "Why?" she cried out loud to God, lifting her face to the sky. "Why? Satan, you're so sneaky," her voice was more like a growl. "And predictable. Always sex, isn't it?!" That's what angered her most and made her unwilling to even listen to John. She realized she had lost her composure, but she could feel no other way. *God, please don't let Satan have the victory over us in this!*

* * *

John went to his bathroom and slammed the door shut. He began to splash water onto his face as he stared at himself in the mirror. He looked as bad as he felt, with red blotches on his face and dark rings under his eyes. "What is happening?" he said to his reflection, hoping it might have an answer. He dropped his head and closed his eyes, then slowly opened them again. He had barely noticed it, but his eyes spotted something on his right leg. He lifted his foot, placing it on the toilet cover. There on his right thigh sat a large red whelp. He touched it and winced in pain, it was a burn. Then he remembered the coffee. He ran into the living room and stood over the couch where he discovered splatter stains and the empty mug on its side on the floor. His mind was racing; had the coffee burned him? It had to be the coffee. It was the last thing he had done, drank and tried to think...then nothing. Had he been drugged?

It happens all the time in the movies, he thought, but this was no movie, this was reality, and that girl was no actress, she had been scared, he was sure. However, he was equally sure that he *had* gone to sleep on the couch, not his bed. She had to have drugged him. She'd had plenty of time to put it in his drink while he was getting her clothes. That would explain why he didn't remember anything, how he could have been moved to his bed, and – this was the clincher – why his head was killing him. But she couldn't have lifted him herself. She'd had help. Who? Ricardo's face came into his mind, but he couldn't believe it. Why? Was it robbery? Nothing appeared to be missing.

Frank Logan.

As soon as the name entered his mind he knew it was the answer. They had stripped him down. There was no telling what they did or could have done. He felt sick, but also for the first time in his life, John wanted to kill a man; he wanted to kill Mr. Logan. He told himself to relax, he had to be calm and go and tell Maggie. Before he moved, there was another knock on the door. John hoped it was her as he headed toward the door, but then stopped for a few seconds to collect and calm himself. The last thing he wanted was another verbal confrontation to erupt. Just as he was about to reach for the doorknob, the door suddenly burst open and three police officers rushed in, grabbed him and threw him onto the floor. They yelled out orders in Spanish as they flipped him over onto his stomach and yanked his hands behind his back. He didn't resist. He also felt no shock or fear. At this point nothing could surprise him.

"You are arrested for rape," an officer much older than the other two said in thick accented English as he stood over John. John never looked up, but laid still and silent as the cuffs cut into his wrists. This had been the craziest morning in all his life. Perhaps they were going to shoot him in the head right then and there like in all those martyr stories he had read.

At least they died for the truth, he mused to himself. *Not a stupid set up!*

There was still no fear. The only emotion pulsating through his veins was anger. He was burning again. His muscles twitched causing his wrists to jerk apart. The handcuffs cut deeper. He felt on fire. He wasn't ready to die or be arrested for something he had not done. He closed his eyes to pray, realizing it felt like years since he had last done so, but he didn't know what to pray. What did God know that he didn't? *Everything,* he told himself and that relaxed the tension a bit, but hardly quelled his anger.

God, you've got to control everything inside me now, or I could really mess this up. Take control, Lord, of all my emotions and judgments and lead me now. I just want to follow. I can't even risk one step without your guidance. As John prayed, the officers looked around the room and spoke quietly. Then the older one gave what sounded like an order, and the young officers lifted John to his feet and led him to their Jeep.

They drove off just as Maggie came running from the Rec and others parents came running over the hill above. The older officer stayed behind to greet them all; he was enjoying himself.

54 THE SWING

Maggie sat alone outside on her porch swing sipping coffee and staring at the starless sky above, her nerves still far from calm. The same thought replayed over and over... *What a mess.* She thanked God that day had been the kids' field trip to the museum in Trujillo. She thanked Him again that they had driven away only moments before all the chaos started. Forty minutes later and the children would have seen John being arrested by the police. This thought sent a shudder through her body and left her feeling sick to her stomach. Now the kids were all back in their beds, exhausted from a long day of walking around the capital city. The parents all agreed not to tell them anything until the next day. It had been almost unbearable to say goodnight to her sons as if everything was normal, but she knew nothing would be accomplished by unloading such news on them at this hour. It seemed like an eternity had passed since she had watched them driving away that morning, smiling and waving goodbye. No one could have imagined the mayhem about to strike their neighborhood. She longed to take the boys and run away from all that was going on, leaving the troubles forever behind them, but she couldn't run, and she couldn't protect the children from the truth. The truth?

Have you already made up your mind? She asked herself. "I don't know" was the only answer she had for now. Suddenly she thought of her home and family back in the US. How she longed to be with them. How deeply she missed them. So many good friends they'd had, but it was all so long ago. The old question returned. *What are you doing here?* She never would have dreamed to find herself living in Venezuela one day, and yet it had all seemed so right at the time. A mission opportunity and the chance to make money, but instead of being missionaries themselves, they used their money to buy one and for their own families! The irony was obvious and convicting. *What had happened?* In the beginning she and Paul had both been so sincere about serving the Lord overseas, but neither of them could have guessed what struggles lay ahead. They never imagined themselves falling prey to greed and worldly success. They never dreamed the world would seduce them away from their faith. Looking back, Maggie realized how naive and foolish they had been. Christ Himself had warned them that no one can serve both God and money. More dangerous than the gripping materialism was the slow wedge of indifference that began to divide her and her husband. Paul became so obsessed with overseeing every aspect of his business ventures that it was nothing for him to be gone away on business trips for 2 or 3 days a week. He would come home and spend hours and hours with the boys to make up for being away so much, and of course Taylor and Robby didn't know any better than to accept it all as standard father behavior. But Maggie knew this was not the kind of family life she had dreamed of. She began to despise Paul for placing business success above family. What she despised even more was her own desire for more of what Paul's success was buying and earning them — material wealth and social status. It was a cruel irony that ate at her soul. The warnings that she sensed deep within were ignored. She didn't want to take responsibility for what they had become. She fought back the guilt of being part of a marriage that was failing, but the guilt *was* there, and it only made her more bitter against her husband. Why isn't *he* trying to change? Where are *his* convictions? In time the wedge was so great they no longer talked about anything important at all, but just chatted like acquaintances stuck on an elevator going nowhere. That's when she first began to think of leaving. Many nights she stayed up wrestling with the desire to take the kids and go, but no matter how far they grew apart, something seemed to make her stay. She had committed until "death do us part" and to that promise she would remain faithful, even if it ruined the rest of her life. However, she finally decided that perhaps a short separation might at least scare him into changing, so one night while Paul was away on business, she packed some of her things. Next, she went into her sons' room and packed a suitcase full of their clothes as well. Their flight to the States was booked. Approaching her sleeping sons, she stopped and stared at their peaceful faces. Did she have the right to turn their lives upside down? No. And she couldn't take them away from their father. She shut their door, dropped her things, and fell to the floor sobbing in despair. That night, she spoke with the One who had always been the love of her younger life. The One who had died for her and saved her, made her new and brought peace to her soul and joy to her life. It had been so long since she had last felt His presence in her world, so long since she had prayed to Him, but it was all she could do. There was nowhere else to turn. Like the prodigal son, she found God waiting and running to welcome her home. She fell into His arms. She cried and He comforted. After hours of repentance, restoration, and communion, Maggie lifted herself off the floor and found her entire being freed of a weight she had carried for so long. The anger, resentment, and fears were gone. She spent the rest of that night reading her Bible and praying for her husband, marriage, family, and calling. She asked God to give her once again the vision she had lost, a vision to serve in Venezuela. Slowly, day-by-day, God answered her prayer and restored her desire to minister. It was soon after, she sensed God leading her to propose to the other parents that they hire a youth leader to come and minister to their children. She had been sure of God's leading in that.

* * *

As the swing slowly carried Maggie forward and backward, the symbolism of the moment caused a sad smile to spread across her face. For as long as she could remember, her spiritual life had moved in a similar pattern. Forward progress followed by backward stumbling. An old familiar thought came crawling back into her mind. *You and your family don't belong here. You never have.* Like always, this upset and frustrated her. It was a thought of failure and she knew it. *Are you giving up again? What about all the amazing and miraculous things that have been happening? And you've had a sense of purpose like never before! With John everything's been new...and now this.* She felt she would never be capable of trusting again.

Later that morning, while the parents stood outside John's apartment getting caught up on all that Maggie had to share, the older officer searched inside for evidence. He eventually walked out holding a clear plastic bag of something green. It was a plant. He help it up for the parents to see, and, upon closer inspection, most recognized it was marijuana. Maggie wanted to rip it out of the smirking officer's hand and throw it into oblivion along with the entire day, but she couldn't pretend it wasn't real. She knew, no matter how much she hated to admit it, that they had been duped by John.

The crowd of parents dispersed after all agreed to a meeting in the Rec at 7pm. Maggie wanted to make sure Paul was back and able to attend. Mrs Childress and the children were due back that night around 9pm. Mr. Childress would explain everything to his wife after they returned.

* * *

Twenty minutes into their seven o'clock meeting and the majority had voted for John's termination, regardless of the outcome of the charges. Sad, Maggie thought while looking around at the faces in room, that they had needed a missionary to bring them all together again. When they had all first moved to their new country and home, it had been a weekly occurrence to get together at one of their homes for food, fellowship, laughter, and games, but soon busy-ness and money stole away their commitment and friendships to one another. Their last get together had been at Christmas time. They had all felt like strangers then. Remembering that day sent a chill down Maggie's spine. She had tried so hard to reach out to the families after that night when God renewed His calling on her life. She was sure God had given her a vision of restored fellowship. And though she had felt like giving up many times, especially after the other wives told her it was impossible, she had at least stayed faithful to the call of prayer. One particular night, Robert came into her room and climbed into her bed as she was praying. He listened as she prayed for every family in their neighborhood and then for her husband and sons. Afterwards, he asked if he could pray too. It was during his short and simple prayer that she first got the idea of bringing someone over to minister to their kids. The next day, she shared the idea enthusiastically with the other parents. At first, they found the idea ridiculous and unnecessary. In time, however, as Regina lost more and more control of Brad and his drug habit became public knowledge, the others began to worry one of their own might be next. On top of this, all the parents were aware of a growing apathy and rebelliousness among their children. Their once playful and obedient sons and daughters seemed to walk around with dark shadows hanging over them. Something had to be done. John Parker was the solution.

Though none said it during the meeting, Maggie now felt they all blamed her for the mess they had on their hands. She had wondered how everyone could so quickly forget all that had been accomplished through John's coming, but she didn't say it because she knew in her heart she was no different. She had even thought of the crowds who welcomed Jesus into Jerusalem on Palm Sunday. How they had sung his praises on Monday, but by Friday were shouting for his crucifixion. She kept the thought to herself.

Now she was exhausted. It had been a long day and night, with everyone talking and yelling, trying to get his or her point across at the same time. Ricardo was called in to give an account of what he knew, which wasn't much. As he had said before, the girl came asking for John. He called

John from the security room and told him a girl was there to see him. John came and quickly took the girl up to his place, but first he told Ricardo not to tell anyone about the girl. Although Ricardo thought it strange that a girl like that would come to see John, he didn't want to make John angry so he did what he was told. Then that morning the girl came running to the front gate screaming and crying that she had been raped. He tried to stop her, but she was hysterical and got away from him. He called the police and waited for them to come. That was the end of his story. Ricardo was thanked for his help and information, then told he could leave. The parents planned to call in Fernando and Diego the next day, but they knew the two men would have little if anything to add. Both men had been given the night off because Fernando would be chaperoning the kids all the next day with Mrs. Childress in Trujillo, and Diego would work a double shift to cover for Fernando and let him recuperate.

Maggie mentioned what John had said about Ricardo; at least she thought she had. Maybe she'd forgotten. She had enough on her mind without having to remember every word John had said. She did inform the parents about John admitting he had visited Logan's club. That news had fallen on the room like a bomb. No one said a word for at least a minute or two. From that point on, things only got worse. Mr. Childress hinted that it had been the women's idea to bring John in the first place, so now it was up to them to deal with it. Regina Rollins spent a few moments explaining why she'd never trusted John, then rushed to get everyone's vote on the matter of his dismissal. Maggie could sense on the hearts of many the desire to wait and at least give it some time, but no one spoke up. A vote was taken. Eight hands were raised in favor of letting John go. Only Paul voted to keep him employed. After the vote, their attention and concern shifted to John's arrest. They all knew that law enforcement in many parts of the country was corrupt and that incarceration, even for foreigners, was dangerous. Mr. Cook reminded them that if John was guilty, then he deserved punishment. Though they all agreed, in their hearts they feared for him.

55 THE SIDES

Paul walked out onto the porch and sat down on the swing beside Maggie. She laid her head on his shoulder.

"Well, the boys are in bed and I think they were asleep before I turned out the lights. They said Patty took them all over Trujillo."

"I bet she's exhausted."

"At least we finished before they got back. Of course Taylor, after seeing everyone walking out of the youth room looking dejected, knew some kind of meeting had taken place and assumed there must be a problem. I told them we'll talk about it tomorrow."

"I wonder if the other parents waited? You know they have all their morse code and flash light message stuff, I hope we can make it through the night without a hitch."

"Well, for the moment they're asleep and have no clue that John's in trouble."

"But it's only a matter of time, and once they know it won't take long for the rest of the world to find out about it. I can just see the headlines back in the States – *Missionary rapes girl while trying to convert her.*"

"Maggie, just don't forget who's really behind this."

"I know Satan's working overtime, but I'm more concerned with his partner."

"So it's that easy for you, huh?"

"No, it's not that easy Paul, but there is a victim involved here. A small girl whom no one is really going to think or care much about, and I refuse to let her be forgotten. She deserves someone on her side." Maggie stopped and looked up at the moon suddenly appearing through the breaking clouds. A lone tear rolled down her cheek. "Our poor kids," she whispered. Paul gently wiped the tear away, then turned her chin towards him.

"Honey, I think we'll find more faith in them than we displayed tonight. It was sad to see all of us forgetting so quickly what's been happening here. You know it only took a day for the crowds Jesus healed and fed to start yelling 'crucify.' We may be making the same mistake." Paul paused, staring into the blackness of the forest. "Maggie, if there's one thing I know about John, it's that he's the real deal and his heart for the

Lord is genuine. Tell me if you can think of one time, just one, when you saw him do something out of character with his faith or disobedient to God's word. Sometimes I wanted him to just mess up a little so I could know he was normal, but he didn't."

"Paul, John admitted he went to Logan's club. He admitted he met the girl before! It's not what a person does in public, but what they do in private that matters; this is Father Ramirez all over again. For all we know, John could be some kind of pervert who's even tried stuff on the kids."

"Maggie, please. Come on." She looked down at the ground, regretting she had said it. Paul knew despair was inciting her imagination. "Did he even try to offer any explanation?"

Maggie was silent. She remembered how adamantly John had protested against the accusations. He had practically begged her to give him a chance to explain – just to listen. She had been too upset to do so.

Paul recognized his wife's hesitation. "Maggie, I know confronting John was difficult, and I'm sure it took all your strength to get through it, but I have to ask you — did he say anything else? Anything that you may have forgotten to tell us tonight? Anything at all?"

Maggie couldn't clearly recall what she had told the group of parents, so she started from the beginning and shared everything she could remember that had been said between John and herself that morning. Paul listened silently until she was through.

"There's something going on here that we can't see, Honey. I'm sure of it. The Devil is in the middle of this. John's guilt or innocence will be revealed in time, but until then, I have to trust the fruits that I see in his life. I haven't just gotten to know John over these past months, I've gotten to know the Holy Spirit inside him. You said yourself that he's a rare breed. His obedience to God's call and passion for Jesus has amazed and challenged both of us!"

Maggie knew that Paul and John had hit it off from the beginning, both finding a much-needed friendship in each other. Their respect for one another only seemed to grow with time. She also knew her husband saw a lot of himself in the young John Parker, a lot that he had left behind and given up, but was now discovering again. Her husband had also been sold out to the Lord in college, ready to graduate and go save the world. John had reminded him of that desire to know and serve God.

"You two've had some real male bonding," Maggie said, trying to smile.

"Yeah, I guess you could say that," Paul answered back chucking, "just like the old days."

"The Brotherhood." Maggie said the words knowing they spoke a lifetime of stories to her husband, who, along with his closest friends in college, had chosen that name to describe the intimate friendship they shared. "Male bonding" was what they had called their special sessions with no girls around, lots of pizza, and a few cigars.

Paul looked into his wife's eyes. "It seems like only yesterday when we came to your window that night throwing rocks and serenading you."

"I still can't believe you let Jim play a banjo."

"I can't believe I let Jim come at all."

They began to laugh and continued to do so as they reminisced into the night, remembering faces not seen and stories not told for years. With eyes closed, they debated just sleeping out on the swing. Later Paul sat up and gazed down at his wife. She sensed his stare and opened her eyes. He spoke softly.

"Maggie, all I know is that John's going to be alone, all alone. Everyone is going to assume the worst and be against him. After what Father Ramirez put this town through, they're going to want to crucify John. I have to believe him and stand by him no matter what. I think he's earned that much from me. If he's guilty, then God can judge him, not me."

She found comfort in her husband's words. She knew he would indeed stand by John, and that John would need him there, even if she could not yet make the same promise herself. She looked up at the face of the man who had so captured her heart and blessed her life. They had found each other again.

Paul pulled his wife closer and held her tight in his arms.

"We've got to let his family know what's going on."

"I'll call them tomorrow," she whispered back.

"Do you want me to do it?"

"No, I can do it."

"Are you sure?"

"Yeah, I'm sure. I think his mom and I will have a lot to talk about. I can't imagine what they're going to think, probably that we failed him somehow."

"Honey, don't get hypothetical. Just call. They've been praying all along and they know the enemy's always at work as well. The prayers of his hometown will only speed up the Lord's work in all this. We need them, but most of all John needs them. They know their son. They'll trust the Lord to work it all for His good, just as we must."

"Paul, when John said that Ricardo was the one who brought the girl to him and that he told Ricardo to go and tell us…well, he looked so confused and shocked."

Paul sat quietly, letting her words register. "I'll go and talk to Ricardo first thing tomorrow."

Maggie knew this information had aroused her husband's curiosity and tomorrow he would start digging. For now, he would go alone. She had no strength left to give.

"Let's pray," she whispered, taking her husband's hands in her own. They bowed their heads and prayed together, feeling as young as their eternal souls were. They prayed for their children, for their marriage, for the girl, for John, for his family, and for the truth. For a second, before they opened their eyes, they both expected to find themselves back at the old bench in the prayer garden at their university. Many things had changed since those days, but one thing hadn't, God was still in control and He still answered prayers; this they knew.

56 THE NOTE

Taylor heard the rock strike his window followed by a series of short whistles and jumped out of his bed as fast as he could – it was the emergency call. He ran to the window in his underwear and opened it before seeing all the American boys and girls, along with Manuel, already outside. Some of the girls giggled, and Taylor ducked out of view and threw on some clothes. He heard Brad yell, in as much a whisper as possible, for him to hurry up. He looked at Robert and decided to let him sleep, then quietly and quickly climbed out the window and joined the others running to the youth room.

"What took you so long?!" Brad asked in his usual loud voice as they ran through the trees. "Manuel had to come and get me cause you wouldn't wake up. We'd been throwing stuff and whistling for about ten minutes."

"I was out man, too much museum history for one day."

"No joke."

"So what's up?" Taylor asked as he unlocked the Rec room door. The moon was bright and the air cool. They all shivered and pushed Taylor through as the door opened. Once inside, they all formed a semi-circle around Taylor and Manuel.

"Something's wrong, Taylor," Tommy said, shaking his head.

"You're not going to believe this," Robyn jumped in. "It's John."

"What is it?" Taylor was looking around at everyone; he hated being the last to know.

Susan spoke next. "We don't really know, Manuel just said John's in trouble." Everyone looked at Manuel.

"Manuel, what's happened to John?" Taylor asked, then repeated again in Spanish. Manuel walked over to the sofa and took a seat. Everyone quietly followed him. Manuel's demeanor was always reserved, a boy of few gestures and emotional displays. Taylor often wondered if all his difficult experiences hadn't buried part of his personality deep inside. At this moment, more than ever before, Taylor wished he could read something from his friend's expressionless face.

Manuel began speaking softly in Spanish. Everyone scooted an inch or two closer. Taylor and Susan were the only two who could understand him, and only Taylor understood every word. The others waited in anticipation watching Taylor's face for any signs of shock or fear, but he only nodded his head. At one point he took his eyes away from Manuel to glance briefly at Susan who remained even more stone faced. One thing was obvious to the others, Taylor and Susan were hanging onto every word. Finally Manuel stopped, and Taylor put his hand on Manuel's shoulder and said "Thank you, brother." He glanced once more at Susan and then took a long look at all the faces staring back at him. Everyone was quiet, waiting for the news. You could've heard a pin drop in the room. Taylor took a deep breath.

"Okay everyone, here's the story. Today Manuel said he was looking for some firewood in the hills above his house and saw some policemen pull an American guy out of their police car and take him into a jail that's hidden there. It's a small jail that not many people know about." Taylor looked at Manuel, who nodded his head in agreement. "So, since a person rarely sees foreigners around here, especially one who has been arrested, Manuel snuck up close to the back window and stood up on some firewood stacked there to look inside and saw a man sitting on the floor with his head between his knees." Taylor stopped and spoke to Manuel again in Spanish, which caused Manuel to reply with a long speech, too long for everyone waiting.

"Come on Taylor what's going on?" Tommy finally asked.

"Okay, sorry. So at first Manuel thought it was just some unlucky foreigner, then he thought he recognized the shirt as one that John has worn a lot, but still he knew that was impossible. Then, just when he was about to leave, the guy lifted his head and Manuel saw John's face." Immediately everyone started shaking their heads and talking all at once.

Mike yelled "No way!" with a look of complete confusion on his face, which he quickly buried in his hands. He was ready to cry. Tommy stood up and walked away mumbling, "What the heck happened?"

"Oh my goodness!" Jamie exclaimed bewilderedly.

"Tommy get back over here! Let Taylor finish Manuel's story," Susan commanded.

"Let Taylor finish," Robyn echoed.

Both Taylor and Susan noticed that Brad and Stephanie hadn't reacted much at all. Tommy walked back to his seat and Taylor continued.

"Manuel said he whispered John's name and John looked up and saw him through the window. He said John smiled when he saw him, then he pointed with his nose to the officers sitting outside his cell and put his finger on his lip for Manuel to be quiet. Then John stood up and walked to his cell door and asked the officers if he could have some paper and a pen. He tried English then Spanish, but the guards just ignored him. One guard told him to be quiet, but Manuel didn't know if John understood him or not. He asked again and again until one officer finally jumped to his feet and ran to the bars with his stick raised above his head as if he was going to go in and hit John. John didn't even move. He just asked again for a pen and paper and the guard yelled "No!" John said "Thank you" and sat back down again. Then Manuel ran home and got a piece of paper and a pen and took it and placed it on the windowsill. In a few minutes it disappeared. Manuel ran back into the woods and waited for a long time, but nothing happened. He finally left because his father needed him to do some work. Then tonight he went back to the jail and back to the window. He found the paper sitting folded on the sill, but there was no one inside the jail. It was dark and empty. He took the letter, waited for his parents to go to sleep, and ran here as fast as he could."

"Oh man!" Tommy said desperately, standing up again.

"So where's the paper?" Brad asked.

Everyone in the room watched as Manuel pulled a crumpled piece of paper out of his pocket and handed it to Taylor. Their apprehension was growing by the second. Taylor unfolded the paper with trembling fingers.

57 THE CHOICE

Brad walked over and stared down at the paper in Taylor's hands.

"So what does it say?"

"Hurry up and read it!" Tommy blurted out after him.

"Just a second. I'll read it out loud." Taylor finished unfolding the paper and began to read.

Incredible youth group! Brothers and sisters, by now you probably know I'm in a little mess. I don't know what you've heard, but it probably hasn't been good. All I can hope is that you know it's all a lie. I was set up, and I think I know who's behind it. You've got to believe me. I would never even think to let you down like this. Some of your parents already don't believe me, and if you choose not to, I'll understand, but I trust God to help you see that I'm telling the truth. Don't worry. He's in control. Don't do anything stupid or try to help me. Just pray! Remember what Jesus said, "The TRUTH will set you free!"

"What is he talking about, Taylor?" Susan asked, "What's happened?"

"I don't know? He didn't say."

"He thought we'd already know," Robyn added.

"Manuel, do you know anything else?" Taylor asked slowly. Manuel shook his head. Taylor thought for a moment then spoke.

"That must be why our parents were all together tonight."

"You're right. My dad said we'd talk about something tomorrow," Mike said, looking sick.

"Mine too. I was too tired to ask any questions," Tommy said, still looking tired.

"Does anyone know anything?" Susan asked, looking around.

Taylor followed with a similar question. "Has anyone heard anything tonight?" As he spoke, he noticed Stephanie nudge her brother. Brad scowled at her then quickly looked away.

"Brad, do you know anything?" Taylor asked.

Brad hesitated as all eyes turned to him.

"Brad?" Taylor repeated.

"Tell them," Stephanie said.

"Shut up, Stephanie!" Brad suddenly yelled, standing up and stomping away from the group. After a few steps he stopped and stood still with his back toward everyone.

"Brad listen," Taylor said gently as he walked over to his friend's side. "You've got to let us know what's going on."

Brad just shook his head and kept silent.

"Stephanie, what is it?" Robyn asked. Everyone waited.

Finally Stephanie began to answer, "Well, we..."

"Stephanie, I said shut up or you're gonna..."

"You shut up, Brad!" Tommy interrupted. "What's wrong with you? We're a group remember? John needs our help."

"Oh yeah? Well our so called spiritual leader got busted with a prostitute in his house this morning when she came running out crying and screaming and later the police took him to jail for raping her and then later they found drugs under his couch! He's a pervert and a fake and he's been fooling us all along!"

For a few seconds no one moved or made a sound. Brad had spoken so fast that some didn't quite understand all he had said.

"What are you talking about, Brad?" Susan demanded.

Brad spoke slowly and clearly, "I'm talking about John Parker raping a girl in his condo."

"Shut up, Brad!" Mike yelled, tears welling up in his eyes. "None of that's true! You're crazy!" He charged at Brad and struck the much larger teenager on his chest with his shoulder. Brad grabbed Mike under his arms and flung him to the floor. Taylor jumped in between them even though Mike made no move to stand back up. He just sat on the floor crying. Everyone stood up and surrounded Brad. Stephanie sat down beside Mike.

"He's a hypocrite!" Brad yelled.

Now it was Tommy's turn. He rushed at Brad and knocked him to the floor before Taylor even saw him coming. All the girls began screaming as Manuel helped Taylor pull the two wrestling boys a part.

"Stop! Stop!" Taylor yelled. "What's wrong with you two?"

They were finally separated and lifted back to their feet. Both boys' shirts were stretched out of shape and their hair rustled all out of place. They gasped for air.

"It's true!" Brad yelled.

"No it's not!" Tommy retorted.

"You heard mom, Stephanie! She said it's true!"

"Well I don't believe her, Brad!" Stephanie yelled back.

"Brad, please be quiet for a moment. You too, Tommy," Taylor begged.

Tommy sat down, shaking his head. "I can't believe you man."

"Shut up!" Brad yelled again.

Taylor had to get control. "Be quiet, Brad! We'll listen to what you have to say, but you've got to settle down. We're acting like a bunch of idiots. Is this the same group that has been meeting in here every day to sing and pray? Is this the same group that's been going out in God's Spirit and seeing Him change everyone around us? What's happening to us? We're falling apart! Whether all of this is true or not doesn't mean we forget everything that God's been doing. Now, Stephanie, is what Brad said true as far as what your mom told you?"

Stephanie stood and faced the group, "Yeah, we heard her talking on the phone about it and when she got off the phone Brad asked her what she was talking about and she told us that John had been arrested for raping a girl and that the police also found drugs in his apartment, but she didn't tell us any details. She said we'd find out more tomorrow when everyone would know and not to talk about it with anyone until then."

"Why didn't mom and dad tell us?" Tommy asked, looking at his sisters.

"Because our parents were putting it off until tomorrow," Susan answered. "They didn't want to be up all night explaining everything to us."

"So your mom believes it?" Robyn asked Stephanie.

"Yeah, she thinks he's guilty. She made it sound like everyone does…" Stephanie hesitated, looking at her brother, then continued, "But she's never really liked John. I know she's helped out and always seemed to support him, but she's never really trusted him." Again she looked at her brother, then quickly away. Brad's head shook back and forth in disagreement.

Taylor knew there was more. "Why Stephanie?"

"It's okay Stephanie. You can tell us," Susan assured her while staring intensely at Brad.

"Yeah, Stephanie, it's alright," Robyn added.

"When Brad told…"

Brad was sick and tired of them always ganging up against him.

"Stephanie, you better be quiet right now or you'll be sorry."

"Brad, I'm not scared of you, and you better quit listening to mom's lies or you'll ruin yourself again." Stephanie started to cry, but continued. "I don't want to see you get back into that crap again." Brad stood up and walked out of the room slamming the door behind him.

"Brad!" Stephanie yelled, but he was gone. Susan, Robyn, and Jamie put their arms around Stephanie. Jamie even cried with her. Susan thought they should have never trusted Brad, but she held her tongue. Stephanie finally regained her composure and continued with her story.

"Brad told mom about that night we prayed for him and the demon came out. He had been so excited and so changed. He wanted mom to know what had happened. When he told her she freaked out. She screamed and yelled and called John every name in the book. She even called the other mothers and tried to get them upset."

"My mom asked me about it and I told her what happened. I even told her about the graffiti and she believed me," Robyn said.

"My parents asked me about it too, one night," Mike said, looking up at everyone from the floor, "and after I told them all that happened, they said since Brad was changed, they knew it was true."

"I think my parents met with John and talked about it and it seemed like everything worked out," Taylor added. "Plus they were relieved to finally know who was behind the vandalism and threats."

Stephanie continued, "Well, Brad was definitely changed. I told my mom that it's in the Bible, but she couldn't accept that her baby boy had been possessed by an evil spirit. Instead, she decided John was the evil one. But the worst part is that every day she told Brad that John had manipulated him and taken advantage of him to win the group's favor. She told him all the time. He tried to ignore her, but eventually her words began to convince him. I tried to talk to him, but he wouldn't listen to me. That's why he didn't show up at the last outreach and why he made excuses not to go."

Everyone remembered how sick Brad had acted the Saturday before. No one had thought anything of it at the time.

"Mom told him that John would eventually embarrass him again. Now that Brad doubts John, he doubts everything that has happened, even his salvation. I'm scared for him! Please everyone we've got to help him."

Tommy walked over and apologized. "I'm sorry, Stephanie. I had no idea this was all going on with Brad. Forgive me for getting angry."

"I forgive you Tommy. It's my fault too. I wanted to tell all of you, but first I was going to talk to John about it. Now I can't!" She began crying again, wishing John was with them.

"Stephanie," Taylor said, walking over and placing his hand on her shoulder. "God knows what's going on. You've got to trust Him. We're going to pray for Brad and for John and for all this mess. Remember what John said that night about Satan? That he's always trying to ruin us. Things have been going so awesome for so long, we've almost forgotten about the enemy. We shouldn't be surprised he's fighting back. The last time we kicked the devil out of this room, and, with God's help, we can kick him out of Jajo. But first we've got to make a decision. Everybody's got to decide where they stand. You either believe John or you don't. It's your choice. I'm standing by him, and whoever wants to join me can stay and start fighting for John tonight with prayer. If you want to go, you can go. John said he'd understand, so I guess we will too. So what's it gonna be?"

No one moved.

Taylor had to be clear. "Don't be afraid to go if you want to, and don't stay just to be a part of the group. This is not about us, this is about loyalty to John. Make sure you've really got it in you."

"I'm staying!" Tommy asserted, sitting back down on the sofa.

"Me too!" Mike yelled, standing back to his feet and wiping his cheeks one last time.

"So am I," said Stephanie.

Within seconds, everyone had echoed a similar answer. It was unanimous. John had earned their trust and now it was time for them to show it. They would start by doing exactly what John had asked — pray.

After an hour of crying out to God for deliverance, protection and His will to be done, seven boys and girls - spiritual warriors armed for battle - exited the Rec and ran through the trees in all directions. As a cold rain started to fall, they climbed back through windows and into beds, cozy and warm. They would all sleep soundly. God had reminded them they had nothing to worry about. He would see to it personally.

58 THE JAIL

John sat alone in his dark cell, which - especially at night - seemed more like a cave with bars than any man-made room. Rain fell softly outside and he appreciated its rhythmic company until the water began finding its way inside the lone window above him and flooded the dirt floor turning it into a mud pit. His mattress had become an island, and he was stranded. At least they had removed his handcuffs. He gingerly rubbed his wrists where the skin was still raw.

This was the third jail they had brought him to. He had spent the first day in the main jail near the downtown square, then moved to a second smaller building up in the mountains. Finally, he was brought blindfolded to his present location, the smallest of all. He had no idea why they needed to keep moving him, but speculated perhaps so they could torture him in private. There was still no word from anyone, but he *had* seen Manuel. *So cool,* he thought, *what were the chances of that happening?* It was confirmation that despite the authorities' best efforts to hide him, his Heavenly Father was looking after him.

His mind continued to jump back and forth from the kids to his situation. Neither topic gave him much encouragement. He couldn't imagine what they must be thinking and feeling, how they must have reacted. He prayed over and over that they would believe his note and not the accusations, but felt in his heart the odds were against it. The parents, he was convinced, had already decided to fire him by now – Maggie's reaction serving as a good indicator. This thought upset him far more than his current surroundings. The officers didn't know him, they were just doing their job, following orders. Maggie and Paul, the Childresses, the Cooks and Littletons, these were families he had just shared the last four months of his life with. They knew him and had become like family. For them to turn their backs on him hurt deeply. He never imagined they would abandon him so quickly. And even though he was certain Frank Logan was involved, he couldn't help but ask God over and over again, *Why Lord?* He wasn't angry at God. He'd grown up reading about men and women who followed God at all costs, Christians whose daily routine was imprisonment or torture. Looking around him, he wondered how similar

Paul's prison cell had been. *And Paul sang while he was chained!* John didn't really feel like singing. The story of Job came to mind next. Job had suffered so much and God had allowed it, had really directed it all. John remembered God's question to Satan in the story, "Have you considered my servant Job?" How John longed for the Lord to be able to speak of him in the same way.

John had no doubt Satan was attacking, but he had to constantly remind himself that God was in control. "If God is for you who can be against you?" John mumbled over and over again. Then he whispered, "Must be tough knowing God uses everything you mess up for His good purpose." He knew either Satan could hear the words himself or a demon would pass the message along.

John remembered the girl's face, Lenora's face, if that was her real name. Those bruises and cuts had been real; the fear in her eyes had been real. Now he realized it was a fear of failing in her task and what Mr. Logan would have done then. He had underestimated Frank Logan's hatred. He should have been more aware of the danger of having an enemy like him. John had forgotten about Father Ramirez, but now the story came back to him. Frank Logan had ruined the priest and sent him running and now Logan was setting John up as well. He was going to take the fall for rape and just like before, everything done in the name of religion would be suspect and despised by the people of Jajo. John realized this was about more than just an old priest or a young youth pastor, this was Frank Logan's war on God. John had to get out. There was more to Frank Logan's plans and John knew it. If only the police would allow him to speak to the girl face to face. He knew he could get her to tell the truth, but she was probably long gone by now. Frank Logan would see to that. There would be no way for John to prove his innocence.

He thought about his family and friends back home who had probably already been told everything. If Maggie was doing the telling, he could only imagine how biased it would be. Surely they wouldn't believe the story. His family, he knew, would never believe he had done this. His friends? For most, he knew the same was true. Rachel would hear about it, too. What would she think? Now he would join the ranks of seemingly normal people who shock the world and fill the newspapers with horrific acts. He could hear the folks in Lewisville already, "So tragic!" "We knew he shouldn't have gone!" "We told you it was a big mistake!" John suddenly felt on fire with frustration. He couldn't let these thoughts destroy him. "Go with

God," his father had told him.

God, I know You're still here. I won't doubt that. But even with God on His side, John for the moment felt alone. *Lord, please send someone who trusts me, just one.*

* * *

Paul left after breakfast to visit Jajo's main jail, but first stopped by the guardhouse and had another chat with Ricardo, who basically repeated the same speech he had given the day before to all the parents. As Paul listened, he determined that Ricardo had most definitely spent some time writing it all out and putting the words to memory. But as a non-English speaker, this wasn't anything out of the ordinary or strange. Anyone would do the same. There were brief flashes of nervousness in Ricardo's demeanor as well, which weren't present the day before, but Paul reasoned it was just the result of all the craziness that had taken place mixed with the fear of losing his job. Before leaving, Paul asked Ricardo to get all the video footage ready for him to watch.

"I don't have video, Mr. Stevens."

Ricardo's words took Paul by surprise. He paused before responding.

"Ricardo, where are the videotapes?"

The guard fidgeted on his stool.

"The police took them."

"You gave the police my tapes and didn't tell me?"

"I thought you know, Mr. Stevens. I thought you want me give them."

"Ricardo…" Paul let out an exasperated sigh and shook his head. He didn't have time for this now. He would find out what was going on once he got to Jajo.

* * *

Paul arrived at the main jail not knowing what to expect, but never figuring on John not being there. What frightened him even more was that no one seemed to know where he was. Whether they were lying or not, he couldn't tell. One of the officers named Antonio, who was a Christian and whose family had been friends with Paul's family for years, assured Paul that no one had been informed of John's location. He walked Paul out to his car.

"Apparently, they are trying to keep this whole case very quiet," Antonio said in almost perfect English which he had learned on his own and practiced often with Paul and his family.

"But they can't hide him, can they? He *will* get a lawyer and a trial, right?"

"Yes, he will, but remember this is not the US. Things are done differently here, and as a criminal he won't be treated as an American tourist."

"What should I do?"

"Contact the US embassy and tell them the situation. They will put pressure on the police and hold them accountable for humane treatment and a fair trial. Also, the press will get more involved and watch everything."

The press were the last people Paul wanted around, but he knew it might save John's life.

"Just realize Paul, once tried, if found guilty, even the embassy can't help him."

"Antonio, I have important video footage of the girl coming and leaving our place, but this morning my security guard told me that the police took all the tapes. They took them without even asking me."

"Amigo. We're a long way from Caracas and we do things our own way here."

Paul didn't like what he was hearing and it showed on his face. "So have you seen the girl?"

Antonio hesitated, and Paul could tell from his expression that he had something he didn't want to share.

"Have you? Don't tell me there's no girl!"

"We can't find her."

"You're kidding!" Paul exclaimed, throwing his hands in the air and actually beginning to laugh. "Antonio, something strange is going on."

"Paul, I understand your feelings, but just be patient. The girl ran away, and is probably hiding. She's scared and confused. We'll find her, and we'll find your tapes." Antonio placed his hand firmly on Paul's shoulder. "We'll find them. Just wait."

Paul wanted to explain to Antonio that a young man's innocence and perhaps even life demanded he didn't just wait, but he held his tongue. He was now in a hurry to find Mayor Velasquez. He said goodbye and climbed back into his Suburban, feeling worse than he had after leaving Ricardo. It was one thing to lose some videotapes, quite another to lose two people!

* * *

Paul had left that morning before the boys woke up. Maggie knew that meant she would have to drop the bomb. She prepared Swedish pancakes for breakfast, their favorite, all the while wondering how she was going to do this. It was late morning by the time Robert came stumbling into the kitchen, his eyes still half shut.

"I knew I smelled pancakes," he mumbled, smiling and taking his seat at the table as if in a trance led by his stomach.

"Is your brother up?"

"I think so."

"Taylor! Pancakes are ready!"

A minute later, Taylor appeared and joined his mom and little brother at the table where the two boys proceeded to slurp up their food in a whirlwind and down two large glasses of milk. Robert smiled from beneath his milk mustache, said "Thanks, Mom" and started to stand up.

"Uh, boys, I need to talk to you about something, and it's not going to be easy, so sit back down for a minute."

"Mom, we know about John," Robert said, obeying her and sitting back down, the smile and the mustache remaining.

Maggie sat still for a few seconds, her mind blank. "You know?"

"Yeah," Taylor replied, "We all do, and we've already had a meeting about it and given it to God."

"Really?" she said, not sounding half as surprised as she felt.

"Yeah, well I didn't get to go to the meeting, but Taylor told me last night when he came back and I gave it to God then."

"You did, did you?"

Well, now what? she thought, then asked, "So you know everything?"

"Yep."

"Yep."

"And you understand everything that's going on?"

"Yep."

"Yep."

"Well, is there anything you want to say or ask me?"

"Nope."

"Nope." Robert was getting a kick out of echoing his brother.

"And I understand why you didn't tell us last night, so it's no big deal," Taylor said, nodding his head approvingly.

"Oh, okay. Thanks son."

"Mom, we just got to wait and see what God does," Robert said, his eyes widening.

He's actually excited about this! Maggie couldn't believe what she was hearing. She wished Paul was there to hear and see it for himself.

"You're right Robert," She said reaching over and rustling his hair. She had to get out of there before she broke down right in front of them, though she wasn't sure whether to laugh or cry.

Taylor and Robert put their dishes in the dishwasher as Maggie went to the bathroom to gain her composure. She returned as they were leaving the kitchen.

"Wait. So how did you find out?"

"Manuel saw John in a small jail outside of town near his house and then Stephanie told us everything because her mom told her and Brad the whole story last night. Of course it was her own unique version of everything. We'll talk later, Mom, with dad too. Right now we gotta go meet with the group."

"Alright," she replied as they ran up the stairs, "Your father will be back for lunch."

Paul will never believe this, she thought. *Or maybe he will, maybe I'm the only one of little faith. Hmph. Well, one thing's for sure, Lord, the more you get a hold of our boys, the easier this parenting stuff gets!*

The boys came running back down the stairs, yelled goodbye, and went out the front door. Seconds later Taylor stuck his head back around the corner.

"Mom, just tell me this — dad went to help John, right?"

"Yes, Taylor, he did," she answered assuringly.

"Thanks Mom!" and he was gone.

Maggie stood still for a moment longer, then walked to the phone. *Now if only this could be as easy... God please help me.* With a shaking index finger, she dialed the number on the paper sitting beside the phone.

59 THE HOMETOWN

The phone rang early in the morning in the Parker house and Megan, as she had succeeded to do for three straight years in a row, managed to once again reach it before anyone else even moved. She was even faster when she was expecting a call.

"Thank You," Mrs. Parker said with just a hint of condescension as she took the phone from her daughter's hand. Megan remained nearby as her mom exchanged greetings with the caller and then grew suddenly quiet. Megan could tell that whoever was talking had her mom's full attention.

"Oh, no! Oh Lord, John," Mrs. Parker exclaimed, sitting down on a bar stool beside her daughter.

Megan sensed trouble and ran to the study to get her father. Thirty minutes later Mrs. Parker slowly hung up the phone and turned to her family who had been standing nearby, waiting quietly and patiently.

"That was Maggie Stevens. She said that yesterday morning John was arrested for..." Mrs. Parker stopped and looked at her daughter. How could she say this in front of her? Mr. Parker knew immediately why she was hesitating. "Megan, can you go to your room for a little while? Until your mom and I finish."

"Dad, please let me stay."

"Megan, I promise I'll be there in a few minutes," her mother said as Mr. Parker took his daughter by the hand and led her out of the room. He quickly returned and took a seat next to his wife. She took a deep breath.

"A girl was seen running out of John's house early in the morning. She went to the police and reported that John had…raped her." Mrs. Parker covered her mouth with trembling hands, but continued speaking. "The police then arrested him and later found some drugs in his place. Can you believe this story Todd?!" Hearing it again from her own lips caused her anger to swell.

Mr. Parker sat in silence shaking his head. Not for one second did either of them entertain thoughts of their son's guilt; rather they were dumbfounded as to how it had all happened. It was quiet for a moment then Mr. Parker spoke,

"Well, it goes without saying that our son did no such thing. The question is who is behind this and why?"

His wife nodded her head, then added, "John's never mentioned any trouble with anyone."

"But dear, there's a hundred things going on over there that we probably don't know about. He couldn't possibly tell us about every person he knows and all that's been happening. "So Maggie Stevens told you all this?" he asked.

"Yes."

He wanted to call her back himself that minute.

Reading her husband's mind, she added, "She said her husband is doing everything to get all of it cleared up and get John out of jail. She said he would be back soon and would call and talk to you."

"Okay, well, I'm going to call about tickets, we could be there by tomorrow night."

"I'm going to call the folks and let them know the situation, then call the church and get some prayer started."

First they went to Megan's room and sat with her on her bed. Megan gripped a photo of her and John tightly in her hands. She was crying and trembling. Both parents suddenly realized how terrible it was for her to have had to wait without any idea of what was going on. Mrs. Parker quickly sat behind her daughter and wrapped her in her arms.

Mr. Parker sat in front of her and took her hands in his. "Honey, John's not hurt or sick or anything. He's in trouble because some people are saying things about him that aren't true."

"What are they saying, Dad?"

Mr. Parker looked at his wife then back at his daughter. He saw no benefit in telling Megan the details of John's situation, but at the same time, desired to be honest. He felt she could handle a certain degree of the information. "Megan, a person has said that John hurt them, and so the police have taken him to the police station. We know it's not true. We know the person is lying, but the police have to investigate. We have to pray that they will also see that John is innocent."

Mrs. Parker looked down at her daughter. "Megan, you'll have to go stay with Peepaw and Meemaw for a few days. Dad and I are going to go help John."

Megan understood. She wanted to go too, but knew it wasn't possible. She nodded her head and then stared down silently at the picture in her hands.

"Are you alright, Honey?" her mother asked, brushing her hair out of her eyes.

"They think John hurt a person?"

"Yes Megan, but..."

"Why? He would never do that!"

"We know."

"But why are they telling lies!" Tears began streaming down her face.

"Shhh. Honey, it's going to be alright," Mrs. Parker said softly, slowly rocking Megan back and forth. "Shhh. God's going to take care of all this mess."

"Your mom's right Megan. John's going to be okay."

"Do you believe that?" Mrs. Parker asked, lifting her daughter's face and wiping the tears off her cheeks. Megan nodded, closed her eyes, and bowed her head. She didn't waste any time, but began praying for her brother and for the police to let him go. Mrs. Parker remained with her daughter, rocking her in her arms and praying with her until she finally dozed off for an early nap.

After praying with his wife and daughter, Mr. Parker returned to the den where he sat and tried to think of a plan of action to take. He would contact those in the church involved with overseas missions and get their input. He would call the State Department and get them involved. *They must know what to do in this kind of situation,* he thought. All he wanted was to be with his son. If only he knew someone in Venezuela, had some friends there, but there was no one…except the families that John was staying with. Now Mr. Parker couldn't help but question their loyalty to his son. He was frightened at the thought of what could happen to his boy in a Venezuelan jail. Upon returning to her husband's side, Mrs. Parker raised all the same questions.

"Todd, I forgot that Maggie Stevens told me the girl was a dancer from a strip club in town and that John told Maggie he knew her, had been there before."

"What are you saying Linda?"

"I don't know Todd. It's just what she said."

"Listen, I don't care what Maggie Stevens says. It doesn't matter whether John was there, inside or outside, whether he knew the girl from visiting that place or just knew her from the town like he did hundreds of people — our son did not rape that girl, and he was not doing any drugs.

We know that." He looked into his wife's eyes and touched her chin, "We know our son, Linda."

"I know, Todd." She was thankful for his confidence, which she herself had lost as Maggie's words replayed in her head. Though Maggie Stevens had tried to sound comforting and sure, Mrs. Parker had heard a hint of despair under the surface. "Todd, let's pray and wait until you talk with Mr. Stevens before we do anything else or talk to anyone else."

They prayed together, then Mrs. Parker went and checked again on Megan who was still asleep. Next, she went to her room to pray alone. Everyone was still separated in the house when the phone rang again. This time Mr. Parker was the first to reach it. Once again the others gathered around. Mr. Parker talked little, mostly listened. Eventually he began to ask questions. His wife helped by whispering many of her own into his ear. Mr. Parker, who had been intensely serious throughout the entire hour-long conversation, suddenly smiled at the end and even laughed briefly before saying goodbye to Mr. Stevens and thanking him for his call. The girls were already relieved.

"Please tell me it's all a mistake," Linda begged as he hung up the phone.

"I'm afraid not girls. Our son is in jail and it seems that the evidence against him is pretty stacked."

"So there's no good news?"

"Not really, actually it even gets a little worse."

"Oh Lord, I don't even want to know."

"Well, first off, it seems some key evidence is missing. Mr. Stevens said that the videotapes which would have recorded the girl coming and going, were taken by the police and cannot be found. On top of that, the girl who accused John is also missing, and finally…"

"Todd?!"

"They're not exactly sure where John is. Which jail he's in."

"Are you serious? How can they not know? What if he's being tortured or..."

"Linda, please don't start thinking the worst."

"This is unbelievable! So if things look even worse now, why do you suddenly look less worried?"

"Yeah, Dad," Megan added, ready to cry again, "you don't sound worried like before."

"Well, I guess it's because at least now I know that someone over there believes in our son and is doing everything he can to help."

"Mr. Stevens?"

"Yep. Besides telling me what's going on with John's arrest, he also explained what's been going on with the Holy Spirit. It seems our son has been pretty humble with the emails about what God's been doing. Mr. Stevens talked forever about how God has used John to change not only all those kids and all the families, but the entire town where they are staying. You know those Saturday night outreaches he's told us about?"

His wife and daughter both nodded their heads.

"John failed to mention the 1000 plus people who have been going every week and the hundreds of people who get saved every time. Mr. Stevens said the Holy Spirit is moving in powerful ways throughout the whole region. He also said that John has made a few enemies. A man named Frank Logan owns the club where the girl works, and he has apparently been losing a lot of business due to the increasing number of men who are getting saved. Satan is losing his hold on people, and this situation, Mr. Stevens assured me, is obviously his attempt to put a stop to it. Now with all these crazy things happening, especially the girl disappearing, it's only a matter of time before the truth comes out."

There was a hint of excitement in her husband's voice.

Men! Mrs. Parker thought to herself. *Always loving a good fight.* "So, we've got to get this part of the world praying for our son!" she said, not with excitement, but determination.

"That's right," her husband responded. "Praying for his release along with the release of that town from Satan's hold."

Mrs. Parker wasn't too concerned for the town at that moment. She could only think of her son, but she understood her husband's thinking. There was much more to all of this than they could ever know.

"Satan is busy, but God is in control, and He's got our boy in His hands."

She heard her husband's words and knew he was right. She also knew that God's hands were the safest place to be. What worried her was the fact that God's hands never guaranteed a happy ending on this side of eternity. She wouldn't stop worrying until her son was free, but first they had to find him.

"Todd, they've got to at least know where he is!"

"They will soon. Mr. Steven's asked the US embassy to get involved and they'll find him and make sure he's treated properly.

"Did he tell you anything else?"

Mr. Parker repeated every detail that Mr. Stevens had shared and as he did so, Mrs. Parker wrote everything down then got on the phone and spent the rest of the day asking others to join in prayer for their son. Those closest, relatives and long time friends, were given more details about John's situation while most were simply told that John was in trouble and needed their prayer. Soon word had spread through their entire church congregation. It didn't take long before those who never went to church heard from someone that John Parker was in trouble. It was enough to get people all over *Lewisville* on their knees.

Word spread fastest, however, where John was still missed the most. Students, faculty, and staff at Tennessee Christian University began lifting up prayers on John's behalf the moment they heard he was in trouble. Bill's room was bombarded with visitors and calls, but he knew even less than others. He spent the afternoon at the Parker's house visiting with them and getting caught up on exactly what was happening, which took awhile, since they were so busy talking on the phone and with concerned visitors. Most of the time he just kept Megan company.

* * *

Mr. Parker made reservations for him and his wife to fly to Venezuela the following afternoon. Until that time they spent all afternoon visiting and praying with friends over the phone and in their house. Of course, those who needed to know as well as those who didn't, learned the details about John's predicament. There was speculation about his guilt and innocence and some, those still holding grudges from all that had been said and written before John had left, voiced the opinion that perhaps he shouldn't have gone after all. The Parker's knew that many would choose to believe he might have actually done it. They were well aware of the shock value of such a story and that for some, believing such accusations was more exciting than seeking the truth. For most, however, John's innocence was fact. His committing such crimes wasn't even a topic for discussion.

* * *

Pastor Larry arranged an emergency prayer service at the church that night. Mr. Parker shared with everyone in attendance, almost the entire congregation, most of what he knew, along with their plans for flying to Venezuela the next day. They would also be flying from Caracas to a local airport in the city of Valera to save time. His update was followed by an hour of intense intercession for them and their son.

* * *

President Pierson, along with Richard and other faculty and staff from TCU, visited the Parkers at their home later that night to pray some more. It seemed as if the Parkers did nothing but eat, sleep, and pray until finally saying good-bye to Megan at Meemaw and Peepaw's house, then heading to the airport.

* * *

Later that evening, as the Parkers flew over the Caribbean Sea, there was a packed house inside the TCU gymnasium where the Lumberjacks were up 38-33 at half time. Instead of the usual pomp and music, the announcer for the game, a longtime friend of John Parker's, informed the crowd of John's need for their prayers. A moment of silence was then given for that very task. Center Eric Williams and a few other players took a knee and remained in prayer long after the moment of silence was over and the crowds resumed their conversations. They prayed until Coach McKenrick shouted for them to get back to the bench.

60 THE CHILDREN

On Saturday morning, the Rec was filled to capacity. Some youth even had to stand outside and look in through opened windows. The room seemed like unfamiliar territory now. John had been gone for over 48 hours. It felt like an eternity to the kids; things just weren't the same without their leader. They all believed John was innocent, and nothing could change their minds. The problem now was not a question of what John had done, but of where he was. On Friday, Taylor, Tommy, and Manuel had all gone back to the jail where Manuel had first seen John. They wanted to be absolutely sure he was gone. He was. It was obvious to them that for some reason the police wanted John out of town. Manuel told them he'd heard of other secret jails in the mountains, but he'd never seen them. They all agreed John couldn't be too far. Two-dozen youth spent that afternoon and night combing the hills for any building, structure, or cave that could be used as a jail. Soon that number had doubled as more and more of the local kids joined in the search. Manuel asked around in the town and in the hills, but no one admitted to seeing or hearing anything. The youth had come to a dead end. The next morning, Taylor talked with his parents and discovered they knew even less. He had never seen his father so upset.

"The Police aren't talking, the mayor's vanished, and the embassy's dragging their feet! Don't they realize a young man's life is at stake?!" his dad had yelled before walking outside and slamming the door. Moments later Taylor and Robert had come to the Rec for the scheduled meeting.

Taylor stood up on a chair so all could hear him. Manuel climbed onto a chair beside him to translate and save him the trouble. All other voices grew quiet. Taylor decided not to share his father's comments with the group. Morale was low enough as it was. As he looked out over all the faces, he thought how moved John would be to see such a show of support. Taylor felt a rush of excitement and courage swell up within him.

"So what are we gonna do, Taylor?" Mike asked, standing outside and looking in through a window.

"We can't just sit here all weekend doing nothing," Jamie voiced drearily.

"We're not Jamie. I'll tell you what we're gonna do. We're gonna do exactly what we would if John were here with us. Look around everybody." Taylor spoke loud and slowly while Manuel translated as quickly as possible.

All heads lifted.

"Look at our group. We've come a long way, and God has done it all. He's made us grow in numbers and strength. This is what John hoped for. John came to teach us about God's love and he hoped to see us share that love with others. Today is Saturday — tonight's our outreach and we're gonna reach out for Jesus because that's what John would want us to do."

Some of the youth began to clap and cheer.

"Are you ready?" Taylor yelled, clinching his fist in the air.

"Yeah!" the group shouted in one voice.

"I said, are you ready?"

"Yeah!" the one voice grew louder.

"Are we gonna give up?"

"No!"

"Is Satan gonna win?"

"No!" Everyone's fist was in the air.

"For John!"

"For John!" they echoed.

"For Jajo!"

"For Jajo!"

"For Jesus!"

"For Jesus!"

"Praise God!" Taylor yelled, jumping off the chair and moving among the group, personally encouraging and touching all those present. Manuel and many others followed his lead, echoing praises to their Savior while slapping hands, hugging, and patting one another on the back. Their solemn gathering had become a pep rally. They were charged. Soon Taylor climbed back onto the chair.

"Okay. We're ready and, God willing, more lives will be changed tonight." He had everyone's full attention.

"Here's the plan..."

Taylor gave instructions to divide up the groups. Robyn and Maria would be in charge of the drama. Mike and Raul would share their testimonies. Susan, Angela and Tommy would lead the music, and then Taylor and Manuel would close. All the leaders came to the front of the room and began choosing those who would make up their team. Soon all the groups were complete. After agreeing to meet back together in six hours for a full rehearsal, they split up to practice and prepare for their parts.

The drama team headed to the basketball court while the music team stayed in the Rec room. Those who were sharing their testimonies went off into the woods by themselves to collect their thoughts. Taylor and Manuel went back to Taylor's house and sat on the floor in his father's study. Taylor already had a message in mind. It would be short, simple and purely evangelistic. Even though his Spanish was improving every week, Taylor decided it would be better if Manuel translated this time. Manuel had trouble speaking English, which was mostly the result of insecurity, but his listening skills were almost flawless. The Venezuelan teenager got a lot of listening practice with these loud, talkative Americans. Taylor shared his ideas and Manuel listened. Whatever words Manuel had trouble with, Taylor would try to explain, find in his Spanish dictionary, or just abandon for an easier one. In the end, the basic meaning of the message was nailed down, and Manuel could express Taylor's ideas using both Taylor's words as well as some of his own. They practiced over and over again.

The other groups prayed and discussed, thought and brainstormed, then prayed some more, until someone volunteered an idea they all agreed on. The songs were chosen and practiced, testimonies thought out and shared, dramas rehearsed and the props prepared. No church in the world had more unity than this body of young believers. They worked hand in hand. No arguments were heard; disagreements were settled quickly and constructively. Everyone shared input. The fact that two languages were being spoken hardly seemed an obstacle. They broke for lunch, ate quickly, then practiced more. At 3 pm the teams met back together and went through a full rehearsal of the night's performances. They were ready. Taylor asked Jamie's friend Carlita to close their meeting with a prayer and then they dispersed. They ran home eager to eat dinner and return. Smiles were on all the faces as they waved and said goodbye to each other.

* * *

"So are you boys doing okay?" Paul asked his sons, staring at them across the dinner table. He had quickly regretted his earlier outburst of frustration with the embassy people. He knew his sons were paying close attention to everything going on. He didn't want his anxiety and stress to become theirs.

"Yep. You know, Mom and Dad, God's really moving in our youth group," Taylor answered cheerfully in between bites. That was not the response his parents had expected.

"We know, Son," his mother replied, "We've seen and heard."

"And it's more than just good things," Taylor continued. "It's more than just what we're doing, it's what God is doing to us and in us. He's changing us, Mom. He's really changing us and making us more like Jesus! Can you believe it?"

"Yeah, Mom, Jesus is changing me too!" Robert shouted, causing a few green beans to explode out of his mouth. After laughing with the others, Maggie leaned over and rustled Robert's hair. Tears were in her eyes.

"I know it," she tried to say but choked on the words. "I know it," she whispered again, looking at her husband, who was thinking and feeling the same things. No matter what happened, they would forever be thankful to John Parker for what he had done in the lives of their children.

Mr. Stevens set his fork down and looked both boys in the eyes. "Boys, you're learning things about God that most people never try to know. God wants to change us and make us like Jesus and He'll never stop. He'll never give up on you, and if you'll stay close to Him, He'll be real to you everyday of your life."

"We love you boys more than anything in the world," Mrs. Stevens added. "But God loves you even more."

"Your mother and I want to take care of you and protect you, but we can't do that forever. God is the only One who will always be with you."

"We know, Dad," Robert said smiling, then dug into the mashed potatoes in front of him.

Taylor looked long into his mother's eyes and then told her he loved her, something that would have seemed strange only weeks before, but now felt necessary and normal. "You too, Dad."

"Thanks, Son. Those are our favorite words to hear." Mr. Stevens winked at his son. "Now eat your food before your mom starts crying again."

Maggie and Paul were both surprised at how little the boys seemed to want to talk about John's situation. Instead of forcing the topic, which would only cause them all more anxiety, they just decided to let the boys bring it up if and when they wanted.

Only Maggie was aware of Paul's plans to pick up Mr. and Mrs. Parker from the airport as he quickly finished eating and told his family goodbye. The boys knew their dad was busy trying to help John, and that's all they needed to know.

* * *

Mr. Garcia, Manuel's father, had disliked John from the first time he had literally run into him at Mr. Logan's club. After that incident, his dislike only grew as he continually heard story after story about what John and those stupid American families were doing. They were the butt end of all jokes at Logan's club. It hadn't helped that his own son had become friends with him, followed by his wife and mother. Everyone knew how Mr. Garcia felt about John, including John himself. As the outreaches began and more and more of his friends disappeared from Logans' club, his dislike turned to hate. No matter how friendly John was, no matter how much his own family spoke well of him and loved him, he kept right on hating him. He had no choice. It was either hate John or hate himself – hate the sin in his life. Hating John was easier. But that day John faced him down in his own doorway, something strange occurred. He had expected to want to murder the cocky boy, and perhaps attempt to do so, but instead, after slamming the door, he collapsed into a chair thinking how tired he felt. *You're so tired,* a voice repeated over and over. He didn't understand. Tired of what? *Tired of hating,* it answered. *How long have you been angry? How long have you lashed out onto your wife and kid senselessly, with no worry or care as to what others think?*

For the first time, he had been confronted. John had threatened to get the police the next time he hit them, which before would have been nothing more than a joke, but now things were different. John was changing everyone. The mayor, some of the officers, not to mention everyone in town, were confessing and believing in this Jesus person. He had already watched his whole family follow along. They went faithfully to their Saturday night meetings while he remained faithful to his favorite places. The difference was, they always returned home with peace and joy to share, while he came back empty and with nothing to give. They were changing. Everybody was changing. He wasn't. What was happening to his friends? Those he had always been able to count on for a night of drinks, women, and crude jokes? Where were they now? He had heard they had "given their lives to God", but had no idea what that meant. Had God really changed them? Could God possibly change him? His heart, so long ignored and silent, was beginning to speak once again, and it was telling him that John was a good man and that his words about God were true. This voice he couldn't so easily run away from, command to shut up, or lash out at. It went with him wherever he went. Not surprisingly, it gave him the most displeasure as he sat every night in Mr. Logan's club. *You should go home to your wife,* it whispered. *You shouldn't be here.* He begged it to stop, but it wouldn't. *Look around. Where are your old friends? They've found a new life. It's time you did, too.* Then the words his old drinking buddy, Ramon, had shared with him came back to haunt him. "The Bible says you should love your wife and only her." He had laughed at the strange sentence coming from his friend's mouth. A friend who, just a week before, had been a paying customer like himself. But Ramon, like so many others, had not been seen in Logan's again. *Go home to your wife. She loves you. John told you so.*

As the Garcia family ate dinner together that evening, Mr. Garcia looked at his wife across the table and realized again how beautiful she was. Not just her figure or her appearance, but a deeper beauty, one that came from within. She was so good to him. Tragically, it had been her goodness that drove him farther and farther away. The more he cheated on her, the guiltier he felt, and the less he could stand to see or be near her. All he wanted to do was hurt her for her goodness, and so he began to hit her. What had he done? How had he been so vile? He admitted to himself for the first time that the alcohol was destroying him. And after all the women he'd had, he was lonelier than ever before. He stared at her, and the thought came, striking him hard in the pit of his stomach, physically taking his breath away. *Why is she still with me? I've rejected and hurt her for so long. She should've left me a long time ago. I've never deserved her.*

She looked at him and he smiled at her. They both blushed.

Confused and uncomfortable by the look she had received from a man who had stopped looking at her altogether years before, she quickly stood up and went into the kitchen. Manuel watched her go then looked curiously at his father.

The husband and father was going to try.

"Son, you know Mr. Logan, the man with the club?"

Manuel just looked at his father, not knowing if he should be dreading this conversation or not.

"I know," he finally said.

"I think he's trying to hurt your friend John. I think he's got a bad plan to ruin him and all those kids. All the Christians…they're ruining his business and he hates them."

"What do you mean?"

"I don't know much, but those of us still hanging around have seen a strange and dangerous looking man coming and going from Logan's. Someone said they heard him talking with Mr. Logan about John and the kids. He's from the jungle..."

Manuel jumped from his chair and sprinted to his room. He grabbed his Bible and was running for the door.

"Manuel!" his father's voice was serious and loud. Manuel stopped and looked at his father, who hesitated then spoke as tender as he knew how, "I...I'm sorry."

"I know, Dad," Manuel said, "and I love you. God loves you, Dad!" Then he was gone. He didn't get to watch his father walk into the kitchen and put his arms around his wife and whisper that he was sorry, that she was beautiful, and that he loved her so much.

61 THE BLUFF

John stared through the iron bars into the forest. He hoped that Manuel would appear again and give him some message from the kids, but he doubted if even Manuel knew about this jail – if that's what you could call it. He looked at his wrist, forgetting once again that the officers had removed his watch. He doubted he'd ever see it again. With each passing moment, his track of time slipped further and further from his mind.

After what he assumed were hours of staring, he finally laid down on his cot and slept. When he awoke, his eyes immediately scanned the windowsill hoping to see something, anything. He was tired of lying down. He stood up and walked again to the window, his every thought on his kids. The two officers playing cards glanced his way, chuckling. He took hold of the bars and closed his eyes. The faces of his youth flashed across the darkness and he smiled to himself. They were all so unique and special to him. They were so full of faith! His kids were sold out to their Savior. They were sold out… Suddenly that thought arrested his attention, followed by a question. *What day is it?* He looked at his bare wrist again. He had been arrested on Thursday morning and spent two nights behind bars. Or had it been three? He had been moved so many times, incarceration was playing tricks with his mind. *I'm sure it's been two nights,* he concluded. *Which makes this the third evening…Saturday evening. Saturday! The outreach!* He suddenly realized why he was in jail. He jumped to his feet and yelled at the two officers.

"Hey, you've got to go…"

"Silencio!" one yelled back, John didn't even hear him.

"…to town and tell my kids..."

One of the officers stood up and rushed at his cell, "Shut up! Stupid Americano!"

"I know you speak English. You've got to listen to me!"

"Shut up or I'll come in and make you quiet!"

John's hands were clenched on the cell bars, which were vibrating as every ounce of his will and strength attempted to rip them out of the ground.

"You better have more than that stick," John said coolly, looking into the officer's eyes, inches below his own. "You touch me and everyone will know. You won't have a job another day." John figured he had no protection at this point, so he was completely bluffing. He was also desperate. "You can kill me if you want, but you're going to listen to me."

The guard removed his gun, but then his partner walked up beside him and talked into his ear. John could tell the one was trying to calm the other down and convince him to put his gun away. John didn't have time to wait. He spoke again.

"You have to go to town and stop the meeting in the plaza."

"There is no meeting because you are in here."

"The American kids will still go to the plaza."

"They will not. Not without you."

"They don't need me!" John shouted then dropped his head. Getting his anger in check, he looked up at both the officers and spoke firmly. "I know they'll have one."

"Well. If you correct then let them go. They don't need you, so sit down and shut up!" The officer began to laugh and was joined by his partner, though the latter hadn't understood a word of what was said.

"Listen to me! They're in danger. Mr. Logan's going to do something!"

"Oh, yes. Mr. Logan, your good friend. You like his girls don't you? You like to hurt them don't you? You make me sick hiding behind your god!" The officer wasn't laughing anymore.

John let the man's words pass through him. He noticed the CB radio sitting on the edge of the table.

"Just call the station and tell them to go and make sure the kids are okay."

"They'll be fine," the officer said, returning once again to his poker game. "They're in god's hands. You're in mine, so shut up!"

62 THE RESOLVE

Taylor, Tommy, Mike, Robert, Susan, Robin, Jamie, and Stephanie all walked the trail to town that evening as they had a hundred times before. Brad hadn't been seen or heard from since he stormed out of the Rec two nights earlier. Stephanie informed everyone that her brother refused to come out of his room and wouldn't talk with her or her mother. Her mom was really freaked out, but Stephanie assured everyone that Brad was okay. He'd acted that same way a hundred times before…and so had her mom.

At the bottom of the final hill, they met with all the locals who were going to be involved in the main performances. A little farther on they were greeted by about thirty more local youth, some of whom would also participate in small ways in the program, but most who just wanted to say hi and hang around and help all they could with the setting up. Saturday night had truly become the most exciting part of the week for most of the people in Jajo, young and old alike.

As they entered the town and walked through the streets, the Americans noticed many of the faces stared at them with a look of surprise, but others with disdain. The youth had been coming every other week for almost two months now, and never had their arrival been watched and whispered about the way it was that evening. The kids understood that probably everyone in the town, if not the whole country, knew about John and his arrest. The older ones also knew the situation was volatile. They had heard every juicy detail about the Father Ramirez scandal and had witnessed firsthand the chaos that followed. They knew many of the townspeople were already fuming and would possibly try to sabotage their outreach. They hoped some still believed John was innocent. Regardless of what anyone thought, the youth were going to preach the gospel.

Taylor heard his name being called and all eyes turned to see Manuel running towards them. Everyone stepped back out of the way so Manuel could get to Taylor. Manuel skidded to a stop and immediately bent over gasping for air. Taylor patted him on his back.

"Manuel, buddy, you didn't have to kill yourself getting here. You know we wouldn't start without you!"

Manuel shook his head and stared at the ground then took a few deep breaths and stood up straight.

"Taylor you must leave. You all go! It's danger here!"

"Slow down Manuel. What are you talking about?"

The other American kids crowded around them. Manuel was too worked up to continue in English, so he switched to his Spanish. A minute later, Taylor translated to the others.

"Manuel's father said that John's not in jail by accident. That Mr. Logan hates John and he set him up. Also, he's seen Mr. Logan talking with a tall dark man from the jungle, a dangerous looking man…" As Taylor spoke these last words, he looked long and hard into the eyes of all the American youth. Hearts were suddenly thumping inside of chests, and four boys in particular found it hard to swallow. Images of that night by the fire had already begun to replay when Taylor interrupted these thoughts with more information.

"His dad also said that someone heard Mr. Logan talking about us and our outreaches. He told Manuel it's not safe for us to be here."

* * *

A moment earlier, as Manuel delivered his message to Taylor, he recognized the steely resolve in his American friend's eyes and knew before even finishing that Taylor wasn't going anywhere. An old fear had gripped the Venezuelan boy as he ran out of his house and it had intensified with every step towards town, but once he was back among his brothers and sisters, he felt the fear fade away and his courage return. After speaking, a slight rush of embarrassment had washed over him. He didn't even give Taylor time to respond, but did so for him. "I know you not scared. I go with you."

Taylor looked at all the others and was told the same thing. No one was going anywhere.

"But you will not leave in haste or go in flight; for the Lord will go before you, the God of Israel will be your rear guard!" The verse from Isaiah came out of Taylor's mouth, surprising even him. Although he had come across the verse during the previous week and thought it powerful at the time, he had never attempted to memorize it. "We don't go alone!" he shouted, rejuvenated by God's promise.

All the kids echoed together "We don't go alone!"

"Let's pray," Susan said and all the youth joined hands as onlookers passed by on all sides.

Over fifty young people sensed an awakening of power and strength within their souls as they once again prayed for John and the people of Jajo. They prayed to be empty vessels for the Holy Spirit to fill and work through. They prayed that God would give them the courage to speak out boldly. Something happened during that prayer, and every heart knew it and every hand felt it. It was a powerful feeling that caused some of the youth to fall onto their knees and others to raise their hands into the air. They prayed collectively and individually, each in their own language. Prayers of love rose up into the evening sky, spreading out over the town. Prayers of deliverance and freedom from Satan's oppression were launched confidently into spiritual orbit. At the end, Taylor's voice lifted up above all the rest.

"Christ, all we have to give is ourselves and all we ask is that others might see You in us and receive Your salvation! Amen!"

Another "Amen!" echoed up from them all.

As faces lifted and others stood back to their feet, shouts of joy and laughter filled the air. Everyone took turns hugging and encouraging one another. Finally, they all walked to Plaza Bolivar side-by-side, hand-in-hand, ready for whatever God had planned.

63 THE COUNTDOWN

Paul arrived at City Hall just after lunch. He had spent the morning speaking with police officers and embassy staff, trying figure out where John was being held. Mayor Velasquez climbed into Paul's Suburban, and the two circled the town square just as the crowds began filling the streets for the weekend markets. A Jeep with two police officers, the mayor's personal bodyguards, followed behind. They reached the small airport about half an hour before the Parker's scheduled arrival. They sat a while and discussed the situation. Paul was feeling more and more relieved by the second. Even though they still hadn't found the girl, and although the mayor hadn't heard anything of the video tapes, he *had* promised to personally visit the arresting officers and find out where the tapes were and what was on them. Far more important was that the mayor himself was beginning to see, along with Paul, that there was more going on than just a simple case of rape. The best news by far, however, was that Mayor Velasquez knew exactly where John was being detained and was taking Mr. and Mrs. Parker to see their son as soon as they arrived. Paul was thankful for the good news which he would soon share with John's parents.

* * *

The children set up the stage and took their places like it was second nature to them. As if on cue themselves, crowds began to approach the stage and fill in the plaza area: shoppers and shop keepers, buyers and sellers, strangers and friends, believers and mockers, locals as well as many from neighboring towns and villages who had heard strange and wonderful tales of God moving mightily in Jajo. The crowd was alive with inquisitive stares and whispers. Almost everyone had heard about John and the rape. Those who believed he was guilty and whose rage had been growing all day suddenly felt nothing but pity for these poor kids who had been so misled. Others, who weren't so willing to accept the stories they were hearing, were waiting to hear from the children themselves about what was going on. Both groups couldn't believe the children had the courage to come and continue the outreach on their own.

John sat dejected on the stone slab, his head lowered, his eyes focused on the floor. The light outside, like the hope inside, was fading. He couldn't look at the officers for fear of murderous thoughts arising. *What do you expect from me, God? What can I do with my hands tied like this?!* John's fists were clenched and his face crimson. It was either stay full of rage or be sick with fright. He chose the former, but slowly the two emotions mixed together, creating an explosive reaction. The room seemed to be growing smaller. He couldn't take it any longer. He couldn't just sit by and let something go wrong. Did he have a choice? A thought came to him, and before he even analyzed it, his voice daringly filled the room.

"How much money is Logan giving you boys to keep me here?" The officers didn't look at him. "He controls you, doesn't he? He's got you scared?"

The officer who spoke English turned his face and glared. The other officer had no reason to pay John any attention.

The thought that perhaps they were in the take with Logan really began to make more and more sense as John spoke. First, Ricardo had been bought, and now them. That would explain why he was out in the middle of nowhere and not even in an official jail. John wondered if Logan had the whole town under his control. John's anger reached a new magnitude. They could kill him and no one would know it and that's probably what they were going to do anyway. He risked it all and glared straight back into the officer's eyes.

"How much?" John asked again, his voice full of mockery and contempt. "Some free time with his girls? All the cerveza you can drink? You're just another one of Logan's servants, aren't you?"

As John spoke, the officer's eyes never flinched or blinked. John had no idea the two policemen were true loyal officers whom the mayor himself had appointed to protect him. He couldn't have guessed that he had been hidden in the mountains for his own safety. He didn't know most officers on the force despised Mr. Logan for all the trouble he caused in their town and that this officer in particular hated Mr. Logan. That his younger sister, to the disapproval of the entire family, had begun working for Logan as one of his dancers, then suddenly disappeared after only a few weeks. John could never have imagined the suffering this officer had experienced as he and many others investigated Logan's, spending countless sleepless nights searching for his sister with no results. And that after three grieving years, with Logan more prosperous than ever, the officer, certain that his little sister had been murdered, never failed to think of her every day. John had no idea the rage his words were inciting.

"How many girls does he give you?"

The officer stood and walked over to John's cell. John likewise stood up and grabbed the bars. They stood face to face silently for a few seconds. John saw something like pain in the officer's eyes.

"American. Mr. Logan does not control me. And if you say that one more time, you will never speak again."

It wasn't the threat that caused John to back off, but the watery eyes that stared back at him, cold and deadly.

John spoke slowly, "Sir, I don't know you, and I don't know your pain. All I know is that Mr. Logan has declared war on me because of what I've been telling people in this town, that Jesus Christ can change lives. Because, when Jesus changes people, they don't need Mr. Logan's drinks or Mr. Logan's girls anymore, and Mr. Logan can't let that happen. Tonight American children and your own children will be in town telling people about Jesus' love, and I know Mr. Logan is going to do something bad. I know that's why I'm here. I didn't touch any of his girls, but I don't care if you believe me; just please radio the station and tell someone, tell the mayor that the kids are going to have the outdoor meeting. If you don't, Logan's going to cause us all more pain."

The officer stood silently and continued staring at John.

John felt as if the man was looking into his soul, searching for any sign of deception. John had spoken from his heart and his words slowly found their way to the officer's as well. The man in uniform finally nodded his head, and John nodded back. Then the officer turned and walked over to the radio. His partner stood up and stared at him and then at John in disbelief. As the officer spoke urgently into the CB, John let out a sigh of relief.

He just hoped it wasn't too late.

* * *

The officers held the few small bags that Mr. and Mrs. Parker had brought as everyone made introductions. After a guarantee from the mayor that they would soon be with John, the party headed briskly to the suburban, not wanting to waste another minute. The Parkers had so many questions, but for the moment were silently praising God for the assurance of their son's safety, as well as the encouragement they received in discovering the respect and support John had from the mayor of the city.

"I truly regret," Mayor Velasquez said, turning to face the Parkers in the back seat behind him, "that you couldn't have the chance to visit our country and town under better circumstances."

"So do we, Mayor," Mr. Parker replied. "Hopefully God will bring all this mess to an end soon so we can enjoy some time together."

They all hoped for the same thing, but wondered just how possible a fast resolution was. No one voiced any doubts.

"You know," the mayor continued, "it was a Saturday night like tonight that my wife and so many others recently came to know Jesus Christ because of the outreaches that John and the children have had in our city. I'm eternally grateful for their obedience and boldness for the Lord"

Todd and Linda smiled.

Paul's eyes were focused on the dark rode before him. He had been thinking to himself, turning scenarios over and over in his mind, when the mayor's words brought him out of his trance. It was Saturday night. Why did that suddenly trouble him? *Of course it's Saturday night…it's been Saturday all day…it's Saturday night!*

"You don't think..." Paul began his question to the mayor then stopped, answering himself with a verbal "No, surely they wouldn't."

"What Paul?" the mayor asked.

Paul just sat still a minute, once again listening to his thoughts. *Would they still go? The boys hadn't said anything about it, but we didn't ask either. Please God, tell me they didn't.*

The mayor saw the worry on Paul's face and asked once more if anything was wrong. Paul reached for his car phone in the console without responding. It rang to life before he picked it up, causing everyone to jump in their seats.

64 THE GROWING PANIC

Maggie hung up her phone, more concerned than after the previous two calls. Mrs. Childress had been the third parent in a row to ask if she had seen or heard their children playing or hanging around nearby. Now that she thought about it, she hadn't seen or heard from her boys in about two hours, since they ran out the door after an early supper. Maggie had assumed they were all hanging out in the Rec together, but Mrs. Childress, who lived closest to the Rec building, said that from from her kitchen window it looked as if all the lights in the Rec were out.

"You don't think they went to town, do you?" she had asked.

"No, of course not. They're somewhere around Patty."

"You realize it's Saturday night."

"They could be up at the waterfall. Don't worry," Maggie had responded convincingly, then hung up the phone and doubted her own words. *Would they possibly have all gone without any of us knowing? Surely not.* But she admitted it would have been easy for them to do with all the things going on. She herself had been busy preparing for the Parker's arrival. All the parents had assumed the same thing: that without John leading them, their kids would know better than to hold an outreach. Taylor had said nothing about it at dinner. *As if he would ask so we could say no!* She remembered their conversation at dinner and realized her boys were definitely as spiritually prepared as they had ever been. *Only one way to find out.* Maggie exited her house in the direction of the Rec with her heart racing. Even from the bottom of the hill she could see the lights were indeed off, and there were no signs of life. She immediately turned around, ran back home, and began calling all the parents. She dialed Regina Rollin's number first. Brad answered the phone and confirmed what she already knew in her gut – the children had gone to town. Within minutes all the parents were at the front gate in their vehicles. Regina rode with Maggie, gripping her seat belt strap tightly as the Range Rover raced down the mountain rode to town. Maggie pulled out her car phone and called her husband. When he answered she quickly informed him that the children were gone and most likely holding an outreach in the plaza by themselves and that all the parents were already on their way to town. Paul let her know that he had the Parkers in his car and they were heading to town as well. She hung up to focus on the winding road. Now that she had time to think, a growing panic began to grip her heart. She remembered what her husband had said on their porch swing - the Devil is in the middle of this - and her foot instinctively pressed down harder on the gas pedal.

* * *

John stood and watched as the officer quickly unlocked and opened his cell door. He was as confused as the officer's partner, but wasted no time asking questions.

"We must go now! Quickly!" the officer yelled, leading John from his cell by the arm.

The other officer followed them both as his partner updated him on what was happening. John had no idea what the policeman had found out on the radio or who he had talked to, but obviously something was up. He would find out soon enough. John did as he was told and climbed into the backseat of the police car as the English-speaking officer cranked the engine and his partner slid into the front seat beside him.

"Thank you," John said as the car lurched forward in a cloud of dust.

The officer behind the wheel gazed at John in the rear view mirror.

"My name is Carlos."

* * *

Frank Logan sat reclining in his oversized leather chair behind his immense mahogany desk, smoking a jumbo cigar, when there was a knock on the door.

"Come in!" he yelled, wondering how successful and accomplished he must look at the moment. Only *he* knew that both pieces of furniture were imitation and falling apart.

Rico appeared in the doorway then stepped to the side, making way for a small, nervous looking man to enter.

"Bernadino! Amigo, what news do you have?!" Mr. Logan looked more friendly and appreciative than Bernadino had ever seen before.

"Senor, I just come from the plaza and want to tell you that everything has started and everything is ready sir."

"Splendid amigo! Thank you very much and remember not a word to anyone and you'll get what was promised every time you come!" Bernadino knew exactly what Mr. Logan meant.

"Thank you Senor." he answered and stood still, continuing to smile. Beads of sweat quickly formed on his forehead. Mr. Logan took another long drag on his cigar then asked, "Yes, Bernadino?"

"Senor, um...the money?"

Mr. Logan hated to hear those words coming from anyone's mouth but his own.

"Not until it's over, amigo," he answered dryly, waving his hand to Rico who immediately grabbed the small man's shirt and threw him out the door.

"Go have a beer on me!" Mr. Logan yelled, then saw Bernadino come back and whisper something to Rico who quickly shoved him away again.

"What did he say?" Mr. Logan asked.

"He said he's going back to the plaza to watch."

Mr. Logan's face momentarily lost its glow. He knew if he were to go downstairs, he would find the same thing he found every Saturday night – an almost empty bar. That's why he was content to just sit in his office and pretend business was good. It had all started so subtly then...bam! Hardly anyone was left! Even his most loyal customers were being lured away. How was it possible that some church kids were enticing his customers more than his dancers? How could God junk compare with his girls? But he could no longer deny it or say it was a passing thing, and that's why he had listened so carefully to the stranger's plan. Actually, he'd already begun thinking of his own plan to ruin John Parker when the dark skinned man had walked into his office and scared him half to death. His fear subsided slightly as soon as the stranger explained the reason for his visit. Their plans fit together perfectly. He would get John out of the way, and the man from the jungle would put a stop to the outreaches. Removing John had been easy. Even fun. Rico never failed in his services, and the others agreed to help for much less than he had expected. And as for the girl, his girl, she didn't have any choice. Soon she would have to be disposed of for good...something else Rico would take care of. Bernadino and two others, probably the last three customers he had, were in the services of the witch doctor, or whatever the man was – he put little stock in such primitive and ridiculous titles – and even though finances were tight, he would pay the three well. It would be worth every penny. Strangely, the witch doctor said nothing of money. Mr. Logan was aware that the man had some score of his own to settle, but it troubled him little that he had no idea what the witch doctor planned on doing. In fact, he didn't want to know and had ordered Bernadino and the others to tell him nothing. Deep in his gut, he knew it wouldn't be pretty, but it wouldn't be on his hands. He had done his part and the kids, well, they were the ones who started it all. His smile returned, and he laughed out loud while looking at Rico who, like always, only stared back. There was a trace of nervousness in his laughter, and both men in the dingy office noticed it. They were both wondering just what the witch doctor was going to do. Even Rico recognized pure evil.

* * *

After Rico headed back downstairs, Frank Logan pulled open his desk drawer and looked down at his shiny, stainless steel Smith & Wesson .38 special revolver. He had never used it before and never planned on needing to as long as Rico was around, but he suddenly felt the urge to make sure it was nearby and loaded. The witch doctor had him spooked. A phrase his abusive old man was fond of sharing suddenly popped into his head.

When you partner with the Devil, death's not far behind.

* * *

If it came for him, he was ready, or so he thought.

65 THE SHOTS

The music washed over Plaza Bolivar and rose into the sky. The people in the crowd, even those few who disliked singing, found themselves at least trying to follow along with the words on the overhead screens while their bodies swayed back and forth. The music team performed like a single organism. No one looked at their music sheets or the instruments in their hands. All eyes were closed and all voices charged with emotion. The drama teams followed and performed flawlessly except for a slight goof up by Robert, where he exited the stage too early then had to come back on and finish his part. A light chuckle rippled through the square. Everyone was somehow at ease and yet anxious to see what would take place that night. The two dramas accomplished their desired effect. As the second drama team left the stage, many hands in the audience were wiping away tears. The expectancy was building.

Those who had prepared testimonies to share now decided it would be better for Taylor and Manuel to just get to the gospel message. There would be other opportunities. At that moment, everyone involved felt an almost unbearable urgency to get the lost home. Hundreds of pairs of eyes followed Taylor and Manuel as they walked out with microphones in their hands and took their place at the center of the softly lit stage. Taylor nodded to Manuel then lifted his microphone to his lips…

"Ahhhh!!!!!"

From the middle of the plaza screaming erupted. Faint at first, it quickly grew louder and louder as the crowd parted down the middle and a woman approached the stage running wildly. All of the Americans rushed to Taylor and Manuel's side to see what was happening. Taylor had hesitated to speak and now remained still and silent, watching, waiting, and praying. The woman stopped a few yards from the stage, and the crowd around her backed away. She was tall with long black hair that, at the moment, fell wildly over her face. She wore a light colored sleeveless garment that extended below her knees. It was torn in places and covered in dirt. Even from the stage, Taylor and the others could see blood oozing from an assortment of scrapes and cuts extending up both arms. She had yet to stop screaming. Obscenities and profanities against God began to spill out of her mouth as her face twisted and contorted in rage. They all knew the voice was not hers, they had heard it before. Thoughts of Brad came to everyone's mind. In the heat of the moment, none of the youth realized the woman was speaking in her native tongue. They didn't realize it because all of them understood every word she said.

Susan stepped forward and spoke adamantly in Spanish, "You have no authority here demon, by the..."

"You tell lies, lies all lies!"

"By the power of Christ's blood I command you to leave this woman!" Susan finished, shouting louder than she had begun. The other girls and boys joined in, their words rolling off their tongues as fluently as if they had been born and raised in Jajo.

"In the name of Jesus Christ we bind you and all who are here with you from this place!"

Christians all throughout the crowd and on the stage began praying for the young woman. Most of the onlookers were transfixed on the scene playing out before them. The fact that all the American youth were suddenly speaking fluently in their native language shocked and amazed them.

Taylor spoke into the microphone. "Demon, what do you want?"

The woman had slowly crouched down. She looked up at Taylor and hissed, "We want your soul!"

Taylor knew all ears were listening; he spoke again, always into the microphone.

"Can you have it?"

"No! No! You know we can't have it! You pathetic..."

"Why demon? Why can't you have it?"

"You know why!"

"You tell me why!"

"You know! You know!"

"Why?!"

"Because Jesus Christ lives in you!"

"Praise God!" Taylor shouted and was suddenly joined by others on the stage.

"Praise God!"

"Amen!"

Everyone was clapping and cheering. Those in the crowd also began shouting out with praises and cheers. Realizing it had just been used as a prop in their outreach efforts, the demon screamed in hatred and began to turn when Taylor yelled with an authority that was not his own.

"Stop!"

The demon slowly turned the woman back to face Taylor. White frothy foam dripped from her mouth like a rabid dog. Her eyes narrowed as the demon assessed its adversary. It would teach this kid a lesson. It never got the chance.

"You forgot something," Taylor continued with a faint smile. "Jesus Christ wants her soul!" He jumped off the stage and rushed towards the woman as the demon began to scream "No!" and every believer prayed against it.

"This is Holy Ground!" Taylor shouted. "In the Name of Jesus Christ, be gone!" He repeated these words until finally the woman collapsed and fell to the ground trembling. To the astonishment of everyone, screams began sounding off from every direction as people all through the crowd began falling to the ground.

"This is holy ground! The Spirit of Christ reigns here!" Susan now held the microphone and echoed Taylor's words as he took a seat next to the woman and comforted her with the help of others who were standing nearby. Most of the crowds had backed away from those who had collapsed while the members of the outreach team all jumped off the stage and ran to their aid. Minutes passed as the youth spoke to and comforted them. The plaza was alive with talk and emotion, and Taylor realized he had to get things back under control. Susan came to his side and he carefully placed the woman into her arms then jogged back to the stage. Manuel quickly joined him. Taylor once again lifted his microphone to speak.

No one in the plaza or on the stage that night could have ever guessed to pay particular attention to two men dressed completely in black clothes as they slowly approached the stage from behind. In the chaos of the scenes unfolding throughout the plaza, no one noticed them take out black masks and pull them over their faces. Nor could anyone have imagined that little Robert Stevens at that very moment sat in the arms of a killer who had orchestrated the perfect opportunity. The witch doctor's prayers to his master had been answered, and the woman had served her purpose exceptionally well. He too had fallen to the ground only to be lifted back to his feet by an American teenage girl and small American boy. A blonde haired, blue-eyed boy he gently picked up and held tightly in his arms. No one expected it.

Taylor spoke. "Tonight we have come to once again share with you the good news of God's love for you. That He loved you so much, He sent His Son, Jesus, to die on a cross for your sin. If you believe in Him, you will be saved from hell and spend forever with God in heaven. We have all disobeyed God in our lives, and we all deserve to be punished for it, but instead of giving us what we deserve, Jesus took our punishment onto Himself. For many weeks now, and especially tonight, you have seen with your own eyes the power of God. He is stronger than any evil and any enemy. He is stronger than the Devil, and the Devil knows it. That's why the Devil doesn't want us to tell you about God's love for you. He wants you to live in ignorance and doubt and disobedience to God so that when he is sent to hell you will be there with him. But tonight God has given you an eagerness to hear the truth — that Christ died on the cross, was buried for three days, then rose from the grave and lives today! And you can know Him!" Taylor now stood at the very edge of the stage as Manuel kneeled behind him in prayer. Standing on tiptoes, with his free hand raised in the air, Taylor shouted boldly at the top of his lungs.

"You can know him personally tonight. You can be saved for eternity! All you have to do is trust and believe in Jesus!"

Pow! Pow! Pow!

Three shots rang out in the night air. Everyone recognized the sound of the bullets whizzing just above their heads and scrambled from the plaza area screaming in hysteria. People pushed, shoved, and ran as fast as they could. Taylor turned to find a gun pointed at his forehead. Two small black eyes peered at him through slits in a black face mask, eyes that assured him he might soon die. The man spoke harshly in Spanish and motioned with his gun for Taylor to move. Taylor's heart and mind were flooded with fear; he suddenly couldn't understand a word the man said.

"Move Taylor!" Manuel yelled in English, "or they kill us!"

Taylor nodded his head and began to walk. The gunmen moved behind him, and that's when Taylor saw another figure dressed in black holding a gun to the back of Manuel's head and shoving his friend towards the back of the stage. The man behind Taylor yelled out more words and Manuel translated again.

"He says to run or die!"

"Then run!" Taylor yelled, jumping off the stage and hitting the ground in a sprint. The gun barrel never left his back. He tried to look back in the direction of the crowd, but the gunman shoved him again making him trip and fall to his knees. He was almost kicked, but managed to get up just as the gunman's foot flew by. He would run perfectly from then on.

66 THE ESCAPE

They sprinted down a few small dirt roads as the sounds of shouting and screaming voices died off in the distance. Soon they came to the edge of town and the beginning of the woods. Taylor's initial panic had lessened and the only fear he had now was for his little brother and the rest of the team. Were they safe? Had anyone been shot? Were these the only men involved? God, what was happening?

Into the deep brush they went, no longer running, but walking briskly. The gunmen were each behind one of the boys. A few times Taylor tripped over some roots and stones in the path, but he managed to stay on his feet. Even the gunmen had a tough time of it. Only Manuel seemed to know the trail perfectly.

"Taylor, I think I know where..." Thud! The gun came down on Manuel's shoulder and caused him to grunt and fall to his knees.

"¡No hables Ingles!" his captor yelled down at him.

"Manuel, are you ok?!" Taylor yelled, turning toward his friend. He was quickly jerked back around and pushed forward. Manuel nodded to Taylor then slowly climbed back to his feet. There would be no more talking, only thinking. Taylor had recognized Manuel's efforts to tell him that he knew where they were going. Did he want him to think about it? Had he been here himself? No one else would possibly know where they were. What were their options? Did they have any? The men obviously needed them for something because they hadn't shot them yet. Taylor thought he could probably bolt and make a run for it. He was sure he could leave these men behind in the thick brush, but how would Manuel know to run at the same time? Any flaw in the attempt would be disastrous. Neither of them could outrun a bullet. Taylor decided it wasn't worth the risk. Still, the image of a mad dash replayed through his mind over and over until they came out into a large clearing and were told to stop. It was too late now.

* * *

Plaza Bolivar sat eerily quiet and still. The officers standing in the back had almost been trampled by the stampede. Although quickly drawing their weapons, they had been forced to turn and run with the rest, missing any opportunity of locating the origin of the shots. Now they had all crawled back to the edge of the plaza wall and were peering over in the direction of the stage. Only one officer who had moved forward earlier to see what all the screaming was about, was then able take cover behind a small statue a few yards from the stage when the shots were fired. He was certain the shooters were close. There were a few bodies strewn about motionless on the ground. One began to slowly drag itself forward, but stopped when the officer told them to remain still. The crowd had run in all directions and emptied the area in less than 60 seconds. Most everyone made it to cover unharmed, but those slower were not so fortunate and had fallen down and been trampled by the crowd. A lone moaning sound rose up from one of the motionless figures.

People were crowded into the woods, streets, bushes, buildings and few houses around the area. No one dared move. Everyone whispered the same question, "Where are the shooters?" Most were sure there had been at least two, maybe more. The disturbing fact that they could be anywhere kept everyone hidden and still. The lights on the stage looked threatening now as if daring someone to expose themselves. It was impossible to see if anyone was around the area. The closest officer would wait only a few seconds longer.

* * *

The vehicles arrived to town simultaneously, but at different locations.

* * *

As John, Carlos and the other officer drove down a dirt road into the back of town, people sprinted past them running in the opposite direction. A voice came yelling over the police radio, and Carlos immediately stopped the car and jumped out, yelling orders at his partner, as he ran down the road in the direction of the plaza. The other officer quickly climbed over the console and took a seat behind the steering wheel.

"What's happening?" John yelled out the door at Carlos, who disappeared around the corner. "What's going on?" he said to the other officer who didn't even look his way, but drove the car down another street towards the police station and city jail where they had been told to take John. John knew something was wrong. He repeated the question two more times before finally realizing the man really couldn't understand him. As they neared the police station, some teenagers suddenly appeared in the middle of the street and were almost run over before the car came to a screeching halt. The headlights shone brightly on four faces covered in sweat and fear. The officer jumped out of the car yelling, then quickly stopped as one of the teenagers began crying uncontrollably. The others began talking all at once to the officer who tried to calm them down. John noticed they were all pointing in the direction of the plaza. Then he heard the words he had feared as the smallest boy in the group yelled "¡Americanos!" over and over. Without any hesitation John opened the passenger door and slid out, crouching beside the car. The officer's back was towards him. He had to go now! He ran in the direction of an alley a few yards away and had just entered its shadows when he heard the officer yell angrily, which he assumed was on his account, but wasn't going back to find out. He sprinted through the streets, weaving in and out of cars, bushes, and even other people who were either walking or running in the opposite direction. He didn't care if he was caught again – he had to reach the plaza. He wasn't trying to escape, just help.

* * *

A line of descending lights zig-zagged and filtered through the hillside trees. Within seconds, a caravan of four vehicles came over the last hill and down into the town, straightening out onto the connecting main street. The vehicles came to a halt as a swarm of running figures and frantic faces flew by. Maggie lightly stepped on the gas as her motherly senses screamed terror in her ears. She soon had to stop again for fear of running over someone in the street. Regina rolled the window down and kept asking people what was wrong, but none stopped to answer her. Maggie realized they were never going to get through the crowds to the plaza in their vehicles. Soon all the American parents were on foot, pushing their way through to the plaza area with the same prayer on each of their minds — God, please let our children be safe!

* * *

Paul, Mayor Velasquez, and the Parkers drove into Jajo already expecting the outreach to be underway. Carlos had radioed the mayor and informed him of John's statements and fear, at which time the mayor ordered them to bring John back to the main jail to wait for them. The mayor's two personal officers had been sent on ahead as Paul tried to keep up without scaring his passengers too much.

* * *

They arrived on a street that followed alongside the plaza wall in a large half circle and immediately wondered if all the worry had been for nothing.

"It looks like there wasn't an outreach after all," Paul said, staring in the direction of the empty and dark plaza.

The mayor said nothing, just scanned the area as they slowly drove around to the main entrance. The mayor looked at his watch.

"It's too early for this place to be so empty."

Paul heard the sentence and looked down at his own watch when the mayor suddenly yelled, "Stop!"

Paul slammed the brakes and everyone flew forward in their seats. One of the mayor's personal officers was running towards the suburban waving his arms. The mayor jumped out, followed by Paul and the Parkers. After listening quietly to the officer, the mayor asked for the parents to follow him. He led them, jogging, around the last part of the outer plaza wall. They came to a stop outside a group of officers and a few townspeople. The mayor took Paul by the arm and spoke slowly. The Parkers, who had been updated in the suburban on what they had all thought was the most current situation, stood nearby, listening carefully. As the mayor translated what the officers were saying, some voices yelled out.

"Mr. Stevens! Mr. Stevens!" Susan, Tommy, Stephanie and Mike all came running towards Paul with more officers following behind them.

"Kids!" Paul yelled and began to run in their direction. They collided into him and latched on, burying their faces in his shirt. He pulled them all close. They were all crying. Tommy looked up.

"Mr. Stevens! Taylor was on the stage! Taylor and Manuel!"

They all began to talk at once.

"Okay, slow down." Paul tried speaking calmly, but inside he was a nervous wreck. He had immediately noticed that neither of his sons were with them.

"First, are you kids okay?"

"We're okay," Susan answered, backing away and wiping her tears away.

"We're alright," Tommy repeated, "but Taylor..."

"Tell me what happened." Mr. Stevens interrupted, knowing he had to get to the bottom of everything as fast as possible. Susan pointed in the direction of the plaza.

"While Taylor and Manuel were on the stage, two men with black masks came up behind them and shot their guns at the crowd. Then I saw them push the boys off the back of the stage and disappear."

Inside, Paul questioned whether he had heard Susan correctly, but didn't waste time asking her to repeat it.

"And Robert?"

Susan was still staring in the direction of the plaza. She turned and looked at Paul. "We haven't seen him."

Tommy shook his head. Stephanie and Mike, who were still holding on to Paul, began to cry louder.

"Shhh. It's okay kids. You all stay here with the mayor and Mr. and Mrs. Parker."

"I'm right behind you Paul," Mr. Parker responded gravely.

Paul looked him in the eyes and nodded his head. He was glad.

Mrs. Parker stepped forward and said hello to the youth as Paul and her husband disappeared in the direction of the stage.

"You're John's mom?" Stephanie asked, a look of disbelief on her face.

"Yes," Mrs. Parker answered smiling, "And your name, sweetheart?"

"Stephanie."

"Of course!" Mrs. Parker replied, pulling the girl and Mike Littleton into her arms. "John has told us a lot about all of you."

"We wish he were here now!" Susan responded, stepping closer.

Mrs. Parker took hold of her hand and whispered, "Me too, dear. Me too."

* * *

A hundred feet away behind a large trash bin on the side of the public restrooms, John stood in the shadows and scanned the plaza area. He had watched Paul and the mayor arrive with his parents, but it had taken him a moment to realize it was them. He had never dreamed of them coming, but as he watched them in the distance he realized he should have expected it all along. He had also seen the children appear and then watched Paul and his dad jog away. Soon he saw another group of people approaching from the right and when they were within sight of his mom and the children, both groups began to run towards one another yelling and crying. It was the rest of the kids and parents. The members of each family were reunited and huddled together crying and hugging each other tightly. Seconds later, John watched one of the women walk over and embrace his mother. Afterwards, they stood close together, face to face in conversation. It was Maggie. He then realized Taylor and Robert weren't among the group. For some reason John remained still, although every nerve and muscle in his body twitched in anticipation of running to them. He couldn't mistake the small voice whispering within. *Wait. Just wait.* Suddenly Paul's voice was heard over the plaza speakers.

"It's okay everyone, there's no one here. Mayor Velasquez, the plaza is safe."

The mayor yelled some orders and all the officers and medics who had arrived, came out from behind the walls and statues and ran in the direction of the stage. This was John's chance. He prepared to run quickly to his parents, but stopped just as he planted his hind foot. His eyes were frozen on the dark corner of a building not thirty yards away. He stood up straight and strained his eyes. There it was again. Movement. He saw a dark shadow crouching against the wall. Soon the figure stood upright and began to carefully back away. At one point a beam from the streetlight flashed across the body and face long enough for John to recognize the person. Though he didn't know him personally, he knew one thing about the man...he was a regular of Mr. Logan's and one who had always refused to have anything to do with the outreaches.

John admitted it was highly possible that the short Venezuelan man was just another curious onlooker like the hundreds of others standing and crouching around in the dark, but that small voice whispered again and John began to doubt the man's presence was a coincidence. As the man began to walk quickly down a street, John jogged off after him. He had a hunch. The man went exactly where John had anticipated and disappeared into Logan's club. John waited around the corner, glancing at the entrance every few seconds. Minutes passed by and then John heard the creaking sound of swinging doors. He peeked again and saw the man walking slowly down the middle of the road with something in his hands. As he got closer, John realized it was money – paper bills – the man was holding out in front of his face. He was smiling and talking to himself. He tucked the cash into his pocket as he turned the corner. He didn't know what hit him.

67 THE PARTNERSHIP

Realizing his anger had only served to cause problems for as long as he could remember, John decided to try a different tactic with the small Venezuelan he now held by the collar two feet off the ground in front of him. Bernadino had screamed out when John first jerked him around the corner and now he continued to yell while also kicking and struggling to get free from John's hold. John put his hand over the man's mouth, muffling his cries for help, and carried him deeper into the shadows. He gently set the squirming man back down onto his feet. John laid his index finger over his lips. He had a plan, but first needed to find out what Bernadino had been paid to do.

"Shhh. Do you speak English amigo?"

Bernadino shook his head "no", but in doing so, John knew he could understand a little, maybe just enough.

"Well, I'm going to talk very slow and all you have to do is listen. I know you are a friend of Mr. Logan's, and you probably know who I am, right?" Bernadino said nothing and made no gestures, but John recognized a hint of comprehension in the man's dark beady eyes.

"I can see you're a man who likes money," John said, smiling and looking down at the few remaining bills in Bernadino's hand. Most of it was scattered over the ground. Bernadino held the money out for John to take. John pushed his hand back down.

"I have an offer for you, amigo, and if you help me you could never have to work for money again. You can be rich for the rest of your life."

Bernadino's eyes told John he was definitely listening.

"I suppose Mr. Logan's paying you to help him scare the Christians, right? To help him get rid of those kids and their meetings." John spoke as if he no longer had anything to do with them. For the moment he was anything but Christian. He was a criminal and evil. "But you see, friend, Mr. Logan doesn't know what I know about the Americans. He just wants them gone. I want their money and I know how much they have and where they keep it." Bernadino was now nodding his head, no longer concerned with playing dumb.

"Mr. Logan's trying to scare the families away so his business won't suffer, but he's a fool! He doesn't realize where the real money is!" Bernadino had never heard anyone call Mr. Logan a fool before, and the sound of it both scared and excited him. The small man looked around, half expecting Rico to emerge from the shadows.

"If we could get our hands on a few of the kids," John continued, "then we can use them to get their parents' money. I know they'll pay and pay big. Pay cash."

"How much?" Bernadino asked smiling, now happy he'd practiced his English as a boy.

John's smile grew even wider. "Ha! Now we're talking amigo. You're a man who asks the right kind of questions. Well, I know they have at least $50,000 cash in each house," John was having fun now, "And I've seen a safe full of gold bars in one of the houses, but probably each family has their own safe."

"Really?" Bernadino exclaimed, "I knew those Americanos tienen mucho dinero!"

"Mucho! So, you want in?" John asked, at the same time thinking when this was all over his new partner in crime had better go to jail for a long time and the American neighborhood would have to beef up security. Bernadino hesitated, scratching his head.

John quickly added, "You can't tell anyone. No one! It's just you and me. Split everything 50/50."

Bernadino's eyes twinkled. "60/40," he replied coolly.

John didn't mind losing imaginary money and he didn't have time to pretend to care. "Deal."

Bernadino grinned from ear to ear, at the same time wishing he'd demanded more.

"Are you in? John asked again, "We don't have much time!"

"I'm in!" the little man said, holding out his hand. John shook it quickly.

"Okay partner, here's the plan. We get our hands on at least two kids and then take them up to a place I know in the mountains. I'll write a note to the parents and tell them how much money we want. We won't even give them time to get the police involved."

"What if they won't pay so fast?"

"They'll pay, or they'll lose some kids." John said the words, his voice flat and without emotion. Bernadino believed him. This John Parker was more evil than he would have ever dreamed.

"Partner, what's your name?" John asked.

"Bernadino."

"Well, Bernadino, we've got to get our hands on some kids or they'll be no money. Did you go to the meeting tonight?"

"Si, but it's over." Bernadino was still grinning. Now that they were partners he figured he could trust John with everything. "The jungle man and two of mis amigos scared away everyone with guns and took two American ninos into the jungle."

John felt sick, like he had just been struck hard in the pit of his stomach. "Who took the boys?" he asked, trying to sound unaffected.

"I don't know who he is. He's Curandero from jungle and he's bad. I think he kills those boys. Mr. Logan paid me and two others to help with the job.

"Dammit Bernadino!" John yelled, venting his anger under the guise of simple frustration, "If he kills those boys we'll never see a penny!" John cursed again for dramatic affect.

"We can just get some other kids. There's many."

"Listen Bernadino, if those boys are killed, there will be no money because there will be no families. They will all move back to America. Every one of them. And they'll take their money with them." John's last sentence was the clincher.

Bernadino knew John was right. They would most definitely leave and take their money far away. He would never have another chance to be filthy rich. They had to stop the jungle man. Mr. Logan's plans meant nothing to him now. He could open his own club with the money he was about to get!

"We stop them!" Bernadino yelled.

"We've got to hurry!" John responded. "Show me the way."

"Come!" Bernadino shouted and began jogging back in the direction of the plaza. John stayed right behind him. They kept close to the buildings and deep in the shadows avoiding all others as best they could. Bernadino led them down some small narrow lanes, over some fences, and through a few backyards. They arrived at the edge of town and quickly disappeared into the neighboring woods. They picked up their pace, weaving in and out of trees, bushes, and rocks. Bernadino found a trail that led them in a half circle around the town. At times the trees thinned and John could see the plaza and stage in the distance. People were moving and running about. Police and ambulance lights flashed all over. He imagined Paul, scared and searching. *I'll find them,* he whispered under his breath.

They circled behind the stage then came to a stop where the trail turned abruptly to the right, disappearing deep into the darkness of the forest.

"This where they took the boys," Bernadino said, gasping for air and pointing down the trail. He thought he was going to die.

"Okay, Let's go," John said, beginning to walk towards the darkness. He stopped and turned around. Bernadino remained hunched over.

"Are you coming?"

"You go yourself. I too slow." Bernadino had no intention of meeting up with the man from the jungle and his two accomplices. He had his doubts that John would make it back alive. Though the thought of all that money was alluring, it was no good to a dead man. If John was killed, Bernadino would try his luck with another American kid at another time if any of the families stayed around.

John wasn't surprised by Bernadino's cowardice and he didn't have time to belittle the guy.

"So where did they go?" John asked, looking down the trail.

"Just run straight and you come to a big open place. They make a big fire."

John suddenly remembered the boys' story about the witch doctor and the fire. *Is he the man from the jungle?* If so, he had the boys again and was obviously going to finish what he had started! John disappeared at once.

"Where we meet later?!" Bernadino yelled as John sprinted into the shadows. After another minute of catching his breath, he turned back towards town and slowly made his way to Logan's for a drink. Along the way he thought about the money. If John somehow managed to survive and get the kids, he would surely need Bernadino's help to pull off the ransom. But what if his American partner double-crossed him? He felt uneasy and on edge, and that didn't change after he had sat down in Logan's with a cold beer in his hand. Why was he so paranoid all of a sudden? Deep down he knew exactly why. What if the witch doctor found out that he had helped John? Suddenly, the beer in his hands lost its taste and he felt sick to his stomach. For the slim chance of making a fortune, but more importantly for his own safety, Bernadino prayed for John's success. For now all he could do was wait. Wait and worry.

68 THE SACRIFICE

Taylor and Robert stood with their arms stretched behind them and their backs pulled tight against the trunk of a tree. Their hands were tied so they couldn't move. All they could do was look across at one another and wait. They weren't crying, they weren't hysterical, but they were scared. All they thought about was one another; each wishing the other could get away. At the moment, however, they were both more worried about Manuel than themselves. He hadn't been tied up, but stood in the middle of the three men who had kidnapped them.

* * *

Moments earlier, when they had arrived to the clearing where a fire was roaring, Taylor immediately saw Robert tied to a tree and tried to run to him. He was blocked by a tall dark figure who stepped in front of him and struck him across his face. He heard Robert scream then everything went black. He awoke to find himself tied the same as his brother, only feet away from him. The man who struck him was standing before him, gazing down and smiling. All Taylor could see were the whites of his eyes and his dull, yellowish teeth. The rest of him was as black as the night around them. He had found them.

"So you see child," the witch doctor said slowly, his voice low and crackling, "he's brought you back to me."

"Who's brought me back?" Taylor mumbled. His jaw and cheek hurt terribly.

"This slave of mine!" The witch doctor turned and waved his hands at the large fire behind him and the flames leaped high into the air. "Now we will finish what we started," he snarled, "but first…" he turned and walked away. The two men in masks appeared, dragging Manuel between them.

"You don't need him!" Taylor yelled, "You don't need my little brother! Please let them go! You just need me!"

The group of men acted as if they heard nothing. Soon the two jerked Manuel around and led him back into the trees, their guns held at his head.

"Manuel!" Taylor yelled "Manuel!"

Robert yelled with him. The dark man walked back over to the boys. Taylor continued to plead with him.

"Please don't hurt him. You've got me! Let them him go! Let my brother go!" Tears were running down his face. "Please!"

Seeing his brother's tears caused Robert to begin crying as well, but he remained silent, just shaking and whimpering.

The witch doctor walked around behind Taylor and untied the rope around his wrists. Gripping one arm, he jerked Taylor away from the tree, scratching the teenager's back against the jagged bark. Taylor winced in pain and fell to his knees.

"Stand!" The witch doctor yelled, yanking Taylor back to his feet. He moved behind Taylor and tied his wrists together again. Taylor's resistance did nothing to slow the man's movements.

"I know who you are Witchcraft," Taylor said. His crying suddenly stopped and his voice was calm. "You answer to *my* master and you bow before *his* name."

"Shut up, fool!" The witch doctor yelled, pulling Taylor behind him, leading him towards the fire. "Tonight, you'll bow before me and beg for mercy!"

"You'll never beat my God, and you know that."

"But I'll beat you." The witch doctor shoved Taylor backward onto a long flat board that was lying in the dirt, one end was propped up on another piece of wood. Taylor understood immediately. It was a crude altar and he was the sacrifice.

"Where is your God now?"

"If you kill me," Taylor answered, looking up into the man's eyes, "You still don't win. As soon as I'm dead, I'm alive. Don't you know?"

The man stared down at the face of his prisoner. He saw courage and sensed peace within the small body. For a moment he was impressed, then quickly his respect turned to hatred. Hatred of the fact that Taylor spoke the truth — he could never have his soul. He picked another rope up off the ground and as he did so, two simultaneous gunshots were heard in the distance. Taylor's heart broke.

"He's still alive," Taylor said, choking back the tears, "He's still alive! Manuel go home my friend! Wait for me!" Taylor heard Robert crying and yelled to his brother. "Robert, I love you! Remember Jesus is Lord!"

Robert shouted in reply, "Jesus is Lord! Jesus is Lord!"

"That's right Robert!" Taylor yelled, crying and smiling all at once. The witch doctor had never seen anything so strange in his life. He began to wrap the rope around Taylor and the board underneath him, pinning him to it.

"Greater is He that is in you than he that is in the world!" The words poured from Taylor's lips and Robert repeated them.

The witch doctor had heard enough. He let go of the rope and removed a piece of cloth from his side and stuffed it into Taylor's mouth.

"Greater is He that is in you than he that is in the world!" Robert continued shouting alone.

The witch doctor began walking towards Robert, ready to silence him once and for all, when another gunshot sounded in the woods. He stopped, waiting. Another shot followed. Something was wrong! He had to hurry.

"Greater is He that is in you than he that is in the world!"

The witch doctor turned and saw that Taylor was sitting up. Somehow he had managed to loosen the rope and was squirming to get free. The man ran over and slammed Taylor back against the board so hard that it nearly cracked his skull. He grabbed the loose rope, pulled it tighter and began to wrap loop after loop around Taylor and the wood until there was no more rope to hold.

The witch doctor quickly walked to the fire and removed a long machete from a strap on his side.

"Greater is He that is in you than he that is in the world!" Robert's eyes were closed and pouring tears.

He held the end of the blade in the fire until the tip began to glow orange and red. He returned to Taylor's side, closed his eyes and began to chant the same words he had that night long ago.

Robert yelled louder, "Greater is He that is in you than he that is in the world!"

Taylor eyes blinked open and he stared up at the killer above him. As he lifted the machete high over his head, Taylor strained to see his little brother one last time. His eyes met Robert's and time suddenly stopped. Both of them smiled at each other, sad, heartbreaking smiles that spoke messages of love and hope and ultimate victory.

"I love you." Taylor's lips moved, but no words came out. The machete began it's descent...

* * *

The witch doctor yelled. Robert screamed. Taylor held his breath.

69 THE WOUND

As the two armed men led Manuel away with his hands still tied, he knew he was about to die. There was no other reason why they would be taking him so deep into the woods. He had tried to run away twice, but only made it a few steps before they caught him and knocked him to the ground, kicking and hitting him, then pulled him back to his feet to walk further. Now he just wanted them to hurry and finish it. All he could think about was Taylor and Robert. He knew what the witch doctor was going to do with them. He also knew that all of it was his fault. He had been the one to introduce the boys to the crazy man. He wondered if God would forgive him.

A few more steps.

"Stop!" one of the men yelled then kicked Manuel's leg, causing it to buckle and drop him onto the ground. He laid still with his eyes closed, waiting for the bullet. Seconds passed.

The men took their stance over their prisoner and raised their pistols together. They both aimed at the head. They both squeezed the trigger. At that very second a large thick branch struck across both of their backs, shattering in pieces and causing the two men to fire in opposite directions before their pistols flew out of their hands. They crashed onto the ground landing on top of Manuel, who opened his eyes and saw John standing over him lifting one of the men into the air. Manuel kicked and scrambled out from under the other man, then climbed to his knees in time to see John draw back his closed fist and strike one of the would be killers across his chin. The man crumpled to the ground instantly. John turned and walked back towards the other man who was slowly sitting up, wondering what had hit him. On the way, John stopped and leaned over Manuel, touching his face.

"Are you okay Manuel?" he asked in between breaths.

Manuel nodded his head. "Gracias, John."

John nodded back, then turned and looked at the man crawling away in the dirt. Manuel noticed a change come over John's face. It was a look he'd never seen on John before and one he hoped he'd never see again.

As John approached, the man quickly stood up and lunged at him with a small knife in his hands. John grabbed the man's wrist and shook the knife loose like it was in the grip of a doll. Then John took the man and lifted him into the air above his head. He grunted and threw the man as hard as he could into a tree. The man's head struck against the thick trunk and he fell limp onto the ground.

"No!"

John recognized Manuel's voice and turned to see the boy wrestling with the other man, their arms intertwined and their hands both locked on the killer's pistol. They fell over onto the ground and began rolling.

"Manuel!" John yelled and ran in their direction. He lunged at them both just as a shot cracked through the air.

"Manuel!" John yelled again, knocking the man away from Manuel who had instantly become motionless. The man scrambled to his feet and began to run. John saw the pistol on the ground, took it in his hands, aimed and fired. The man screamed, dropped to one knee then slowly stood back up. John lifted the gun again, aiming it carefully at the back of the man's head. The man turned and looked at John, then cried out with a hopeless shriek and began hobbling away, holding and dragging one leg. John's hand shook as his finger tightened on the trigger. The fleeing man closed his eyes, waiting for the bullet to hit.

"John…" The voice that spoke was faint and weak.

John watched the man disappear into the darkness then dropped the gun to the ground. He quickly moved to Manuel's side. The boy lay curled up on the ground with his eyes half closed. John noticed the blood soaking through his shirt above his stomach.

"Manuel, hey little buddy," John whispered "you're gonna be okay." John sat on the ground and put Manuel's head in his lap, "Listen to me amigo. You hang in there. You're gonna be alright." Tears fell from John's chin, dropping onto Manuel's cheek. As John wiped them away, Manuel opened his eyes a little wider and whispered.

"John…help Taylor…I'll be..." he coughed, then continued weakly, "I'm okay. Hurry!" As he said the last word he lifted his hand and pointed in the direction for John to go. John hesitated, looking down into Manuel's eyes. Manuel nodded his head and John knew he had to go. He removed his shirt then carefully lifted Manuel's head and set it gently back down onto the homemade pillow.

"I'll be back Manuel," John whispered into his ear and then ran off in the direction Manuel had shown him.

70 THE BATTLE

In less than a minute John could see fire light glowing on the tops of trees. He heard the witch doctor's voice and began to run harder. He broke through some branches and rushed into the clearing, quickly taking everything in. His eyes bore down on the witch doctor's back just as the man raised his machete over his head and yelled. Robert screamed.

"Ahhh!!!! John shouted, leaping over the roaring flames of the fire and striking the man at his midsection. The large knife flew from his hand, sticking into the dirt inches from Taylor's head as both men slammed to the ground, rolling over and over again. The witch doctor's body was long and slippery. Lightning quick, he squirmed out of John's hold and jumped to his feet. John stood up equally fast.

They faced each other, circling slowly. The dark man's eyes glowed red in rage. John's eyes narrowed. The light from the fire reflected on John's shirtless body, causing the sweat to glisten and shine. His chest heaved in and out violently. He was covered in dirt, scratches, and blood. His muscles were flexed and twitching. The witch doctor looked tame in comparison.

"We meet again!" the satanic man snarled, "This time, you will die!"

John recognized the voice spitting out. Witchcraft had found a new home.

"You can't have my boys," John said, "and you can't win. You're through."

"Your life is over!" the witch doctor screamed, then rushed at John with his hands outstretched.

"Ahhh!!!!"

They collided with a thud! Both men wrapped their hands around the other's throat. The witch doctor's fingers were long and his nails sharp. He dug them into John's skin, squeezing with a supernatural strength. But John's neck was thick, and solid and his hands were large and strong and they gripped the possessed man's neck with ease. He squeezed harder and harder. Both of their faces turned red, then slowly the killer's turned purple. A gurgling sound trickled out from his mouth as he slowly dropped down to his knees. John stood over him and continued to squeeze. He saw the killer's eyes widen and twitch in horror, then they began to change; the rage was fading.

Up to this moment, John's ears had been full of a constant roar, the roar of rage that had overtaken him the second he saw the two men standing over Manuel. Now, as he choked the life out of this man, the roar became a sharp piercing scream.

"John stop! Please stop!

John blinked his eyes, looking at the almost lifeless body below him.

"Don't kill him, John! Stop!

The man's eyes closed and John knew only seconds remained.

"Please John!"

Another older voice joined in. "Robert, what's happening?"

"John's killing him!"

John blinked again. The screaming inside ceased. He suddenly heard the voices calling to him. Robert! Taylor! He released his hold and let the witch doctor's limp body fall to the ground. Robert's voice turned him around.

"John, is he dead?"

John ran over to Robert and untied him from the tree. Robert fell into his arms, crying uncontrollably. Seconds later, they ran over and untied Taylor, lifting him to his feet. All three hugged, crying and laughing at the same time. Relief washed over them, but heartbeats continued to pound. John held Robert tightly with one hand while wiping Taylor's tears with his other.

"It's okay boys. It's over. It's really over."

They looked over at the witch doctor lying on the ground.

"Is he dead?" Taylor asked.

"I don't know," John answered.

"John choked him to death, Taylor," Robert exclaimed. "I saw it!" Then Robert grew quiet with a confused look on his face. Inside, the small boy was torn between joy and sadness.

John prayed Robert was wrong. He silently cried for God to let the man live. He looked down at Robert and knew either way, the nightmares would last a long time for them all. Then he remembered Manuel.

"Taylor, Manuel's hurt. We've got to get him help right away!"

"Manuel's alive? I thought they killed him!" Taylor said, already beginning to run in the direction the men had earlier taken his friend. John lifted Robert into his arms and followed behind. They had only taken a few steps when a low wheezing sound filled the air, followed by a sharp choking cry. John turned and they both saw the witch doctor roll over onto his back and place his hands on his throat. His chest lifted and sank rapidly.

Robert let out a short cry, jumped out of John's arms, and ran behind a tree.

"It's alright Robert. We're okay."

"John stay away from him!" Robert shouted.

John did exactly the opposite and walked over to the witch doctor, stopping on his way to pull the machete out of the ground. Standing over the choking man, John waited. The man's breathing returned to normal and his hands dropped back to his sides. His eyes slowly opened, staring up at John, and, for a moment, John couldn't believe what he saw…eyes soft and innocent, like the eyes of a child. In fact, the man's entire appearance was frail and weak, and John could hardly believe this was the same violent person he had wrestled with only moments before. John's heart was filled with pity. He put the machete down and gently lifted the man to his feet, then wrapped the man's arms over his shoulder and dragged him to a tree. He set the man down against the trunk, took the ropes that were lying on the ground and bound him to the tree with as many knots as he could tie. John looked down at the man and thanked God for answering his prayer. John knew the man had only been used by the Devil, and in the end was to be discarded. He also knew God was not through with the man yet. The thought that he had almost sent this poor soul on its way to hell sent a chill through John's body.

Robert came and stood behind John, peeking through his legs at the man.

"You helped saved his life, buddy."

John picked up another discarded rope and then lifted Robert into his arms. As they ran from the clearing, the small boy looked over John's shoulder at the man who had almost killed his brother. A man he for some reason, now loved as much as any person he knew. Their eyes met and Robert was sure he saw the faint trace of appreciation.

Minutes later, they found Taylor sitting on the ground with Manuel propped up and leaning back against his chest. Taylor's arms were wrapped around his friend's stomach and covered in blood. Manuel's eyes were closed.

"He's not breathing, John." Taylor mumbled between sobs.

John set Robert down and placed his fingers against Manuel's neck, checking for a pulse. He felt nothing.

"Why, John? Why, *God*?" Taylor looked up at the sky. "He just wanted me. He just wanted me!"

John's heart broke. He didn't know what to say. Robert walked over to his brother, got down on his knees, and as his eyes filled with tears, leaned over and kissed Manuel on his cheek.

"He's still alive Taylor. He's just gone home."

"I know, Robert. I know."

* * *

The masked man John had thrown against the tree was still lying motionless on the ground nearby. With the rope he had picked up, John hog-tied the man's wrists and ankles. The man was still breathing and would eventually wake up, but he wasn't going anywhere. When John finished, he picked Robert up and set him on his shoulders.

"Taylor, we need to find your parents and get help. Do you want to wait here?"

Taylor nodded his head.

"Alright. We'll be back soon."

"See ya soon, Taylor," Robert repeated as he and John jogged away.

* * *

John found the trail quickly, and within minutes they were met by a group of lights moving back and forth through the trees. Search teams had been sent out to comb the woods in every direction. Most of the town had been recruited for the job. The gunshots had brought them closer.

"Hey! Over here!" John and Robert yelled together.

Soon lights converged upon them and whistles and shouts filled the night air.

John handed Robert over to Paul and Maggie, who embraced him at the same time, squeezing him in between them with laughter and tears of joy.

"Taylor's okay, but Manuel's been shot and needs help right away. Taylor's with him." As John was speaking, a police officer grabbed him from behind and handcuffed his wrists. John didn't fight or argue. Paul yelled for the officer to let him go.

"Paul, it's okay," John said calmly. "Get help to Manuel. Straight down that trail. Less than a mile. Go now!"

Paul shouted for the medics to follow him and then took off down the trail with a group of medical workers and police officers running behind.

* * *

Maggie walked over to John, holding Robert in her arms. She gazed into John's eyes and for a moment said nothing. Tears began to spill down her cheeks.

"Forgive me," she whispered, wiping her tears and runny nose on her shirtsleeve.

"Of course, Maggie," John said, smiling.

She looked down at her youngest son and whispered, "Thank you."

John nodded and then the officer turned him and led him back towards town. Maggie and Robert continued down the trail in the direction her husband and the others had gone.

71 THE CLOSURE

Taylor held onto Manuel's motionless body, whispering into his friend's ears.

"I'm gonna miss you brother. You're my best friend. I'm so glad I came to Venezuela. I'm so glad I got to be your friend. I'll never forget you."

"Taylor." The voice was faint and soft. "Taylor."

Taylor quickly pushed himself upright and leaned his ear over Manuel's shoulder.

"Manuel? Are you alive?"

Manuel's eyes blinked open and his head lifted slightly. Taylor felt his friend's chest rising and falling.

"Taylor, tu eres mi hermano…my brother."

"Si. Siempre…forever." Taylor began to cry. "You're gonna be okay Manuel. You stay with me. Don't go."

"Shhhh Taylor, it's okay. Jesus says it's time I go home." A smile spread across Manuel's face. "He's waiting."

Taylor began to sob uncontrollably. He was overwhelmed with both joy and grief, and his heart felt like it was going to explode.

"But I don't want you to go…"

"Taylor…it's Jesus. I want Jesus."

Taylor suddenly realized his Venezuelan brother was being beckoned into heaven by Jesus Himself. For Manuel, there was no conflict about whether to stay or go.

"Tell mi familia I love them. Tell everyone — todos en Jajo, todas en mi country — that Jesus loves them. Tell mi padre I wait for him."

His head dropped to his chest and his eyes closed.

"I wait for you," he whispered with his final breath.

"I'll tell him, brother. I'll tell everyone." Taylor looked up at the sky, blinking away the tears. "He's all yours, Jesus."

* * *

Paul arrived first and found his son lying on the ground with Manuel in his arms. Both boys appeared to be sleeping peacefully. Within seconds the first medics arrived. They quickly checked Manuel's vitals then placed him on a stretcher and carried him off at a brisk pace without a word to Paul about his condition. Police officers likewise carried away the unconscious masked assailant. Paul lifted Taylor into his arms and walked slowly through the woods, singing his son's favorite song softly in his ears.

"As the deer panteth for the water so my soul longeth after Thee. You alone are my heart's desire and I long to worship Thee."

They met Maggie and Robert and walked back to Jajo together.

John was taken to the front of the plaza, and by the time he and the officers with him had arrived, there was a large crowd following behind. Those with radios had informed the other search parties that the boys had been found and were safe, so most had returned and were waiting. As soon as he was in sight, John was rushed upon by his mother and all the other children and families. The mayor quickly ordered for his handcuffs to be removed and once off, he hugged and caressed them all. The last search party returned and John's father was with them. He met his son with an embrace full fear, joy, and relief. They held each other tightly, crying and not saying a word.

Later, John and his parents went to the city jail where John explained everything to the mayor, Carlos, and the other officers who were there. His own thoughts and suspicions, as well as what he had learned from Bernadino, were more than enough to get the mayor's order, sending most of the entire police force in the direction of Logan's Gentlemen's Club.

Bernadino sat at the bar watching the beautiful girls dancing on the stage across the room. He had a beer in one hand, a cigarette in the other and a smile on his face. He was thinking about money and opening his own club with the best food, drinks, and women that his future fortune could buy. He saw his name in lights, "Bernadino's House of Style." He was overcome with delight and ordered a round of drinks for everyone.

They were never served.

* * *

The police entered Logan's club, shouting orders and throwing Rico to the floor, breaking his nose. It took four officers in all to restrain and cuff him. Bernadino screamed and ran for the door. He only required one.

There was so much screaming and crashing of furniture from patrons and dancers alike, no one heard the sound upstairs. Carlos ordered everyone to get on their knees and place their hands behind their heads. Officers continued to file in through the swinging doors. Carlos walked up the stairs and knocked on Mr. Logan's door. It creaked opened. Smoke floated around the room, twisting and twirling up into the air from a cigar that rested in an ashtray on a large mahogany desk. Below the smoke, in his large leather chair, Mr. Logan sat with a thin smile on his lips and his eyes closed. His head leaned to one side and was covered in blood. Carlos walked over and removed the revolver from Mr. Logan's lifeless hand. It was over. Logan's was closed.

"Still not even," Carlos said, then turned and left.

72 THE INVESTIGATION

The next few days passed by like a blur. John was considered innocent by almost everyone in the small police department, as well as the mayor's office. All of the known facts pointed clearly to a set-up, but since his accuser had disappeared, he couldn't officially be released from custody. The mayor ordered him to be kept under house arrest, which involved two officers keeping guard outside his apartment. His parents stayed in the adjoining guest apartment. John spent most of his time at the police station where he, Carlos, and the police chief pieced together everything that had taken place. The kidnapper John had thrown into the tree, a local thief and drunkard, suffered a concussion and was taken to the hospital, where he slowly recovered, but still seemed confused about a lot of things. It was unlikely he would be of much use before going away to prison. It was the second morning, when a babbling and disillusioned Ricardo came crawling out of the woods near the edge of town begging to be arrested and taken to the doctor, that the certainty of John's innocence came to light. The ex-security guard whom John had unknowingly shot in the leg had not only lost a lot of blood crawling through the jungle all night, but his senses as well.

* * *

The identity of the witch doctor remained a mystery. He would neither speak nor change expressions, but sat hours on end with his lips tight and eyes closed. Everyone had a theory. Some said he had been abandoned in the woods as a child and raised with the wolves. Others, that he had been kidnapped and raised in Europe where he learned to speak fluent English before finally escaping his captors and returning to Venezuela. Of course, he murdered them all before escaping. One of the police officers was from the Guarijo indigenous people, and he was certain their prisoner was, as well. He had spoken to the prisoner in the native Guarijo language and noticed a flicker of understanding. When Paul learned of the possible Guarijo connection, his heart sank, and he felt sick to his stomach. He could no longer pretend his hands were clean. Had this been a plot of revenge for the harm Paul's company and others like it were causing to Lake Maracaibo and the livelihood of the Guarijo people? If so, then Paul had put his own children's lives at risk. Even if it turned out to be just a theory, Paul knew his days in the oil industry were numbered.

* * *

One morning, Taylor and Robert surprised their parents by asking to visit their attacker in his cell. It took a lot of persuasion, but the two boys finally convinced even their mother that it was something they felt God wanted them to do and that it would be safe. Paul called and spoke to the Police Chief and he guaranteed their safety. That afternoon, after handcuffing the prisoner's legs and feet and strapping him into a bolted down chair, Paul walked his two sons into the man's cell escorted by three officers. Maggie waited outside with John and a handful of other officers. With their father right behind them, the boys approached the prisoner, stopping a few feet away. They knew the man could understand English. Robert spoke first.

"Sir? Mr. man?"

The witch doctor didn't move or open his eyes, but they all knew he was listening. Robert looked at his older brother, who nodded for him to continue.

"I...I just want to tell you sir that even though you've done bad things and hurt people, God still loves you and Jesus loves you and I forgive you. I really do." Robert looked up at his father with a mixed expression of relief and uncertainty. Paul put his hand on his youngest son's shoulder and squeezed. Taylor took a step forward.

"I don't really know why I had to come here today. You killed my friend, and for that I want to hate you. But even though I don't know why you kill, I know it comes from hate you have inside, and I don't want to be that way, to hate like you. God forgave me of all my sins, and He'll do the same for you. My friend would want you to know that. Manuel..." Tears began streaming down Taylor's cheeks "would forgive you..." Taylor rubbed his eyes and sniffed back his runny nose. "I forgive you, too. I don't want you to go to Hell." No matter how hard Taylor fought back the tears, they continued to pour. He could barely speak another word and after mumbling, "Jesus loves you", he turned and buried his face in his father's shirt. Paul slowly led both boys out of the room. After the door shut, the stillness in the room lingered until two eyes opened, blinking at the door. Inside that quiet room, a heart was pounding. A heart touched for the first time by unconditional love.

* * *

Rico wasn't talking either. Even after the severe beating he took at the hands of some of the officers, his lips remained shut. Carlos had asked John to join in the interrogation, but he declined the offer, fearing what might take place.

Bernadino, on the other hand, spilled his guts before they laid a finger on him. He hoped to cooperate and be released as soon as possible. He had learned of Mr. Logan's suicide and was more than willing to place all the blame on the deceased criminal. During one interrogation he even tried convincing an officer he had been an informant all along; the officer couldn't help but laugh out loud. Of course, Bernadino didn't say a word about John Parker's offer or their agreement. He still imagined his new American partner was free and preparing to reap their fortune. John decided not to spoil his fantasy. He knew the conniving little fellow would have plenty of time for contemplation in prison, and Rico would be there to help him sort it all out.

Ricardo awoke one night in the hospital, his faculties regained, covered in sweat and begging for forgiveness. No one quite knew what brought about his transformation, but the next morning he was submissive and forthcoming. His detailed confession, combined with Bernadino's information, provided the authorities with a clear picture of Frank Logan's and the Witch Doctor's scheme. Most important of all, Ricardo had overheard a conversation between Mr. Logan and Rico about Lenora's whereabouts, the girl who had visited John on that stormy night. The police located a hidden trap door behind Logan's bar counter that led to a secret basement where they found her tied up, gagged, and unconscious. It was days before John was able to meet with her in the clinic and, through tears, she pleaded for John's mercy and forgiveness. As everyone had assumed, she hadn't had a choice. Mr. Logan never offered choices. John cried with her and took her tiny hands in his own. She had nothing for him to forgive, he whispered. John asked Carlos, the police officer whose sister had disappeared long ago, to translate for him as he shared the love of Jesus with her, and she listened, amazed. Never before had she heard anything like it.

She longed to know more. John promised to visit her daily. Afterward, Carlos pulled John aside.

"I found this in Mr. Logan's pocket."

John looked down at the small booklet Carlos was handing him. He recognized it immediately.

"John. I have no peace in my life since my sister disappeared. My heart turned to stone that day, and I have been enslaved by bitterness and rage. I want freedom amigo. I want Jesus. I want to know where I will go when I die."

John looked down at the title printed on the front of the small tract and then up at Carlos with his mouth hanging open and astonishment all over his face.

"I read it." Carlos said, with a grin.

They prayed together right then and there, and all of Carlos' burdens were lifted from his weary frame. The new follower of Christ opened his eyes and with a smile on his face that no one had seen in years, he gave John a hearty embrace and slap on the back. They would meet many more times in the following days to pray and read the Bible together.

The final piece to the puzzle came a day later when Carlos located a batch of videotapes in a secret compartment in the floor of Frank Logan's office. In less than an hour, half the police force, the mayor, John, and Paul Stevens were all gathered in front of a large television in a conference room at the police station. Everyone sat transfixed as black and white images that had been captured on the American neighborhood security cameras began to play. Each tape provided a different area and angle of footage. First, at exactly 1:45 a.m., Rico was recorded approaching the front gate with Lenora at his side, the metal doors swung open, then closed again behind them. Another tape showed Ricardo meeting the two inside, speaking briefly with Rico then escorting Lenora away into the darkness in the direction of John's condo. Still another tape filmed Rico sitting in the guardhouse smoking a cigarette until Ricardo's return at 2:00 a.m. Rico waited around until 2:48 a.m. and then disappeared in the same direction Ricardo had taken Lenora. At 3:57 a.m. Rico returned, spoke briefly again with Ricardo, and then exited through the front gate. After a long stretch of nothing except Ricardo sitting nervously and checking his watch again and again, the tapes were fast-forwarded until a blur of activity began. At 7:30 a.m. Ricardo hit the button to open the gate, and a few seconds later, Rosarita's face appeared in the guardhouse window. She checked in, writing her name and time of arrival on a clipboard and then after a minute of small talk, went on her way. At 7:45, Ricardo hit the button again, and Fernando walked into the guardhouse, smiling, with two cups of coffee in his hands. Ricardo took a cup and the two security guards chatted casually as if nothing out of the ordinary was going on. John and Paul were sitting on the edge of their seats looking for any sign of guilty involvement on Fernando's part. Paul prayed silently that his long-time protector was a genuine friend. At 8:00 a.m. Mrs. Childress drove up to the gate with a shuttle-bus full of kids on their way to the museum tour in Trujillo. Fernando climbed aboard, and Ricardo waved goodbye as they drove away. Based on the footage, Paul felt sure Fernando had no clue what Ricardo was up to. At 8:27 a.m. with the morning sun well into the sky, Ricardo suddenly darted out of the guardhouse and returned seconds later with Lenora in his grasp. She kicked and screamed as Ricardo, his face full of wicked delight, slapped her across the jaw and threw her to the floor. He violently wrapped her wrists together with tape, blindfolded, and gagged her. Then something unexpected occurred. At 8:36 a.m. Ricardo quickly stood up and stared out the back window. He drew his gun and pointed it at Lenora's head and put his finger over his mouth for her to remain silent. Then he walked just outside the doorway as a black Suburban pulled up in front of him. The driver side tinted window lowered and Paul stuck his hand out to shake Ricardo's. They spoke for moment, at one point jokingly, as Lenora lay motionless at the bottom corner of the screen. Then Paul waved goodbye and drove out of sight. Ricardo came back into the guardhouse. His amiable smile immediately returned to the sadistic one he had worn moments earlier.

At this point, Paul leaned forward in his chair and rubbed his hands over his face. He couldn't believe he had actually been that close to Lenora as he had left that morning to make a run to town. He bristled at the thought of it. He also felt nauseous.

John placed his hand on Paul's back. Paul looked over at John.

"She was right there," he whispered hoarsely through clenched teeth.

"You couldn't have known, Paul. There's no way."

Without another word, both of them focused their attention back on the television.

Ricardo took out a cell-phone and dialed a number. He spoke only a few words then jerked Lenora to her feet. Within a minute, at 8:45 a.m., Ricardo hit the button again, Rico entered the guardhouse, flung Lenora over his shoulder, handed Ricardo a thick envelope, and walked out. The questions surrounding Lenora's disappearance were finally answered. Afterwards, Ricardo took a seat in front of the wall of monitors. At exactly 8:48 a.m. all footage suddenly turned to snow, and then black. All except one tape. The camera mounted inside the guardhouse continued to record Ricardo sitting in his chair as he began to remove the other tapes and stack them inside a box – for some reason he forgot or purposely allowed the camera to continue recording. No one in the room could figure out why or why he had even recorded everything in the first place. It seemed he could've played it much safer by claiming equipment malfunction or even sabotage. Why run the risk of the tapes being found? Someone proposed he may have had blackmail plans in mind, but as the tape continued to play, it seemed more an ignorant accident than a plan. John and Paul wondered if it wasn't an act of Divine intervention. Eventually, the police arrived on the scene and then later the two officers left with John in custody. Someone commented that Ricardo never even phoned the police. Paul remembered Maggie saying she hadn't called them. Something more was going on. Everyone in the room began discussing all they had just witnessed. No one was paying much attention to the television screen when a lone police officer suddenly appeared in the guardhouse doorway, smiling and shaking hands with Ricardo. Immediately Ricardo walked back over to the wall of monitors and recorders, picked up the sack of videotapes, then stopped. He looked up at the guardhouse monitor with an expression of both shock and frustration on his face. His hand moved forward and the final screen went black as well. The meeting room grew suddenly quiet. It had been a blunder and a costly one for the officer who had appeared in the final seconds. He was the older officer who had remained behind to talk with the parents and gather evidence – evidence such as the bag of marijuana he had paraded before all the parents. The marijuana had been delivered and registered at the station, but the videotapes never made it. Shuffling was heard in the room as a figure made a mad dash for the door. He didn't have a chance. A dozen officers, the first of whom was Carlos, pounced on him, pinning him to the floor. Whatever opportunity he would have had to explain the reason for the tapes getting into Mr. Logan's hands was now blown. He was quickly thrown in jail along with the others. The mayor, determined to sniff out any other corruption in his police force, called for a massive internal investigation.

73 THE GATHERING

Maggie and Taylor spent hours at the Garcia's house with Manuel's mother and grandmother. His father couldn't be found. Many local friends also stopped by to express their condolences. There was a heaviness over the whole town. The plaza and park sat empty and silent. Even the mountains were solemn. The usual calls and sounds of wildlife seemed distant and faint. The American neighborhood was also quiet and still. All of the families remained inside their homes together. The fathers cancelled all appointments and itinerary for the week. Wednesday night, all the families gathered in the Rec.

Although tired and weak, John stood at the front of the room, ready to take up the task of leadership once more. He smiled at his mom and dad who sat in the back holding each other's hands. He looked at the others. They had all apologized and asked his forgiveness continuously throughout the week, and he had quickly granted it, assuring them it was all over and not to worry another minute.

* * *

Surprisingly, Regina Rollins had even invited him over to eat dinner with her and her children. She opened the door that evening, and for the first time John believed he was actually seeing her for who she truly was. Her make-up was light and her hair fell softly and naturally over her shoulders. Her voice was full of warmth as she welcomed him. John prepared his famous spaghetti with the kids' help. Brad remained standoffish at first, but in time began cracking jokes and laughing along with his sister and mother. After dinner they all sat in the living room and began a discussion that lasted for hours. Near the end, John apologized for not telling Regina about what happened with Brad that night in the Rec, but she assured him she wouldn't have believed or accepted it anyway. God had been doing a lot of work on her heart, she explained, and she had finally given Him charge of her emotions. The insecurity and rejection she had suffered for so long was gone, replaced by peace. For the first time in a long time, she was happy, and one could see it on her face. Her children were equally thrilled to see their mother in such spirits. Most of all, she was forever grateful for what John had done in the lives of her children. John received her gratitude with a lump in his throat, and when her son followed with his own apology, John had to fight back tears. He held his hand out to the young boy, and Brad shook it firmly. Stephanie displayed her famous grin.

* * *

Standing before everyone, John could see on their faces they still felt ashamed for their behavior and judgement. He expected that if given the chance, they would apologize again long into the night. He would not give them the opportunity.

"We gather together tonight a very changed group. I praise God for every face I see in this room." John's voice cracked as he finished the sentence. He silently thanked God again for keeping the kids safe. There were sniffles all over the room, and mothers dabbed their eyes with tissue.

"But we also meet together missing someone who is very special to us. Mrs. Garcia has accepted our offer to cover all the funeral expenses, but also asked that we be in charge of planning the service. Maggie and Paul are going to share some ideas."

John walked to the back and sat down with his folks as Maggie, Paul, and Taylor walked to the front. Maggie spoke first.

"I want to thank everyone for offering to help Mrs. Garcia during this time. She's a strong woman and the Lord is comforting both her and her mother right now. Please pray for God's peace to surround them. Also, pray for Mr. Garcia who hasn't been seen since the night of the shooting. Mrs. Garcia told me that during their final meal with Manuel, her husband changed. He asked her forgiveness and cried for the terrible things he had done. He wanted to know about her Jesus, but soon neighbors came screaming about the shooting and a terrified look came over his face and he said his son's name, then left. That was the last anyone saw or heard from him. Pray for his safety. She's already lost her son. Losing her husband would be...well, I can't even imagine it. Pray for Mr. Garcia's safety and salvation. Mrs. Garcia said he's very close to becoming a Christian."

Everyone nodded their heads, already silently lifting the requests to the Lord.

"Before Paul talks about the arrangements, Taylor has something to share."

Taylor stepped forward.

"I think all of you have heard about the last conversation Manuel and I had together in the woods. He was at peace when he died because he saw Jesus and heard Jesus calling him home. I didn't want him to go, and I still don't know why God allowed him to die. I don't understand it at all, but his death hasn't weakened my faith. Being with him and holding him as Jesus called him home, has only strengthened it."

More tissues were out, in the men's hands as well.

"Manuel asked me to tell his father he would be waiting for him. We've got to find Mr. Garcia and let him know he can see his son again!"

Taylor took a seat with his mother and brother as his father proceeded to share the funeral arrangements he had thought of, as well as ask for suggestions from the group. They discussed and planned long into the night. Afterwards they prayed even longer.

74 THE ENTOURAGE

Saturday arrived with many unwanted companions. The early morning skies were dark and ominous. Rain fell sporadically. It even seemed the colder winds of autumn had decided to make an unofficial early visit. Hardest of all, the afternoon would bring closure to the life and death of a child. In a matter of hours, a town would say goodbye to one of its own, a farewell that had come far too soon.

As Maggie stood on the back porch looking off into the woods, she felt as gray as her surroundings. The birds were still silent. Her every thought was for Manuel's mother. It seemed so unfair that one mother could suffer while another rejoice. Even though fighting it back, the thought of what could have happened to her boys came rushing over her again, and she fell to her knees sobbing and feeling sick.

* * *

John sat outside in a lawn chair sipping coffee and gazing out over the sloping hill behind his condo. He also noticed the absence of life and color in the normally fluorescent and breathing landscape. After finishing his coffee, he prayed out loud for almost an hour. There was anticipation in his voice as it streamed out into the trees. Manuel's death would not be in vain. John knew God's Spirit was ready to pour down on the people of Jajo if they were willing to receive Him. The funeral plans were set, the day was upon them. Now, John prayed for God's will to be done.

* * *

The mothers and children walked with umbrellas in hand and climbed into the waiting vehicles the men had parked in front of each house. They descended the mountainside slowly. When they arrived at the plaza, Mayor Velasquez and his family, along with other police officers and townspeople, greeted them. They were also greeted with hundreds, perhaps thousands, of flowers and bouquets that had been, and were still being, placed in arrangement all over the plaza. Men and women, boys and girls, arrived constantly with flowers in hand, setting them in place, creating a garden in the heart of the town. The colors began to bring life back to Jajo. The American families walked through the plaza greeting others and inspecting the floral assortments. They themselves had ordered many of the flowers, which had arrived special delivery from Merida the night before and had been set in place by the mothers and daughters. Now seeing them for the first time in daylight, the women and girls beamed with pride and joy.

* * *

A caravan of dark luxury vehicles descended from the Via Niquitao, the main road leading into and out of Jajo, which connects the mountain town to the highway and the rest of northern Venezuela. The vehicles drove slowly into town and rolled to a stop at the plaza entrance. Before anyone had stepped out of the vehicles Mayor Velasquez had already walked over and extended his hand. A group of men in dark suits and a few women in similar color soon formed a circle around the mayor and took turns introducing themselves and shaking hands. The mayor led the group over to where the American families were standing and introduced them.

"Paul, this is Governor Rodriguez of Barquisimeto who has come with his wife, to express his condolences to the Garcia family."

Paul stepped forward and shook the Governor's hand firmly.

"It's a pleasure to meet you, Governor."

"Likewise," the Governor answered nodding his head, "this is my wife, Esperanza." A tall, attractive woman stepped forward, smiling, and shook Paul's hand.

"Mrs. Rodriguez, it's a pleasure."

"Thank you," she answered kindly.

"And this is my wife Maggie and my sons Taylor and Robert." As Paul spoke, his family stepped forward and shook hands with both the Governor and his wife. Robert put on his best smile and delighted them both with his acquaintance. The other families followed suit, and minutes passed before everyone had been formally introduced. The other women and men in the group were politicians and businessmen from Merida, Valera, Barquisimeto, and even the capital city, Caracas, who had heard of what happened to the young boy in Jajo and desired to express their support to the Garcia family. A few in the group were born again believers who knew about the outreaches that the American children had put on. They knew that the Lord was moving in their country and this knowledge excited them.

The last man to step forward was a tall, broad shouldered elderly man who looked to be in his early seventies, with silver thick hair, and bronze wrinkled skin. As he moved to the middle of the group everyone stopped their conversations and gave him their full attention, his presence seemed to silently demand it.

"This," Governor Rodriguez said, lifting his hand in the gentleman's direction, "is Paulo Ruiz."

Most of the Americans immediately recognized the name and face and were speechless. Paulo Ruiz was the Billy Graham of South America, a man who had traveled the globe holding crusades and revivals in every country and language. He was a theologian and scholar, respected by even the most passionate of secularists. With a powerful voice and commanding presence, few dared to challenge him or the message he shared, one that had changed little during the forty five years he had been sharing it. A message of God's love for a lost world. The most amazing, or frustrating to his critics, characteristic of Paulo Ruiz was the humble and simple way he lived while constantly surrounded by fame and popularity. While so many other big name evangelists with big name ministries allowed themselves to be smeared and tarnished by indiscretion, Ruiz had remained true to his calling and true to the One who called him. He often referred to himself as "a regular Joe" and always spoke to people on their level, never looking down on them. This caused all who listened, to trust and respect him.

Mr. Childress remembered listening to him once or twice on the radio. The Littleton's had watched one of his crusades on television years before. Paul and Maggie had actually attended one of his crusades in St. Louis, Missouri, while they were university students. John and his parents had also watched him speak on television before, and John remembered his professors refer to Paulo Ruiz as "a great man of God."

The American youth were not familiar with him, but could tell from the reaction of their parents, that they were standing in the presence of someone very important.

"Where is the young missionary from the States?" the stately gentleman asked, looking over the group.

John stepped forward feeling very unworthy of the title.

"Young man, I've looked forward to meeting you." As he spoke, the evangelist held his hand out to John and smiled.

John felt his face flush and grow warm.

"It's an honor, Dr. Ruiz." John replied nervously, shaking his hand.

"And your name is?"

"John Parker."

"John Parker, how about we go for a walk."

John looked back at his parents for some sort of assistance, but all he got were smiles and a wink. The mayor nodded his head, and John realized he looked foolish stalling the way he was. He quickly agreed to Dr. Ruiz's request and the two walked slowly away with the evangelist's large hand resting on John's shoulder.

75 THE FUNERAL

For the next half hour, John and the evangelist were nowhere to be seen. All the others finished preparing the stage and getting everything set up.

Mrs. Garcia and her mother arrived and received the condolences and warmth of the visiting guests with many tears as well as smiles. They were completely overwhelmed with all the flowers and beauty that covered the plaza. After walking around and touching and smelling the flowers, Mrs. Garcia sat down in a corner and cried while holding her mother tightly. Maggie joined them and soon the three ladies were praying for the funeral service. Fifteen minutes before two o'clock, a rich dark mahogany casket was carried through the plaza and set in front of the stage. The top portion of the lid was opened. Mrs. Garcia and her mother peered down onto Manuel's small lifeless frame as she straightened his shirt collar and gently brushed the hair out of his eyes. He appeared to be in a peaceful sleep. Mrs. Garcia smiled and whispered to her baby boy. She had wanted an open casket ceremony, giving everyone an opportunity to gaze upon her precious lovely child and say goodbye. As the plaza clock struck two o'clock, the two women joined the mayor and visiting guests on the stage. Looking up at the crowd, they were surprised to see how many people had arrived in just the last fifteen minutes. Already the plaza was as full as it had ever been during any previous outreach. Mrs. Garcia smiled and even waved at all the faces she recognized and knew well. Tissues were already constantly being dabbed onto tear-streaked faces. Still, John and Dr. Ruiz had not returned. It was time to begin. The mayor walked to the podium that had been set up and also covered in flowers. He smiled at the enormous crowd and spoke into microphone.

"Dear people of Jajo. It touches my heart to see so many of you here with us today. Your presence shows that we are a city that cares for and loves one another. A town that laughs when one laughs, and cries when one cries. But this love it is not the result of our own doing. It is not something we could produce on our own. It is because the love of God has swept over our town and changed us. Because Jesus Christ has come into so many of our hearts and given us new life, and this is why we are united. Let's pray to God and thank him for giving us his Son, for changing us, and for uniting us." The mayor bowed his head and all others followed.

As the mayor prayed and all eyes were closed, John and Dr. Ruiz silently appeared at one side of stage. John assisted the evangelist up the steps and to his seat and then quickly descended and joined the American families who were all sitting together on the front row facing the stage. As John sat, he noticed many others still arriving and adding to those in the plaza. After the crowd echoed "Amen", the mayor took his seat. Tommy, Susan, and Angela walked up the steps to the front of the stage. Tommy and Angela strapped their guitars over their shoulders and the three took their places behind three microphones that had been quickly placed before them. Tommy began to pick his strings, and the entire plaza was flooded with the beautiful soft sound. Angela quickly joined him with her own unique strumming and the people in the crowd began to move and sway in their places. Next Susan's voice was added to the melodic mix. The guitars grew softer so everyone could hear the Spanish words she sang, words that belonged to Manuel's favorite song:

"You are my strength when I am weak
You are the treasure that I seek
You are my All in All
When I fall down You pick me up
When I am dry You fill my cup
You are my All in All
Jesus, Lamb of God
Worthy is Your Name"

By the second verse everyone was singing out with her. With eyes closed and faces and hands lifted upwards, the words rose into the sky in one powerful voice. By the end of the song, all those on the stage were standing. Tommy and Angela didn't stop, but immediately began the chords to the next song, playing louder, with Susan singing stronger than ever before. Everyone began to clap and sway, some even danced in place.

"You came from heaven to earth, to show the way
From the earth to the cross, my debt to pay
From the cross to the grave
From the grave to the sky
Lord I lift Your Name on High"

There were cheers and prayers spoken out all over the plaza and stage. Hands were outstretched to heaven and fists clinched in victory. Every worshipping heart was bursting from joy in the knowledge that at that very moment Manuel was in the presence of his Savior. When the song ended, shouts and cheers rose up to the sky. Those on the stage smiled and hugged one another while some continued to pray and sing with their eyes closed, completely overcome by the presence of God.

The mayor walked back to the podium as the three musicians headed back to their seats. As he leaned towards the microphone, an amazing thing happened. Suddenly, the top of his head seemed to light up with fire. The startled crowd watched and whispered in amazement as the shimmering flames slowly moved down his face, crawled over his shoulders, chest, and finally enveloped his entire figure in a golden glow. The mayor cupped his hands over his eyes and lifted his face up to the sky. In one movement the crowd did the same. Above the town of Jajo a small thin ray of sunlight had penetrated through the mass of gray cover and lit upon the lone figure standing at the microphone. Everyone seemed to hold their breath as they watched the clouds begin to slowly give way and break apart. More and more rays began to filter through, illuminating the stage and then the entire plaza, forcing the darkness over the land to flee. Suddenly, the long-hidden sun now appeared in all its blinding splendor. Bright energy poured forth. Immediately everything changed.

The flowers that before had sat dull and colorless throughout the plaza were now set aflame in fluorescent pink, yellow, blue, white, red, orange, and purple. Even the leaves and stems became painted in fresher, deeper green. People turned and looked around in all directions. Some of those closest to the flowers backed away in surprise at the sudden intensity of color. The cold, damp air was also pushed away, replaced by a warm fresh breeze that blew across everyone's face leaving smiles in its trail. Many closed their eyes and inhaled deeply. The blue sky seemed brighter than Jajo had ever seen it before and the plush green carpet of jungle that surrounded them breathed with life and growth. Maggie heard the sounds she had missed for so long. Birds were calling and insects picked up their noisy chatter. A flock of geese moved across the sky in perfect triangular form.

"Praise God for moving in Jajo!" the mayor shouted to the crowd, who responded with more shouts and cheers. "Because He came, the spirit of this small boy whose temporal body lays here before us all, is now, as I speak, in the very presence of the greatest love he could ever know. He is more safe and blessed than we could ever imagine. Thank God for taking something as tragic as death and turning it into something as beautiful as eternal life with Him! We cry out in our loss of one so special, but we rejoice in heaven's gain!"

More cheers.

"Today, as we say goodbye to Manuel Garcia, let us not forget that we will again one day say 'Hello'. If you have Jesus Christ in your heart you *will* one day see Manuel again."

More shouts and clapping.

"A great man has come here today with many other special people. People who have heard about what God's been doing in Jajo. People who love the Lord and desire for Him to move the same way in their own towns and cities as well as our entire country."

There was clapping and a few "amens" expressed from those behind him.

"They have come to join us in saying goodbye to this special and brave child of God. Please join me in welcoming Dr. Paulo Ruiz!"

76 THE CELEBRATION

Cheers and applause erupted from the crowd. To many, especially the long-time believers, Paulo Ruiz was a national hero and star. The humble man stood and walked passed the mayor, thanking him for the introduction, then took his place behind the podium. He gripped both edges with his hands and looked out over the crowd. The plaza was overflowing, with many people sitting on the outer wall and even standing in the surrounding streets. Dr. Ruiz squinted his eyes and made out the shapes of many sitting and standing on cars and rooftops. And yet still more and more were arriving. He spoke slowly in his native tongue, his voice deep and resonant,

"When the perishable has been clothed with the imperishable, and the mortal with immortality, then the saying that is written will come true: 'Death has been swallowed up in victory. Where, O death, is your victory? Where, O death, is your sting?'"

Everyone was quiet and still.

John sat with his head bowed and his eyes closed. As Paulo Ruiz preached, John prayed. He knew God was orchestrating something powerful. The Americans had spent hours preparing for the service over the past few days. Originally, the plan was for John to share a message with Taylor translating beside him. Then Paulo Ruiz had arrived. The evangelist's coming had been an unexpected, but pleasant surprise to the Americans. His coming meant God had plans of His own.

As John listened to Ruiz's voice booming from the plaza speakers, the conversation they had shared alone only moments before replayed in his mind.

* * *

"John, the reason I asked you to come on this walk with me is because God told me to come here to Jajo to share something with you."

John felt a lump in his throat.

"Mayor Velasquez told me on the phone about everything that's been happening here since you arrived. I listened to the stories of basketball games and outreaches and people coming the know Jesus Christ because of the way you and the American children have loved them with God's love."

As John listened, it seemed as if Dr. Ruiz was speaking of another place, another time, and most of all – another John. He'd made too many mistakes along the way.

"But son, as I hung up the phone the Lord told me that you weren't acknowledging your role in everything."

The two men were walking slowly when Ruiz's last words stopped John in his tracks. John looked at him, then up at the sky, then back at the smiling evangelist.

"God put it on my heart to share this with you: that He is glorified when you honor Him for what He accomplishes. Accomplishes through others, but also what He accomplishes through you. When you fail to see His works in your life, especially through some false sense of self-humility, you are robbing God of His due worship and robbing yourself of needed fellowship with Him. Son, I know you've had struggles."

John had a feeling he probably knew every sinful detail.

"Know that God's grace is sufficient in your weakness."

John stared down at the ground.

"John?"

Slowly John lifted his face and met Ruiz's eyes.

"Know that."

John was overcome with repentance. Tears began to run down his cheeks. Dr. Ruiz's hand rested on John's shoulder and gave him an encouraging squeeze.

"Let's take a seat."

The two men sat down on a nearby park bench.

"I'd like to pray with you, John, if that's okay?"

"I'd love to."

Paulo Ruiz closed his eyes and began to pray. He asked for God's direction and authority over the life of John Parker, and John, in turn, asked for God's protection and continued blessings on Dr. Ruiz's ministry. When they finished and stood to their feet, John realized that in a matter of minutes he had bonded with a complete stranger in a way he had never experienced with anyone before. He began to feel embarrassed for having cried like a little child, but as soon as Ruiz's strong hand rested once again on his shoulder, all insecurity vanished, and they walked back together, both encouraged and grateful.

It was only seconds before reaching the stage that John had asked Dr. Ruiz if he would please share a message with the crowd. John knew God had brought the man to Jajo for the people as much as for himself. The evangelist agreed to John's request. After sitting down, John informed the Americans of the change in the service. No one complained.

* * *

"In the gospel of Mark, chapter 10, Jesus said, 'Let the children come to me. Don't stop them! For the kingdom of God belongs to such as these.'" Ruiz paused, scanning the crowd with a penetrating gaze. "Isn't that an amazing statement? According to Jesus, children have an advantage over us adults when it comes to spiritual matters. Because of their humility, simple faith, and uncomplicated trust in God, they have special access to His kingdom power. How foolish we are to think God has more important things to do than call our children to His side. Nothing could be further from the truth." Ruiz smiled down at the American kids on the front row. "Thank you, young people for showing us what true faith looks like."

The American children smiled at Ruiz, then at one another and their parents. Taylor felt goose bumps on his arms.

"'The kingdom of God belongs to such as these'. What did Jesus mean by this phrase? In one sense, Jesus is pointing out that God's kingdom belongs to the nobodies, to those who do not approach His kingdom on the merits of their own status. And in another sense Jesus is saying that children have an important role to play in God's kingdom work here on earth. Children can serve and testify and love and teach and preach in their own unique, simple, and powerful ways right now! And from what I've been told and what I'm seeing for myself today, God has been using children to show the people of Jajo His power and His truth. You have all been witnesses to the power of uncompromising child-like faith!"

Many in the crowd clapped and shouted "amen" in agreement.

"Today we celebrate the life of a young boy whose final request was for his father and all the people of his town and country to put their trust and faith in Jesus Christ. People of Jajo, learn from the life of Manuel. Learn what matters most. Even in his death, he was thinking of your eternal salvation! Just as Jesus, as he died on the cross, was thinking of and providing for your eternal salvation! If anyone here does not know the Lord Jesus Christ as their Lord and Savior, let him or her come to him now. His peace will never leave you, and his love will lift you one day - just as it lifted the soul of this young child before us - up to the heavens and into the very presence of God. Now is the time for salvation! Now is the moment God has provided!" With every sentence, Dr. Ruiz's voice grew stronger and louder. "Come to Him! Lift your hands into the air and call on the name of Jesus Christ!"

Arms raised and hands shot up into the air all over the plaza. There were so many hands going up that many had to twist and squirm before finding enough room to raise one. Some who were still approaching from far away but able to hear what was being said, began running towards the plaza with their arms in the air. It was a sight that caused every American, from the oldest to the youngest, to bow their heads and begin praying. Even though the majority of them couldn't understand Ruiz's words, they understood the significance of what was happening.

Dr. Ruiz continued. "You are responding to God's Spirit. If there are any others, please, now is the time."

Ruiz waited. There seemed to be some movement in the back of the square.

"Listen carefully to the words I'm about to pray to God and if you agree in your heart and mind and soul, then repeat them after me as your own."

There was an area in the middle of the square where people seemed to be stepping to one side or the other.

"Father God, I stand before you now…"

Many arms near the front of the plaza were dropping out of sight. Paulo Ruiz stopped. It was quiet, except for the faint sound of whispering and feet shuffling on sandy pavement. Most of the Americans had opened their eyes and were staring in the direction of the commotion. Suddenly it became obvious that someone was making their way to the stage, a realization which sent panic into the hearts of the kids. For them, the sight was all too familiar and the tragedy which followed, still too recent and painful. John saw the fear on the children's faces and stood to his feet. As he did so, Mrs. Garcia also stood with her hands crossed over her chest. Those nearest to the stage finally parted, turning and backing away from a man who slowly walked through the opened path.

He wore nothing but a dirty T-shirt and jogging pants. His black hair was all disheveled and his face unshaven. Also noticeable were scratches and cuts on his arms and bare feet. He walked slowly up to the casket and stared dejectedly inside. He sank to his knees, weeping and shaking uncontrollably. Mrs. Garcia ran to the front of the stage and down the steps crying out her husband's name. She fell onto her knees, wrapping her arms around him, and they both cried together, whispering each other's names and the name of their son. Mrs. Garcia's mother had begun to follow after her daughter, but then stopped after realizing her son-in-law had come back. Maggie quickly walked onto the stage and over to the elderly woman and held her in her arms. They both cried and smiled. In the crowd and on the stage people began praying once again. Many arms were still in the air. Paulo Ruiz waited patiently, smiling down at the couple and praying to God. He, too, was moved to tears. Mr. Garcia stood back to his feet, taking his wife's arms and lifting her up as well. Then they stared into each other's eyes whispering words they alone needed to hear. Next, he took her into his arms and pulled her close against himself, holding her tight – something it seemed he had been waiting an eternity for. After a moment, they slowly separated and turned once again to the casket, reached down and placed their hands onto their son's heart. From their front row seats, the Americans heard Mr. Garcia's words and though few understood them, everyone knew he was saying goodbye.

"Thank you Manuel. My brave son. I love you. I miss you, but I will see you again."

Taylor, who had been crying softly ever since everyone's hands went up, now really lost it and sat back down in his chair burying his face in his hands. Seeing the love of God at work in his best friend's family was more than his heart could handle. Mr. Stevens squeezed his son's shoulder and Robert placed his own small hand on his brother's back.

Mr. and Mrs. Garcia leaned over and kissed their son on his face, then, taking hold of each other's hands, stood up straight and gazed at Dr. Ruiz behind the podium. Mr. Garcia closed his eyes and raised his free hand into the air. All eyes closed again. The evangelist's booming voice once again flooded over the plaza and surrounding area.

"Father God, I believe in You."

As one voice, hundreds echoed.

"I know I have sinned against you and I am sorry. I know that sin leads to death...but thanks be to Jesus for dying on the cross in my place. He purchased my forgiveness and my freedom. I believe He rose again and is alive today. I give my life to Him. I put my trust and faith in Him. Come into my heart now and fill me with Your Spirit. Fill me with Your love and change me. Use my life for Your glory, both now and forever!"

When Paulo Ruiz said "Amen" there were shouts, cheers, whistles, and claps of celebration never heard before in the town of Jajo or perhaps the world. Strangers took hold of one another, laughing and crying. Families formed circles of prayer. Friends and enemies shook hands and praised God together. Dr. Ruiz asked the music team to lead everyone in another song, which they did gladly. John was handed some small conga drums and played into the microphone providing everyone a rhythm to sing and dance along with. It was a celebration.

They played, danced and sang long into the afternoon. Afterwards, Paulo Ruiz spent almost half an hour talking to the crowd, challenging them to grow and stay committed to the things of God. He warned them against returning once again to old habits and thoughts and promised them if they would be faithful to read and study God's word and pray, that the change would be permanent and growth would come.

77 THE FAMILIAR FACE

As evening fell on Jajo, those who knew the Garcia family and even many who did not, formed an endless line to pay their respects to the family and their son.

* * *

John looked out over the crowd. It was an ocean of believers, a mighty sea of faith. As the stream of people continued passing Manuel's casket and saying goodbye, one figure in the distance caught John's attention and held it. It was a man standing inches above those around him with broad shoulders and long arms. A man with a kind face that suddenly met John's gaze and smiled.

"Hector." John whispered and jumped off the side of the stage, running through the people, zig-zagging in between them. He came to the place where he thought he had seen the tall man standing, only to find a group of elderly people smiling up at him and saying "God bless you," in Spanish. He smiled and echoed the words back to them, then cupped his hand over his eyes and scanned the entire area. He was gone. Gone again. Maybe it hadn't even been him, John thought. Suddenly a hand tugged gently on John's shirt. He looked down into the eyes of a Venezuelan woman whose snow white hair dangled in front of an old and weathered face. She smiled and lifted her other hand. Below her long crooked fingers a whistle hung dangling on a tiny rope. John took it from her and slowly looped it over his head and around his neck.

"Hay un angel aqui," she whispered.

John understood enough to know she'd seen an angel.

Maybe he had as well.

* * *

It would be long after dark before the plaza was empty and silent. Plaza Bolivar would never again be the same. It would always be considered holy ground, a place where God visits His people. More outreaches would follow, along with prayer vigils and music celebrations. The annual basketball tournament would become a reality, allowing boys and girls of all ages to participate. Paulo Ruiz would return again to hold a crusade and hundreds would be healed of diseases and disabilities and thousands more would give their lives to Jesus Christ. Plaza Bolivar would never be the same again because the people of Jajo were never the same again.

78 THE NEXT ADVENTURE

John walked up the boarding ramp towards the door of the airplane, waving to the American families who stood behind a far-off fence waving back. At the top of the stairs he stopped to have one last look at them all.

* * *

He was going home. Seven weeks had passed since the funeral, and his six months were officially over. The parents had begged him to return earlier with his mother and father, who, after spending a few days relaxing and taking in the sights and sounds of northern Venezuela, finally returned to Tennessee. But John insisted they allow him stay and finish out his full six months. His parents understood his decision, were even proud of him for it. After seeing his parents off, John spent days on end visiting and saying goodbye to all those in the town and surrounding area. He visited the shops and stores, the parks and school, even the police station, where he now knew every officer by name. He ate lunch with the mayor and his wife and prayed with them for the spiritual growth of their town, state and country. He attended Jajo's first official church service that was held in the simply renovated building formerly known as "Logan's Gentlemen's Club." A banner stretched across the front that read in both Spanish and English "Jajo's House of Worship." John wondered what Mr. Logan would think of his place now. In his heart, John would always regret not doing more to get through to the broken and lost man. During the service, John shared one last message with the congregation. His challenge was simple: keep sharing the good news, keep making disciples, and God will keep moving and changing lives. His short message was followed by one final drum solo. He received a standing ovation afterwards with shouts of "¡Otra vez (again)!" The praise team rushed the stage, picked up their instruments and launched into one final medley of praise songs with John leading the way.

Later during the service, Mr. Garcia was publicly ordained by the packed house as their official pastor. Only days before, he had been invited by Paulo Ruiz to join him in Caracas for an evangelistic crusade. It was there that he began to discover the power of the Holy Spirit in his life, a gift for preaching, and a great mentor and friend in Paulo Ruiz. Pastor Garcia's first challenge that afternoon was for the Christians to pray for the salvation of the man who had murdered his son. He would be going to visit the criminal condemned to die, to share with him how he might have eternal life. Pastor Garcia's love and compassion would soon be his congregation's as well.

In the months and years to come, Jajo's House of Worship would become less of a traditional church building where people gather to hear a pastor teach the word of God and more of a missions campaign headquarters where people were trained and equipped to carry and share the word of God to the lost in neighboring towns, cities, states and even countries throughout South America and beyond. The Jajo Revival was on the move and with it, a disciple-making movement that would one day span the globe.

* * *

John's final days and nights were committed to the families who had brought him over and changed his life. Eating and sharing, playing outside and roaming the trails, singing and praying together for the last few times, they did it all and treasured every second.

The night before his departure, John and the youth had a "lock in" in the Rec, but didn't officially lock themselves in until they had spent most of the night running around outside playing capture the flag and lying in the grass looking up at the stars. Once inside, they reminisced on all that had happened since his arrival. Laughter often mixed with tears as they relived every adventure, every trial, and every miracle. One after the other, they all dozed off, content and full of gratitude. John, however, never slept that night, but prayed over each one of the youth until the sun appeared. The next day all the families piled into the Swan for the trip to the Merida airport. As the large shuttle bus made its way through the street of Jajo, John stuck his arms and head out the window to wave and yell goodbye. Many in the town, especially the children and teenagers, followed, chased, and cheered him on his way. He would be back. The American families demanded it, and he promised it.

* * *

After hugging each and every adult and child, Paul Stevens walked John to the security checkpoint.

"When you come back to visit, our situation might be a little different."

"Why's that?"

"You remember that night we flew over Lake Maracaibo together?"

"Of course."

"Well, what you *didn't* say that night really got to me."

John smiled perplexingly. "What I didn't say?"

"That's right. What you didn't say. I heard you *not* say, 'how can you live this way?!' So I've decided not to live that way anymore. Maggie and I are ready to finally answer God's call to do missions full-time. So pray for us as we seek His leading and direction. I'm about to really start learning some Español!"

John felt a kindred connection with Paul like never before.

"So our house might be a little smaller, we might be on a moped and you might be sleeping on a futon, but you're welcome any time!"

"Be sure to read that moped manual!"

They shared a hearty laugh and then John extended his hand and Paul gripped it firmly. "His will. His way. His glory, brother."

"His will. His way. His glory."

One final nod of agreement between them and then John entered the security checkpoint line as Paul walked back over and joined all the others waving goodbye.

* * *

"I love you!" He shouted before disappearing into the terminal.

"We love you too, John!" They shouted back in unison.

* * *

John took his seat on the plane. A middle-aged woman sat next to the window already lost in the pages of her magazine. She didn't look up.

Should be quieter than the last flight, John thought to himself and smiled. Still, he had to at least say hello.

"Excuse me?" he said, causing the woman to turn her face in his direction. He noticed the magazine was some kind of Science Journal. She continued holding it open in front of her as if saying this had better not take long. She leaned her face down and peered over the top of her reading glasses.

"Sorry to bother you ma'am, but if I don't get the acquaintances out of the way at the beginning, it's always harder to do later; My name's John Parker." John smiled and extended his hand as the woman lowered her magazine with one hand while removing her glasses with the other. A thin smile appeared.

"I'm Ruth Blair."

They shook hands slowly. Ruth Blair momentarily forgot about her magazine. She was amused at this young man who had so quickly removed the barriers that strangers often hold up between them.

"It's nice to meet you, Ruth Blair."

"It's nice to meet you as well, John." She felt herself wanting to continue the conversation. "So what have you been doing in Venezuela?"

"I'm a missionary," he answered simply, wondering how much she would really like to know. "And you?" he asked back, sincerely curious.

She paused for a moment, thinking how effective he must be at his craft, then finally answered,

"I'm here with a team of archeologists and paleontologists working together on a site in the Andes Mountains."

"Really!" John replied, with images of Indiana Jones flashing through his mind. He was amazed. Perceiving the obvious intelligence his new friend possessed, he asked the only question that came to mind. "So Ruth, do you believe in God?"

"I'm an atheist actually," she answered, with a look of bemusement.

"Really!" John responded, thinking to himself, *Here we go again Lord!*

ABOUT THE AUTHOR

D.C. Lee began his own life of missionary adventures in high school with a 20 hour train ride from the border of Texas to Aguascalientes, Mexico. Since that first trip, he has traveled to 22 countries around the globe (so far) where he has shared the good news and labored to build up the body of Christ. He and his wife are the parents of three amazing children who are growing up on the mission field and learning to partner in Great Commission work. The Lee family splits their time between Texas and Asia (with as many trips to Colorado as they can fit in between).

DISCOVER MORE BOOKS BY D.C. LEE AT

WWW.RESONATEBOOKS.COM

Coming in 2021!

God Sees Beautiful

A True Story Of Loving The Unloved In China

Left To Die

One afternoon, as she often did after English class, Hannah went for a walk around the orphanage to see if any children had left or any new children had arrived. The three story orphanage was full of dark hallways and empty rooms. Hannah climbed the stairs to the 3rd floor and found herself standing in front of a door she had never seen before. The door opened into a low-lit room where several small cribs were lined up along the walls. She took a few steps into the musty smelling room and scanned the empty beds. She turned to leave and was just closing the door behind her when she heard the soft whimpering of a baby. Had she missed something? She walked across the room to a crib in the far corner and discovered a tiny baby lying on its back. She examined the child closely. The baby boy had Down syndrome and appeared just a few days old. He was so tiny and cute, but the skin on his face was dry and peeling off and there was thick black liquid coming out of his mouth, coating his lips. Hannah's heart cried out in deep compassion for the child. She looked around the room again, perplexed that this baby had been left completely alone. Then a slow and nauseating realization came upon her. The baby was alone because no one wanted to watch him die. Hannah knew the orphanage workers were overworked, underpaid and under skilled. More importantly, they were superstitious. Being responsible for a baby that dies could prove ominous for their own families and children, or so many of them believed. Hannah felt a righteous indignation rising up within her and she quickly went in search of someone who could tell her more about the baby's condition and situation. She grabbed the first young woman she saw and led her back into the room.

"What is wrong with this baby?" She asked in Chinese.

The woman explained that the baby had been abandoned on the side of the road because of his many serious birth defects. In addition to having Down syndrome, he had also been born without an anus and because of this, they were unable able to feed him. When Hannah asked how they were planning to help him, the woman shook her head and said they had already taken him to the local hospital, but the doctors could do nothing for him. Hannah was stunned. This poor baby, already abandoned by his family, was now being abandoned to die alone. Hannah decided she could not let that happen.

"Please stay here and wait for me to come back." Hannah told the worker as she exited the room. She ran downstairs and found Susan.

"Come with me!"

As Susan followed along behind, Hannah told her about the baby. They entered the room and Hannah led Susan over to the crib. When Susan saw the baby's peeling face and mouth full of black puss, she gasped and placed a hand on her chest.

"We've got to help him." Susan whispered, reaching down and gently stroking the baby's head. She closed her eyes and began to pray.

Hannah turned to the orphanage worker.

"Can we take this baby home?"

Never in a million years did Hannah believe the orphanage would actually let them take the baby home, but she still had to ask. Even though his future looked grim, they could love on him during his last days on earth and make him as comfortable as possible.

The orphanage worker walked out of the room without saying a word and Hannah's heart broke. She didn't understand. Why had God let her find this dying baby if she couldn't do anything to help him? Susan continued to pray silently. Hannah closed her eyes and prayed one short sentence.

"We need your help, God."

Hannah heard the door open and looked up to see the orphanage worker standing in front of her with a piece of paper in one hand and a pen in the other.

"You must both sign this document to take the baby home."

With trembling hands and hearts thumping in their chests, Hannah and Susan signed their names at the bottom of the document and immediately became the child's legal foster moms.

"I will make a copy for you." The woman left again and Hannah and Susan, in tears and laughter, began to jump around the room while hugging each other.

"I can't believe it!"

"Praise God!"

The two women decided not to wait for the worker to come back, but quickly wrapped the baby up in his blanket and made their way downstairs to the main lobby and offices. Their hearts were still beating wildly. They were certain the orphanage leaders would change their minds at any moment and the baby would be taken from them. Susan went into the main office to retrieve their copy of the document while Hannah exited the building and walked briskly to the main road. Susan caught up with her within minutes, waving the paper that had just changed their lives.

Inside the taxi, they decided to take the baby to Scott and Julia's house to discuss the whole situation with them. Hannah silently worried that the older couple would scold them and tell them how crazy they were, but the moment they walked into the Harper's home, her anxieties vanished. Julia carefully took the baby from Hannah and gently bounced him in her arms as she and her husband listened to the women's unbelievable story.

When they finished, Julia looked at them with a seriousness they had never seen on her face before.

"What do you plan to do now?"

Hannah and Susan looked at each other and then slowly turned their gaze back to Julia. "We don't know!"

"So let me tell you. We are going to fight for this baby. We will not just sit and wait for him to die. We must take him to Kunming where the hospitals are more equipped and the doctors are more trained. If he needs life saving surgery, he'll get it."

Julia's words brought tears of relief to their eyes.

* * *

The very next day, Susan climbed onto a bus with the baby in her arms for the three hour journey to the capital city airport. She was going alone. Scott and Julia couldn't go because Grace needed their constant care. Hannah would stay and look after Timmy. The small team waved goodbye as Susan and the baby drove away. Standing on the sidewalk together, they held hands and prayed for a safe and successful trip. On the bus, Susan prayed too. One simple prayer, over and over again:

"Please don't let him die, God. Please don't let him die."

HERE'S A SNEAK PEAK OF ANOTHER EXCITING NEW NOVEL COMING SOON!

1998

Prologue

Dawson Reyes knew this was his one and only chance at a normal life. He knew that he would never, ever meet anyone like her again. He also completely understood that she deserved everything she was hoping for, which was what every other husband and wife dreamed of — a family of their own. That is why, as he stepped out of their house into the predawn darkness and walked the path leading from the front door to his jet black vintage 77' Bronco parked in the driveway, there was a knot in his throat and the metallic taste of approaching vomit on his tongue. He cursed himself, but didn't turn around. Instead, he climbed in, turned the ignition and quickly backed out of the driveway, pausing briefly in the street to take one last look at his picture-perfect home. She was in there asleep, or maybe she had been pretending and was now once again screaming into her pillow. Her tears had run dry long ago. More than likely, she was already packing her things.

You made a vow. Don't leave her.

He didn't know what to make of this voice inside his head anymore. His conscience, if it was his conscience, was thoroughly confused and screwed up because the same damn voice telling him to stay was also telling him to go. He had to go because someone innocent and weak and helpless needed him more than anyone else needed him; even his wife. The voice would hound him and push him and not let him sleep or rest until each child was found safe…or dead. One voice with two opposing messages; He simply couldn't do both. His choice was always to go because he knew - with no pretense or ego - that he was the best hope any of them had. He was committed, some might say ruined, for life. Dawson punched the gas pedal and shot off down the street as if he could somehow leave his thoughts behind; but they weren't going anywhere.

Amy Harrison was 6 years old with brown hair, brown eyes and a face covered in brown freckles. Thus, it was only natural for her parents, siblings and everyone else who knew her to call her "Brownie".

"Our little Brownie!" her mother had cried out, crumpling into her husband's arms as Dawson sat stone-faced, staring down at their most recent photo of their smiling daughter. She looked like she had some spunk and spirit in her, and Dawson said as much to the distraught couple who managed to smile amidst their tears and respond with, "if you only knew!"

"A bit strong willed?" Dawson stated as much as asked.

"And smart as a whip." Her father whispered.

Dawson smiled. He believed every abducted child had a chance at survival and the more spirit, fortitude and ingenuity they possessed, the better their chances. He had seen and experienced some amazing examples of wisdom, bravery, and endurance. Amy had been last seen riding her scooter down the sidewalk towards the stop sign at the end of the block. A stop sign that stood just over 150 feet from their front door. Squealing tires had been heard by more than one neighbor. Her scooter was found in the middle of the street. No one had seen the vehicle. Just like that, Amy Harrison was gone…as if she had vanished into thin air.

The same thought came to Dawson's mind every time he stared at one of these photos — humanity is lost when children are taken, abused and discarded like property and trash. There was less and less room for optimism in Dawson's life, and those closest to him, his wife especially, could sense his grip on anything resembling happiness and peace slipping away.

The days following a new case were particularly crucial for finding leads before trails turned cold and memories spotty. These initial days were especially hard on Dawson's marriage because he was up all hours of the night with thoughts that locked him up and rendered him emotionally detached from the needs of his wife. After three long days and nights there were still no leads in Amy's case. And then, the tip came in and with it, hope. Dawson didn't even tell her parents or his wife about it or about his plans to fly to Nashville, Tennessee, the next morning.

As he exited his neighborhood and crawled into the early morning commute towards LaGuardia Airport, he was hopeful for the lead that had come in and despondent about leaving his wife without saying goodbye.

Within an hour of landing in Nashville, Dawson met with the local detectives and brought them up to speed on the case and then interviewed the clerk of a local convenience store who had called in the tip. Two days prior, the clerk had learned about Amy Harrison's abduction on the national news and decided to print out and display her missing person flier on the front door of the store. The following night, he went outside to do his rounds of emptying the trash cans between the gas pumps when a car pulled in to get gas. When he stepped out from behind one of the pumps, the car suddenly sped away, sending rocks and dust into the air, but not before the clerk caught a glimpse of a small girl's face sitting in the back seat. It wasn't until he was walking back into the store and looked at the photo on his door that he realized it was her! He rushed to the phone and called the police. By the time they arrived, the car and the girl were long gone. However, the clerk already had video surveillance footage ready to show and hand over. In it, a camera mounted on one of the pumps caught a clear image of a '98 black Ford Mustang and the license plate on the back. The license plate number quickly produced a name and local address.

18 hours later, in the dead of night, Dawson, the local detectives, and a SWAT team were all in position. The black Mustang had been discovered under a large camouflage tarp in the woods nearby. Three SWAT officers had spread out around the residence and taken up positions near the doors and windows. A fourth SWAT officer entered the crawl space below the mobile home with a head-mounted flashlight and mini high definition video camera. As expected, a trip wire attached to a pile of aluminum cans (a red neck home alarm system) was slowly and quietly circumvented. The officer continued his crawl beneath the structure until his headlamp revealed a plywood box extending from below the floor down to the ground near the back left corner of the home. This image appeared on a set of monitors mounted on the inside wall of a black delivery truck where Dawson and the rest of his team were waiting, watching and listening from less than a mile away. From the schematics they had acquired of the exact make and model of the mobile home, they quickly determined the box was located directly below the master bedroom. The officer quietly drilled a hole through the plywood with a silent drill. An officer outside the master bedroom window confirmed through his radio mouthpiece that the TV in the bedroom was on, but their perp was sound asleep in his bed. The officer outside the living room window reported that the window was not locked. The officer positioned outside the front door reported that it was. Down below, the officer finished drilling the small hole and ran a thin surgical wire through the hole on which was mounted another high-def video camera set to night-vision mode. Turning the camera to the right, there was only a green shadowy darkness. To the left, wooden steps came into focus leading up to the bedroom which was lit up by the glow of the TV. Dawson instructed the officer to turn the camera back towards the right and hold.

"Light up?" The officer whispered into his mouthpiece, using as few words as possible. There was a small, but powerful light attached to the side of the thin camera which could brighten the entire area.

"Negative," Dawson replied. "If she's down there and sees it, there's no telling how she'll respond."

If she's down there. God, please let her be there. Dawson didn't believe in God, but sometimes he entertained the possibility in the vain hope that he could one day curse someone for putting humanity, especially the most vulnerable, through such hell on earth. Despite his animosity towards all things spiritual, he silently prayed for a lucky break. The officer held his position. Everyone settled down for a patient wait. They needed probable cause to get the search warrant to enter the suspect's home. If they could somehow get a visual on the little girl being held captive in this underground space, a local judge was on 24-hour standby, ready to immediately sign off on the warrant. The team had one more hour until daybreak, when they would have to pull back and start new surveillance measures all of which were a waste of time in Dawson's mind. By now, most who worked with him on a regular basis knew that he hated protocol because it made an almost impossible job all the more impossible. Ten slow, grueling minutes passed, and then something amazing happened. There was a click and then a soft, green glow filled the screen and slowly a small dark figure came into focus. It was a small figure sitting down with a flickering cigarette lighter in one hand and a book in the other. That was it. Dawson felt the heat crawling up his back and he gripped the table with such force that the monitor vibrated.

"Get the judge."

Within minutes, a signed copy of the judge's warrant came rolling out of the wall mounted fax machine.

"We're a go team. Repeat. We're a go."

* * *

As the sun slowly rose over the horizon and streaks of pink and purple melted into a light blue sky, the black van slowly rolled into the circular dirt driveway. Dawson and the two detectives exited and approached the front door. The SWAT officer posted there had already placed small explosive devices on the hinges of the door and around the door frame. Now the officer quickly and quietly moved around to the back of the structure, joining the officer outside the master bedroom window. Dawson stepped up onto the small porch while the two detectives remained a little behind and on both sides of him. It was obvious the girl's captor left the trap door open to let air flow down into her space and to keep a constant eye on her, but Dawson knew that if anyone came knocking, the trap door would be slammed shut. To make sure the girl was shut in for safety, Dawson knocked on the door, announced that he was with the gas company, and then backed away from the door and down the porch steps. The officer outside the window who had eyes on their suspect quickly radioed that he was on the move and armed with a handgun. The officer monitoring the little girl radioed that the trap door had been shut with the girl still down below. Dawson counted to three and then shouted "Now!" There was a loud explosion on the backside of the house where small explosives had also been mounted on the flimsy wall of the master bedroom. The two officers crashed through the wall and took up defensive positions in the master bedroom as smoke and pieces of wood paneling and insulation floated in the air like confetti. Their perp was now completely cut off from doing any harm to his victim. The officer beneath the mobile home quickly removed one of the side panels of wood and stuck his head into the dark space.

"Amy. This is the police. You're safe. We'll get you out of here really soon." In case of a pending shootout, the agent didn't remove her from the crawl space yet.

As the perp stumbled his way into the living room and kitchen, flash grenades and smoke bombs were tossed into the area through the dining nook window. Explosions shook the structure and smoke began to trickle out of the spaces around the front door. Within seconds, coughing, wrenching and cursing could be heard inside, right behind the front door. Dawson and the detectives were kneeling around the small porch with their guns aimed at that very spot.

"Carl Williams! This is the police! You're surrounded! Come out with your hands in the air!"

* * *

When Amy's parents came to the hospital and found her safe and cleaned up, with only a few scratches and bruises on her smiling face, they completely collapsed onto her bed and let loose a flood of moans and tears that the poor young child could barely comprehend. These sounds were very familiar to Dawson, and, even though he had never made them himself, his large childhood home had once been full of them. Mr. Harrison walked over to Dawson and, with eyes red and swollen, grabbed Dawson's shoulders and gave them a firm shake and mouthed the words "thank you", but no sound came out.

These were the most gratifying experiences Dawson had ever known and probably would ever know. And all the more so because they rarely happened and were such a stark contrast and complete reversal of how these final meetings usually went when a lifeless body was found or when the trail grew cold and there was nothing more to be done. This brought everyone involved to the brink of insanity.

* * *

Before his flight back to New York City, Dawson had called his wife to share the good news, but she didn't answer and her voicemail never picked up. A few long hours later, as he stood on his front porch with his hand on the doorknob, he already knew that she was gone and the normal life he had dreamed of had left with her. He didn't want to go inside, didn't want to spend another day in this now empty and lifeless house. He slowly stepped into the darkness of his entryway and imagined her coming down the stairs with a smile on her face and that look in her eyes — the look of wanting to devour him right there on the hardwood floors. He flicked on the entryway light switch, turned towards the large decorative mirror hanging on the wall, and stood transfixed at the message he found scrawled in the delicate handwriting of his wife:

"It's finally over, D. I will always love you. I pray God will set you free."

Dawson felt his eyes burning and a tear already streaking down his cheek. He wiped the tear away and looked at the moist mark on the back of his hand. He hadn't seen or felt one of his own tears in years.

I'm sorry Amber. He didn't blame her at all. How could he? All she wanted was him and a family to call their own. He had been a fool to fall in love in the first place and the worst of human beings to promise her forever. This thought hurt and angered him most. He had known all along that there was no chance for happily ever after, but had refused to admit it when it mattered most. Dawson had long known that his chance for a normal life had been robbed from him years before, and now each time another child was taken he entered the nightmares of the victims' families. Families who lay in bed in the dark of night begging God for mercy, for a miracle, for a reprieve from the claustrophobic thoughts of what could possibly be happening to their missing child. Sleep comes, but only after the mind has completely exhausted itself of possibilities. Such endless nights go on for years and years until a body is rescued or discovered, and even then they can last a lifetime. For those whose children are never found, only the sleep of death brings true rest. These families trusted him because he knew what they were going through and because he reacted with a bulldog tenacity that the families were desperate for. Every victim was his younger sister and every family his own.

* * *

Dawson snapped out of his thoughts, went to the kitchen, dropped his things onto the dining table, grabbed a beer from the fridge and collapsed onto his leather sofa. He took a long sip of his beer and then suddenly smiled. As destroyed as he felt inside, the sudden image of Brownie and her parents smiling and laughing together in each other's arms filled his mind, and, for a brief moment, he relished in the goodness of that image. He felt a joy rising up within his heart and another knot in his throat and then more tears fell. First, tears of joy and relief but then tears of grief, regret, and frustration. *Amber…if only you could've seen and experienced for yourself the reunion of Brownie with her parents.*

Dawson closed his eyes and the last conversation he'd had with his wife began to echo off the walls of his mind.

"Let them go, Dawson! You can't save them all, and you surely can't bring them back to life!"

"Hell, Amber. If it was you, would you want me to let you go? If we had a daughter, would you want me to let her go?" As soon as the words had shot from his mouth, Dawson regretted them.

"If we had a daughter! You son of a…" Her voice trailed off. She shook her head from side to side as if trying to dislodge the fury that had consumed her. She looked directly into her husband's eyes. Her voice was calm, but firm.

"Don't ever talk to me about having a daughter! Don't talk to me about children at all!" She rushed into the bathroom, slamming the door behind her.

How could he bring a child into this crazy world where evil seemed more powerful and active than good, seemed to mock and toy with good for its own amusement? There was no possibility of utopia on earth. He'd seen it all. Buddhist monks, Catholic priests and youth pastors, politicians, professors and police officers, teachers, bus drivers and the local handyman…they were all polluted and perverted and deserved justice and suffering the same as – no, worse than – their victims. Heaven was a dream that Dawson prayed existed for those who truly deserved it — innocent children. Everyone else, himself included, could go to hell.

* * *

As if a presence unseen had been waiting for that very thought to materialize in his head, Dawson looked down into his left hand and surprisingly discovered his 357 Magnum in its grip. He didn't even remember taking it out of its holster. He closed his eyes and slowly raised the barrel up under his chin. Would he finally see his sister again if he pulled the trigger? His finger tightened on the trigger. Wouldn't that be just the pitiful ending her abductors hoped for?

Her voice filled his ears. *Don't give them the satisfaction, brother; just stop as many as you can from doing it again.*

He lowered his gun and set it on the table. *I can't stop them all, Stephanie. You don't understand. It's like a plague now, as if humanity has been flushed down the toilet, I can't look at anyone the same; everyone is a suspect and it's going to drive me insane!* Dawson walked to his bedroom and collapsed onto his bed fully clothed. He reached for his wife's hand, but found only empty sheets. He grabbed hold of them, and his grip was still tight when he fell asleep.

* * *

News of Brownie's rescue and the successful capture and arrest of her abductor had already made it back to the Missing Persons Department of the NYPD where Dawson worked. Other details of the arrest were not so commonly known. Dawson had spent the entire morning with his direct supervisor and then with Internal Affairs. Once again he was put on administrative leave for "use of excessive force". This time he had crushed the windpipe of the perp and dislocated his arm. Details of the report described how it had taken four other officers to pull Dawson off of the man and by the time they had done so, his arm was dislocated, his windpipe crushed and blood was everywhere. As always, Dawson just regretted leaving the man alive. Internal Affairs was ready to throw the book at this young hot-shot detective who seemed to believe he was above the law. Everyone knew his story. Everyone sympathized with the nightmare his family had been put through. Everyone understood this was personal for him, but that is exactly what made him so unpredictable. And at only 27 years of age not only was he one of the youngest detectives ever to serve at the NYPD, but he was just getting started. Internal Affairs was preparing to bring his promising career to a sudden end. They had enough evidence to put him away for a few years, giving him plenty of time in close proximity with many of the felons he had helped lock up over his short career span. The clock was ticking and it was only a matter of time before he would face his own day in court. His supervisor's hands were tied and the department – fully aware that he was the best detective on their force, if not the entire country – could no longer handle the liability he brought them. Dawson was sitting at his desk in his small office when his phone vibrated and he looked down at a text message, hoping it might be from Amber.

* * *

I think your time here is done. If you're interested in a career change that better suits your skills and overall objective, then give me 20 minutes over a cup of coffee. A black sedan will be waiting for you outside in 10 minutes. Your sister would be proud of you, Mr. Reyes.

* * *

And that is how Dawson Reyes found himself sitting across from a very intriguing Mr. Alexander Petrod Schuster, whose extended hand, Dawson shook firmly.

"You have my full attention Mr. Schuster."

"Please, call me A.P."

2002

Chapter 1

It's strange, the thoughts that go through a man's mind as he's running for his life. Dawson Reyes came flying down the final steps onto Nathan Road, jumping over a sitting, snuggling couple before his feet planted onto the pavement and launched him forward again. He firmly held onto a tightly wrapped bundle with one arm and knocked people out of his way like a running back with a bad case of stiff-arm with the other. As he ran, his nostrils breathed in the familiar smell of fried vegetables and beef noodle soup and his stomach told him it was time for another feeding. *Of all the times to be thinking of eating! Idiot!* Dawson dove into a sea of bodies moving through the Temple Street Night Market in Hong Kong's Yau Ma Tei district. He ran, lunged, twisted and glided through the crowd as if his movements were choreographed to a supersonic waltz. In any other crowded location on the globe, he would've been cursed and perhaps even grabbed and thrown to the ground; but not in Kowloon, Hong Kong, where one's personal bubble ended at the tip of the nose. From a bird's eye view, The Temple Street Night Market was a two mile stretch of descending, zigzagging cobblestone that nightly hosted one of the largest outside shopping sprees in the world. Vendors squeezed together side by side selling every imaginable good and service. The street was a cacophony of sound, with television sets blaring pirated DVD movies, stereos booming everything from rap to heavy metal to Chinese aboriginal flutists, and sellers standing on chairs and shouting through megaphones like televangelists on speed. With all the noise around him, Dawson was simultaneously aware of the silence. It was a silence he had been trained to perceive.

They weren't on him yet, but they were coming. Silently and steadily they were coming for him. Suddenly Dawson broke through a small crowd gathered in the middle of the lane and managed to look down just as his running shoe pressed onto the tiny tail of a black lab puppy walking around in circles. The puppy yelped in pain and a man next to a small cage full of other puppies stood up and shook his fist yelling, along with a handful of other onlookers, but Dawson had already disappeared into another wall of bodies. He shouted "sorry" in Cantonese and truly meaning it. The flow of people grew thicker and their movement slower. Dawson looked to his right, debating whether or not to duck into one of the dozens of alleys that ran away from the street down towards the harbor. It would be good if he could catch a ferry to Hong Kong and lay low there for a few hours, but there were huge risks involved in such a course of action. Even though he knew most of the alleys like the back of his hand, if he was caught in one, there would be no way out and he'd be toast. Here in the crowds of the bustling night market, he would be somewhat safer. However, it wasn't a question of his own safety that burdened him; his thoughts were ever on the bundle, and there was nothing that was going to keep him from delivering his "package" unharmed. Dawson continued to move. A man on a mission, he refused to be distracted by haunting images, clamoring thoughts, and surging emotions. Tragedy had struck, but there was nothing he could do about that now. All remaining hope lay wrapped up in his arms, and he would protect it with his life. Soon he would release it and gather up furious vengeance in its place. It was the constant bittersweet cycle of a life that had chosen him.

Dawson entered a section where the street began a steep decline. On either side sat some of the best dumpling dives in the city, crowded with people hunching over hot bowls of steamed dim sum and wonton soup. Many customers sat on stools or squatted outside loading their mouths. He glanced over and caught sight of his blurred reflection flying past the large glass windows of the "WORLD'S BEST NOODLE SHOP!" and the image immediately brought buried words back to the surface.

"You're just a blur, constantly running everywhere. You never stop moving for one second to have me." Even after all these years, his ex-wife's voice could come out of nowhere at the most unexpected moments and squeeze another drop of guilt and regret out of his dried up heart. Of course, she had been right and he was still running. Luckily, Dawson was a bit too preoccupied at the moment to sit and wallow in self-pity and replay the demise of his marriage all over again. He pulled the bundle closer to his chest. His eyes narrowed into slits of darkness and his lips spread into a thin smile. This is exactly why she had left — because there was no denying that he completely fed off the adrenaline of moments such as these. It had pushed him then, and it still propelled him now. The hunt, the chase, the fatal threat, the ultimate risk – these were his identity and contentment. Dawson suddenly slowed down to a brisk walk and glanced around in all directions. Then he felt something bump into his leg and seem to stick there. He looked down to find a small Cantonese girl moving alongside him stride for stride, though she was practically sprinting to keep up. With one hand she held up a dozen or so roses for inspection as her other hand brushed her long black hair out of her grimy, precious face.

"For girlfriend?" she asked with a pleading smile.

Dawson stopped and pulled a wad of bills out of his pants pocket. He spoke quickly, but clearly in the local Cantonese dialect, "Here, child — I want you to go buy yourself something delicious to eat, a large ice cold milk tea, and then take the rest of the night off, okay?"

The girl's already large eyes opened even wider at the sound of this foreigner's perfect Cantonese. Her amazement turned to sheer shock when Dawson handed her a $500 Hong Kong Dollar bill and grabbed all the flowers out of her hand just to make sure she didn't continue working any longer. She stared at the wrinkled up bill in her hand and then up at Dawson. Others were beginning to crowd around them and stare as well.

"You better put that in a safe place and do what I said; buy yourself a meal and go spend the rest of the night playing with friends. Then go home and sleep well. Okay?"

She nodded her head and smiled.

"God bless you," she whispered in English.

"Your smile already has," Dawson said and darted back into the moving crowd. He picked up his pace, distancing himself from another face that would haunt him. They always did. He had seen too many young faces like hers — gazing at the sky, lifeless and silent while at the same time screaming horrible suffering and injustice at the top of their lungs to any who would dare listen. Dawson had chosen to listen. To hear the pain and the pleading for justice — the demand for vengeance. Soon the voices consumed him and in the process drowned out and pushed away everything he held dear, including his wife, family, and friends. They hadn't understood that he had peered behind the veil that separates the normal world from the unimaginable, and he could never be the same. While the masses traveling through the Temple Street Night Market saw a simple young flower seller with her whole life before her, Dawson saw another young victim waiting to be snatched up and carried away. The standard questions were shouting in his mind: Who is she selling the flowers for? Her parents or some abusive lao ban (boss)? Is she safe? Does she need protection? He took her flowers, but had wanted to pick her up and carry her away to a safe place…though he wasn't sure if such a place even existed.

Chapter 2

Dawson heard voices yelling up ahead, and his mangled thoughts dissipated, leaving behind an all too familiar ache in his heart. He stopped in the middle of the street. He saw a group of men approaching about 100 yards below him. There were seven of them. He glanced behind him in the direction he had just come and caught a glimpse of five more. They were closing in on him. He came to the realization that he was stuck and cursed himself. Here, at the Jordan Road section of the night market, a continuous line of restaurants sat on both sides. He considered crashing through a restaurant into a back alley, but knew all of them were walled in. He also knew that if he entered a restaurant with the intent of riding the elevator or taking the stairs, he would eventually come to the roof and once again be stuck. Two policemen stood twenty feet away pestering a vendor about his selection of DVDs, and Dawson couldn't help the sudden rage that filled his veins.

Useless fools.

Here he was in a situation that needed – demanded – the law intervene and do its job, but he knew the officers would only make the situation worse…they had done it before. However noble his intentions, however heroic his accomplishments, he was a foreigner and his motives, to quote one detective who had interrogated him, "are misguided shit that get you locked up". At least the cops in Hong Kong knew how to throw in an English expletive or two.

As Dawson assessed the situation, he knew for certain that one more brush with the law and his ability to work and move in Hong Kong would be jeopardized indefinitely. Deciding there was no reason to stick out like a sore thumb in the middle of the street, he ducked inside a noodle shop and headed for some tables near the back corner. Not taking his eyes off the front door, he took a seat at a booth, squeezing in with a group already there, mumbling "excuse me" in Cantonese. It was common for complete strangers to share a table in Asia, so Dawson was ready to ignore his companions when one of them cleared their throat and he looked up into a pair of blue eyes, the likes of which he had never seen before. Looking to his left, Dawson scanned the faces of a total of six Caucasian girls with large round eyes and an assortment of hair colors. He had just stumbled onto a group of female foreigners who he immediately assessed to be tourists or students. The girl to his left, the one he had practically sat on trying to get into his seat, was gazing at her friends wide-eyed while the others giggled. The one in front of him, with the piercing blue eyes, held a steady gaze and a slight smile in his direction.

"Méi wèntí," she said coolly, wondering if this ruggedly handsome, yet ridiculously rude stranger understood the Mandarin phrase for "no problem."

"Bù hǎoyìsi." He replied, "Guǎngdōng huà hé pǔtōnghuà nǐ dūhuì shuō ma?"

Maria knew he had just asked her if she spoke both Cantonese and Mandarin, but she was caught off guard by his perfect tone and local accent. She quickly gathered her thoughts and responded in the typical Chinese humble fashion that she was learning Mandarin and only knew a few Cantonese words and phrases. Now it was Dawson's turn to be impressed. Most foreigners he had come across studying Mandarin either butchered up the tones or only listened and refused to attempt complete sentences. He was instantly curious about this one. By the look on the faces around them, it was obvious he and blue eyes were the only two following their conversation.

"Hello, ladies," Dawson said, switching to English and turning away from a gaze that had begun to unnerve him. He smiled at the girls sheepishly, trying to appear totally at ease, but his loud, rapid breathing testified otherwise. "Mind if I join you?"

All of the girls looked at their blue-eyed leader. Dawson figured them all to be either high school or college students, while the one across from him had to be somewhere in her mid to late twenties.

"Not at all," she responded with a thin tight smile that told Dawson she didn't trust him at all around her younger friends. Dawson met her gaze with an understanding grin. He took quick note of the fact they were almost eye-level, which meant she was either in a booster chair or close to 6 feet tall. She had light blonde hair pulled back in a ponytail and light blonde eyebrows, but dark eyelashes that were the perfect frames to eyes that he had already decided were masterpieces. Her nose was slender and pointed, her lips small but full, and her chin reminded him of a smooth vase he had kept on a windowsill once. Her cheeks were fleshy and pale like the moon and covered with small copper colored freckles. Either because he was at the moment running from a very serious threat or because he had just stumbled upon the most captivating face he had ever seen, he was momentarily speechless.

"Um..."

"Do you mind if we pray?" The girl with blue eyes asked, glancing around at her companions and then down at the steaming bowls of soup on the table.

"Of course not. Please, go ahead," Dawson responded, glancing past her towards the front door as everyone around him closed their eyes and bowed their heads. The next thing Dawson knew, he heard the girl with the blue eyes speaking in another foreign language. He wasn't sure exactly what it was, but narrowed it down to something Scandinavian, perhaps Swedish or Norwegian. With his eyes glued on her once again, Dawson felt something rising up in his chest. He took a deep breath and as he exhaled he heard the soft voice, like a whisper, but plain as day:

You can trust her.

If he had felt speechless before, now he was tongue-tied. The girl with blue eyes said something that sounded like "Amen," and the others echoed it. She looked up at Dawson, and this time his heart skipped a beat.

"Are you okay? You look like you could use a cold drink?"

Dawson wiped the sweat from his forehead with his forearm. And then the voice spoke again.

Trust her.

Dawson felt his stomach drop. He had never heard anything like this before. It wasn't like a thought had come into his head, but an actual audible voice speaking into his ear, which he knew was ridiculous!

"Sorry? Did you say "trust"?"

Now it was blue eyes' turn to look confused. She gazed at the others who were either making strange faces or trying hard to hold back laughter.

Dawson immediately knew he had just sounded like a fool. He had to calm down. He gazed past the girl with blue eyes towards the front door again and felt certain he was just about out of time. She shrugged her shoulders and then turned her attention to her soup, wrapping noodles around her chopsticks like an oriental pro. A waiter came over and asked Dawson in broken English if he could take his order and without thinking, Dawson responded in fluent Cantonese that he was on his way out. The waiter scowled and walked away as the girls looked at one another and giggled again.

"Listen, I'm sorry I crashed into you all like that." Dawson stood up and began to back away from them towards the door.

His eyes quickly rested on hers. *I've got to get a hold of myself! So she's pretty, okay she's gorgeous, not the first…*

"You ladies enjoy your wonton soup."

"Thanks. Will do," the young woman replied, noticing for the first time the large bundle he was holding up against his chest. She thought it odd, but since coming to Asia, she had run into a lot of "oddballs", most of them ex-pats from the West. This guy was quickly moving to the top of her list.

A few steps further from the table and Dawson turned away as a chorus of laughter and Scandinavian voices erupted.

He walked to the front door and peered out through the glass. He saw them immediately. All twelve of his pursuers were standing in a circle out in the middle of the street. One of them pointed towards a few of the nearby restaurants and they all split up in different directions while two stayed put. It would be only minutes before some of them entered. Dawson made the decision without even consciously thinking about it. He glanced back to the table and saw the woman with blue eyes still staring after him, her head slightly tilted to one side and a curious look on her face. He walked over to the cash register counter and grabbed a pen and a paper menu. He wrote quickly but carefully then walked back over to the table as all eyes lifted up and mouths clamped shut. He stopped directly in front of the woman with blue eyes and asked her for her name. Even before he'd finished the question, Dawson noticed a red hue wash over her face.

"I'm Maria."

"Maria, I need you to do something for me." Dawson leaned forward and carefully placed his bundle into the woman's hands. She took it willingly, without protest. One of the other girls gasped in surprise. Dawson looked around at them all and then back to her. "You have to get what's wrapped in *this* blanket to *this* person at *this* place as soon as possible." Dawson put the menu down on the table and pointed to the words he had written.

"Do you understand Maria?"

Maria stared at the menu, taking in his words, taking in their meaning…

"Maria, do you understand?"

The girl next to Maria gave her a nudge with her arm and Maria suddenly looked up just in time to see Dawson walk away and disappear through the front glass door.

They all sat in silence. A few were smiling, most looked dumbfounded. Maria scooted back in her seat and looked down at the bundle in her hands as the size and weight of what she was holding began to register. Then she felt something shift inside. With her heart thumping in her chest, she pulled back on layers of folded blanket and suddenly found herself staring down at a tiny little scrunched up Asian face. Maria caught her breath and then bit her lip as everyone began gathering around to look at the small precious package in her arms. The tiny baby moved its head back and forth with quivering jerks. Two little arms unfolded and tiny hands with miniature fingers stretched out towards Maria's face. By now all of the girls had surrounded her and were practically on top of her gazing down. The baby, with a small shock of jet black hair on its head, slowly opened its eyes, blinked twice and then let out a muffled cry. All at once, every last one of the girls let out a cry of her own. Maria quickly stood to her feet. "Wait here girls."

"We're coming with…"

"No. I said to wait here." The authority in Maria's voice caused all the girls to sit back down, close their mouths and quietly watch her walk to the front door of the restaurant where she stopped and stared out through the glass. She saw the man who had given her the child walking out into the middle of the street. She took a deep breath and began to push the door open, ready to confront this stranger who had just done the unthinkable, when suddenly all hell broke loose right before her very eyes.

Made in the USA
Columbia, SC
27 May 2021

38606041R00243